# LONDON'S TERMINI

# LONDON'S TERMINI

ALAN A. JACKSON

———
Second Edition
———

DAVID & CHARLES
NEWTON ABBOT   LONDON   NORTH POMFRET

*British Library Cataloguing in Publication Data*

Jackson, Alan A.
    London's termini.——2nd ed.
    1. Railways——England——London——Stations
    ——History
    I. Title
    385'.314'09421          TF302.L6


ISBN 0–7135–8634–4

First published 1969
Second edition 1985

Printed in Great Britain
by Redwood Burn Limited, Trowbridge, Wilts
for David & Charles (Publishers) Limited
Brunel House   Newton Abbot   Devon

Published in the United States of America
by David & Charles Inc
North Pomfret   Vermont 05053   USA

# Contents

# List of Illustrations

IN TEXT

The publishers are grateful to the editors of the Railway Magazine for giving permission to reproduce the line illustrations which appear on pages 36, 47, 64, 65, 82, 100, 121, 135, 164, 178, 180, 184, 200, 228, 261, 270, 273, 283, 292, 306, 307, and 323.

# Preface to the First Edition

London's railway termini fit awkwardly into the motor age. Designed for the steam locomotive and the horse cab, and built in profusion in the days of *laissez-faire* capitalism, when the railway was the main means of land transport, they now have to serve a unified and attenuated railway system operated by diesel and electric traction. The inevitable changes, long postponed, have at last begun. Surprisingly, none has yet been closed, but the days of Marylebone are surely numbered. Euston has been completely rebuilt; Holborn Viaduct and Cannon Street have undergone drastic modernisation; the reconstruction of Victoria is under active consideration; a major upheaval is almost completed at Paddington; and there has been talk of discarding St Pancras after a proposed rebuilding of Kings Cross. With the passing of the steam locomotive from the great train sheds built to disperse its exhaust there has been a transformation; to those who knew them even ten years ago, stations such as St Pancras and Liverpool Street are now almost unrecognisable on a winter's afternoon.

Time then to set down a record. The original idea came from Mr Michael Higson, and when he offered it to me, I accepted with enthusiasm, eventually producing a far longer book than first envisaged. An attempt has been made to present the development of the existing main line termini and their predecessors in a fairly straightforward and orderly fashion on a chronological base. After an introductory survey, a chapter is devoted to each station or station group, beginning with Euston, the first London terminus for long distance traffic, and proceeding in a roughly clockwise direction to end with Marylebone, the last to be built. This arrangement, together with a detailed index, is designed to render the book an easy and convenient source of reference.

It is perhaps as well to apologise in advance to those who find their specialised interests skimped or neglected. Baker Street has been left out because the Metropolitan Railway, for all its pretensions, was never a main-line company. Train services have not received much attention because this topic has been thrashed to exhaustion over the years in the amateur railway periodicals; where services are mentioned, the emphasis has been placed on local workings—this is essentially a London book. I am aware of the inadequacy of the signalling notes which follow each chapter, but hope they will serve as a guide until a specialist in this subject gives it the detailed treatment it deserves.

There are many to thank for advice and assistance. The staff of the excellent Westminster Public Libraries met my requests with their customary calm efficiency; the public relations officials of the London Midland, Eastern, Western and Southern Regions of British Railways replied promptly to my enquiries about current events and plans, and supplied statistics; the staff at the Clapham Transport Museum, notably Mr Bob Cogger, gave me the greatest assistance in my quest for illustrations.

Friends, and fellow members of the Railway Club, were, as ever, generous with their time and help. Mr Charles E. Lee went to much trouble to find illustrations from his own collection, and courteously allowed me to make use of his published articles on some of the stations (detailed in Appendix VI); Dr Edwin Course, of Southampton University, who has done so much to foster my interest in London railways, looked through the typescript and offered suggestions; Mr J. T. Howard Turner contributed valuable advice from his extensive knowledge of railway engineering and the southern systems; Mr G. T. Moody read the book as it was written, his lifelong study of London railways providing a very substantial contribution of suggestions and comments; Mr H. V. Borley, Librarian of the Railway Club, another Londoner who knows his railways well, worked with his usual patience and care to check facts and dates. I am also grateful to the Rev P. W. Boulding for allowing me to use illustrations from his collection, and to Mr J. N. Slater, Assistant Editor of the *Railway Magazine*, for permission to use plans originally published in that journal.

My intention has been to provide a book that will be read and used not only by the railway-minded, but by the student of nineteenth and twentieth century London. Should it prove helpful to both, stimulating further interest and inquiry, I shall be well content.

Ashtead, April 1969                                                   ALAN A. JACKSON

# Preface to the Second Edition

Since this book first appeared a decade and a half ago, two of London's termini have been almost completely rebuilt, whilst others have undergone piecemeal improvement in the traditional manner. For the rest, indecision and hence neglect and decline, have prevailed. It is remarkable that 15 years on, all 15 stations existing in 1969 still survive, although the fate of Marylebone at last seems to be firmly sealed. Holborn Viaduct, now open for a short day on Mondays to Fridays only, could be replaced economically with a two-platform facility on the old Snow Hill site, and this may well come about before much longer. The fragmented remains of Broad Street, bordered by grass-grown wastes, await the long-postponed, but now imminent redevelopment and integration with Liverpool Street.

London Bridge and Blackfriars have received their desperately-needed rebuilding. At Kings Cross, there is a modern concourse, albeit somewhat inadequate, whilst the muddle of approach tracks has been sorted out and resignalled. Waterloo, Paddington, St Pancras and Liverpool Street have undergone a number of minor changes and improvements, with the latter on the threshold of major rebuilding. Modern Euston has worked well, requiring few changes and substantially increasing its traffic. Fenchurch Street is being altered in connection with commercial development of the space above its platforms. Beleaguered by constantly growing rail-air traffic, Victoria, the third busiest terminus, seems almost continuously in the throes of reconstruction, yet somehow remains unsatisfactory and frustrating to the user.

All the main termini now have modern departure and arrival indicators of the airport type, combined with rebuilt barrier lines. 'Fast-food' outlets imported from the USA have replaced many of the traditional catering facilities and with one exception, self-service rules. So quickly have fashions changed in this area that some stations have seen refreshment facilities gutted and rebuilt twice in the 15 years.

Electric traction has arrived at Kings Cross and St Pancras, although as yet only on short distance services, and both stations have lost most of their suburban traffic to new services to Moorgate via the old Great Northern & City tube and the City Widened Lines. No more has been heard of the cross-London proposals mentioned on pages 23 and 206, but the tunnels and right of way between Farringdon and Blackfriars have been retained for possible future use and their potential is being investigated at the time of writing. Grandiose proposals for main lines across London and new main line facilities still break surface occasionally; we have been regaled with plans for Channel Tunnel termini at White City and Waterloo in place of the original suggestion that Victoria would be suitable, and for full size tunnels between Victoria and Euston, but these also soon began to accumulate dust.

There has been an overall decline in traffic handled at the termini in recent years, attributable in large measure to the fall in central London employment. The reduction averages just over $10\frac{1}{2}$ per cent since 1967-68, but within this figure it is interesting to see that four of the stations have won more passengers, the most notable increase being at Euston (an additional 27,200 daily, or 68 per cent over 1968). In total the 15 termini still deal with over a million passengers every weekday.

Looking to the future, the completion of the M25 motorway around the outside of London seems to offer a threat to the termini's 'in-across-and-out' traffic, which British Rail could meet with development of cross-London facilities over existing tracks and 'Parkway' stations where the main lines intersect the motorways. In general we can expect to see further rationalisation and contraction of the lavish inheritance from uninhibited Victorian private enterprise, so much of which surprisingly survives as we near the end of the 20th century.

In this Second Edition I have made some minor amplifications and corrections, but the original text is substantially maintained, supplemented by a new chapter to record the detailed changes at each terminus up to date. Some additions have been made to the bibliography, which I do not claim to be comprehensive.

It is sad to record the passing of three of those who helped me so much with the original work – Charles E. Lee, G. T. Moody and the Rev. P. W. Boulding; they are much missed. I am most grateful for assistance rendered this time by Messrs. H. V. Borley, J. N. Faulkner and R. H. G. Thomas.

Dorking, July 1984                                    ALAN A. JACKSON

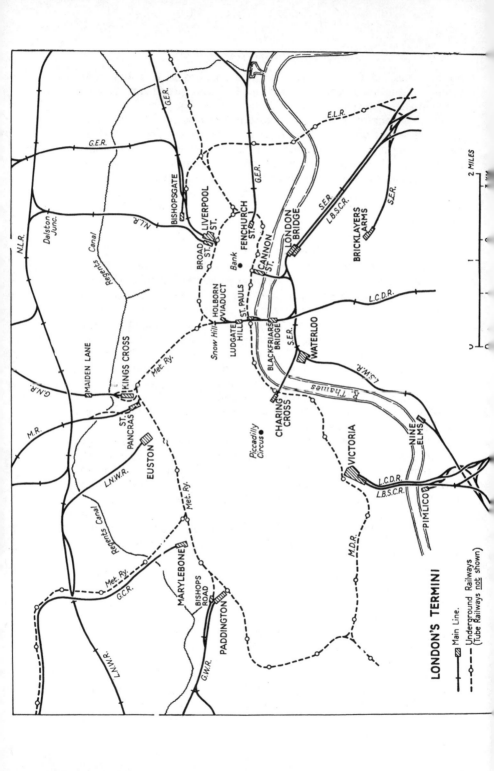

LONDON'S TERMINI

—|— Main Line.

---o--- Underground Railways
(Tube Railways not shown)

2 MILES

G.E.R.
G.E.R.
E.L.R.
Dalston Junc.
N.L.R.
Regents Canal
BISHOPSGATE
BROAD ST.
LIVERPOOL ST.
FENCHURCH ST.
G.E.R.
CANNON ST.
LONDON BRIDGE
S.E.R.
L.B.S.C.R.
S.E.R.
BRICKLAYERS ARMS
Bank
Holborn Viaduct
St. Pauls
Snow Hill
Ludgate Hill
BLACKFRIARS BRIDGE
S.E.R.
L.C.D.R.
WATERLOO
L.S.W.R.
R. Thames
N.L.R.
Maiden Lane
KINGS CROSS
Met. Ry.
CHARING CROSS
Piccadilly Circus
G.N.R.
M.R.
ST. PANCRAS
EUSTON
L.N.W.R.
Met. Ry.
VICTORIA
NINE ELMS
Regents Canal
Met. Ry.
G.C.R.
MARYLEBONE
BISHOPS ROAD
PADDINGTON
G.W.R.
L.N.W.R.
M.D.R.
L.C.D.R.
L.B.S.C.R.
PIMLICO

# CHAPTER I

# Surveying the Scene

## NOT ENTIRELY HAPHAZARD

It is at once clear, on looking at a map of central London, that the great railway termini were not arranged in accordance with any predetermined plan. Yet there is certain evidence (the array of northern stations along a more or less level line, and the strange shape of the Inner 'Circle' railway) that development was not entirely haphazard. A closer examination reveals a distinct difference in pattern between the northern and southern lines; the latter are seen to probe much more closely to the centre, and to have the best sites.

At first, the most important, and almost the only restraints were the crude disciplines of finance. North of the river, Euston (1837), the first Paddington (1838), Shoreditch (1840), and Fenchurch Street (1841), were all sited either on the edge of the built-up area or on the outer rim of the higher value property. In the south, where the property was neither valuable nor fashionable, the first terminus was brought close in, right up to the river at London Bridge (1836). It is true that the second, Nine Elms (1838) was further out, but by 1844 the owning company was preparing to go forward to Waterloo Bridge and London Bridge. Bricklayers Arms (1844) was also distant, but as a passenger terminus it was but an expedient and really is a special case.

In the middle forties the Railway Mania was in full flush. Capital was available for almost any scheme that seemed in the least hopeful, and for many that were not. A whole clutch of termini were daringly projected into the very heart of the metropolis, including a central terminus on what is now the Victoria Embankment, served by lines linking Paddington to Fenchurch Street through Westminster and the City. At this, the government took fright, and a Royal Commision (the Commissioners on Railway Termini within or in the immediate vicinity of the Metropolis, 1846) was

B

appointed to review the various schemes affecting central London and to consider:

> whether the extension of railways into the centre of the Metro-
> polis is calculated to afford such additional convenience or benefit
> to the public as will compensate for the sacrifice of property, the
> interruption of important thoroughfares, and the interference with
> the plans of improvement already suggested.

Unable to foresee the importance that railway traffic into London would assume, the Commissioners were not impressed that the convenience of passengers weighed very heavily against the immense disturbance and expense which would follow a decision to bring the main-line railways into the central area, and to do so for the sake of short distance passengers seemed to them quite unjustifiable. They saw no advantage in a single central terminus for all the railways, pointing out that the number of through passengers across the centre was negligible, and that the congestion which would arise both within and without such a station would be intolerable (they also rightly stressed the many difficulties that would stem from divided management).

### GUIDANCE GIVEN

In their report, the Commissioners recommended that on the north side of the Thames, no railway should enter the central area as defined in their terms of reference (using modern names, the limits were: Edgware Road, Marylebone Road, Euston Road, Pentonville Road, City Road, Finsbury Square, Bishopsgate, Gracechurch Street, London Bridge, Borough High Street, Borough Road, Lambeth Road, Albert Embankment, Vauxhall Bridge, Vauxhall Bridge Road, Grosvenor Place, Park Lane). If in future it should be deemed advisable to admit railways to this area, the Commissioners thought this should be done in accordance with some uniform plan 'carefully laid down under the authority of Your Majesty's Government and sanctioned by the wisdom of Parliament'. On the south side of the river, the property to be disturbed was thought less valuable, the main roads to be crossed fewer and less important, and the street system better able to cope with the traffic created by railway termini.

Accordingly the Commissioners looked with favour upon the schemes then before Parliament for an extension from Waterloo to London Bridge, and an extension of the railway from the southeast (either the SER, or the North Kent Railway, whichever Parliament considered had the most merit) to a terminus at or near Waterloo. They noted that London Bridge and the proposed NKR terminus at Union Street were convenient for the City, both as regards passengers and goods, and that the authorised LSWR terminus at Waterloo Bridge would be equally convenient for the West End. Finally, they recommended the construction of a line outside their area which would connect all lines approaching London with each other, and with the docks, crossing the Thames at some point west of Vauxhall Bridge.

Further guidance was given by Select Committees of Parliament. That of 1855, the Select Committee of the House of Commons on Metropolitan Communications, decided that the termini ought to be connected with each other, with the river and the docks, and with the Post Office. It was to this Committee that Sir Joseph Paxton[1] proposed an imaginative if somewhat nebulous scheme for an inner circle railway in a glass arcade, which he called the Great Victorian Way. Another smaller railway boom occurred in 1863, with particular attention to London, and in that year, a committee of the House of Lords, the Select Committee on Metropolitan Railway Communication, 1863, considered the problem of the capital's communications. They reported against the idea of a large central terminus, said that any new lines in the central area should be underground, and proposed an 'inner circuit' north of the river to link the termini. It was also recommended that the limits of the 1846 Commission should be extended further out, as far as ordinary railways were concerned. The Joint Committee on Railway Schemes (Metropolis) of 1864 endorsed the inner circle railway proposal.

Lines built from the north after 1846 respected the Royal Commission's forbidden zone. Kings Cross (1852), the second Paddington (1854), St Pancras (1868) and Marylebone (1899) all came up to or close to the frontier, but no further. The 1863 Committee had considered that the Great Eastern Railway might be allowed to come nearer the centre, which it did in due course, opening Liverpool Street, just inside the central zone, in 1874. Meanwhile the North London Railway, aided and abetted by the London & North Western, had also put a foot across at Broad Street in 1865; but it was only a technical breach.

In the south, the position was altogether different. Accepting the freedom of action implied by the findings of the Royal Commission, the southern lines proliferated termini, each company striving to establish a station in both the City and the West End. In doing so, they spanned the river and entered the central zone on the north bank. In 1866 the London Chatham & Dover Railway even opened a link with the northern lines which passed right across the forbidden zone, mostly above ground, with a cheeky bridge over the bottom of Ludgate Hill, in the very shadow of St Paul's Cathedral.

There was good reason for all this activity. These southern companies had no great mineral or industrial traffics to keep them solvent; three-quarters or more of their revenues came from passenger traffic. Their main lines eked out a precarious living on a mixture of military, Continental and pleasure traffic, and such bread and butter as they could get came from the suburbs. For this suburban business, access to the City and West End was of prime importance. And, by 1860, the authorities had begun to realise that transpontine termini for the southern lines would help to reduce congestion on the road bridges and in the narrow City streets.

Already established near the City at London Bridge, the LBSCR reached the West End at Victoria in 1860. The SER also managed the ideal, with well-sited termini in each .part of the centre. Both inside the central zone, Charing Cross (1864) and Cannon Street (1866), were in bridgehead positions involving no serious destruction of valuable property. Even more successful (though at the cost of financial ruin) was the LCDR, with a West End station at Victoria adjacent to that of the LBSCR (1862) and a City establishment at Ludgate Hill (1864), later supplemented by two more, Holborn Viaduct (1874) and St Paul's (now Blackfriars) (1886), all well within the forbidden zone. As for the London & South Western, its new Waterloo terminus (1848) had already been deemed convenient for the West End by the Royal Commission, but it never succeeded in reaching the City on its own tracks, first making do with services projected over other companies' lines, then eventually constructing its own tube railway from Waterloo to the Bank.

North of the river, the Great Western, Midland and Great Northern companies provided their suburban passengers with City access by linking their terminal approaches with the Metropolitan Railway and running through trains to Moorgate and beyond. The GWR also took a share in Victoria, but the approach was circuitous and of little practical value to its passengers. Some of the quite heavy GNR suburban traffic was siphoned off by North London trains running to the City at Broad Street, and the LNWR also made use of the NLR to carry its passengers to the City. But to none of these big northern companies was suburban traffic of anything but marginal importance; indeed it was often regarded as something of a nuisance.

With a heavy suburban traffic consisting largely of City workers, the GER was content to stay at Liverpool Street and Fenchurch Street, making no attempt to use its physical connection with the Metropolitan at the former station after the initial negotiations had broken down. However, from 1912, GER passengers were offered direct access to the West End via the Central London tube railway. Fenchurch Street's other user, the London Tilbury & Southend, obtained its West End access by fostering a link with the District Railway (the Whitechapel & Bow Joint, opened in 1902).

## FROM ONE TO THE OTHER

Those who advocated a combined central terminus were fond of emphasising the vagaries and difficulties faced by passengers moving across London from one terminus to another. It was many years before such journeys became reasonably convenient. From its opening in 1863, the Metropolitan Railway afforded direct connection between Paddington and Kings Cross, and six years later, circuitous communication was available between those stations and Victoria, via Gloucester Road and the Metropolitan District Railway. In 1870 the District pushed east to a station near Charing Cross (sufficiently distant to require a cab or outside porter were the passenger encumbered with luggage). The Metropolitan reached Liverpool Street in 1875; Cannon Street received its District station in 1884.

It was not until that latter year that the officially-recommended Inner Circle was finally joined, offering stations adjacent to eight of the fourteen termini then existing, and also serving Charing Cross, Fenchurch Street and Euston after a fashion. Despite the congestion of the streets, journeys between termini at opposite points of the 'Circle' were more expeditiously made by road transport, and most of the main-line companies operated or subsidised cross-centre horse bus services, usually free of charge to passengers booked across London.

Speedier and more convenient movement between the termini came in the 1900s with the arrival of the motor bus, the motor taxicab and the electric tube railway (the Inner Circle was also electrically worked from September 1905). By 1913 all the termini except Fenchurch Street, Ludgate Hill and Holborn Viaduct were served by at least one underground electric railway route.

Although the Midland Railway introduced a motor bus service between St Pancras and Victoria via Charing Cross in July, 1905, the inter-termini services operated on behalf of the railway companies were gradually rendered superfluous by the expansion of the motor taxicab fleet and improvements in public transport.

During the 1920s, railway-inspired inter-termini services briefly flourished for the last time. In 1928 and 1929, the SR, LNER and GWR began to work buses between their termini for the convenience of Pullman and Continental passengers*. About 1932 the operation of these services was handed over to a contractor. After the formation of the London Passenger Transport Board, they disappeared and a regular bus link was established between the major termini. From 1 October 1936, the Board worked an inter-station service, using eight specially-built 20-seater Leyland Cubs painted royal blue and cream, with large luggage boots beneath their raised rear seat decks. A flat fare of 1s single was charged. Withdrawn in 1939, these buses were revived in December 1943, working only in the evenings and at night. A remnant of the service still survives; on week-end nights normal double-deck buses provide an hourly connection between Waterloo, Victoria, Paddington, Euston and Kings Cross—St Pancras.

For those who could afford the fares and the all but obligatory tip, cabs have always been a popular means of transport between the termini and to and from destinations in town. Their importance is demonstrated by the elaborate arrangements made to accommodate them; at all termini except Fenchurch Street, Broad Street, Blackfriars and Ludgate Hill, facilities were provided to enable cabs to set down passengers near the booking offices and to collect them from alongside or near the arrival platforms. From the earliest days, most railway companies preferred to license certain 'privilege' cabs to pick up passengers at the termini. By so doing they could control the service, insisting that an adequate number of cabs meet all long-distance trains whatever the time of day, and that the best type of cab be used, driven by the most reliable men. The agents providing the privilege cabs had to leave a deposit for each vehicle and make a weekly payment. At Euston in 1877, the deposit was £2 per cab and the weekly toll, 2s. In case of complaint, the deposit would be forfeited. In 1897 all companies except the LSWR agreed to an interchange system whereby any cab privileged by one company could ply for hire at

---

* The SR/LNER service between Victoria, Kings Cross and Marylebone started on 9 July 1928 on a shared cost basis. From 8 October 1928 it was extended to Waterloo for Southampton-le Havre passengers. A universal fare of 1s was charged. The GWR started a similar service between Paddington and Victoria, using 15-seaters, in 1929.

any other terminus without extra payment. At Waterloo, apart from a handful of cabs privileged to use the main-line departure cab yard, any cab could use the station on payment of one penny. The privileged cab system at London stations was generally abolished by Sec 2 of the London Cab and Stage Carriage Act, 1907, made permanent by the Expiring Laws Act, 1925. The Act did not affect the liability of cabs and drivers to comply with the railway companies' regulations as to conduct, fitness, numbers admitted at any one time etc, and provision was made for continuation of the system if a company could prove to the satisfaction of the Home Secretary that without it an insufficient number of cabs would be available.

After its reconstruction in 1916, Paddington became a popular station among the cabbies. Its well-planned approach roads and ramps accommodated 127 cabs outside (over platforms 11 and 12), with room for another 40 in the roadway between platforms 8 and 9. There was no toll, and the cabs entered the arrival side in strict order. A cab would take anything between twenty minutes and two hours to pass through the station, according to the time of day and state of traffic. As late as 1936 horse cabs were still occasionally seen in the rank and according to the *Great Western Railway Magazine*, July 1936, one was still meeting a 'regular' on his arrival from the country each Wednesday and Friday morning, as it had done for 37 years.

DIRECT LINK ACROSS THE CENTRE

Only one direct railway link was completed across the centre of London. This was the LCDR—Metropolitan connection of 1866, already mentioned. Severely restricted by sharp curves and steep gradients, it has not been used by regular passenger services for many years. Since the 1860s many more similar direct connections have been proposed, but such schemes have always foundered on the grounds of high capital cost. As recently as 1966 British Railways offered two possible links for the London Transportation Study: Victoria to London Bridge, and Paddington to Liverpool Street. It was suggested that these might share intermediate stations at Covent Garden and Ludgate Hill, the latter also serving refurbished north–south facilities via the 1866 link.

SOCIAL EFFECTS

Once built, the termini with a predominantly long-distance

traffic slowly influenced their immediate surroundings. A certain seediness crept up. This degeneration, sometimes all around, sometimes in a sector of neighbouring streets, was most marked at Paddington, Victoria, Waterloo and the Euston—St Pancras—Kings Cross complex. It was seen to a lesser extent alongside Charing Cross, but hardly at all at Marylebone, a sign perhaps of that station's distinct lack of success as a long-distance terminus.

It was not simply a matter of steam and smoke. Rather did it arise from the nature of the traffic. Travellers far from the restraints of the family home were often easy, even willing victims to certain temptations, and these were made available. Shops were opened to dispense cheap souvenirs, contraceptives and provocative literature (though rarely all three at once), whilst public houses were thick upon the ground, and of the large and noisy kind. Cheap little hotels provided shelter for commercial or clandestine lust. Near Waterloo, with its heavy naval and military traffic, a small brothel area grew up. Petty criminals of varying skills congregated to take advantage of the opportunities offered by the crowds, or by isolated and confused strangers to London. Others, who would consider themselves benefactors rather than criminals, preyed upon young country girls arriving to work in London, luring them to occupations more lucrative than domestic service.

But this was only part of the social impact. In constructing the termini and their approaches, the railway companies swept away some of London's worst slums, but nothing was done to rehouse those who were displaced until the middle 1880s, when Parliament eventually came to insist upon it,[2] and by then most of the destruction had been wrought. As the new lines swathed through the little houses and crowded tenements, consciences were eased by the provision of cheap trains at the beginning of each working day, sometimes voluntarily, sometimes by statute. These trains were not in practice much used by the displaced poor, who crowded into adjacent streets, aggravating the housing problem, but they did encourage a great exodus of clerks, artisans and shop and warehouse workers to new suburbs such as Tottenham and Walthamstow. This had been foreseen as early as 1861, when the Rev William Denton, of St Bartholomew, Cripplegate, in a pamphlet (*Observations on the displacement of the Poor by Metropolitan Railways and by other Public Improvements*), described the forcible eviction of the poor by the proposed new railways, and pointed out that cheap trains were no solution, as they were used only by artisans. He argued that the poor must live on top of their work, and the railways ought to provide dwellings for them, administered by trustees.

## ARCHITECTURE AND DESIGN

And what of the visual contribution; did the termini enhance the appearance of the great city they served? Alas, with a few notable exceptions, they cannot be described as a particularly inspiring collection of buildings. Foreign visitors, accustomed to monumental structures set in large open squares, must find the London termini rather an anti-climax. Almost all are hidden away behind main thoroughfares, or so placed that their architectural impact cannot be absorbed or appreciated. Waterloo is hopelessly strangled by the Charing Cross line viaduct, Marylebone skulks behind a huge hotel, the Siamese twins of Victoria hide shyly round a corner, and Liverpool Street, Broad Street, Fenchurch Street and Cannon Street abut on to streets little wider than country lanes. Where fine architecture did exist, it got scant respect. At Euston, Hardwick's screen, which must have looked splendid for a few years whilst it stood alone against the Hampstead ridge, was gradually suffocated by building all about, then mauled, to make room for dreary, straight-faced offices and finally, destroyed. Kings Cross, with a frontage of considerable merit, suffered for many years the indignity of a ghastly mess of forecourt buildings, provisional and permanent, from which it has only recently been freed.

Appearance, internal design, and fitness for purpose are normally the business of the architect; but not so here. In the nineteenth century, architect and engineer lived in separate worlds, working with their backs to each other, almost literally so. Thus no London terminus emerged as a unified aesthetic concept, although perhaps Kings Cross, in its original state, with its honest functional frontage, spoilt only by a silly clock tower and grim side offices, can be said to have been a near miss. Euston's classical screen was magnicent, but behind it the railway buildings were from the first uninspiring and mean, and the Great Hall, splendid in itself, only succeeded in emphasising the dichotomy.

Elsewhere, architects titivated the basic engineering structure (Paddington) or contributed offices or heavily ornamented hotels to close off one end of the train shed (London Bridge, St Pancras, Cannon Street, Charing Cross, Holborn Viaduct). In other cases there was no master architect; the frontage was designed by an engineer or builder, and ornamented by an 'architectural assistant' or consultant (Waterloo, Victoria, Liverpool Street, Broad Street, Fenchurch Street, Marylebone). Left alone to fulfil basic requirements, the great Victorian engineers often succeeded in creating functional beauty of a high order (the roofs at Paddington, St Pancras, Cannon Street and Liverpool Street, the concourse at Waterloo).

Requirements dictated the fundamental design. A primary requirement for the early terminus was ability to handle a departing and an arriving train simultaneously. To meet this, many of the first termini were built with a single departure and arrival 'stage' on opposite sides, the space between filled by spare tracks where carriages could be stored, cleaned, and examined under the shelter of the overall roof (the short, light coaches could easily be manhandled from one track to another by the use of turnplates). Nine Elms, Shoreditch, Bricklayers Arms, Euston, Victoria (LCDR), Paddington and Kings Cross were all of this pattern, the last five with their main offices alongside the departure platform, so that after walking through the booking office, the passenger found himself facing the centre of his train. The main-line part of Liverpool Street, built as late as 1874, followed the same plan. Most of these stations, but not all, had separate carriage roadways for vehicles serving the departure and arrival sides, either within the station walls, or down one side.

When, with the growth of traffic from the 1870s onwards, the need for more platform accommodation arose, the empty carriage tracks in the middle of the station were abolished, and separate buildings were provided outside the terminus for the cleaning and storage of rolling stock. This created an operational problem because by then the nearest available land was often several miles away, and the shuffling of empty carriage trains to and from the depots congested already inadequate approach tracks. In some cases at least, the ECS traffic must have tipped the balance in making the expensive decision to widen terminal approaches.

When such widening works were undertaken, in the late nineteenth and early twentieth centuries, special tracks were occasionally provided for ECS working; and at all major termini complicated arrangements eventually existed for these movements.[3] Nowadays the problem has largely disappeared; many trains are turned round quickly in the terminus and sent out again in traffic after a perfunctory cleaning, whilst the remaining workings between termini and carriage depots no longer have to compete for line occupation with a procession of steam locomotives moving to and from their depots or yards.

Despite the increase in platforms, and the associated construction of cross platforms behind the buffer stops, the rigid separation of arrival and departure 'sides', often with separate signal boxes, continued for many years. It survived at Paddington until 1967, and continued to some extent even later at Kings Cross.

Most stations built after 1860 had their booking offices and other amenities placed in a central position across the end, sometimes under a hotel which formed the frontage and closed the train shed. Stations of this type were Charing Cross, Cannon Street, Holborn Viaduct, Blackfriars, Broad Street, Fenchurch Street and Marylebone. St Pancras was an odd exception in that its booking office and some other accommodation was placed at one side, although near the street frontage, whilst the remainder of the facilities and main gateways were positioned centrally under the hotel.

With the single exception of the original Greenwich terminus at London Bridge, all designers considered it proper to protect passengers and rolling stock from the weather by means of an overall roof. The early roofs were low and unprepossessing, but beginning with Kings Cross in 1852, the high arched roof gained favour. This not only assisted the dispersal of smoke, but clearly added grandeur. Two years after Kings Cross, the first modest single-span arch appeared at Fenchurch Street, and gradually this was developed into an almost monumental feature, far larger and grander than sober necessity required, through the riverine spans of Charing Cross and Cannon Street to a climax in 1868 with Barlow's noble 240 ft arch above St Pancras. After that, the column-supported roof returned to favour, but with variations and improvements such as Jacomb-Hood's column-free passenger concourse at Waterloo. Curiously, architects and the general public continued to regard the high arched roof as *de rigueur* for an important terminus, and the roofs at Marylebone and the rebuilt Waterloo were criticised as mean and ugly. As late as the 1930s, the 'modern' model terminus sold for Hornby Trains perpetuated the old tradition of the high segmented arch. Now economy dictates design, and with the disappearance of the smoke nuisance, a terminus can be built under an office block, or hotel, passengers having to make do with a roof only a little higher than the trains, as at the new Euston.

Only five of the termini (Victoria [LBSCR], Waterloo, Euston, Blackfriars* and London Bridge*) have been completely rebuilt. Elsewhere traffic growth, particularly suburban, enforced piecemeal expansion and reconstruction, extending as far as complete

* The original train sheds survive here.

rebuilding of platforms at Fenchurch Street. A great deal more rebuilding and enlargement would have been inevitable but for the arrival of electric traction and the development of automatic signalling, two factors which afforded enormous increases in capacity without moving a brick. The underground loop termini below the main platforms which were on the drawing boards of several railway companies in the 1890s and 1900s were never needed.

CHANCES MISSED

For another type of rebuilding, the railways bestirred themselves too late. In the second half of the 1950s, central London experienced an office building boom without precedent which made fortunes for an astute band of private developers. Holding at its termini some of the most attractive sites in the capital, the British Transport Commission remained virtually inactive. No effort was made to change the statutory restriction which prevented the Commission from developing its own property for other than operational purposes, leaving it only able to recoup ground rent from any land sold. Sites at three termini were leased to a private developer on extremely favourable terms without finding any way of taking an equity stake in his schemes. When other similar schemes (to be mentioned later in this book) were stamped upon by the LCC and the City of London, the Commission always gave in without much of a fight.

It was 1959 before the Minister of Transport was asked whether he would be willing to introduce legislation to enable the railways to develop their property on a commercial basis, and eventually, in the Transport Act of 1962, this freedom was given. Schemes existed, or were produced, for almost all the London termini, but alas, by the time they began to come forward, the planning permission tap was being turned off, and in November 1964 a virtually complete ban was imposed. Only the three schemes mentioned earlier came to reality; sold by their original owner to Town & City Properties Ltd in 1962, these were for offices on the York Road side of Waterloo (finally completed in 1969), in front of Holborn Viaduct (1963) and in front of Cannon Street (1965).*

Reviewing what remains after the devastation of German bombs and post-war rebuilding, it is apparent that of the original structures, St Pancras, Paddington and Kings Cross are to be, or rather, should be, treasured—for different reasons. The order of merit can be left to personal taste.

---

* Subsequent developments, following further policy changes, are mentioned in Chapter 16.

At St Pancras, Scott's hotel is an almost overpowering exercise in high Victorian Gothic, splendid in its roofline and profusion of ornament, its interior almost as intricate as the outside. Demolition would be a crime on the scale of Euston or the City Coal Exchange, a crime which with luck, it may already be too late to pull off. That said, I must confess that there is no joy for me in looking at the Midland Grand, perhaps because the bricks, now very dirty, were the wrong colour anyway, perhaps because it all comes from the drawing board, not from the heart. And its dreary surroundings depress the spirit: particularly Midland Road, with the Goods Depot on one side, and the dark bricks of St Pancras on the other, one of the most dismal vistas in London, looking for all the world as if it had been lifted bodily from the middle of some nineteenth-century northern town.* But once inside the station, there is indeed unalloyed pleasure to be had from the triumphant spread of Barlow's great roof, a demonstration that superb architecture can be achieved through magnificent engineering.

In unique contrast alongside, Kings Cross presents its bold straightforward screen, its new forecourt clutter some improvement on the old. Here the interior is a great disappointment. The accommodation is cramped, there is little to inspire. It is to me an unfriendly, cold-hearted place, but the front makes up for it.

Paddington's riches, not to be denied, all lie within, like those of a plain girl. The hotel fails to attract the eye, only a part of the train shed can be seen from the front. Enter and you are uplifted by Brunel's elegant perspective, gently curving, broken so happily by the 'transepts'. Closer scrutiny will reveal Wyatt's bizarre and delicate ornamentation, combining so nicely with the work of the master engineer.

These three are now firmly accepted as worthy of preservation, and although it is now unlikely that they will suffer the fate of Euston's screen and Great Hall, vigilance cannot be relaxed. Of the others, each has its redeeming features and special charms, and the reader will have his own favourites. Mine are Waterloo and Marylebone, still ignored by the architectural historian and the guide books. Edwardian-Imperial, blatantly extrovert, Waterloo has a fine, solid dignity; a spacious place, offering a perfect backcloth for marching troops and Great Occasions, it was built to a sensible design that still works well. A complete opposite is unassuming little Marylebone, a very feminine building. Nondescript architecture perhaps, but there is an almost domestic tranquillity about its well-cared-for appearance and appointments, a tranquillity

* Since this was written in 1968, the scene has lightened somewhat. *Some* of the brickwork has been cleaned and the Goods Depot has been razed.

which emanates a subtle, civilised charm. There is no bustle or confusion here. The trains serve only quiet suburbs and the beech-covered hill country beyond, where in the autumn, leaves cover the tracks. All this, together with its hopeless past and even more hopeless future, make Marylebone quite the most romantic of all the London termini.

# CHAPTER 2

# Euston

It is appropriate to begin with Euston, for it was London's first main-line terminus. Planned by the engineer Robert Stephenson, and graced by the noble architecture of Philip Hardwick,[1] the London & Birmingham Railway's terminus was opened to the public on 20 July 1837. Hardwick's Doric portico and screen, and the Great Hall, designed by his son, Philip Charles,[2] were splendid monuments to the abounding confidence of the Railway Age. Surrounded and almost overwhelmed by the unworthy accretions of later years, they survived almost intact until 1961. Now the old Euston is gone, and in its place is a new terminus built to accommodate the slick electric trains which are affording London such excellent communication with Birmingham, Manchester and Liverpool that they have attracted many hundreds of new passengers from the motorways and internal airlines.

A number of sites were considered for the terminus of the London & Birmingham Railway. At first the intention was to finish up in Islington, conveniently near the Regent's Canal, for transhipments to and from the docks. Then Stephenson suggested another route into London, further to the west, with a terminus at Marble Arch, but the provisional committee objected to this as unsuitable for freight traffic, agreeing a compromise site at Maiden Lane, near Kings Cross, from whence the line could later be extended to the docks. This proposal was rejected by the Lords in 1832. In his plans for the 1833 session, Stephenson took account of economy cuts ordered by the directors, achieving a saving by terminating the line at Camden Town, just north of the Regent's Canal. This was authorised in 1833, but in the following year the board decided to venture a little nearer London and agreed plans to go forward another 1¼ miles to Euston Grove.

This extension involved a crossing over the canal which created a fairly severe gradient between there and the terminus at 1 in 68 and 1 in 77. It was considered that the outward climb might present difficulties to the light steam locomotives then in use, and arrangements were made to haul the trains up to Camden by continuous cable. Power for the cable was supplied by two 60 hp Maudslay & Field condensing engines placed underground beneath two tall chimneys either side of the line.

At Camden the engines of incoming trains were detached and the passengers' tickets collected. Trains then descended the bank unaided, attached to the cable, and controlled by 'bankriders'. A complete section of the Rules & Regulations was devoted to these men and their duties. From this we learn that:

> The Bankriders are to have the control, management and responsibility of the Inclined Plane and of the Trains passing down it . . . The speed on the Incline must never exceed 10 miles per hour, but a lower speed is necessary when the Train is heavy, or the Rails in bad order.

On the outward run, the bankriders pushed the loaded coaches to the 'Messenger', the rope which attached the train to the winding cable, and fastened it. When all was ready, and the policemen with their red, green and white flags had signalled the line clear, the men in the engine-house at Camden were alerted by the 'wailing whistle', an organ pipe operated by compressed air let into the connecting main at Euston. This air main was also used to sound a similar pipe at the terminus, giving warning of the approach of an up train. When the whistle was heard, a bell was rung to carry the message on to the porters and cabmen, and it is said that the noise would cause the cab horses to raise their heads from their nosebags and preen themselves for action.

At first the cable was not ready, and until 14 October 1837 trains were worked up to Camden with steam locomotives at front and rear. Cable working lasted until 14 July 1844, but the coasting into the terminus continued for a few more years. Maudslay's engines found useful employment at a Russian flax mill.

Steam locomotives almost always needed assistance to bring trains out of Euston. In the early days this was given by a pilot engine, which was normally detached from the train near the Canal Bridge. Running forward, it was diverted to a short siding beyond the bridge, while the intrepid pointsman, with the second engine almost upon him, reset the points for the main line. This pointsman was enjoined by the regulations not to move the points unless he saw the engineman of the pilot locomotive 'motion to the left with his hand (by night with his handlamp)'. Later, the

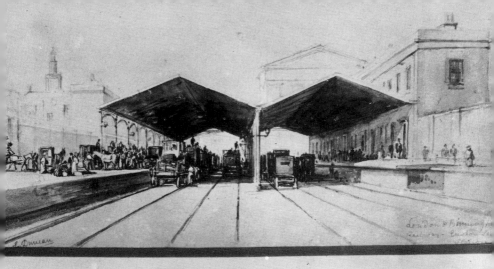

n a train arrives it stops close to the parade at the up side and passengers step out
it, and may, if they are disposed to ride to any part of the town enter the omnibusses,
or cars that are waiting for them."

(Osborne's London & Birmingham Railway Guide, 1840)

Page 33

(above) *Euston, looking south c 1840. The outline of the portico is seen behind the train
shed, right, and the tower of St Pancras New Church is in the left background. A train
has just arrived, with a private carriage on a flat truck at its rear. From a watercolour
by E. Duncan;* (below) *Euston, portico and lodges c 1901. The Western Lodge has been
demolished to make way for offices, and the Arrival Train Shed can be glimpsed between
the two Eastern Lodges*

(above) *Euston, platforms 4, 5 and 6 looking north c 1938 with Watford electric train in No 4;* (below) *The new Euston's airport-like concourse on 9 November 1968*

LNWR adopted the conventional banking engine at the rear.

In these early years, passenger working was confined to the two easternmost tracks, and only they had the cable. The outer of the two western lines was used by engines moving between Euston and the engine yard at Camden in both directions, whilst the remaining line accommodated empty carriages, for which purpose it was roofed over south of the Park Street (now Parkway) Bridge.

This first Euston had but two boarded platforms, the 'arrival stage' and the 'departure stage', on the site of what were later Nos 3 and 6 in the old Euston. These platforms were about 420 ft long and between the platform tracks were two empty carriage roads. Small hand-worked turnplates were provided to move carriages from one line to another. Similar turnplates afforded access to a 15-road carriage shed in the north-east corner of the station yard.

The railway accommodation was on the eastern half of the large site that the company had purchased fronting Drummond Street. To the west, beyond a central granite roadway, was the land reserved for the Great Western Railway's London terminus. That company planned to bring its Bristol line to a junction with the L & BR near Kensal Green, but there were arguments between the two parties about the terms of the GWR tenancy at Euston and the matter was further complicated by the GWR's determination to use the broad gauge. In the end, the Great Western withdrew and built a separate terminus at Paddington. The original Euston therefore presented a decidedly lop-sided appearance, with its railway tracks and platforms at one side behind the main frontage. Unlike Marylebone, which was also lop-sided, Euston eventually generated more than enough traffic to require all the empty space for railway use.

Approaching the station by road, the traveller saw from a distance the breathtaking vista of Hardwick's great portico, with its attendant lodges. This imposing 300 ft screen, viewed without obstruction from the new Euston Road, must have looked really splendid on a summer's day, with the sunlight catching the pristine albescence of its Bramley Fall stone all against the verdant backcloth of Hampstead Heath. One lodge was joined to the portico on each side, and there were detached lodges, with detached piers, on each side beyond. The spaces in the portico and those between the lodges and beyond were closed with lofty wrought iron gates decorated with the company's coat of arms, cast by J. J. Bramah to Hardwick's designs.

C

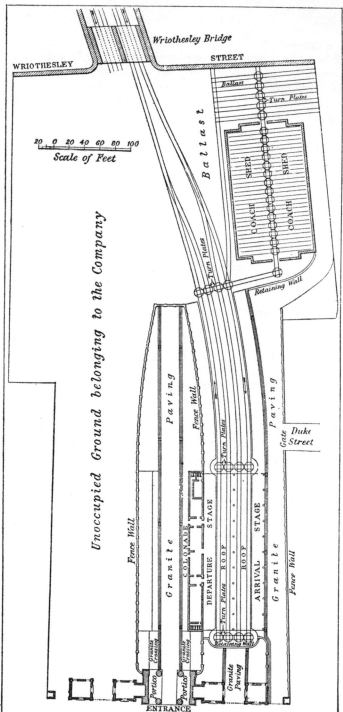

Plan of Euston station 1837. From the Railway Magazine, July 1937

## A GRAND BUT SIMPLE PORTICO

The 72 ft high portico, a true *propylaeum*, had four hollow Doric columns 44 ft 2 in high and 8 ft 6 in in diameter, thus exceeding in magnitude the Athenian *propylaea*. It was completed in May 1838 at a cost of some £35,000. Full of pride at the achievement represented by the completion of the London & Birmingham Railway, the directors had decided that nothing but architecture of the highest classical order was good enough to commemorate it, as they thought, permanently. In a report to the shareholders in February 1837, they explained: 'The entrance to the London passenger station, opening immediately upon what will necessarily become the Grand Avenue for travelling between the Midland and Northern parts of the kingdom, the directors thought that it should receive some architectural embellishment. They accepted accordingly a design of Mr Hardwick's for a grand but simple portico, which they considered well adapted for the national character of the undertaking.' The Hardwick portico was not only a 'Gateway to the North', but a great triumphal arch to mark the arrival of a wonderful new means of transport, a symbol of the solidity and endurable nature of the railway, representative of the successful marriage of steam and progress.

It did not meet with universal acclaim. Augustus Welby Pugin, architect of the Gothic Revival, was snappy:

> The architects have evidently considered it an opportunity for showing off what they could do instead of carrying out what was required. Hence the colossal Grecian portico or gateway, 100 feet high, for the cabs to drive through and put down a few feet further, at the 14 inch brick wall and sash window booking office. This piece of Brobdingnagian absurdity must have cost the company a sum which would have built a first rate station, replete with convenience, and which would have been really grand for its simplicity.[3]

Perhaps he would have approved of the new Euston.

Beyond the screen, a granite paved roadway led into the station yard, to the east of which was a two-storey stuccoed building containing the waiting rooms, offices and lavatories, with separate entrances and accommodation for first class passengers, to ensure they had no distressing contacts with the lower orders. Second class customers had a combined waiting room and booking office, but nothing was provided for the third class. At the roadway side, this building had a one-storey high colonnade to shelter the first and second class passengers arriving by carriage, omnibus or cab.

The double train shed, designed by Charles Fox,[4] was about 200 ft long, its 40 ft spans supported on cast-iron columns. At the east side was the arrival platform, flanked by a roadway for cabs and omnibuses, which passengers could reach under the protection of the roof. The various destinations of the buses were indicated on boards fixed to the columns opposite their stands. A strict control was kept over the cabs. Only forty-five were allowed inside the station at any one time, the proprietor paying the railway company a £2 deposit for each 'privilege' cab. In case of complaint the deposit was forfeited, the driver dismissed from the yard. As cabs left the station, their destination and number were noted by the railway police as a precaution against lost property and an aid in the investigation of crime and complaints.

Facilities were provided for loading the private carriages of the wealthier clients on to flat wagons whilst their horses were led into a box. This was the 1837 equivalent of Motorail, with one small difference—the passengers could if they wished remain in their own carriage throughout the rail journey. It was a tiresome business for the railway staff, as passengers using the service would often arrive at the last minute, causing delay to the train while the loading procedure was carried through.

At first, the resources of the new station were not overtaxed. There were but three outward trains and an equal number of arrivals each day, serving Harrow, Watford, and Boxmoor and covering the 24½ miles in just over an hour. On 9 April 1838 the line reached Watling Street at Denbigh Hall (just beyond Bletchley). Through passengers to Birmingham were then conveyed from Euston, travelling over the uncompleted section between Denbigh Hall and Rugby in the road coaches of Chaplin & Horne. The rail link was completed on 17 September, with nine trains each way daily between Euston and Birmingham, covering the 112¾ miles in 5¼ h or more, against 1½ h today.

At Birmingham, rail connections were available to Liverpool and Manchester. Before the London & Birmingham Railway became part of the London & North Western Railway in 1846, the opening of new lines had given Euston access to Preston, Derby, York and Edinburgh. The west coast line to Scotland was completed on 15 February 1848.

Soon after the opening of Euston, a second and larger office building, containing an open Doric colonnade of eight bays, was erected north of the first. This was subsequently included in the core block around the Great Hall, and the columns, which were in its east wall, survived on platform 6 until the demolition of the old station in 1962.

Two railway hotels, the first of their kind in London, were opened at Euston in September 1839. Simple in style and stucco-covered, they were designed by Philip Hardwick Snr, and placed in front of the portico, one either side, thus initiating the destruction of the vista and the crowding-in of the classical screen. On the west side was the Victoria, unlicensed and unpretentious, officially described as 'dormitory and coffee room'. The superior establishment on the opposite side, the Euston, catering for first class passengers, was managed by the aptly-named Mr Bacon, a former steward of the Athenaeum.

These two four-storey buildings were linked in 1881 by a new block in 'the modern French style', detailed by J. Maclaren, a very second rate affair which utterly destroyed the view of Hardwick's screen from the Euston Road. But by this time the 'embellishment' of which the London & Birmingham directors had been so proud was out of fashion, regarded as little more than a nuisance. As if to mock it, the hotel was supported over the roadway by four rows of horrible cast-iron Doric columns stuck in a poky opening which extended only to first floor level. There were some compensations; the £30,000, 141-bedroom hotel soon earned a good name among travellers. Writing of it in the *Railway Magazine* early in 1914, Basil Mercer said, 'comfort is studied rather than display, and the fact that English waiters are employed ought to gladden the heart of every patriotic Englishman'. After suffering some damage in the second world war, the Euston Hotel was finally closed in May 1963 when it was demolished to make room for the new station.

By 1845 some 140 staff were employed at Euston to attend to the needs of the passengers and mails using the twenty-two trains in and out each day. Some strain on the original platform accommodation was already becoming evident. George Carr Glyn, the L & BR chairman, told the Royal Commission on Metropolitan Termini that in the summer and autumn of 1845, 'the Post Office were so late that the 8.30 pm Lancashire Mail was frequently delayed until the 9 pm departure time of the Yorkshire Mail; the confusion was very great, and the company decided to separate the Yorkshire traffic.'

This separation was achieved in 1846 by the provision of new departure and arrival platforms (later numbered 9 and 10) on the vacant land originally reserved for the GWR, to the west of the 1837 station and cab yard. Platform 9 remained 'the York' to railwaymen until it finally disappeared in 1963, although the main flow of York traffic was diverted to the more direct route of the Great Northern Railway after that line had reached London in 1850. At the same time as the construction of the new platforms, houses in Whittlebury Street, on the extreme western boundary of the original Euston site, were demolished to make room for a long railway office block, running north from Drummond Street. By 1849 the original arrival platform had been lengthened to 900 ft and a third carriage siding had been added between the 1837 platforms.

The second splendour of old Euston, the Great Hall, opened on 27 May 1849, was a combined concourse and waiting room which set the pattern for many similar halls in large stations abroad. It formed part of a 220 ft by 168 ft block erected in 1846-9 by William Cubitt & Co at a cost of £150,000. Despite the employment of an eminent architect, this large complex of buildings was erected with virtually no regard either to the future development of the station or its existing layout. By the nature of its plan and position, it could not but distort the future growth of the station, virtually splitting the whole area into separate parts, and, owing to the shape of the site, making it quite impossible to build anything but short platforms behind it. Given that it was to be a central feature of the terminus, it is also odd that it was not placed symmetrically with the portico, but a little to the west of it.

After passing through the portico and the yard behind, passengers alighted from their conveyances under an awning at the south end of this new building and entered through one of five doorways. These led into an outer vestibule, 64 ft by 22 ft, floored with a mosaic pavement of patent 'metallic lava'. Five more entrances opened into the Great Hall.

This huge chamber was 125 ft 6 in long by 61 ft 4 in wide, and 62 ft high. At its northern end, a curved double staircase in stone led up to a central flight serving a 16 ft wide vestibule and a gallery round the walls. Beyond the vestibule were a shareholders' meeting room, board room, various committee rooms and the suites of the company's principal officers.

The meeting room, with space for some 400 shareholders, was

a beautiful apartment in the Renaissance style, with pairs of marble pillars around the walls. The main features of the board room were a sculptured plaster ceiling and a great yellow pine table.

Few other English buildings could offer anything to match the deeply-coffered ceiling of the Great Hall, embellished with massive curved consoles and plaster bas-reliefs in each corner, the whole beautifully lit by attic windows. The bas-reliefs, measuring 10 ft by 7 ft were in pairs; with busty, long-thighed women and muscular men, they symbolised London, Birmingham, Northampton, Chester, Manchester, Carlisle, Lancashire and Liverpool.

Above the Doric portal of the meeting room was a stone group incorporating a judicious Victorian mix—Britannia, a lion, a ship, Mercury, the Arts and the Sciences. Both sculpture and bas-reliefs were the work of John Thomas.[5] The decoration was completed by mock columns, four double ones at the north end, four single ones at the south, all 24 ft 7 in high. Contemporary accounts described the style as 'Roman-Ionic'. Modern architectural writers have found other influences. Whatever it was, it was undoubtedly impressive, and no other London station had anything to match this huge room.

Such display was inevitably expensive. Every effort was made to cut the cost where this could be done without diminishing the effect. The walls were decorated with grey Martin's cement to simulate granite, and the columns were of plaster, marbled to suggest red granite. In 1852 a Carrara marble statue of George Stephenson by E. H. Baily was placed at the foot of the staircase. Over the years, clutter accumulated, including slot machines and a number of railway models in large glass cases.

To the east of the hall was the main booking hall, 60 ft by 40 ft, matched on the opposite side by a smaller booking hall, 56 ft by 33 ft, for the midlands and the branch lines. West of the Great Hall block, on the other side of what was later platform 10, a new building, long and narrow, housed the parcels office. In line with it, to the south, were the Queen's Apartments, an early example of the VIP lounge, intended to afford privacy and comfort to royalty and other notables using the railway. There were two rooms, one an antechamber, both decorated in the 'Greek' style, with white and buff walls 'painted in large panels with the most fairy-like scroll ornaments and flowers'. The windows of the main room stretched from floor to ceiling, and when they were opened, the privileged users could step straight on to the departure platform.[6] These facilities were apparently scorned, as within a few years the premises were devoted to more practical purposes, becoming an extension of the parcels office.

After the splendours of the portico and the Great Hall, the rest of Euston came as something of an anti-climax. A writer of the 1850s commented:

> . . . as is common in this country . . . the spirit of the pro-
> prietors evaporated with the outworks . . . We cannot bestow
> unqualified praise upon the station arrangements at Euston. Com-
> fort has been sacrificed to magnificence . . . the waiting rooms,
> refreshment stand, and *other conveniences* are as ill-contrived as
> possible; while a vast hall with magnificent roof and scagliola
> pillars appears to have swallowed up all the money, and all the
> light of the establishment. The First Class Waiting Room is dull
> to a fearful degree, and finished in the dreariest style of economy.
> The Second Class Waiting Room is a dark cavern, with nothing
> better than a borrowed light . . .[1]

Apart from the addition of a small bay platform on the east side, behind the Great Hall (later No 7), to accommodate the Kensington (Addison Road) trains in 1863, there were no further substantial changes until 1869-74. Then, stimulated by the arrival in London of its competitor, the Midland, the LNWR set about adding a little grandeur and some more platforms.

A strip of ground was acquired between the hotels and Euston Road to accommodate an 80 ft wide approach drive. At the south end of this, J. B. Stansby, the company's architect, provided square two-storey entrance lodges, faced with Portland stone, panelled and rusticated. Incised and gilded letters on the quoin stones proclaimed the names of the principal stations of the LNWR, many of them, such as Peterborough, Leicester and Swansea, to be reached much more expeditiously from other establishments up and down the road.

In the west lodge, the guide book publishers and tourist agents Norton & Shaw established a branch office, whilst the other was used as a small parcels office.* The new entrance, opened in 1870, was graced by a bronze statue of Robert Stephenson by Baron Carlo Marochetti, presented to the LNWR by the Institution of Civil Engineers, in whose vaults it had been gathering dust for some years. Behind Stephenson, the LNWR later erected a memorial to the 3,719 employees killed in the 1914-18 war.

For eleven years, until the enlargement of the hotel destroyed it, the drive enhanced the vista of Hardwick's screen from the Euston Road. A touch of emphasis was added by placing the station name in incised gilded letters on the architrave of the portico.

* A post office was established in the West Lodge in 1870. Moved to the Great Hall about 1925, it lasted until the building of the new station.

In the station itself, extensive improvements were carried out on the east side. New platforms (1 and 2) were completed in 1873, together with a cab entrance from Seymour Street (now Eversholt Street) at the north end leading to a cab road between them. The space for this enlargement was obtained by demolishing a row of small houses on the west side of Seymour Street and by removing the 1837 carriage shed (a new shed was built on the up side at Willesden). Whilst this work was going on, in 1872, the original 1837 roof was raised 6 ft to provide more room for the dispersal of smoke, not to mention a little more grandeur. An area 900 ft by 130 ft was jacked up hydraulically and all the new pedestals were inserted in the course of a week.

### ADDING DREARINESS

From 1881 onwards, new offices were constructed east and west of the station yard and along the Drummond Street front on the west side. These added greatly to the heavy dreariness of the old Euston and continued the process of destroying Hardwick's work. The westernmost pier and lodge were demolished to make way for them. So difficult was the lodge to remove, that the contractors were forced to blow it up. The London & Birmingham had been built to last.

A continuing growth of long-distance traffic made it necessary to expand the western side of the station to the fullest possible extent, and this was accomplished between 1887 and 1892. It was a major project, involving the diversion of Cardington Street over the burial ground of St James's, Westminster. In disturbing the dead, care was taken that there would be no cause for the kind of public outcry that had arisen during the construction of the approaches to St Pancras. Each corpse was provided with a new coffin and reinterred at St Pancras Cemetery, Finchley, at the expense of the LNWR. Acworth records in *The Railways of England*, that 'a doctor and an inspector were constantly present at either end on behalf of the company, to see that nothing was done which might offend against either due reverence for the dead or due regard for the health of the living'. When it was all over, the ground was probed to make sure nobody was left behind.

The lengthy western departure platforms (12-15) were brought into use on 1 July 1892, together with a separate booking office and cab entrance in Drummond Street. This station within a station caused much confusion, so much so, that in the heat of the moment, comparisons were drawn with the old Waterloo, though

it was never as bad as that. Eventually the situation was put right
by extending the main cab yard westwards under the office block
and by opening a new booking office near platform 12, in a better
position to serve all parts of the station. A casualty of the west side
alterations was the down side carriage shed, replaced by an additional shed at Willesden in 1888. On the east side, the 'wooden
platform' for local trains (Nos 4 and 5) was completed in 1891 on
the site of the carriage roads remaining from the original station.

Euston had now reached its maximum extent of 15 platforms,
numbered from east to west. Arriving trains used 1 to 3, suburban
trains 4 and 5. Platform 6 handled both arrivals and departures,
including royal trains, and (until the very end of the old Euston),
the famous 'West Coast Postal'. Number 7 was another local platform, whilst 8 to 10 were used for parcels and occasionally for
local trains. Served from Cardington Street by an approach road
over platforms 13 to 15, platform 11 was used only for parcels,
milk and fish traffic. Platforms 12 to 15 were allocated to main-line
departures. Between 5 and 6 was a third road, 'the horse box line'.

The area behind the Great Hall, too cramped for passenger platforms, was known as 'the field' and contained several short reception sidings. At the outer end of platforms 10 and 11 were a
carriage dock and an engine siding (later another siding, 'B', was
put in between platforms 10 and 11). Between 11 and 12 was the
'brake pit road' and between 13 and 14, 'road No 2'. Alongside
platform 15 were engine sidings, and, at the outer end, an engine
turntable. The enlargement works were rounded off in 1898 by
the demolition of the two-arch Ampthill Square bridge and its replacement by a girder structure, permitting the arrival platforms
to be extended and the approach curves to be eased.

All this patching and stretching of the 1837 station only served
to emphasise Euston's unworthiness as the London terminus of the
self-styled 'Premier Line'. At least some of the directors were
ashamed of it, and in 1898-9 the board considered a scheme for
complete reconstruction, with the frontage brought up to Euston
Square Gardens. An Act was obtained in 1900, but the financial
disruptions of the South African war enabled the company to post-
pone what must have looked like a very difficult decision. Piecemeal development was to continue for another sixty years.

Until this time, there was but one down running line between
Camden and Euston, a state of affairs that caused much difficulty
and delay and had to be put right, whether or not a new station
were built. Work began in 1901 on the widening of the cutting
and approach lines, continuing until 1906. Some half million tons

of clay were removed, making room for the new lines and two new carriage sheds, one each side of the tracks. These sheds provided cover for some 350 coaches, and with the additional sidings put in at the same time, eliminated many of the unprofitable 11-mile return workings to the Willesden depot. (In 1953 carriage servicing was transferred from Willesden depot to a large new installation at Stonebridge Park.)

A new double line was provided in the cutting for engine movements to and from the Camden depot, and a subway, with a gradient of 1 in 50 was constructed to carry an up engine line and down empty carriage line from the arrival side to the carriage sidings and shed on the west side. 'Backed out' by their own engines through this subway, the carriages of arriving trains, after servicing in the west yard, could be moved direct to the departure platforms without interfering with other traffic. Upon the completion of this work, four running lines were available for passenger trains in and out of the terminus.

From the down to the up side, the arrangement was:

11-road carriage shed,
four ' Backing Out ' roads,
up engine line No. 1,
down fast,
down slow,
up slow,
up fast,
up engine line No 2,
down empty carriage line,
5-road carriage shed.

The last work carried out by the LNWR improved the amenities of the terminus. In 1913-14 a new booking concourse was formed south of the Great Hall by using a 150 ft by 30 ft section of the cab yard. The old booking offices were converted to refreshment rooms. When this work was complete, in 1915-16, the hall was renovated and repainted. Electric light had been installed throughout the station in 1905, but the gas globes in the hall were left undisturbed.

Euston has always been predominantly a main-line station; suburban traffic was sparse for many years, but an hourly service to Watford was started on 1 June 1879 after completion of quadrupling between Camden and Willesden Junction. There was no connection with the Underground system until 12 May 1907, when the City & South London tube railway opened its extension from the Angel. This was followed on 22 June by the opening of a second tube station, on the Charing Cross, Euston & Hampstead Railway. At the insistence of the LNWR, both tube lines had street stations, the CSLR in Eversholt Street (Euston House is now over the site), and the CCEHR in Drummond Street, but there were also lifts to a small booking hall beneath the eastern side of the terminus, with stairs up to platforms 3 and 6. The Metropolitan was a good five minutes' walk away, at Gower Street, renamed Euston Square (a misnomer) on 1 November 1909 as a late reaction to the opening of the tube stations at Euston. The arrival of the tube railways, in particular Parliamentary approval for tube extensions from Golders Green to Edgware and Watford, spurred the LNWR into some serious thinking about suburban traffic.

In 1906 plans were announced for a new electric line alongside the main lines as far as Watford, with a terminal loop in tube beneath Euston. After the LNWR had taken over the management of the North London Railway in 1909, and following negotiations with the Underground company, this scheme was wisely modified. In 1911 it was agreed that the incoming traffic from the new suburban line would be split into three streams: LNWR electric trains to Euston and Broad Street, and Bakerloo tube trains to the West End via a new tube connection between Queen's Park and Paddington. The electric trains into Euston were to run into the existing station instead of an underground loop. To segregate them from the main-line traffic, there were to be further improvements to the approaches, including new twin tubes of 16 ft 4 in diameter through Primrose Hill, and a system of burrowing junctions at Chalk Farm. There would also be a new 955 yd single-track tunnel passing under all lines and the Regent's Canal, carrying the up empty carriage road from the north side of the line at Camden to the west carriage yard, on the other side some way down the bank. These works were delayed by the first world war, and were not finally completed until 1922. A public service of 630 volt dc third and fourth rail electric trains between Euston and Watford began on 10 July 1922. In the terminus, platforms 4, 5 and 7 were electrified.

At the 1923 grouping, the LNWR was absorbed into the London Midland & Scottish Railway, a company soon proud to call itself the largest private enterprise in the British Empire. Despite this boast, it did not make any very impressive changes at Euston, at least not until 1935, when it proposed to tear the whole place down and rebuild.

During 1927 the Great Hall was renovated for a second time. On this occasion the advice of Sir Edwin Lutyens, the eminent archi-

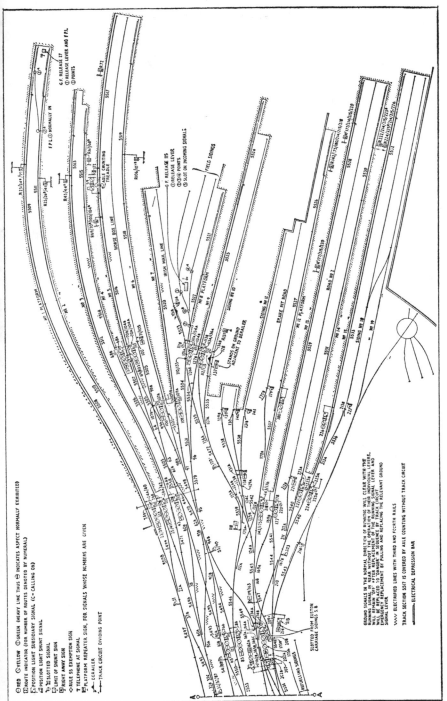

*Plan of Euston 1953. From the Railway Magazine, March 1953*

tect, resulted in the walls and pillars being coated with 'imitation red Egyptian porphyry'. Electric light replaced gas in the original globes. Three years later, 'as a further step forward in its modernisation',[8] the hall received in its midst a large and hideous enquiry and reservation bureau. Very little else happened. Platform loudspeakers were installed in 1934 and a year later, platforms 12 and 13 were lengthened.

### RUMBLINGS OF RECONSTRUCTION

But behind the scenes great plans were being made. As early as 1933, at the annual dinner of the Royal Institute of British Architects, Sir Josiah Stamp, chairman of the LMSR, had flown the kite, mentioning the difficulty of rebuilding Euston without demolishing the Great Hall, and wondering whether he would be accused of vandalism if he scrapped Scott's St Pancras 'obsolete as an hotel and useless as offices' (the significance of this last point will be seen in a moment). At the end of 1935 it was announced that Euston station, hotel and offices would be rebuilt with the aid of a government loan guarantee under the Railways (Agreement) Act of 1935. Percy Thomas, president of the Royal Institute of British Architects, was appointed consulting architect to co-operate with the company's architect and chief civil engineer in preparing plans and designs. These duly emerged, and showed that the vast new terminus would have an hotel and office frontage on the Euston Road. Helicopters would be accommodated on the roof (a suburban service for directors?) and there would be sufficient room for the traffic of St Pancras. The Great Hall, which stood in the way, would have to go, but it might prove possible to re-erect Hardwick's portico along the Euston Road front.

On 12 July 1938, Sir Josiah sat down in the shareholders' meeting room of the doomed Great Hall complex to throw a switch which set off charges at Caldon Low quarries, releasing 100,000 tons of limestone to build the new station. After this little drama, nothing more was done apart from the erection of some flats at Kentish Town to accommodate those who would be displaced by the new works. Once again a war had intervened.

Air raids in 1940 damaged the roof of the Great Hall, and a bomb which landed between platforms 2 and 3 wrecked offices and part of the hotel. All in all, the Germans made a pretty poor job of demolishing the old place. Battered by heavy wartime use, the shabby hole-and-corner muddle that was Euston passed into the hands of British Railways with a great deal of other property in similar state. Unable to obtain the capital necessary for complete reconstruction, BR continued the patching up policy. Surprisingly it spent over £500,000 on this.

One of the first of BR's gifts to Euston was a large train arrival bureau erected at the south end of platforms 1 to 3 in June 1951. Here, in almost cinema-like atmosphere and comfort, 92 people could sit, watching train information back-projected on to a 12-panel screen, savouring the widespread disruption, railway and personal, that lay behind the bland announcements that the train from X and Y was 70 minutes late at Rugby, and that from A and B, 90 minutes late at Watford.

The next step was to get the awkward track layout sorted out. Long trains standing in an arrival platform fouled access to other platforms, holding up incoming trains outside. Nothing could be done about this until the Ampthill Square bridge at the north end of the station and the old No 2 signal box were moved out of the way. The offending bridge was demolished in January 1952 and the signal box disappeared when the signalling was modernised later in that year. This done, the track layout was simplified, and the number of diamond crossings reduced from eighteen to five. At the same time, platforms 1 to 3, 6, 7 and 15 were lengthened, the extensions varying from 40 ft on 15 to 190 ft on 1. In 1954-5, platforms 12 to 15 were repositioned and widened, the siding between 14 and 13 becoming 13 platform road after 13 had been widened; 12 was moved similarly, the old platform 12 line becoming a siding. New cantilevered supports for the building on the extreme western side of the station provided room for the new platform 15 road.

In view of what was to come, it is poignant to record that the Great Hall and shareholders' meeting room were carefully re-decorated to Hardwick's original designs during 1951-3. The general appearance of the hall was much improved by the removal of the intruding LMSR enquiry bureau.

A 'Continental refreshment terrace' was opened at the south end of the departure platforms in September 1958. Here passengers were able to sip BR tea amidst coal smuts and diesel fumes—a scene worthy of the pencil of Osbert Lancaster.

Attention was next directed to the ticket-issuing facilities. A new suburban booking office, equipped with a Westinghouse-Garrard ticket printing and issuing machine, was installed on platforms 4 and 5 in 1958. Two years later, new main-line booking offices, with ten AEG Multiprinter machines, were opened either side of the main entrance to the Great Hall. Euston thus became the first London terminus to have fully-mechanised ticket-issuing equipment.

These improvements did little to alleviate the dreary, soot-be-grimed squalor of the old station. To the ordinary passenger, it was a place to get away from as quickly as possible, yet for those with hearts to feel and eyes to see it was heavy with history, a station of character. There was still a thrill to be had as one stood at the buffers of platforms 1 and 2 watching powerful locomotives roll-ing in round the sweeping curve with well-filled expresses from the north; and the redecorated Great Hall seized the imagination, evoking as it did the awesome dignity of the 'Premier Line' and the great Victorians who built it up. But the portico, with a tobacco kiosk wedged incongruously into its east side, was filthy and sad; crowded about, it could not be properly seen and many must have passed through the station unaware of its existence.

When we heard in 1959 that all this was to disappear, that at long last a new Euston was to be built, no one was much troubled. The old place would go without many tears, and everyone assumed without a second thought that some way of saving the Great Hall and the portico would be found.

### OLD GLORY DESTROYED

An integral part of a great scheme for the electrification of the lines to Birmingham, Manchester and Liverpool, the new station was to be a terminus worthy of what was virtually a new railway. As the LMSR planners had already realised, Euston could not be enlarged without removing the Hardwick screen and the Great Hall, for the only possible space for expansion was to the south, and the historic buildings were in the path of new platforms. So it was that late in 1959 BR gave the London County Council the re-quired two months' notice of its intention to demolish the portico and the hall; both were on the statutory list of buildings of archi-tectural and historical interest. The LCC gave permission, provided the screen was re-erected in an appropriate dignified and open setting, but their consultants could find no way of preserving the Great Hall without impeding the operational requirements of the railway.

Half its battle won, BR strongly opposed the LCC's re-erection stipulation, pointing out that the portico could not be moved and rebuilt for less than £190,000, whereas the cost of demolition was but £12,000. The baby was then placed firmly in the government's lap, with the LCC bravely promising financial help if others would

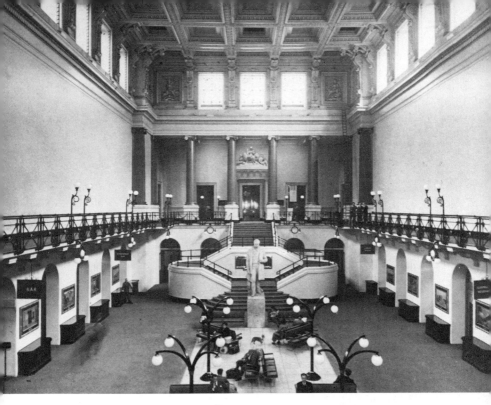

Page 51

(above) *Euston, the Great Hall, after restoration by British Railways in 1953, looking north. The entrance to the Shareholders' Room is seen at the top of the stairs; (below) St Pancras interior, looking north c 1869. At left, by the Spiers & Pond refreshment cabin, a local train awaits departure. Girders for the hotel screen are seen in the centre road, whilst an express arrives on the right*

St Pancras in pristine splendour, about 1885, shortly after the completion of the west wing and cab ramps. Kings Cross is seen at the extreme right. The site for the Somers Town Goods Depot has been cleared at the extreme left

do likewise. In July 1961, the Minister of Transport, Ernest Marples, announced that the preservation of the portico did not justify the expenditure involved; but this was not the end of the story.

A strong opposition was organised. Many experts questioned the estimate of £190,000, and it was said that a Canadian firm would undertake to move the portico on rollers for less than half that sum. The Earl of Euston, the Earl of Rosse, John Betjeman, and many eminent architects led the battle against what the Conservative *Daily Telegraph* had called 'a disgraceful action'. On 16 October 1961, with scaffolding already erected around the great Doric columns, seventy-five architects and students demonstrated inside the Great Hall, hanging placards on the portico. Eight days later, a 15-man deputation, led by the president of the Royal Academy, Sir Charles Wheeler, attended upon Prime Minister Harold Macmillan in his room at the House of Commons. But it was all to no avail.

In his reply to Sir Charles, the prime minister pointed out that not only would the removal cost £190,000, but even if it were thought right to spend such a sum, there was no suitable site where the re-erected portico would not look incongruous. It could not be placed in front of the new station, as this was to come right up to the Euston Road. Its fate sealed, the 'Arch' felt the first blows of the breakers on 6 November 1961. Four months later, it had disappeared from sight. In case of a miracle, the contractor carefully numbered the stones.

### REBUILDING BEGINS AT LAST

Taylor Woodrow Construction Ltd was awarded the contract for stage one of the new Euston in the summer of 1962. Slowly, the process of platform reconstruction proceeded across the station site from east to west; down came the Great Hall and its less worthy surroundings. With that wonderful calm ingenuity that is a professional characteristic of railway civil engineers, a new station was erected amidst the ruins of the old while train services continued through it all.

An 11,000 sq ft temporary building, containing ticket offices, waiting room, shops, a post office and an enquiry office, was opened on 1 April 1963 to serve the needs of passengers during the rebuilding period. There was some inconvenience, and many passengers were diverted to other stations, but Euston remained very much alive throughout the whole operation.

D

By 1966, fifteen passenger platforms had been completed, together with parcel and restaurant car docks on the Cardington Street side, twenty platforms in all. Lengths varied from 1,300 ft to 700 ft, the main platforms being 37 ft wide. The first regular workings of main-line electric trains began in November 1965,* to be followed on 3 January 1966 by the full electric service. In conjunction with the construction of the new platforms, the approach tracks were rearranged to give complete interchangeability of routes.

Platforms 8, 9, 10 were fitted with conductor rails as well as overhead wires to accommodate the Watford suburban trains (the conductors were removed from 8 in 1967). Most main-line electric trains were turned round at the platforms, only night trains, Pullmans and certain day expresses going out to Willesden carriage depot. It was soon found that there was insufficient stabling space for the electric locomotives and some use was made of platform 11 for this purpose.

Above platforms 3 to 18 in the northern part of the station was a fully-mechanised parcels depot, five acres in extent, opened on 7 August 1966. Road vehicles reached this from Barnby Street via elevated roadways, leaving at the north end of Cardington Street. Parcels were moved to and from the platforms by ramps and goods lifts.

At the bend of Cardington Street, on the site of the locomotive turntable, a four-storey Signals and Telecommunications Centre was opened in September 1965.

From the time the new station was first planned in the late 1950s, BR had hoped to find a large part of the expenditure from the proceeds of commercial lettings, but the LCC frowned on the idea of offices over the station. The BR plan involved four tower blocks, one 365 ft high, together with a 300 ft high hotel between the station frontage and Euston Road. It was unfortunate that the final proposal went to the LCC just one week after the government had issued a White Paper stating that the rate of office growth in central London could not be allowed to continue without more effective control, and that in future, most new offices would have to be outside the central area. A few weeks later, in March 1963, the LCC told BR there could be no offices at Euston other than for BR staff.

## A NEW GREAT HALL

Fresh plans were then prepared, with the possibility of a hotel tower block still in mind, and Taylor Woodrow began work on the

* The last steam trains had worked into Euston in 1964.

passenger building in May 1966. Designed by R. L. Moorcroft, the London Midland Region architect, this long, low unassuming structure flanked Euston Square, just south of Drummond Street, part of which was covered. Between the building and the square was a paved open space, known as the piazza, above a parking area for 230 cars.

Completed in large part by September 1968, the new passenger building was opened by the Queen on 14 October. On the Euston Square frontage, passengers approached a 647 ft colonnade through which they passed from the piazza to the concourse hall. This colonnade was a neat link with the Euston of 1837, which had a similar feature on the street side. Harmonising with the great grey mass of the station behind, the frontage elevations were in black and white, polished black granite cladding on the rectangular columns, and white mosaic horizontal facings, with glazed screens between.

The passenger hall, some 200 ft wide by 150 ft deep under a 36 ft high main roof, was quickly named the Great Hall, after its predecessor. Well lit and air conditioned, it was entirely free from the trolley traffic that is such a great nuisance to passengers at some other termini. The ticket barriers to platforms 1 to 15 were on the north side, at the head of gently sloping ramps; also on this side, below the clerestory, was a large electro-mechanical departure indicator set between illuminated advertisement panels. To the west of the hall was the self contained travel centre, with its information, reservation and booking facilities. Along the north and east sides were various shops, refreshment rooms and lavatories, some of those on the east at first floor level. Shops were also to be found in the colonnade either side of the hall, altogether offering a greater variety of services than at any other British station, including a tailor, a hairdresser, a bank, book and record shops, an off-licence, a travel agency, a betting shop, and a photographic shop. The post office however was not replaced, although there were posting and postal vending machines in the hall.

Immediately below the concourse was the large new Underground booking hall, reached by escalators, but also linked directly to the suburban platforms by subway. From 1 December 1968, Victoria Line service was available from Euston, in addition to the Northern Line. No connection was made to the Metropolitan and Circle Lines at Euston Square; should a subway eventually be built, it will need a travolator, as the Euston platform ends are still a long way back from Euston Road.

Apart from the parcels facilities already mentioned, all vehicular traffic was confined to basement level. Taxis and private cars entered from the west side, and after setting down at a platform with direct access to the concourse, could leave for the outgoing station taxi rank, the basement car park, or the street, as appropriate. In the northern part of the basement, reached by a service road from Eversholt Street, were unloading docks for mail, newspapers, and shop and catering supplies.

Two relics of the old Euston were preserved in the new. The Stephenson statue adorned the piazza, and John Thomas's Britannia group from the doorway of the shareholders' meeting room was to be found just inside the entrance to the Sprig buffet.

When the last of the old buildings were demolished in 1969 and the final dispositions could be seen, there was no doubt that room could have been found for the portico between the frontage and the main road. Instead we now have the station frontage completely obscured by the office blocks allowed by a later planning about-face.

## SIGNALLING AND ACCIDENTS

Until the last decade of the nineteenth century the signalling arrangements at Euston were distinctly primitive, but on 27 April 1891 as part of the general improvements to the west side, a new main signal cabin, Euston No 2, was opened in the yard, opposite platforms 7 and 8. This contained 288 levers in two long frames, at which the men worked face to face. The old No 1 box, or 'bell house', with 20 levers, strung above the cab road between platforms 2 and 3, dated from the 1870s. It remained in use to control the workings of platforms 1 to 5. Communication between Nos 1 and 2 boxes was effected by means of a ringing code and describers; the former was necessary as the signalman in No 2 could not see the arrival roads, and there was no track circuiting.

With the approach lines improvements of 1901-6, subsidiary boxes Nos 1, 3 and 4 were converted to electric power signalling, with point motors and solenoid-worked semaphores and discs. No 3 box ('Port Arthur') was situated at the station end of the backing out roads on the down side, and No 4 was between up engine line No 1 and the subway. Later, many of the signals controlled from the main No 2 box were changed to the same electrical system, and in March 1906 this box was given two new tappet locking frames designed by A. M. Thompson, arranged along the windows at either side of the cabin, 255 levers in all.

A serious accident occurred in 1924, shortly after the inauguration of the suburban electric services. At 7.53 am on 26 April, a
six-car up electric train struck the rear of the 5.30 am Cup Final excursion from Coventry, made up to fourteen coaches. Five passengers were killed in the main-line train, which was standing at the
up slow home signal for Euston No 4 box. The motorman of the
electric train was trapped in his cab for five hours. As a result of
what the Ministry of Transport inspecting officer described as a
'false mental impression', the signalman had given *train out of
section* for an up Scots express which had been standing on the up
fast line alongside the excursion, on his up slow instead of his up
fast instrument, subsequently accepting the electric train on the
line already occupied by the excursion. Owing to smoke and steam
under Park Street bridge, the motorman had not been able to see
the tail light of the excursion until he was within 16 yards
of it.

On 10 November 1938, 23 people were injured when a suburban train at platform 15 was hit by empty coaches mistakenly
directed into it because a bell signal was misunderstood.

Although some colour-light signalling was installed by the LMSR
in 1934, this was on a very limited scale, and Euston's signalling
remained crude for such a large and important station.

Just how crude was illuminated by the inspector's report of an
accident which took place fifteen years later, on 6 August 1949. On
the morning of that day, empty stock was being propelled from
one of the backing out roads into platform 12 when it was
wrongly directed into platform 13, occupied by stock for the
8.37 am Manchester train, which it ran into at about 5 mph. The
inspector noted that there was no track circuiting and nothing in
No 2 box to show which platforms were occupied, apart from a
slate on which the signalmen were supposed to chalk up platform
occupation, rubbing out the entry when the train left. Track circuiting was installed on platforms 12 to 15 soon after.

Modern signalling came at last in 1952. The new box, opened on
6 October, had 227 all-electric levers in a Westinghouse frame (61
point levers, including 2 ground frame releases, 126 signal levers,
including 50 for ground signals, and 40 spares). The box, on the up
side just north of the Hampstead Road bridge, replaced Euston
Nos 1, 2 and 3, and the main line controls in Euston No 4. It
worked the station's whole new complex of colour light signals
and electro-pneumatic points (the first at any London terminus) as
far out as Camden No 1 box. There were 32 long range multi-
aspect colour light signals, 26 position-light subsidiary signals, 21

short range yellow aspect signals (for movements from running signals to sidings without track circuits) and theatre type route indicators.

This expensive equipment remained in use for only thirteen years. The new box, opened in September 1965 as part of the re-built station, was on the west side between Cardington Street and Ampthill Square. It had a Westinghouse control panel split into two rings, allowing two signalmen each to set up a route simultan-eously. Working with Ericsson train describer equipment, the panel was of the entrance-exit type, combining operating controls and indications for 755 routes. Signalmen and panel were in an air conditioned room. Control of the main lines extended as far as South Hampstead, that for the dc lines as far as Queen's Park No 3, and that for the North London route as far as Primrose Hill. In all, the station and control area contained 67 colour light signals (only four of them automatic), 82 ground signals, and 84 sets of points. Euston No 4, which had become Euston Carriage Shed box in 1952, and Camden Nos 1 and 2 were all closed, as was the 1952 box.

# CHAPTER 3

# St Pancras

### MISTAKEN FOR A CHURCH

It is said that an American tourist staying at a Bloomsbury hotel once asked for the nearest place of worship, and was directed to St Pancras Church. Taking a wrong turning, he found himself confronted with St Pancras station, which he duly entered, sufficiently deceived to doff his hat. On meeting a resplendently-attired individual whom he took to be some sort of beadle, he enquired the time of the next service, and was somewhat abashed to be given the departure times of half a dozen trains. This story does not strain credulity too far; St Pancras is a most impressive building, with Gothic architecture that imparts a distinctly ecclesiastical flavour. Its structure provides undeniable impact, for not only is there the intricate, imposing frontage, but inside, and in some ways more precious, is a beautifully-engineered train shed, one of the finest in the world. In truth a worthy temple for the steam locomotive, St Pancras was the Midland Railway's contribution to the London railway scene. Its splendours were not surpassed by any terminus built subsequently.

The Midland had reached Hitchin in May 1857, and from the 1 February following, its trains ran into London over the Great Northern main line. Freight and minerals were flowing south in increasing quantity over the Midland, but because the GNR jealously imposed a cruel toll of 1s 9d a ton on coal carried over its line, compared with 2d for other minerals, most Midland coal continued to come south over the London & North Western, which had handled the Midland's London traffic for many years.

Little satisfaction was to be had from these arrangements. The coal was delayed at Rugby, and over the single pair of tracks between Hitchin and London, the GNR naturally gave priority to its own trains. Matters came to a head in 1862, when both Midland and GNR were handling a very heavy excursion traffic into London for the Great International Exhibition in South Kensington. Most of the special exhibition trains, including those of the Midland, were accommodated in the GNR goods yard at Kings Cross, where amenities were sketchy, and platforms inadequate or non-existent. This, and the delays were bad enough, but as summer came and the pressure on track space grew, the GNR demanded that the Midland make use of their own coal depot, which they had all but finished nearby. There was some hesitation on the Midland's part as to whether this was feasible, when, to show their temper, the GNR summarily cleared a number of Midland wagons from their yard.

Utterly humiliated by the events of 1862, the Midland board confirmed a decision already half-made—that the railway must have its own access to London. A bill was prepared for a 49¾ mile line southwards from Bedford, presented to Parliament in the following year, and passed, despite not unexpected opposition from the GNR and the LNWR.

Mention has been made of a Midland coal depot at Kings Cross. Even before the decision was taken to build the London Extension, the Midland was busy providing itself with extensive facilities for its metropolitan goods traffic, which had outgrown the accommodation the GNR was able to offer. Opened in stages between 1862 and 1865, the Midland goods and coal depot was sited between the North London Railway and the Regent's Canal, immediately to the west of the GNR yards, and to the north of Agar Town, a slum area from which it took its name. Naturally, in consenting to these arrangements, the GNR had hoped to stave off any ideas for a separate main line to London.

Despite the fact that coal and goods traffic provided the greater part of the Midland's revenues and the main incentive for the London Extension, the prestige value of a well-sited passenger terminus was not overlooked. To be fully competitive with its rivals, the LNWR and GNR, the Midland realised it must bring its passengers to the Royal Commission boundary at Euston Road, despite the necessity to cross the Canal and break open an already built-up area. The matter was clinched when the company was able to obtain for a moderate price the eastern part of Lord Somers' estate, on the north side of Euston Road.

William Barlow,[1] the Midland's consulting engineer, decided to bring the line south from Camden Square on the level, passing under the North London Railway, through the reeking slums of Agar Town, and over the Canal and the Fleet River. This meant that the platforms of the terminus were to be some 20 ft above the

Euston Road, despite a slight falling gradient into the station, which was to cause a number of buffer stop collisions over the years and require shunting engines to assist outgoing trains from the rear. During the first half of 1866, several thousand houses in Agar Town and Somers Town, almost all of them mean and squalid, were demolished to make way for the railway. Evicted without compensation of any kind, some 10,000 people crowded into adjacent areas, making new slums and breeding grounds for epidemic disease. At the southernmost point, seven streets were demolished to make room for the 4½ acre terminus. Also on the site of the station was St Luke, Kings Cross, a brand new church, which had to be rebuilt in Kentish Town at the Midland's expense.

A corner of the much overcrowded burial ground of the old St Pancras Church stood in the path of the works, and the human remains, which existed in stratum to a considerable depth, were reinterred in other cemeteries. Working conditions amid the foetid ground, saturated as it was with decomposing matter, were indescribably repulsive and difficult. At first, little reverence was shown; bones were left lying about to become the playthings of street urchins, and open coffins were seen on the working site. A great furore arose in the newspapers, and after protests in high quarters, more care was taken.

This havoc among the dead was largely the result of a decision to construct a double track link between the Midland and the Metropolitan Railway, leaving the main line on the east side, just north of the North London Railway, at a point later known as St Paul's Road junction. Almost at once the line dived into a tunnel at 1 in 75, and it was the cut and cover work for this tunnel that broke into the graves. After passing diagonally under the main line, the tunnel recrossed it beneath St Pancras, joining the widened Metropolitan Railway just west of that company's Kings Cross station. The widening of the Metropolitan (City Widened Lines) extended from Kings Cross to Farringdon Street, and was opened, for GNR passenger trains, on 17 February 1868.

Another tunnel was built beneath the frontage of St Pancras station, parallel with Euston Road, in anticipation of a widening of the Metropolitan westwards to Paddington. No such widening took place, and this work remained unused until 15 March 1926, when a track was laid in it, connecting the Circle Line with the City Widened Lines, to afford some relief to the former. The spur was closed in 1935, and the tunnel incorporated in the new Metropolitan and Circle Lines station at Kings Cross, brought into use in 1941.

### BASIS OF A FINE DESIGN

Work on the new terminus began in 1866, an early task being the enclosure in an iron pipe of the Fleet River, then virtually an open sewer.

Barlow's first plans for the station were for a double or even triple span roof above the elevated platforms; he intended to fill the air space below the rails with spoil from the tunnels. Discussions with James Allport,[2] the Midland's general manager, brought forward the suggestion that this basement area offered valuable storage space, readily accessible from the surrounding streets, and it was then decided that the whole area beneath the station should be vaulted and available for cellarage.

It was this decision that led Barlow to think of a single span roof, so it is perhaps not too great an exaggeration to say that St Pancras owes much of its grandeur to Burton beer. The problems and solutions were lucidly expounded by Barlow in a paper read to the Institution of Civil Engineers on 20 March 1870. In order to make the best possible use of the basement space, columns and girders were employed instead of brick piers, and the spacing between the columns was that in the Burton beer warehouses, that is to say, the beer barrel became the unit of measurement. A roof of two or more spans would need to be supported by columns of large diameter which would penetrate the basement and thus interfere with this neat plan. Moreover, such columns would require extra strong foundations, presenting great engineering difficulties where they came over the tunnel beneath the station. Barlow realised that the station floor would form a ready-made tie for a roof of single span, and dared to propose this. Although the cost of a 240 ft span roof would be higher than that of a double span, he was encouraged by Allport's desire to have the maximum freedom of movement within the station, with flexibility to alter the platform and track plan to meet changes in traffic needs.

St Pancras was thus provided with its magnificent roof, still admired today as an outstanding piece of engineering. Barlow created the main design, but he left much of the detail to R. M. Ordish, an engineer who specialised in cast iron roofs and suspension bridges. This breathtaking roof was 689 ft long, towering 100 ft above the rails at the apex of its ribs. At the crown, the arch was slightly pointed, as this was thought to offer some advantage in resisting the lateral action of the wind; by curious coincidence, this feature anticipated the Gothic architecture of the frontage. Each of the

25 channel and plate iron ribs weighed almost 55 tons, and each was 29 ft 4 in from its neighbour. No support was provided by the side walls, the ribs being held to their brick piers by massive curved iron anchor plates, and tied by the main floor and 3 in diameter rods below. The tops of the brick piers were level with the platforms. To give the maximum headroom near the walls, the curvature of the roof arch was diminished from 160 ft to 57 ft radius at the haunches. The result of all this was a clear space of 245 ft 6 in across the station.

Before St Pancras was opened, the strength of the new structure was amply tested. As there was some delay in obtaining bricks, the partly completed roof, boarded, slated and glazed, was left for a time without the protection of the side walls. During this period it withstood severe buffeting by the wind without any perceptible movement. When erecting the framework of the roof, the Butterley Company used two large timber stages; with a load of two iron ribs, workmen and impedimenta, these imposed a deadweight of some 350 tons on the station flooring. Again there were no ill effects.

After the opening of the station, an iron and glass windscreen was completed across the outward end of the roof. At the other end, the plan had been to close the roof off with the frontage block, but later, to avoid any risk of smoke and steam entering the hotel, a second gable and another glazed screen were provided to form a barrier.

When finished, the roof was painted dark brown, which did not please Allport. He thought it looked 'exceedingly dull and heavy, and . . . marred, to some extent, the grand appearance which the station would otherwise have exhibited';[3] it should, he considered, be the colour of the sky (presumably he did not mean the dark yellow so frequently seen in NW1 in the long winters of the steam age). Allport's suggestion was taken up; in 1877, F. S. Williams wrote in *The Midland Railway, Its Rise and Progress*, that the roof had 'recently' been repainted and decorated with 'a blue sky-like appearance'. Blues and greys were used for subsequent repaintings.

We have already seen something of the strength of the station floor. Carried on girders and 720 cast-iron columns, it was formed of Mallet's buckle plates, and strong enough at any point to carry a locomotive, thus providing the maximum flexibility of track and platform arrangement. Beneath were the beer vaults, served by a network of tracks and turnplates, over which the wagons were moved by capstan and rope after descending in an hydraulic lift

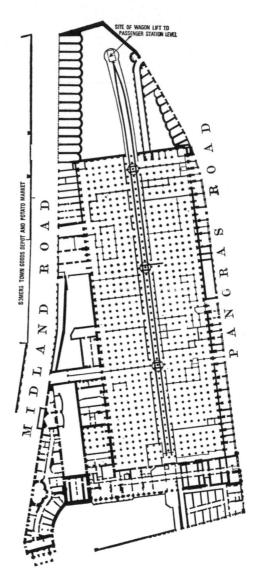

*Plans of St Pancras c 1958. From the* Railway Magazine, *October 1968*
    *(above) street level*
    *(right) platform level*

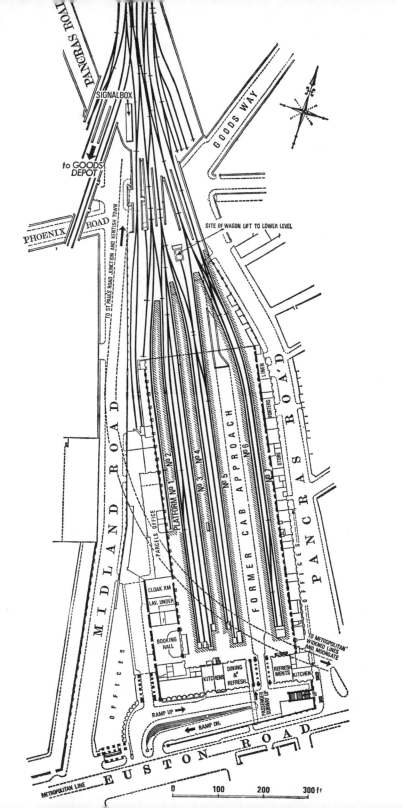

PANCRAS ROAD

SIGNALBOX

to GOODS
DEPOT

GOODS WAY

PHOENIX ROAD

TO ST PAULS ROAD JUNCTION AND KENTISH TOWN

SITE OF WAGON LIFT TO LOWER LEVEL

MIDLAND ROAD

PLATFORM Nº 1
Nº 2
Nº 3
Nº 4
Nº 5
FORMER CAB APPROACH
Nº 6

LINEN
PORTERS
Nº 2 STORE
Nº 1 STORE
OFFICES
PANCRAS ROAD

PARCELS OFFICE

CLOAK RM
LAV. UNDER

BOOKING
HALL

OFFICES

KITCHENS
DINING
&
REFRESH.
REFRESH-
MENTS
KITCHEN

PASSENGER SUBWAY UP

TO METROPOLITAN
WIDENED LINES
AND MOORGATE

RAMP UP
RAMP DN.

METROPOLITAN LINE

EUSTON ROAD

0    100    200    300 ft

at the north end of the platforms. For many years the beer traffic flourished, requiring daily trains to the terminus, but road vehicles gradually eroded it after the 1920s, until it ceased altogether in the early 1960s. By 1967, all track and other salvageable material had been removed from the vaults so that they might be let for other uses, or perhaps filled in.

As the London Extension approached completion little more than the bare bones of the terminus were ready to receive it. The first regular freight trains on the all Midland route reached Agar Town goods station on 9 September 1867. Next came passenger trains on local service between Bedford and Moorgate, using the tunnel under the terminus from 13 July 1868. Finally, in the early hours of 1 October 1868, without ceremony of any kind, St Pancras itself was opened to traffic. Booking offices and other amenities were incomplete. Of the hotel which was to form the frontage only the foundations could be seen.

### THE MIDLAND GRAND HOTEL

This hotel was to be the grandest, plushiest of its kind, a veritable palace to pamper and flatter the self-esteem of the industrial tycoons from the burgeoning Midlands and North. Above it the Midland intended to place offices for its headquarters staff. An architectural competition was held for this building in 1865.

'After more than once declining', Sir George Gilbert Scott[4] was persuaded to enter by his friend Joseph Lewis, a Midland Railway director. In September 1865, whilst the family were at a small hotel on Hayling Island, Scott's son fell ill; the architect stayed on with his family throughout that month and the following one, putting the time to good use by preparing his design. His entry was successful, but in the interests of economy various modifications were later made to his lavish plans. Of these, the most important was the elimination of the top storey, no longer necessary after it had been decided to leave the headquarters staff at Derby.

Economies and deferments were the result of financial pressures arising from the need for heavy expenditure on the London Extension; not only did this far exceed the estimates, it had to be met during the difficult times which followed the failure of the Overend & Gurney discount house in May 1866. For these reasons the work was taken in sections and progress was slow. Work did not begin until 1868 and it was not until 5 May 1873 that the first part of the seven-storey hotel could be opened. Another three years elapsed before the completion of the west wing.

With its castellated fringes, scores of dormer windows (each with finial), its myriad pointed-arch windows below the cornice, the multitude of chimneys on its steeply-pitched roofs, and its every corner marked by spirelet or pinnacle, the Midland Grand Hotel was one of the finest and largest examples of high Victorian secular Gothic. From the elaborate *porte cochère* at the west end, the 565 ft frontage curved back and round to parallel the Euston Road, terminating in a 270 ft spire-capped clock tower which was a worthy rival to that of Barry and Pugin at Westminster. The clock was supplied by John Walker of Cornhill in 1872; after showing increasing signs of old age, it stopped altogether in 1967. Over the elevations, Edward Gripper's patent bricks were varied with dressings in several different kinds of stone, and red and grey Peterhead granite. Frontage and skyline together offered a treasury of delights and surprises in which the erudite could find details of Salisbury and Winchester, the merely patient discover a statue of Britannia crowned by a lightning conductor.

Seen from close quarters, it was perhaps a little overwhelming, but from the heights of Pentonville on a winter's afternoon, with a low sun behind to enhance the magic and disguise the excesses, it could be superb. John O'Connor captured something of this in his 1881 painting, now in the Museum of London.

The outward extravagance of the Midland Grand was matched inside, where Scott was assisted by F. Sang and others. From the main entrance hall in Euston Road, a pointed arch led into a Minton-tiled corridor round the curve of the west wing. On the right, following the line of the building, was the general coffee and dining room, which overlooked the cab roadways and steps up to the station. This room, 100 ft long, 30 ft wide and 24 ft high, was later to be despoiled by partitioning and changes in décor. At the far end of the corridor, on the left, was the double intertwined grand staircase, decorated with iron scrollwork and ascending to the third floor under a beautiful vaulted ceiling 80 ft above the ground. Tucked into the well of this staircase was a tiny Moorish style booth where Turkish coffee was dispensed. On the first floor was a vast reading and drawing room, with its own arcade and windows overlooking the Euston Road. Nearby a smaller coffee room was kept 'select' by the imposition of higher tariffs. Altogether there were some 400 sitting rooms and bedrooms. Everywhere were pointed arches, carved oak doors, marble faced walls.

Scott had opened all the stops, for he was venting a powerful frustration:

It is often spoken of to me as the finest building in London; my own belief is that it is possibly *too good* for its purpose, but having been disappointed, through Lord Palmerston, of my ardent hope of carrying out my style in the Government Offices, and the subject having been in the meanwhile taken out of my hands by other architects, I was glad to be able to erect one building in that style in London.[5]

There is little doubt that Scott made good use of the many studies of fourteenth-century Gothic detail that he had prepared for the Whitehall offices, but St Pancras was, of course, a completely fresh design. No expense was spared in providing all the latest devices, such as gasoliers, electric bells, dust chutes and hydraulic lifts. Following complaints, rubber surfaces were placed in the cab roadways to deaden the noise at night.

Under the management of R. Etzensberger, late manager of the Victoria Hotel, Venice, and of the commissariat of the Nile steamers, the Midland Grand prospered. Baedeker thought it one of the best of London's railway hotels, and noted in 1911 that bed and breakfast prices started at 7s, compared with 8s at the Euston and 12s 6d at the Ritz. Carefully choosing his words, George Augustus Sala declared it to be 'the most sumptuous and the best conducted hotel in the Empire'. Service and amenities were always up to date, even in advance of the times, and in many ways a pattern was set for other big hotels to follow. As early as the 1890s there was a ladies' smoking room, a very daring innovation at a time when it was considered positively *fast* for a woman to smoke, even in secret. At the turn of the century, it had the first revolving door to be installed in London, and a curious type of telephone enabling guests to listen in to theatre and concert performances.

Although some businessmen remained faithful, the hotel's serious lack of modern comforts (notably central heating and an adequate number of bathrooms) caused patronage to decline steeply after the first world war. In 1935 the LMSR gave up the unequal struggle and converted it to railway offices.

Within what is now prosaically known as St Pancras Chambers, some of the original splendour survives. The grand staircase, with its 1873 carpet held in with great brass rods, amid dark red walls patterned with gold *fleurs de lys*, remains a show piece; and there are other surprises, such as an alcove mural of the *Garden of Deduit—Romance de la Rose* by T. W. Hay, great mirrors, marble mantelpieces and fine mahogany panels at the lift landings. Light modern colour schemes no doubt brighten the working day for the clerks and typists, but they have drowned the dignity of the interminable, dead straight corridors that stretch out from each landing of the grand staircase. Until 1983 British Transport Hotels Ltd occupied most of the building, not inappropriately, as their main office.

## UNDER BARLOW'S ROOF

The station itself was entered through an imposing archway under a 55 ft wide tower where the frontage block joined the west wing. Incoming cabs went through this arch, and after unloading, left down a ramp parallel with the platforms. Along the front of the hotel, serving another of its entrances, the cab road continued as far as a second arch, used by cabs coming away from the arrival side (these had their own separate entrance at the back of the station). Here the front roadway bent back on itself and descended to an exit gate next to the entrance. At the eastern end, by the bend in the cab road, a small staircase, greatly widened and improved in 1895, led down to Pancras Road and Kings Cross station.

Once through the entrance arch, the passenger alighted from his vehicle in a glass-roofed yard, where waiting porters attended him. Through one of three doorways, he then entered a handsome booking hall, completed in 1869, lit by six pairs of pointed arch windows and panelled with oak in lincnfold. Secreted in the capitals of the columns around the walls, as if to demonstrate that it was not a church after all, were some charming little carvings of railwaymen.

Two doorways led from this hall to the cross-platform between the buffer stops and the hotel. Now, at last, the traveller was under the great roof. He was a dull man if his imagination was not stirred. For let there be no doubt, St Pancras before the diesel age was an experience never to be forgotten. Entering it on a foggy afternoon, the visitor received the full impact of the steam railway, assaulting all his senses at once. Smoke and steam rose slowly to a roof almost out of view, whilst at the far end the atmosphere concentrated to a muddy dark yellow, obscuring the gasometers. In the great cavern between, where the electric lighting always seemed to fight a losing battle with the murk, all locomotive sounds were amplified. When, as often happened, a safety valve could restrain itself no longer, and sent a roaring blast of steam to cleanse the Butterley ironwork, women and children would all but jump from their skins, and many a man would flinch.

Originally there were eleven roads and five platform faces: the short local platform (now No 1) faced the west wall, its opposite

E

face, was the full-length main departure platform; then came six carriage storage roads between the present Nos 2 and 5, followed by the main arrival platforms (now 5 and 6) either side of a 25 ft wide cab road; against the east wall was the excursion platform, now No 7. In 1892, a wooden platform, the present Nos 3 and 4, was inserted in the carriage roads, giving the final total of six 800 ft platforms and a short bay. There were now two sidings between platforms 2 and 3, and another, ending in the hoist to the beer vaults, between 4 and 5. Platforms 1 and 2 were used for both arrivals and departures, including local trains, while 3 and 4 were allocated to departures and 5 to 7 to arrivals.

Beyond the ends of the platforms were four tracks, east and west departure, east and west arrival, merging quickly to form an up and two down passenger lines which continued as far as Cambridge Street Junction, the end of the first block section. From this point there was only a plain double passenger line as far as St Paul's Road Junction, where the two tracks from the Metropolitan came in on the up side. To the west of the passenger lines there was now a double goods road, also used to work empty carriage trains to and from the sidings at Kentish Town or the carriage depot at Cricklewood. Although there were engine sidings and turntable on the up side near the gasometers, the main locomotive depot was at Kentish Town, about 1½ miles out, also on the up side. Despite improvements carried out in 1907-8, when some coal bays on the up side were removed and the layout over the canal widened, these arrangements remained troublesome to operate, not least in crossing empty trains from the arrival platforms to the down goods road and bringing them over to the up side again at Cricklewood to reach the depot. Another cause of delay came with increased train lengths in later years; it was physically impossible to lengthen the platforms without costly engineering works, and any train longer than twelve coaches would block movements to other platforms.

Arranged along the sides of the station at platform level were various offices, notably on the west side, where a parcels depot was later added. Here too was the splendid gentlemen's court, one of the most impressive in any London terminus, with its stalls arranged in tasteful clusters around the roof columns. At street level, along the front and sides of the buildings, shops and coal offices provided a useful rent income.

## TRAIN SERVICES

Apart from the additional platforms already mentioned, no alterations of substance were made to the original structure, which remained more than ample for the traffic. In 1902, there were 150 trains in and out daily: 'At no time of the day can St Pancras be called a busy station in the sense in which the word is understood at Waterloo or Liverpool Street. The long distance expresses leave at stated—and stately—intervals, the only approach to bustle being at midnight, when three important trains leave within five minutes of each other.'[6]

For many years suburban traffic was virtually non-existent, almost all the local trains working to and from Moorgate. In 1903 only fourteen suburban trains arrived between 5 and 10 am, but from 1910, some attempt was made to develop outer suburban traffic to St Albans and beyond by accelerating and augmenting the service.

In pregrouping days St Pancras offered variety to the railway observer, with Great Eastern, and London Tilbury & Southend engines mixing with those of the Midland. The GER ran trains as far as Yarmouth, Norwich and Lowestoft via Kentish Town and South Tottenham between 1870 and 1917, St Pancras serving tenuously as that company's 'West End' terminus in exchange for Midland running powers over the GER to the London docks. In the years immediately before 1914, St Pancras had the fastest service to Cambridge (71 min). The GER trains were suspended in 1917 as a wartime economy measure, and never restored, apart from a brief revival in the summers of 1922 and 1923 when one express daily ran to Hunstanton and back. This GER route was patronised by both royalty (to Sandringham) and racegoers (to Newmarket), and the company maintained its own booking office at the Midland terminus.

Opened in 1894, the LTSR connection provided St Pancras with boat trains, which conveyed passengers via South Tottenham, Barking and Tilbury to Australia and Scandinavia. The link was made possible by the opening of the Tottenham & Forest Gate Railway (promoted by the Midland and the LTSR), from South Tottenham to a junction with the LTSR at Woodgrange Park, on 9 July 1894. Previously the Tilbury boat trains had worked from Liverpool Street or occasionally from Fenchurch Street. From 1895 the Midland also ran a few through trains daily from St Pancras to Southend via Barking, at first using their own locomotives, but from April 1899 LTSR engines worked Midland coaches from St Pancras. Boat trains were also operated from St Pancras for the short lived (1930-32) Tilbury-Dunkirk service. Hauled in LMSR and early BR days by the ubiquitous Fowler 4F o–6–o tender loco-motives, the Australian and Scandinavian boat trains lasted until 1963 when they returned to Liverpool Street or Fenchurch Street.

One of the most serious air raid incidents at any London term-inus in the 1914-18 war occurred at St Pancras on 17 February 1918. A stick of five bombs fell across the station, most of them causing no great harm, until one exploded in the cab court out-side the booking office. Here a crowd of people were sheltering under the entrance arch, and twenty were killed. There was no interruption to rail traffic.

## BOMBS AND RENEWAL

Despite their greater destructive power, the bombs and mines of the 1939-45 war failed to shake the rock-solid construction of St Pancras, although there was some serious damage. A land mine wrecked a large part of the roof on the night of 15/16 October 1940, closing the station for five days whilst the debris was cleared. In the night of 10/11 May 1941 a bomb penetrated the station floor at the inner end of platform 3, passing through the beer vaults to explode near the railway tunnel below. Again the main structure and foundations were unharmed, but the station was closed for eight days until local damage was made good, plat-forms 2 and 3 remaining out of use until the first week of June.

British Railways spent a great deal of money on St Pancras after years of near-neglect by the LMSR. Apart from the signalling modernisation to be mentioned later, the track in the station ap-proaches was rearranged and reconstructed in 1947, a new refresh-ment facilities were opened in 1959, and in 1963 a brave attempt was made to smarten up the somewhat gaunt platform entrances by erecting a 240 ft barrier screen with train indicators. Shortly before this, in 1958-9, the glazed area of the roof was enlarged to bring more natural light to the concourse, and the roof struc-ture was repaired and repainted (the glass in the end screens was not replaced after the war). During 1957, the woodwork of the booking hall was cleaned up, restoring much of its former splen-dour; at the same time, the ceiling was lowered and reconstructed.

The desultory suburban service inherited from the Midland and

LMSR was livened up a little. From 28 September 1959 multiple-unit diesel sets took over partially, and steam was entirely replaced from 11 January 1960, when an improved and regular service began (half-hourly off peak to Elstree and beyond, hourly for the inner stations). Despite a series of alarming train fires, the diesels, perhaps the most intensively-worked in the world, did well, increasing traffic by over 20 per cent. Even so, suburban movements at St Pancras remained very light in comparison with those at Liverpool Street and the Southern termini. Steam also disappeared from the main-line trains in the early 1960s.

During 1966, BR began to talk about 'combining' St Pancras and Kings Cross, threatening to replace Scott's hotel with an office tower. This was probably kite-flying, as the memory of Euston was still fresh in all minds. In answer to a question in the House of Lords, Lord Kennet, for the government, said he was aware of the strong feelings about the destruction of Euston's portico and that his Minister 'would take any step open to him to avoid a repetition of any such destruction'. This was followed, in November 1967, by the inclusion of the terminus in the statutory list of buildings of special architectural or historic interest. During 1967, proposals were made for using the terminus as an exhibition or sports centre, or as a transport museum, whilst BR published a somewhat half-baked scheme for rebuilding Kings Cross, closing St Pancras, and diverting the Midland services to Euston or the City Widened Lines. This BR plan was ill-received and much criticised on practical grounds, and eventually, in December 1968, scrapped, as it had not been found cost-effective. Saddled with its historic monument on a potentially lucrative site, BR swallowed hard and retreated, muttering that the interior of the hotel would have to be modernised.

Although the pressure for rationalisation and economy will continue to threaten the long term future of the railway facilities at St Pancras, it now seems most unlikely that the train shed and hotel frontage will be denied to posterity. Nuclear explosions aside, just what will happen to it in its second century remains an interesting question.

### SIGNALLING

From the outset, St Pancras signalling was interlocked, with block working. The first signal box, designed to harmonise with the station building, stood at the north end of the turntable siding, to the east of the station yard. This box was closed in 1873 and replaced by the Station or East box, which was just to the north of the outer ends of platforms 3 and 4. It had two frames, the east with 32 levers, and the west, with 38 (later increased to 41), both parallel to the tracks, and was in fact two signal boxes placed back to back.

After the opening of the Somers Town goods depot on the west side of St Pancras in 1887, a principal box, St Pancras Junction, was erected in the neck of the junction between the lines to the depot and that to the carriage siding on the western side of the passenger station. This cabin was 82 ft long and 12 ft wide and had an 84-lever passenger frame and a 48-lever goods frame, the former facing east, the latter west, and north of the other. A gantry carrying 42 up home and advance starting semaphore arms on 21 dolls spanned the four roads leading out of the platforms, but in 1914 this was replaced by another which had only 16 arms and 8 dolls, each doll with an illuminated route indicator at its base.

The proximity of these two boxes, and of Cambridge Street, the end of the first block section, combined with the nature of the track layout, led to a large amount of signal slotting and a great many signal movements for each train. Despite this, St Pancras was one of the last of London's termini to receive modern signalling.

A scheme was eventually drawn up which provided two and four-aspect colour light signalling and electro-pneumatic points at the terminus, and in the approaches as far out as the country end of Belsize tunnel. Work began in the middle 1950s. On 7 October 1957 a new box was opened on the west side of St Pancras station, at the end of platform 1, replacing the Station, Junction and Cambridge Street cabins. The relay-interlocking route setting installation, with its dc track circuits, was controlled from a console with 205 route switches, 33 switches for individual emergency point operation, and others for ground frame releases. Below the main operating room was a room with 1,400 relays, a battery room, and a linesmen's mess room. Westinghouse supplied the signalling equipment, Standard Telephones & Cables the train describers.

In the modernisation, St Pancras lost a third box, known only to the enlightened few, as it was hidden some 46 ft below the station. St Pancras Tunnel box was a tiny four-lever affair scooped out of the west wall of the tunnel between Kings Cross (Metropolitan) and St Paul's Road junction. Opened in 1889, after a mishap the previous year, it was a block post inserted to shorten the long section between Midland Junction box (Metropolitan Railway) and the Midland's box at St Paul's Road. At first, the tunnel signals controlled from the box were of the armless type, worked mechanically, but eventually colour lights were installed. To reach the box, the signalman entered a small door at the bottom of the cab ramp on the west side of the terminus. On the other side of the door was a small room, with a claustrophobic iron spiral staircase leading down from the middle of the floor. Arrived at the bottom, he could see the lights of the box across the tracks, dimly shining through the soot-begrimed panes of its semi-circular window. Although signalmen are used to lonely vigils, Tunnel box must have been an unusual, even eerie duty. In later years, trains were relatively infrequent; between them, a deep silence reigned in these sooty depths, broken only by the distant rumble of the Metropolitan and the hum of the ventilation fan at the back of the box. Eight hours there could never have been much fun. When the box was closed on 2 February 1958 the operation of the signals in the tunnel was taken over by London Transport's Kings Cross 'C' box. Subsequent signalling changes are mentioned in chapter 16.

# CHAPTER 4

# Kings Cross

## TWO SIMPLE TRAIN SHEDS

In common with some of the other termini, Kings Cross is more than one station. The main and original part consists of two simple train sheds closed across the street end by a plain screen. Once derided, but now, with changing tastes, much admired, this screen for many years concealed railway and passenger facilities greatly in need of reconstruction. Accretions of later years, collectively known as the Suburban station, were a drab untidy mess, mercifully hidden round a corner.

When the Great Northern Railway arrived in London in 1850, its trains were accommodated in a temporary station adjacent to Maiden Lane (now York Way) whilst the line was being pushed under the Regent's Canal to the permanent terminus at Kings Cross, through the 528 yd Maiden Lane or Gas Works tunnel. Referred to in the timetable as 'Kings Cross', this temporary terminus, opened on 7 August 1850, consisted of two timber platforms on the down side between Gas Works and Copenhagen tunnels. Its spartan amenities had to cope with the excursion traffic of the Great Exhibition of 1851, and, in August of that year, with the embarkation of Queen Victoria and Prince Albert on a journey by rail and road to Scotland.

Built over a ten-acre site formerly occupied by the Small Pox and Fever Hospitals and a number of houses, the permanent terminus was sufficiently advanced to permit opening for public traffic on 14 October 1852. At first, there were twelve down trains between 7 am and 8 pm, only three of them expresses, and a similar up service, with a last arrival at 10 pm. Buses connected with all trains to convey passengers to Paddington, Waterloo and London Bridge at a fare of 6d, which included up to 40 lbs of luggage.

Lewis Cubitt,[1] working with the engineers William and Joseph

Cubitt[2] designed a straightforward, elegant and economical station. At the south end, two train sheds were closed by a 216 ft façade of London stock bricks incorporating two arches which revealed the cross section of the interior. Almost devoid of ornament, this south front was crowned by a central square clock tower 112 ft high, the clock set in an Italianate turret which spoiled the stark simplicity of the design. Dent's clock had been exhibited at the 1851 Exhibition; it had four 9 ft diameter dials, but the north one was blocked off as it could not be seen from the ground after erection at Kings Cross. The minute hands moved every half second instead of the more customary 30 second jerks, although this hardly explained why it rarely if ever agreed with Walker's clock on neighbouring St Pancras. Also in the tower were a tenor, a bass and a treble bell, the largest weighing 1 ton 9 cwt. Silenced in 1914, the chimes were heard again between 1924 and 1927, then stopped for good; twenty years later they were taken away.

The two arches of the south front were flanked by quite plain square buttress piers finished on top with flat brick fascias. Along the front, at street level, was a projecting porch with six arched openings (the ugly iron and glass canopy was a later addition). On the east side, a wide arched entrance led to the cabway alongside the arrival platform. To the west, there was an undistinguished masonry block containing offices and the usual station amenities.

Each train shed was 800 ft long and 105 ft wide, and 71 ft above the rails at centre. They were joined down the middle of the station by a strong brick wall carried on abutments. Along the west side of the station was a departure platform (now No 8), and along the east, the arrival platform (now No 1); between them were fourteen carriage roads.

About three-quarters of the roof area was glazed. The roof arches, at 20 ft intervals, were supported by laminated wood girders which exerted a very powerful thrust on the outside walls. This pressure was of no great moment on the west side, which was thoroughly buttressed by the office block, but on the east, the flying buttress arrangement over the cab road was much weaker. By the late 1860s this east wall was showing signs of strain. During 1869-70 the timber trusses on the east side were replaced with wrought-iron girders. A similar operation was carried out in the departure shed in 1886-7.

The long building between the departure platform and the outside carriage road on the west of the station contained a refreshment room, first and second class waiting rooms, first and second class ladies' rooms (there were no third class *ladies*), parcels office, and the general offices and board room of the GNR. No facilities were provided for third class passengers, who had only one train a day each way in the initial service. About one-third of the way down the platform was the 'pay office' or booking hall, 100 ft long by 40 ft high, and occupying the full 40 ft width of the building.

At the time of its opening, Kings Cross was the largest station in Britain, and much admired. So much so, that some GNR shareholders were moved to complain of extravagance. Their grumbles were answered by Edmund Denison, the chairman, who told them that it was 'the cheapest building for what it contains and will contain that can be pointed out in London'. For a construction cost of £123,500, Denison thought the company had done well, as indeed they had, for the Euston portico and Great Hall had alone cost much more.

Lewis Cubitt also designed the five-storey Great Northern Hotel, which was opened in 1854 and is still in use. A plain, uninteresting building in white stone and brick, arranged on a curved plan, it is set apart from the station, to the south west.

USING THE CAPACITY

Denison's suggestion that the capacity of the terminus would be put to good use was soon borne out. There was a steady growth of traffic. When Kings Cross opened there were only four stations (Hornsey, Colney Hatch & Southgate, Barnet, and Potters Bar) on the $17\frac{3}{4}$ mile stretch between London and Hatfield, but additional stations were opened at Holloway Road in 1856, at Wood Green in 1859 and at Seven Sisters Road (now Finsbury Park) in 1861. From 1 February 1858, room had to be found for the London trains of the Midland. In 1863 connections were established with the Metropolitan Railway (which had opened on 10 January 1863, with a station at Kings Cross slightly east of the GNR terminus). All GNR local trains were diverted to Farringdon Street from 1 October. On reaching the surface at Kings Cross, down trains had to set back into the departure platform of the terminus, but in the up direction, from the end of 1865, before descending to the lower regions, the local trains stopped at a specially-provided platform called York Road, just outside the terminus.

An additional arrival platform was inserted into the main station during 1862, one face (later No 2) of full length, but the other with a short platform stepped into the northern end, forming a

bay (later No 3). The full width portion at the inner end was sufficient for a short train.

Further strains were imposed on the Kings Cross approaches by
the construction of a connection between the Metropolitan and
the LCDR in 1866. From thenceforward a heavy coal traffic left
the GNR at Kings Cross bound for South London and beyond via
Ludgate Hill and Herne Hill. Also, from 1 January 1866, passenger
trains were worked between Kings Cross and Herne Hill, and
from 3 January between GNR suburban stations and Ludgate Hill.
A Hatfield to Herne Hill service started on 1 August. GNR trains
across London were diverted to Victoria from 1 March 1868. Ten
years later, from 1 June 1878, through services were established
over the same cross-centre route between Enfield and Muswell Hill
and Woolwich Arsenal, initially worked by the GNR, but taken
over by the SER on 1 August 1880.

A year after the inauguration of through services between north
and south London, on 22 August 1867, another thirty-six trains
were added to the daily tidal flow by the opening of the Finchley
and Edgware branch.

All trains had to be worked over the single up and down tracks
in Gas Works Tunnel. An additional impediment was present at
the north end of the tunnel, where all up goods trains had to cross
over the running lines on the level before they could reach the
Kings Cross yard. It was small wonder that the Midland trains
were delayed.

When the City Widened Lines were constructed alongside the
Metropolitan, new junctions had to be made at Kings Cross and
to enable the work to proceed, the GNR service was suspended
from 1 July 1867. These alterations were completed early in 1868,
and a limited passenger service resumed on 17 February. In the
following year, on 1 June, the GNR suburban trains were extended
eastwards to Moorgate.

Although some relief was felt when the Midland trains departed
for their own line after 30 September 1868, this was short-lived.
With the opening of branches to Enfield in 1871, to High Barnet
in 1872 and to Alexandra Palace in 1873, suburban traffic continued to expand. From a mere nineteen in 1855, the number of
departures from Kings Cross had grown to eighty-nine in 1873,
all but twenty of which were suburban, almost all off the Metropolitan.

## SUBURBAN ACCRETIONS

All this time, Kings Cross had been worked with a single

departure platform used not only by main line and local trains, but backed into by every passenger train leaving the Metropolitan. This somewhat absurd situation was now gradually put right. First came the opening, in August 1875, of what was rather long-windedly known as 'Kings Cross Main Line (Local) Station', consisting of three short platform faces and two tracks outside the western wall of the terminus, under its own overall roof. This local station, used only for departures, was opposite the north end of the main departure platform, occupying the site of a carriage repair shop. A small yard for turning and coaling locomotives was built at the same time between the local station and the down line to the Metropolitan.

This Metropolitan connection remained without a platform until 1 February 1878, from which date the tedious backing into the main-line station was at last ended by the opening of 'Kings Cross (Suburban)'. Yet this created new difficulties, for great was the anxiety (and embarrassment) of the less skilful drivers as they struggled to start well-loaded trains from its sharply-curved, steeply-graded platform. Traffic from the Metropolitan was heavy, and it was usual for the tunnel mouth to be wreathed in smoke; although a repeater signal was provided at that end of the platform, it was necessary after dark to assist drivers of through trains by giving hand lamp signals.

The tunnel, known as Hotel Curve, was detested by all engine crews, who no doubt had their own picturesque names for it. Not only was there a wicked curve of 7 chains (154 yd) radius, but part of the climb was at 1 in 35. An unfortunate GNR employee was obliged to spend his working hours within this fearsome hole, spreading sand on the rails after the passage of each train. Freight trains could not be banked except in special circumstances, as the second engine had to be crossed over all the busy lines into the terminus before it could return. Double-heading was out of the question, as the loading gauge of this single line tunnel was so tight that the crew of the second engine would be unable to work in the fumes and smoke from the pilot. Some light was thrown on conditions in Hotel Curve by the Ministry of Transport report of an accident which took place in July 1932 (the passing of time had led to no improvement). A train had slipped back so badly on the upward climb that it had run into another in its rear. The inspector commented: 'The signals only become visible just as the engine reaches them, and it is only by touching the tunnel lining with an outstretched hand that trainmen can be certain they are travelling in the right direction. Even breathing is at times diffi-

cult, and drivers have little or no chance of rectifying an error.'
After this, following the inspector's recommendation, lights were
provided at short intervals to help drivers preserve their sense of
location, speed and direction.

Between 1867 and 1873 the number of GNR season ticket holders
had increased from 2,500 to over 6,000, and there was every sign
of continued growth. As most of the local trains still went through
to the Metropolitan, the congestion was experienced in the double
track approach tunnel rather than in the terminus itself. The difficulties of working the approaches further increased with the opening of a GNR goods depot at Farringdon Street in 1874. At this time,
it was not uncommon for rush-hour trains to take up to 30 minutes
to cover the $1\frac{1}{2}$ miles between Holloway and Kings Cross. In those
days passengers' protests were formally summarised in 'memorials'
which they presented to the railways' directors.

The harassed management rested its hopes on a connection to
the North London Railway at Canonbury, permitting diversion of
many GNR suburban trains to Broad Street. Alas, the LNWR-domin-
ated North London would not have GNR passenger trains on its
tracks, and the only acceptable solution was for the North London
to run over the GNR suburban lines on a mileage basis. This began
on 18 January 1875, mopping up much of the traffic, and enabling
Henry Oakley, the GNR general manager, to boast that his suburban
trains were 'running with improved punctuality'. But as traffic
continued to grow, optimism was quickly dispersed. The remaining
land around the inner stations was rapidly covered with new
houses designed to attract the Pooters and the Cummingses. By
1881 the season ticket army had swollen to 14,400.

Great efforts were made to improve the terminal approaches. A
skew bridge and duplicate Copenhagen tunnel were provided in
August 1877 to keep trains entering Kings Cross goods yard out
of the way of passenger movements. In the following year, a second
Gas Works tunnel was completed beneath the canal, to be opened,
together with a resited York Road platform, on 4 March. A third
Copenhagen tunnel, on the east side, was ready for traffic on
20 June 1886.

## SERIOUS DELAYS

Despite these works, up trains were still subject to serious delays, especially in the rush hours. There were several reasons why
this was so: tickets were collected and examined while trains

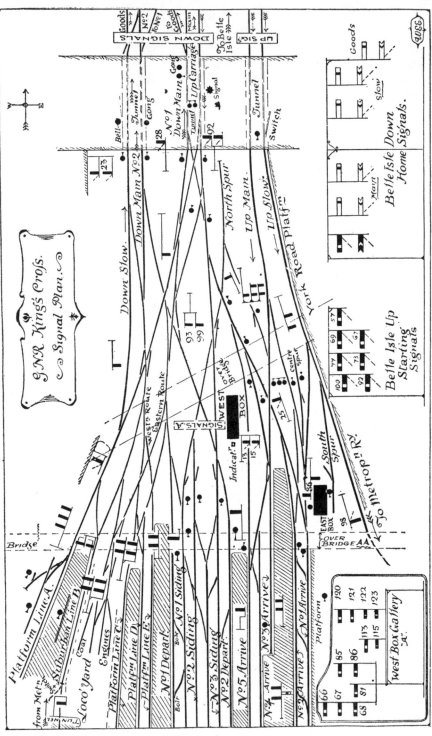

Plan of Kings Cross 1905. From the Railway Magazine, March 1905

stood for this purpose at Holloway (until 1897, when the Holloway ticket check was abandoned. York Road and Kings Cross [Metropolitan] were 'open' stations and many a small boy enjoyed a free ride between them); there were only two up roads through Gas Works tunnels, and all empty stock for down departures had to be worked through them with the passenger trains; and finally, as some Moorgate trains had coaches for Kings Cross terminus, delay built up whilst the portion was detached at York Road.

The inevitable third tunnel under the canal was finished in June 1892. Situated on the west side, it accommodated two down roads (down slow and down main No 2), the westernmost road in the 1852 tunnel becoming down main No 1, and the other a shunting road. This latter line was converted to an up line for empty passenger trains and light engines on 29 August 1898, enabling empty trains to run direct into the departure platform for the first time. After this, shunting from the arrival to the departure side was usually accomplished by using the down roads.

As the tracks in the station yard were still an inflexible muddle, these shunting operations presented a considerable hazard. It only needed the derailment of a single coach in the cramped space between the tunnel mouths and the platforms to cause more or less complete chaos. Such incidents were apt to occur at holiday times when the station staff were always under great strain. Another handicap was the down-under-and-up alignment of the Gas Works tunnels and the subsequent one mile climb at 1 in 107. Not only were run backs to be expected (some are mentioned in the note at the end of this chapter), but the tunnels and yard were liable to flooding after heavy rain. A typical incident occurred on 25 July 1901, when all traffic was completely suspended for $4\frac{1}{2}$ hours after a flood. Such indignity was suffered by no other major London terminus.

Towards the end of the nineteenth century, Kings Cross was handling some 250 passenger and freight trains daily, as well as empty carriage workings and other movements, the total load being near to saturation point for the layout with traditional signalling methods. (Empty carriage trains were worked to and from sidings at Holloway, Finsbury Park, Hornsey, and later, Bounds Green. There were also light engine movements to and from the locomotive depot, situated on the west side of the Kings Cross goods yard.) Although much of this traffic was on and off the Metropolitan, as late as 1892 the terminus was still being worked with only one main-line departure platform. As there were over forty departures daily, the situation was becoming intolerable.

In 1893 new platforms (later 5 and 6) were built either side of the central wall between the two train sheds. These were opened on 18 December, the westernmost one at last giving a second platform for departures. At the same time, an iron girder footbridge was erected, connecting all platforms in the main station about half-way down their length, and linking the old general offices on the departure side with new offices built in the early 1890s over the cab road on the arrival side.

This cab road was a rather sinister place, and as at Euston and Paddington, the number and destination were recorded by a railway policeman, as the cab left. 'A precaution against the kidnapping of children' a child would be told, only to receive a further shock on peering out of the back of the cab, where he would almost certainly see an unkempt, unshaven figure loping along behind, following it all the way home, and sometimes stealing a precarious ride on the bar at the back. Could this be a kidnapper, or was it perhaps a burglar? The truth was less romantic. In those hard days, men were prepared to go to all this trouble for the few pence to be earned in carrying bags from the cab to the house.

### MORE ADDITIONS

Alterations were made to the local station in 1895, when an additional track was placed between the platform and a new island platform, 500 ft long and 20 ft wide. To make room for this, the locomotive yard, with its 50 ft turntable and coaling stage, was moved west, and the curve from the Metropolitan somewhat flattened. The platform on the Metropolitan connection was rebuilt, with a short terminal platform at a higher level on its west side.* This together with new milk and horse and carriage docks, filled the triangular space between Cheney Street and the back of Culross Buildings. The new platforms were opened on 7 April 1895.

The local platforms were now designated A to E, from west to east, A and B being known as 'suburban' platforms to distinguish them from C to E in the 'local' station. Platform E, which was accessible from the main-line departure platform, both at its north end and through an intermediate passageway, was sometimes used for main-line departures. The local station had its own booking office, circulating area and refreshment room, all fronting Cheney Street. There was also a small buffet on platform B, offering a

* There had been a terminal platform here since July or August 1880. This platform, used for peak hour departures, became No. 15 in 1921, 17 in 1924 and went out of regular use in 1940.

Page 85

(above) *Kings Cross in its early simplicity c 1853. From a watercolour published by R. B. Fleming & Co Ltd; (below) Kings Cross in the last days of steam; left to right 60131 Osprey, A1 Pacific; 61379, B1 4-6-0; 60064 Tagalie, A3 Pacific. 15 February 1958*

Page 86

(above) *Bishopsgate, c 1865;* (below) *Liverpool Street west side, about 1904*

refuge from the discomforts of that smoke-bound outpost. In the main station, the arrival and departure sides were still rigidly separated, even to the extent of separate platform numbering (1 and 2 departure, and 1 to 5 arrival), a situation which was to persist until 1921.

When Kings Cross was first opened, both the station and hotel were in line with the St Pancras Old Road. About 1872 that road was diverted to run alongside the new St Pancras station, bringing it to a right angle junction with Euston Road, and leaving an open space in front of the terminus. This space remained unoccupied for a time, but it was later used by a vendor of garden furniture, who filled it with a display of rustic seats, arches and summer houses designed to catch the eye of the homegoing suburbanite. Subsequently, permanent and semi-permanent buildings were erected, including a left luggage office. On Sunday 11 May 1902, fire broke out in one of the wooden buildings. Fanned by a north east wind, it spread rapidly, destroying a large part of the garden furniture, the left luggage office and some GNR road vans and buses.

After this, more buildings were erected, and by 1914 the area was thoroughly cluttered. There were the mail office, the Jubilee cloak room (used for heavy parcels), the emigrants' transit shed, the excursion office, a timber office for railway staff, a cab shelter, and, plonked right at the front, the 1906 station of the Piccadilly tube railway in the standard dark rhubarb terracotta blocks. As if this wasn't enough, the LNER added some crudely-designed single storey shops either side of the tube station in 1934, and shortly after that, Laing's erected a specimen of a desirable suburban residence in front of the Great Northern Hotel.

In addition to the through services to Metropolitan Railway stations, access to the Metropolitan platforms at Kings Cross was available through a long subway from the main-line concourse, opened on 20 June 1892. Subways from the southern end of the departure platform gave ready access to the underground booking hall of the City & South London tube railway, which was extended from Angel to Euston on 12 May 1907. The Piccadilly tube station, already mentioned, was opened on 15 December 1906, and connected to the Metropolitan-GNR subway.

During the first world war, it was the practice to draw main-line trains into the tunnels as far as possible when enemy aircraft were overhead. In fact no damage was inflicted on the station, which was fortunate, as it had considerable strategic importance. Very heavy freight traffic was passing south almost continuously

F

through the Metropolitan connection, so much so that the slack-hour trains between the Metropolitan and the GNR were taken off in January 1915 to provide more paths. A large amount of high explosive was carried through Kings Cross, much of it by passenger train, and a special store for it was constructed on the main departure platform.

MAJOR CHANGES

Some important changes were made in 1922-4. They were largely designed to facilitate the working of the increased number of local trains terminating there instead of running through to the Metropolitan (with a few exceptions, the slack-hour cancellations of 1915 were never restored).

As the up carriage road in the centre Gas Works tunnel was mainly reserved for the working of empty carriages and light engines into the terminus, it was not always available for shunting local trains from the arrival side to the local station, and the down lines then had to be used instead. This also applied when engines were moved from the arrival side to the engine yard on the down side. The remedy adopted involved the conversion of the permissively-worked up carriage road to an up relief running line, together with signalling improvements. From 22 January 1922, up trains could be directed into all the departure platforms except the present 16 and 17 and up suburban trains began to use 11 to 13.

Although providing considerable benefits, this change by no means cured the basic defects of the Kings Cross layout. Departures from platforms 1 to 5 still blocked all inwards movements, those from the others partially stopping up trains entering. The up slow line was only usable for the Metropolitan connection and platform 1, and the up main for platforms 1 to 5. All trains destined for the west side had to use the up relief road. This sorry state of affairs persisted until 1977. The extremely costly works needed to rectify it were avoided for sixty years only because much of the pressure was taken out of the Kings Cross suburban traffic by the arrival of tube railways and improved street transport in the first decade of the present century.

Relief to suburban and cross-London traffic was first felt in 1906-7; and in the latter year the through trains to south London were withdrawn for lack of patronage. In 1906 the GNR felt

sufficiently relaxed to indulge in a publicity campaign extolling
the virtues of residence on the 'Northern Heights' and encouraging
new traffic to 'Bracing Barnet' (16 minutes from Kings Cross;
season rate 6d a day), 'Healthy Southgate' (13 min; 4½d), 'Breezy
Highgate' (13 min; 2½d), and 'Picturesque Finchley' (17 min; 4d).
The extension of the Piccadilly tube to Wood Green, Bowes Park
and Southgate in 1932-3 made heavy inroads into the Kings Cross
suburban traffic, and another large section of it was removed
when the tube trains of the Northern Line took over the working
of the High Barnet and Mill Hill branches in 1939-41.

When the Gresley Pacific locomotives came into use after the
first world war, it was decided to install a 70 ft turntable at Kings
Cross to eliminate wasteful light engine running. Before the war,
the GNR had bought 5¾ acres of the gas works site, and a new
engine coaling and turning yard was now constructed on this. An
interesting feature of the yard, which came into use in December
1923, was the provision of an underground steam pipe which fed
steam from a locomotive standing in the yard to heat carriages
waiting at the departure platform, thus freeing pilot engines which
had formerly been used for this purpose.

The new works of the immediate post-war era were completed
on 15 December 1924 when a 400 ft island platform (Nos 14 and
15) was opened on the site of the old engine yard. Since 11 July
1921 the platforms had been numbered from east to west right
across the station, including the local and suburban stations, but
with 7 to 9 omitted. This gap was partly filled on 19 September
1926 by the opening of a 945 ft by 12 ft concrete island platform
on the departure side, numbered 7 and 8. In 1938 the width of this
platform was doubled after the removal of the No 9 carriage road;
at the same time, it was connected to the central footbridge. To
provide further room for main-line arrivals and add to the mystery
and complications of Kings Cross platform numbering, the LNER
abolished platform 3 in 1934, extending No 4 to full length.

Like Waterloo and Charing Cross, Kings Cross experienced a
grisly cloakroom incident in the between-war years. The depositor
of the female legs which were found in a case in the cloakroom in
1934 was never discovered; all that the police were able to ascer-
tain was that they neatly fitted a female torso entrusted about the
same time to the care of the left luggage office at Brighton station.

During the 1920s, the LNER carried out various improvements
in the passenger amenities, building new lavatories, bath and dressing rooms under the main departure platform (now 8), and opening a Georgian tea room, a new refreshment room and an enquiry

office at the side. In 1927 this platform was extended at the outer
end by 45 ft to accommodate the longer trains then coming into
use.

More work was done in the 1930s when all the lettering of the
station signs was changed to Gill Sans, a type fount designed by
Eric Gill (1882-1940) and adopted in 1932 by the LNER as standard
for every form of lettering and printing. New platform barriers
with illuminated blinds showing departure times were erected in
the main station. A large enquiry and reservation office was opened
on platform 10 (now 8) in 1936, and in 1938-9 a subway was
constructed to connect all the platforms in the main station with
a new parcels and mail bag depot on the west side.

## A HECTIC WAR

Kings Cross had a hectic war, handling a very heavy traffic in
troops and civilians. Engine shortages caused trains to be made up
to twenty or more coaches, some of which would be outside the
platform, necessitating additional shunting movements and loss of
time. Some trains carried as many as 2,000 passengers.[3] Severe
damage was inflicted on the station by two 1,000 lb bombs,
chained together, which fell on the west side on 11 May 1941, removing a slice of the general offices, the grill room and bar, and
wrecking the booking hall. A large section of the roof was blown
out. It was fortunate that the explosion occurred in the small hours
of a Sunday when the station was deserted, but even so, twelve men
were killed. Temporary booking and refreshment facilities were
soon organised, and there was no necessity to cancel any trains. As
a result of bombing on the Metropolitan lines, services to Moorgate
were suspended from 30 December 1940 until 1 October 1945 (to
Aldersgate) and 6 May 1946 (to Moorgate).

At first there was no restoration of the once intense suburban
services. In 1937 there were twenty-one departures in a typical
peak hour, ten of them from Moorgate; in 1968 there were only
nine, three from the City. But from 1958-9, these trains were
worked by diesel locomotives and railcars, and there was a slight
increase in traffic associated with population growth in the outer
country area. In 1959, 6,953 passengers left between 4.30 and 7.0
pm, but in 1968 the corresponding figure was 8,919. Main-line
workings at Kings Cross became wholly diesel-hauled from 16 June
1963. The subsequent electrification of the suburban services is
dealt with in chapter 16.

## DRAUGHTY AND CHEERLESS

In 1968 Kings Cross was neither a pleasing nor impressive station. The form of the original design, with its separate arrival and departure sheds, and all amenities alongside the departure platform, was ill-suited to modern needs. The little cross-platform that emerged from this design was utterly inadequate as a concourse; hardly wide enough for comfort on the west side, it narrowed down even more on the east, where platforms 1 to 4 extended further south than the others. At the front of the station, large openings allowed a generous breeze to blow through the train sheds, a feature which did not make for passenger comfort, even if it did help to disperse the smoke and steam, or dilute the more insidious exhaust of the diesels.

The main-line booking hall was bleak and uninviting, and the heart of the station, the long platform 10, an untidy and cheerless place in comparison with the similarly situated platform 1 at Paddington. A large bookstall was almost its only bright spot. An exploration of the other end of this platform revealed an increasingly gloomy scene. Near the end, a strangely-isolated waiting room was usually inhabited by layabouts and string-belted tramps; on reaching daylight, one stumbled upon a grim-looking huddle of train-spotters, still mourning steam, yet trying very hard to summon interest in the unromantic manoeuvres of diesel engines and cars. A similar walk down the original arrival platform, permanently barricaded with parcels, was only for the athletic.

Equally depressing, despite smart new platform barriers and information displays, was the Suburban Station, as the extra-mural platforms were collectively known. Here but two amenities remained, a buffet in the veneers and chrome of the 1930s, and a tiny bookstall, open only at peak hours.

In the early 1960s, the construction of the Victoria Line tube station at Kings Cross offered a fine opportunity to give Cubitt's noble frontage a worthy setting. Up went the hoardings and the hopes of those who cared about such things; down came the ugly terracotta tube station and the even uglier 1930s shops. Then, as the Underground men pursued their complicated engineering out of sight, British Railways produced a plan for rebuilding Kings Cross which would retain the original front but erode some of its impact. Across the Cubitt screen were to be slashed the searing horizontals of a two-storey concourse building, projecting at least 40 ft. Within there would be escalators, subways and travolators affording connection with the Underground and City Widened Lines, the latter carrying St Pancras short-distance services after the closure of the Midland terminus. To the west and slightly to the north of the main-line station, a 300 ft tower would provide a new home for BR headquarters' staff.

As mentioned in the St Pancras chapter, this scheme, which never had seemed realistic or acceptable, was torn up by BR towards the end of 1968. Just what *was* done is told in chapter 16.

### SIGNALLING AND ACCIDENTS

At first Kings Cross had no block working. Points were worked by hand levers, and signals from pull-over levers operated from a small fenced-off area at the west side of the southern tunnel portal. The main line was equipped with semaphore signals with perforated arms, moved to three positions (stop, caution and clear) to control time-interval working.

This primitive equipment had been replaced by the early 1870s, when block working was in operation. A new box, later called West, was opened in 1881, with 140 levers (10 spare). This was supplemented in 1886 by East box, with 100 levers (21 spare). West box, which was at the north end of what are now platforms 5 and 6, dealt with departure movements and station shunting. East box, situated near the north end of platform 1, controlled arrivals and York Road. Both boxes had tappet-interlocked frames supplied by McKenzie & Holland.

It was not feasible to provide ground signals to cover all possible moves over the complicated and difficult layout in the station yard, and it was not unusual for a shunting move into one of the tunnels to be signalled back by a gang of shunters with hand lamps.

Owing to the presence of two road bridges over the station yard, the signalmen in East and West boxes did not have a clear view of the tracks they controlled, and a form of track circuiting (the first in Britain) together with electric fouling bars, was installed on some lines in the tunnels as early as 1894. The bridge immediately north of the station carried Battle Bridge Road, the other an access drive into the gas works. The latter was removed in 1912, but

Battle Bridge Road survived until 1921, when it was demolished and replaced by Goods Way, constructed over the tunnel.

As part of the departure side rearrangements mentioned in the main text, power-operated three-position upper quadrant signals were brought into use in six places on 22 January 1922. These signals had illuminated roller blind route indicators showing at front and rear, and were supplied by Siemens. Full track circuiting was completed in 1923.

On 3 October 1932 all the semaphore signals in the station area were replaced by Siemens colour lights. The new signalling, which also included 73 point motors, was controlled from an all-electric power frame of 232 levers. This frame was in a new box, which replaced East and West and was centrally situated at the north end of platforms 5 and 6. Precautions were taken against flooding; signal cables were run overhead on light gantries, some point motors were mounted on concrete blocks clear of the usual flood level, and point detector boxes were made watertight.*

Situated at the bottom of a long gradient, Kings Cross could hardly hope to avoid accidents of a particular kind. The first occurred in 1860, when an excursion train from Manchester mounted the buffers after a tipsy guard had overlooked the need to give additional assistance by applying his handbrakes. Fortunately no one was killed, but the mess was considerable. This incident was followed on 2 November 1865 by a spectacular affair involving a coal train. During the passage of Copenhagen tunnel, a portion of this train broke away, rolling down into the terminus, where the guard managed to escape by jumping on to the platform. Some trucks spilled over the end of the track, charging into the roadway, where they spent their load in final undignified collapse. A hurried digging over of the coal was organised for fear that someone might be buried, but there were no casualties.

More serious were the events of Sunday, 4 February 1945. On that day, the 6 pm for Leeds and Bradford, composed of Pacific locomotive 2512 and seventeen coaches, in all about 590 tons load, met trouble in the middle Gas Works tunnel. Here *Silver Fox* slipped so violently that she stalled, allowing her train to run back. A signalman in the Kings Cross cabin, seeing what was happening on his diagram, tried to divert the runaway into platform 15, as the road was set for platform 10, occupied by the 7 pm for Aberdeen. Unhappily, one of the bogies of the last coach had passed over the points before they began to move; two passengers were killed in the subsequent derailment and signalling equipment was extensively damaged. It was not until 23 February that train ser-

* For subsequent signalling changes see chapter 16.

vices and signalling were completely restored. The inspector's report revealed that the track was new, the engine tyres practically unworn—a good combination for low adhesion, causing the heavily-taxed locomotive to perform as it did on the 1 in 105 gradient at the other side of the dip under the canal.

## Broad Street

### VAST EMPTINESS TODAY

Penetrated by occasional trains, which creep in with an apologetic air, the vast emptiness of Broad Street is a reminder that this was once the City terminus of the busy North London Railway, with more daily train arrivals than Euston and Paddington together, more indeed than any other London terminus except Liverpool Street and Victoria. Now sustained outside the rush hours by only one train service, it is a station that has seen little glory and a great deal of hard work. The original building was no jewel of architecture, and the crude accretions in the forecourt have almost succeeded in suffocating it. Yet here and there, compensations are offered to the seeing eye.

The North London began life as the East & West India Docks & Birmingham Junction Railway, a title intended to express its purpose, which was to carry freight between the London & Birmingham Railway and the London docks. Still burdened by this weighty title, the line was opened in September 1850, under the aegis of the London & North Western Railway, who always controlled its main policy. By the time the name was changed to the neater North London Railway in 1853, passenger traffic had assumed an unforeseen importance. Cheap fares and frequent trains encouraged patronage, despite a four-mile detour round East London before the City was reached at Fenchurch Street, by courtesy of the London & Blackwall Railway.

### CITY ACCESS FOR THE NORTH WESTERN

More direct access to the City was an obvious next step, and became possible with the assistance of the LNWR, which was anxious to have a goods depot in the City, and agreed to contribute the larger part of the cost of a new terminus. This was to be

at the junction of Broad Street and Liverpool Street, and reached
by a two-mile line running south from the North London at Kingsland.

Many humble houses had to be demolished in Shoreditch and
Haggerston before the approach line could be built, and to secure
Parliamentary approval, the North London undertook to provide
one morning workmen's train from Dalston and a return working
in the evening, at a fare of one penny. Few of the displaced took
advantage of this generous concession; most of them crowded into
nearby streets, continuing to walk to such employment as they
had.

Terminus and extension together cost £1,200,000. Southwards
from east and west junctions at Kingsland, three tracks were carried on viaducts to the edge of the City of London. A new station,
Dalston Junction, was built at the northern end, and there was
one intermediate station, at Shoreditch (a second, Haggerston, was
added in 1867). The construction and design of the terminus and
approach tracks was the responsibility of William Baker, the first
chief engineer of the LNWR, which was to own the western side
of Broad Street station, as well as the approach tracks on that side
south of Skinner Street junction, the approaches to its goods
depot from New Inn Yard junction, and a goods depot at Shoreditch.

At the site of the terminus, after the demolition of houses and
other property, excavations revealed the existence of human remains in stratum several feet thick. This was thought to be either
a plague pit or the burial pits of the old Bethlehem Hospital.

The frontage was 250 ft long by 110 ft wide, situated at the
western end of Liverpool Street, opposite the end of the street
whose name the station took. No architect is mentioned in the
account in the *Illustrated London News* of 3 February 1866, which
describes the elevations as of 'mixed Italian style' and 'rather more
decorated than most stations of similar kind'. Baker probably
roughed out the details himself, perhaps employing one or two
minor architectural draughtsmen to finish them off. The materials
were white Suffolk bricks, with columns of Peterhead granite, and
capitals, medallions and other decorations in terracotta. In the
centre of it all was a 75 ft clock tower, quite swamping its small
clock. Altogether it was really rather horrid, the only redeeming
feature a pleasing arcaded external staircase on the east side.

Inside, at street level, were two booking halls, one for each railway company, 60 ft high, and either side of the clock tower. The
two conjoint train sheds together measured 460 ft by 200 ft. High

above the street, they at first contained only four tracks, the principal platform being some 50 ft wide.

After a ceremonial breakfast for the Lord Mayor and Sheriffs of the City on 31 October, the terminus was opened to ordinary mortals on 1 November 1865. Trains ran every fifteen minutes to Chalk Farm, at the same interval to Bow (for Fenchurch Street;

*Broad Street as built. From a drawing for the* Illustrated London News, *3 February 1866*

from 1 August 1866, this service was diverted to Poplar) and every thirty minutes to Kew (via Hampstead Heath; there were connections to Kingston via Mortlake, and some through trains; the service was alternated to Kew Bridge and to Richmond from 1 January 1869). Passengers to and from Dalston and points west were better off by a saving of twenty minutes each way. A Watford service was begun on 1 September 1866, and some of the Chalk Farm trains were extended to Willesden Junction on 3 June 1879, but withdrawn from 1 January 1917.

The LNWR goods depot, opened on 18 May 1868, was at ground level, some 60 ft below the passenger station, and on the west side of it. Wagons were raised and lowered from the yard above by means of hydraulic lifts. Everything was arranged as compactly as

possible to make the best use of the highly priced land; passenger
terminus and two-level goods station together occupied only 2½
acres.

It was all a great success. Both passenger and freight traffic
flourished. The North London's own traffic more than doubled in
a very short time, to be supplemented from January 1875 by some
forty or so trains each way daily between Broad Street and Great
Northern suburban stations. During the last quarter of the nineteenth century this modest terminus became one of the busiest in
London.

A fourth approach track, known as No 2 down, was finished in
1874 (the bridge over Great Eastern Street was delayed until 1876
by negotiations with the Metropolitan Board of Works). This work
was followed by a rearrangement of tracks and platforms on the
western side of Broad Street, completed in 1877. In an endeavour
to improve the passenger flow through the station, the interior was
rearranged, a new central booking office at platform level coming
into use on 4 September 1890. At the same time, the appearance
of the frontage was marred by the erection of two covered footbridges over the forecourt, with stairs to the street at one end, and
platform level entrances at the other. The east side of the station
was rearranged in 1891, when a further track was added, making
eight in all.

Varying in length from 419 to 480 ft, and numbered from east
to west, the platforms were of stone, ill-lit by ponderous gas
lamps. The rails of the platform tracks ran over engine pits, full
length on numbers 1 to 4, and extending as far as the cross-overs
on platforms 5 to 8.

At the turn of the century, platform 1 was the home of the
Chalk Farm stopping trains. Poplar and Bow services used 2 and 3;
both 3 and 4 were patronised by the North London trains to and
from the GNR suburban stations; 5 was used by the 'Outer Circle'
and 6 and 7 by services to LNWR suburban stations and the NLR
fast trains to Richmond and Willesden. Platform 8 accommodated
the stopping service to Richmond and Kew Bridge. The Outer
Circle service was operated by the LNWR, first between Broad Street
and Kensington (Addison Road) from 1 September 1867, then onwards to Victoria (LBSCR) from 1 January 1869. It was diverted
from Victoria to Mansion House (Metropolitan District Railway)
from 1 February 1872. After the electrification of the District, it

was cut back to Earls Court from 1 January 1909. It ceased in 1914 when a shuttle service of electric trains began to work between Earls Court and Willesden Junction (High Level).

Each pair of platforms shared a coaling stage, and there were two more stages just outside the station. On the east side, the engine of an arriving train would wait at the buffers whilst another locomotive was brought from the coaling stage to be coupled to the other end of the train, ready for departure. Once the train had left, the incoming engine moved to the coaling stage for coal and water and was then ready for the next departure. On the west side (platforms 5 to 8) there were scissors cross-overs, allowing the immediate release of the train engine, which could leave with the same train after visiting the coaling stage. A ninth platform was added outside the western wall in 1913.

When the Central London Railway extended its tube line from the Bank to Liverpool Street in 1912, a booking hall was built under the forecourt of Broad Street station. Served by two escalators, it was brought into use on 10 October. Access to the main concourse of the terminus was provided from 23 February 1913 when two lifts began to operate between the tube station and the North London platform level. A tube railway booking office was opened by the upper lift landing and through tickets were issued between NLR stations and the tube. Later in 1913, these works were completed by the erection of a Portland stone frontage to the Broad Street station courtyard, surrounding the old footbridge staircases and incorporating a new central entrance for the main station, with entrances to the tube booking hall either side.

Until 1910, Broad Street's traffic was entirely local in character. The services provided in the 1900s worked to Chalk Farm and to Poplar every fifteen minutes, to Richmond hourly and to Kew Bridge hourly. In addition there were the Outer Circle trains to Mansion House, half-hourly, and two trains an hour to GNR stations. (The stations served were those on the lines to High Barnet, Alexandra Palace, Enfield [Gordon Hill from 1910], and Potters Bar. For short periods, Hatfield and Cuffley were also served. In the peak year of 1906 there were sixty-five trains each way daily to and from GNR stations, all worked by NLR engines and stock.) At peak hours there were additional trains and also LNWR services to Watford and Tring. In 1906 Broad Street was handling 712 trains a day, with some 80,000 passengers.

As a challenge to the improved GWR service to Birmingham via that company's new main line, the LNWR introduced a Monday to Friday restaurant car express to and from Broad Street. This 'City

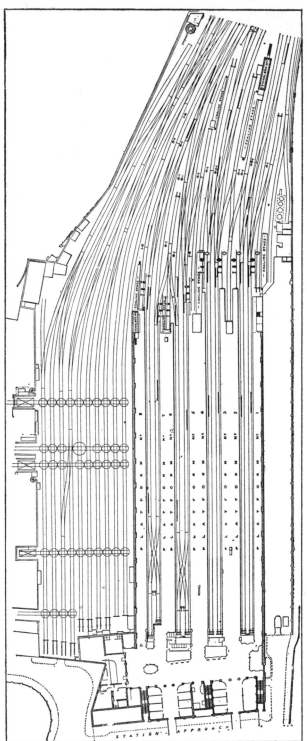

Plan of Broad Street 1906. From the Railway Magazine, September 1906

to City' train began on 1 February 1910 between Wolverhampton and Birmingham and Broad Street, stopping only at Coventry on the up working and additionally at Willesden on the return run. It was designed to attract businessmen and carried a lady typist who would tap out letters to order during the journey. The down train was withdrawn from 13 July 1914 and the up train from 22 February 1915, and the service was not revived after the war.

## CHILLY WINDS

Broad Street's suburban trains early felt the effect of electric tramcar, motor bus and tube railway. The chilly winds of their competition were first noticed about 1901, and despite brave efforts to publicise the doubtful pleasures of travelling by the 'open air route' and the operation of non-stop trains between Broad Street and Gospel Oak, the graphs of revenue and passengers slid downwards. By 1911 the annual total of passengers carried was the lowest for forty years.

Electrification was first considered in 1904 as a means of stopping the rot, but it eventually came as part of the LNWR scheme of 1911, a scheme drawn up two years after that company had taken over the management and working of the North London. LNWR electric trains, operating on the four-rail system, first left Broad Street on 1 October 1916 when the Richmond and Kew Bridge workings were taken over by the new trains. Rush hour services to Watford via Hampstead Heath followed on 16 April 1917. An all-day electric service to Watford via Primrose Hill began on 10 July 1922. At Broad Street, platforms 5 to 9 were equipped with conductor rails, the electric trains running in and out on the No 2 up and down roads between the terminus and Dalston.

Between the wars there were electric trains to Richmond every fifteen minutes and to Watford every thirty minutes, with additional trains in the peak including one to Croxley Green. Steam trains ran every half-hour to Poplar (five in the peak hour). Rush hour services included one steam train an hour to Tring and six to LNER (ex GNR) stations. In the 1920s, Broad Street's traffic continued to decline, particularly that over the former GNR lines, reduced to rush hours only since 1915. More attractive alternatives were provided by motor bus and tube railway, the LMSR assisting the process by retaining in use the old North London four-wheel carriages until 1935. Unheated and gas-lit, with hard back seats and open top partitions, these veterans survived even longer on the Broad Street—Poplar service, where one set was still running, in newly-varnished North London livery, as late as 1938.

To afford some relief to the cramped accommodation in the old Fenchurch Street, the LMSR lengthened platforms 1 and 2 at Broad Street, operating regular services from them to Southend, Grays and Tilbury from 1923 onwards. These trains continued to run until the Fenchurch Street enlargement was completed in 1935.

Broad Street suffered minor damage in the first world war. On 8 September 1915, bomb explosions shattered a thousand panes of glass, demolished a wall and injured some horses in the goods station. More serious disturbances were created twenty-five years later. The lines into the terminus were put completely out of action on the night of 3/4 October 1940 and the station was closed for several days. Similar interruptions were experienced on 13 October and 11 November. Services over the former GNR lines, which had been suspended between 11 September and 3 December 1939 to make room for essential war traffic, were taken off altogether on 4 October 1940 after the previous night's bomb havoc. LNER stock had been used from 5 February 1940, causing much initial confusion among passengers. Heavy air attacks on the East End of London, with subsequent evacuation of many of the residents, finally extinguished the poorly-patronised service east of Dalston Junction, which was not worked after 14 May 1944. Shoreditch and Haggerston stations had closed in 1940. Although the Poplar service was never resumed, the LNER revived the Broad Street trains after the war, using its own locomotives and stock; trains ran to and from Hertford North and Welwyn Garden City from 30 July 1945 in rush hours only.

Main-line trains reappeared briefly at holiday times in 1950 and 1951 when some short-distance main-line services to Cambridge and other places were diverted to relieve Kings Cross.

### A POST-WAR PROBLEM

Apart from the electric rush-hour services between Broad Street and Watford via Primrose Hill, the only trains which now use this terminus are the electrics to and from Richmond via Hampstead Heath, three an hour each way until mid-evening. At slack times, the traffic is so light that one man is sufficient to staff the whole terminus. At the turn of the century there were almost 50,000

Page 103

(above) *Fenchurch Street interior, 24 March 1956,* BR *2-6-4T, 80080 backing on to special train for the Railway Correspondence & Travel Society's East London Railtour No 2;* (below) *Liverpool Street interior, looking north east from above platform 1, 5 May, 1956*

(above) *London Bridge Joint Station of 1844-5. This drawing shows the proposed frontage, not all of which was built;* (below) *Bricklayers Arms. This drawing by S. Sly for* The Illustrated London News *contains a number of small errors and renders the building rather more impressive than reality*

passengers arriving in the rush hours, but in 1968 the daily user was only 9,000, falling to 3,000 on Saturdays and only 1,250 on Sundays.

Traffic thinned out so much that British Railways closed off the main station block altogether in the late 1950s, erecting two small buildings on the concourse, one for the stationmaster and ticket booking, the other for enquiries and 'gentlemen'. These were completed in 1957. Unable to operate the refreshment room profitably, the railway authorities passed it over to private enterprise, who in turn gave up the struggle in 1963. After that there was little to divert the waiting passenger, apart from a charming one-eighth scale model of NLR 4–4–0T No 60. A feature of Broad Street for many years, this model was built at Bow Works in 1888. It once ran on live steam, but latterly suffered the indignity of being powered by an electric motor, which responded when a penny was dropped for the Railway Benevolent Institution.* At the opposite end of the concourse is a sad little cenotaph which the North London Railway erected to commemorate those of its staff who were killed in the 1914-18 war.

In 1967-8 Broad Street was stripped of most of its remaining grandeur when the outer parts of the train shed roofs were removed to reduce maintenance costs. What was left was but a poor thing indeed, just one more of BR's many under-used assets. As related in chapter 16, its inevitable closure was to be long-delayed.

## SIGNALLING

From the outset, Broad Street had interlocked signalling, provided by McKenzie & Holland, in two boxes, one for each side of the station. No 1 box was situated north of the platforms on the east side and worked the NLR platforms. No 2 was at the north end of platform 8. In the 1891 rearrangement mentioned in the main text, the original No 1 box was replaced by a new 75-lever box opened in May 1891. This had NLR standard tappet interlocking, and was situated north of the coaling stage serving Nos 2 and 3 platforms.

Each cabin had an inner home signal to maintain locking and

* This model is now in The National Railway Museum.

prevent reversal of points in front of an approaching train. Further protection was given by a Park & Pryce train protection bar in each platform road, which locked the inner home at danger while a train was standing in the platform on the bar.

North of the station, Skinner Street Junction box marked an intermediate block section and New Inn Yard junction box the end of the first section. These two cabins were also needed to control the freight working in and out of the LNWR goods depot on the west side of the terminus.

Subsequent changes are mentioned in chapter 16.

CHAPTER 6

## *Liverpool Street*

### NOT AS BLACK AS PAINTED

A gloomy low level situation, uninspired architecture, and a con-
fusing, disjointed layout all contributed to Liverpool Street's past
unpopularity. In steam days it always seemed to have more than
its fair share of smoke and grime, not being an easy place to venti-
late or keep clean. Suffering the austerities of wartime travel, Tom
Driberg had been moved, in the winter of 1944, to describe it in
*Reynolds News* as 'almost completely squalid . . . tiringly chaotic
. . . this hell hole . . .' setting off an interesting correspondence in
*The Railway Gazette;* but it was never as bad as *that,* even in its
worst days, and those wartime years were among the worst.
Electrification provided the opportunity of keeping the interior
clean and bright, making Liverpool Street a much more pleasant
place for the ordinary passenger. But many a railway enthusiast
now passed through with a heavy heart, sadly missing the impatient beat of Westinghouse brake pumps and the soft smoke that
lingered so long, mixed so romantically with summer sunlight or
winter fog.

### SHOREDITCH, OR BAD CHARACTERS GOT RID OF

Whatever the real or imagined disadvantages of Liverpool Street,
it was a vast improvement upon its predecessor, the Shoreditch
terminus of the Eastern Counties Railway. That line had been
opened from a temporary station at Devonshire Street, Mile End,
on 20 June 1839 after the formal opening of 18 June, reaching the
permanent terminus just south of the junction of Bethnal Green
Road and Shoreditch on 1 July 1840. As the engineer John Braithwaite[1] had cut through the built-up area by bringing the ECR in
from the Lea Valley over a viaduct of brick arches, the platforms
were above street level. Passengers arriving in London by this route

for the first time must have wondered how they would make their escape, for the line terminated in one of the capital's poorest and most unpleasant quarters. Six years after the opening, the station was renamed Bishopsgate, probably in the hope that it might be thought nearer the City than it was.

Its situation was in truth unfortunate. Within a stone's throw of Old Jago, one of London's foulest slums, inhabited almost entirely by criminals, the terminus was built on the site of Webb Square, 'a sort of receptacle for pickpockets, housebreakers and prostitutes, great numbers of whom were removed; and the same along St John Street, one side of which was taken down, and several bad characters were then got rid of'.[2] As early as 1845 the ECR was proposing to construct an alternative terminus. In supporting a Farringdon Street scheme before the Royal Commission of 1846, George Hudson spoke of the inconvenience of Shoreditch, both for the City and the West End. Nearly twenty years later the terminus was still there, and *The Railway News* was commenting acidly that the site 'has always been an unsavoury and unsuitable locality, and not even the change of name from Shoreditch to Bishopsgate has ever made it one whit more attractive.'

Designed by Braithwaite, the Shoreditch building contained the offices of the Eastern Counties Railway and of the Northern & Eastern Railway, which used the line inwards from Stratford. Incorporated in 1836, this company proposed to build a line from Islington to York via Bishops Stortford, Cambridge and Lincoln. Finding the cost of a London terminus and approaches too much for its financial resources, it made arrangements with the ECR to run over that company's line between Stratford and Shoreditch at a toll of 4d per passenger and a rent of £7,000 a year. The first section of the N & ER, from Stratford to Broxbourne, was opened on 15 September 1840, and the line had only reached Bishops Stortford before the company was leased to the ECR in 1844; it was vested in the Great Eastern Railway, the ECR's successor, in 1902.

Behind a 125 ft frontage were single departure and arrival platforms each 265 ft long, separated by three empty carriage roads. Above the tracks and platforms was a corrugated wrought-iron roof with a 36 ft centre span and 20 ft 6 in side spans. Water from it drained through 34 cast-iron columns which ran in two rows down its 230 ft length. At each end of the platforms, all five 5 ft gauge tracks were linked by turnplates. Both the N & ER and the ECR were converted to standard gauge in 1844.

On the up side, to the east of the station, were two ticket platforms, and, in the yard, a horse and carriage dock. The down side of the station yard contained horse and carriage docks, a 32 ft turntable, an engine pit, a water crane, and a coke platform. In St John Street, on the north side of the line, and east of the passenger station, was a goods yard.

Such a small station inevitably required enlargement before it was very old. A modest rebuilding, incorporating a new frontage in the Italian style by Sancton Wood was carried out in 1848-9. But it was still inadequate and poorly-sited.

In 1862, the ECR became part of the Great Eastern Railway, and consideration was at once given to the question of a London terminus. Attempts to obtain use of the proposed station at Broad Street were unsuccessful, and in a report to the board, dated 17 December 1862, the manager and engineer recommended the construction of a new passenger terminus inside the City of London, the development of suburban traffic by the construction of new lines, and the conversion of Bishopsgate to a goods station. They described the terminus as 'objectionable in almost every feature. In locality it is remote; its approaches are inconvenient; and as regards space, it is so restricted that your traffic can only be carried at great cost, with great delay, and with an absolute restriction on the number of trains which can be despatched'. The extension into the City received the blessing of a House of Lords Select Committee on London's Railways in 1863.

Various proposals were made; first for a terminus at Finsbury Circus, then as far south as Wormwood Street, with approach tracks above street level; but the scheme sanctioned by Parliament in 1864 was for a low level station in Liverpool Street, alongside and to the east of the North London Railway terminus then under construction. Ten years were to elapse before the project was realised. It was a difficult time to raise capital, especially for the GER, then going through an anxious period of financial stress. When a move could at last be made, there were long delays before the necessary properties were acquired.

It was decided to bring the approach tracks down from the old ECR viaduct at Tapp Street (just west of the present Bethnal Green station), maintaining a gradient of 1 in 70 until they were below street level. This provided some saving in land acquisition, allowing the lines to pass under one side of the original terminal site. Beyond, the alignment was to go under Commercial Street and Shoreditch High Street before turning south to enter the terminus, on a site once occupied by the gardens of the old Bethlehem Hospital. Among the major buildings to be demolished were the City of London Theatre and the City of London Gasworks. When giving evidence on 16 May 1884 to the Royal Commission on the Housing of the Working Classes, William Birt (general manager of the GER) mentioned the destruction of 450 tenement dwellings, sheltering some 7,000 people. Some of the houses had been occupied by as many as seven families and were perhaps some of the worst of their kind in London. Their destruction had been anticipated in a clause of the 1864 Act requiring the GER to run a 2d return train daily from Edmonton and another from Walthamstow. In practice the GER provided many more cheap trains but, as elsewhere, most of those thrown out of their homes were too poor to afford new houses in the suburbs. Instead, they spent the few shillings 'compensation' on a bottle or two of gin and the hire of a cart and squeezed themselves into adjacent streets, increasing the already pitiable overcrowding of the Shoreditch area. Birt claimed that the GER always compensated tenants, paying from 30s to 50s according to the circumstances of each family, but whilst this may have been strictly true at the time he gave evidence, such payments as were made a decade earlier did not always reach those levels.

## AT THE FOOT OF AN INCLINE

Many years later, in the *Great Eastern Railway Magazine*, of February 1923, Lord Claud Hamilton[3] related how the GER directors were prevented from taking any interest in the design of the new terminus. Planning and construction were in the hands of Samuel Swarbrick, the general manager, who had the chairman, Lightly Simpson, under his thumb. Swarbrick, who was more interested in financial matters than traffic and operating considerations, had agreed the low-level plan. Hamilton thought this a serious error, and wanted to see the platforms at street level, but he and his fellow directors were not allowed to interfere. 'The result', wrote Hamilton, 'has been a great inconvenience to the travelling public . . . every one of our heavily-laden trains has to commence its journey at the bottom of an incline'.

A part of the new station was opened on 2 February 1874, for the Enfield and Walthamstow services, the remainder coming into use on 1 November 1875, when the old Bishopsgate terminus was closed to passengers. Converted to a goods depot, it reopened in 1881 and survived in use until 5 December 1964, when it was totally destroyed by fire.

Liverpool Street, as opened in 1874-5, occupied an area of ten acres, and had ten platforms, numbered from west to east. At the extreme west side, the tracks serving platforms 1 and 2 were extended in tunnel beneath the station buildings and under the street to a junction with the Metropolitan Railway, just west of what was later to be that company's Liverpool Street station.

The main buildings of the terminus consisted of a 90 ft high block on Liverpool Street, another block attached to this, running back 320 ft from the street, and a third block, 146 ft long, joined to the second at its north end, at right angles to it, and terminating in a massive spired clock tower. Apart from the clock tower, on the west, and a 90 ft high central section in the middle block, these last two buildings were 67 ft high. In the open space formed by the angle of the buildings were four roadways for pedestrians and vehicles. The westernmost of these was above the tunnel to the Metropolitan and led to the separate suburban booking office. This office was later closed, and a five-storey office block erected over it, west of the clock tower.

For many years the pedestrian way remained open, with access to a new low-level suburban booking office, but it is now closed and used as a car park for the Great Eastern Hotel. Next to the suburban approach, descending from the street to platform level, was the entrance way for cabs bound for the main-line departure side. This roadway had a pavement at the west side and formed the most popular entrance and exit for those not using the subways under the street to and from the Metropolitan station. After this came the exit ramp for cabs leaving the departure side, and finally, alongside the west block, a small yard serving the general offices which were situated in this building. At the extreme eastern side of the station, alongside the easternmost platform, there was another vehicle roadway, running the full length of the station from Pindar Street to Liverpool Street, serving main-line arrivals.

Behind the north block and the clock tower was the suburban section of the station, ten platform faces and eight tracks under a 450 ft roof in spans of 46 ft and 109 ft. The main-line departure and arrival platforms (later 9 and 10) were to the east of the middle office block; 900 ft in length, they extended almost up to Liverpool Street under a 730 ft roof in spans of 109 ft and 45 ft.

The train shed, shaped like an inverted 'L', with its four spans of iron and glass reaching up to 76 ft above the tracks, had roof trusses of wrought-iron, with cast-iron ornamental details and spandril fittings. The roof is one of the best points of Liverpool Street; lofty and delicate-looking, it imparts grace to the interior. Later the roofscape was enhanced by two enormous four-faced clocks, which were suspended above the platforms. Despite their Gothic appearance, they were electrically operated.

In the centre of the long west block, at platform level, was the main-line booking office, 90 ft long and 50 ft wide, conveniently situated between the cab road and the departure platform. After the first world war, the GER erected a large mural memorial at the north end of this hall. It was unveiled on 22 June 1922 by Field Marshal Sir Henry Wilson (Chief of the Imperial General Staff, and an Ulster MP), and a plaque next to it recalls that on returning from the ceremony, Wilson was assassinated on his doorstep by two members of the Irish Republican Army. Another plaque on the same wall forms a memorial to the heroic GER marine officer, Captain Fryatt, who was executed by the Germans in 1916.[4]

Either side of the booking hall were waiting and refreshment rooms. Above, all along this middle block, were the general offices of the GER.

The frontage buildings, in white Suffolk brick, with Bath stone dressings and ornamentation, are uninteresting, even dreary in appearance. Edward Wilson, an engineer, drew up the designs for the terminus, and any architectural assistance was at a humble level. The style is a restrained Gothic, the features seemingly taken straight from a copy book of do-it-yourself architecture.

The platforms behind the north block, now numbered 1 to 8, were allocated to suburban services, apart from the two easternmost, which shared main-line departures with the long platform now numbered 9. Against the western wall was No 1, reached by a footbridge, spanning the entrance to the Metropolitan junction tunnel, which received the platform tracks of Nos 1 and 2. The remaining suburban platforms were set further back, the two easternmost tracks having a platform face either side. These faces are now known as 7 west, 7 east, 8 west and 8 east, but at earlier periods were variously known as 6, 7, 8 and 9, or 6, 7, 7 and 8. This confusion is the reason why some accounts give the number of platforms at the original Liverpool Street as 9, others 10. There were in fact 12 platform *faces*. Next came the long departure platform, and opposite it, on the extreme eastern side of the station, the arrival platform (now 10), of similar length.

From 1 February until 12 July 1875, when its own station was completed, Metropolitan Railway trains used platforms 1 and 2 of the GER station. The proposed through workings between the two railways were suffocated by tedious arguments about charges, and after the opening of the Metropolitan station (on the opposite side of Liverpool Street, and known as Bishopsgate until 1 January 1909), the connecting tunnel was used only for special workings. The last of these, a Metropolitan excursion train from Rickmansworth to Yarmouth, ran in 1904. Three years later the junction was removed.

Although the tenemented poor had received little or no recompense, the landowners required suitable rewards. The cost of construction and materials was heavy, notably high prices being paid for the roof ironwork. Altogether the terminus cost some £2,000,000, and in an endeavour to recover some of it, the GER obtained powers in an Act of 1869 to charge fares over the 1¼ mile extension at the 2 mile rate.

In conjunction with the opening of Liverpool Street, a three-pronged group of suburban lines was constructed north of Bethnal Green, as recommended in the report mentioned earlier. These new lines ran through Hackney Downs and Tottenham to Lower Edmonton, where a junction was formed with the original Enfield branch; and from Hackney Downs through Clapton to junctions with the Cambridge line and the 1870 Walthamstow branch from Lea Bridge. Both were opened in August 1872. The Walthamstow branch was extended to Chingford in 1873, and the Tottenham and Edmonton line was given a branch to Palace Gates (Wood Green) in 1878. As these new direct routes to Walthamstow and Enfield were ready before Liverpool Street, and there was no room for more trains at Bishopsgate, a new station, Bishopsgate Low Level, was opened on the approach line to Liverpool Street on 4 November 1872. This was directly beneath the original terminus, and as there was little or no room for smoke to escape, it was decided to fit condensing apparatus to the whole interchangeable fleet of suburban tank engines; the possibility of through running on to the Metropolitan Railway may also have been a factor in this decision. Bishopsgate Low Level station remained open after the completion of Liverpool Street, but was closed as a wartime economy on 22 May 1916, a sad day for the knowing rush-hour passengers who would assure themselves of an evening seat by boarding incoming trains there.

During the 1880s, the suburban services over these new lines, with their very cheap fares and frequent trains, developed a heavy traffic, and it became clear that the accommodation at Liverpool Street would be insufficient for all the GER services, despite the continued use of Fenchurch Street for some routes. As early as 1884, the chairman of the GER told shareholders that the company could fill a thousand trains daily in and out of Liverpool Street, but the existing premises could handle only two-thirds that number.

## EAST SIDE EXTENSION

For some time the GER had been acquiring land between the eastern boundary of the terminus and Bishopsgate. This area, 188 ft wide, and some six acres in extent, was now cleared, and in 1890 construction of what was to be the East Side station was begun. This time, Parliament had insisted that the displaced inhabitants be rehoused by the railway company at low fixed rents. Alternative accommodation was found for 137 in existing property; the remaining 600 went into tenements completed in 1890 at GER expense.

As part of the new works, a third pair of approach tracks was provided between Bethnal Green and Liverpool Street, coming into use in 1891. The westernmost lines, reserved entirely for the Enfield Town, Palace Gates and Walthamstow services were then known as the Suburban lines, the middle pair as the Local and the eastern pair as the Through. These last four tracks continued beyond Bethnal Green, eventually to Romford. Between Bethnal Green and Hackney Downs North junction were four tracks, the Suburban, and, on the east, the Fast lines, the latter joining the Local lines at Bethnal Green.

At Liverpool Street, platforms 1 to 5 (West Side Suburban) were connected to both the Suburban and Local lines, platforms 7 to 14 were served by both Local and Through, whilst 15 to 18 were connected to the Through lines only. The East Side, with its eight 30 ft wide platforms, all slightly longer than numbers 1 to 8, was opened to public traffic on 2 April 1894. During the time when the new platforms and signal boxes were being connected, no trains were cancelled, but from 27 March to 2 April, 132 flagmen worked 800 trains a day, and from 25 June to 2 July, when the new West Side signal box was installed and certain alterations made to the West Side platforms, 140 flagmen managed 871 daily trains without serious incident.

If the number of platforms is taken as a measure of size, Liverpool Street, with eighteen, was the largest London terminus until the opening of the new Victoria in 1908, but both before and after that date it held supreme place as regards the number of passengers handled daily. In March 1907 there were 851 passenger trains in and out each twenty-four hours, together with 224 empty coach trains, ten goods trains and five light engines, a total of 1,090 movements every day.

At this time the normal platform allocation was as follows:

*West Side*
1  Palace Gates and Enfield Town and all workmen's trains on the Suburban Lines
2  Palace Gates and Enfield Town
3  Chingford
4  North Woolwich and evening fast trains on the Enfield and Chingford lines
5  Loughton and North Woolwich
6  Loughton, North Woolwich; Cambridge line departures as required
7 & 8  Cambridge line departures
9  Cambridge and Colchester main-line departures
10 to 12  Main-line arrivals
13  Main-line arrivals as required. Suburban and stopping trains on the Colchester line.

*East Side Suburban*
14  New Cross and Croydon via East London Railway
15-17  Ilford, Romford and Southend lines
18  Barking via Forest Gate junction
Ilford, Romford and Southend as required.
Horse box and other specials as required.

The services to south London through the Thames Tunnel which used platform 14, and sometimes 18, and before that, the original station, had an interesting career. After the completion of the East London Railway from Wapping to East London junction (just east of Bishopsgate) on 10 April 1876, the LBSCR started a service from Croydon to Liverpool Street on the following 1 July. This was joined by SER trains, which worked into Liverpool Street from Addiscombe Road (now Addiscombe) between 1 April 1880 and 2 March 1884. From 1 January 1886, the GER had taken over the workings to the LBSCR stations, operating a service to New Cross, and, from 1 February 1887, to East Croydon. These trains did not run beyond New Cross from 1 June 1911 and ceased altogether when the East London Railway was electrified from 31 March 1913. Apart from these local trains, there had been a daily return working between Liverpool Street and Brighton from 1876 to 1883, with through carriages for a further year.

The frontage of the East Side was formed by the Great Eastern Hotel, which had been completed in May 1884. Designed by C. E. Barry in a vaguely French Renaissance style, this red brick structure was somewhat more impressive than the earlier station buildings. Now the largest, if not the only major hotel in the City of

London, the Great Eastern contains the Abercorn Rooms, an extension of 1900-01 by Col. R. W. Edis, entered from Bishopsgate, and used for banquets, dances and other functions.

## MYSTERIOUS AND MURKY

Beneath the hotel was an area known as the 'backs', penetrated by the tracks of platforms 9 and 10 and one of the two sidings between them, thus providing the building with a railway-served basement. A mysterious and murky place, the backs were the introduction to an equally grim subway which led to the eastbound Metropolitan platform. As a child, the author was often taken this way when visiting relatives in south-east London, never passing through without a shudder, as both subway and backs had entered his subconscious and formed the scenery of many a frightening dream.

There always seemed to be a few trucks in the backs, or on the sidings between 9 and 10, known as the 'yard'. We later discovered that Liverpool Street had a night goods train, the 12.7 am from Stratford, which brought in permanent way material, coal for the hotel and the engine docks, and truck traffic for the hotel and other departments. This 'ghost train', as it was known to the staff, returned with a load of hotel refuse and ashes from the engine docks. In the heyday of steam, the coaling stages of the engine docks at the platform ends needed as much as 15,000 tons a year. The terminus also saw parcels trains from the southern lines via the East London Railway, which were brought into the yard for splitting and reversing before moving on. Interchange freight trains were also worked in and out of the terminus.

Along Bishopsgate, the east side was penetrated by in and out cab roads ending in a small yard opposite platforms 11 and 12. Next came an office block, later known as Harwich House, and this was followed by the rather plain façade which contained the pedestrian entrances to the booking hall, concourse and platforms of the East Side. Beyond this was a large block of offices with shops at ground floor level, stretching almost the whole length of the platforms, and containing the entrance to the parcels depot. This building was later named Hamilton House after Lord Claud Hamilton. The parcels depot extended over platforms 11 to 18, with a parcels bridge as far as platform 8. Flanked by roadways, it was connected by lifts to the platforms, and to a parcels subway below.

Entering the East Side from Bishopsgate, the passenger either descended a stairway into the large concourse at the head of the platforms, or passed into the East Side booking office from which doorways led out on to the footbridge which ran right across the station. The train shed of the East Side consisted of a four span roof (51 ft 6 in, 42 ft 3 in, 42 ft 3 in and 51 ft 11 in), with red brick walls, and a cross span over the 15,000 sq ft concourse. There was a pleasing lightness and spaciousness about this new section of the terminus, which was designed by W. N. Ashbee,[5] head of the GER architectural section.

When the station was first planned, it was apparently not realised that if there were any expansion in the only possible direction, eastwards, the extra length of the main-line platforms 9 and 10 would split the station in two just as effectively as the Great Hall split Euston. When the East Side was built, it was necessary to make the best of this situation and erect footbridges not only across the south ends of 9 and 10, but across the full width of the combined East and West Sides, to provide ready access to all parts of the station. This main footbridge was by no means straight, none too wide, and at two different levels. It was the scene of much confusion at busy times as people struggled to get from one side of the station to the other; from it many a curse must have been uttered, because of it, many a train missed.

But it did have one redeeming feature, for three little tea rooms jutted out from it, offering refreshment and relaxation for the weary. There were two on the West Side, opposite platforms 3 to 6, and one on the East Side, facing 12 and 13. These delightful Gothic gazebos provided many a pleasant half-hour for the railway-minded station saunterer and those given to watching the social scene. Sitting here, with the aroma of tea and buttered toast subtly mixing into the smoke and steam wafting through the open window, it was possible to enjoy a particularly cosy contemplation of the bustle and activity always present below. One of these rooms, refurbished in a pseudo-style, and that much less attractive, remains open on the West Side; the others are used for railway purposes.

Communications across the station were somewhat improved in July 1912 when the Central London tube railway was extended to Liverpool Street. A booking hall was then built for the tube beneath the West Side, and a subway opened to connect it to Bishopsgate, across the station. Taking the view that the Central London would bring extra traffic, the GER made the space required for the tube station available free of charge. In more recent years, the area at the end of platforms 9 and 10 has been tidied up, the

'backs' sidings abolished, and level communication around the ends
has replaced the smaller footbridge.

In addition to the passenger facilities provided by the Central
London tube railway, Liverpool Street was one of the two London
termini to be served by the Post Office tube railway, opened between Paddington and Whitechapel in December 1927. A station
was provided at the south end, under the hotel, with two 315 ft
parcel and letter bag conveyors to platforms 10 and 11. Normal
traffic in the 1930s reached some 10,000 bags daily, with 690 GPO
trains calling.

<h2 style="text-align:center">SUBURBAN JAZZ</h2>

The suburban and outer suburban network was completed by
the opening of the Southend branch (1889), the Churchbury loop,
from Edmonton to Cheshunt (1891) and the Hainault loop from
Ilford to Woodford (1903). Neither of the loops was immediately
successful, and the Churchbury line was closed to passengers in
1909. By the 1900s, the GER suburban service was the most lavish
and the busiest in the world. In 1912 the three pairs of approach
tracks were carrying around a thousand trains daily, with a passenger load of some 200,000 in and out, mostly in suburban trains
of fifteen to seventeen four-wheel carriages. From the earliest days,
Liverpool Street suburban traffic had been deliberately encouraged,
particularly on the West Side. The two cheap trains required by
the 1864 Act had been increased to twenty-three by 1883 and to
thirty by 1900, five serving Enfield Town, providing a return run of
21½ miles for 2d. Supplementing the 2d trains were twelve 3d
trains operating between 7 and 7.30 am and following these, until 8 am, there were about a dozen trains at half the ordinary fare,
The 2d and 3d fares remained in force until 1920, when the cheap
fares were revised on a mileage scale. By 1927 the cheapest return
fare from Enfield Town or Wood Street was 6d (arriving by
7.2 am). In the evening, all cheap tickets were available on any
train after 4 pm (after noon on Saturdays), excluding some fast
trains. A half-hourly all-night service, the first in Britain, was introduced on 21 June 1897 between Liverpool Street and Walthamstow.

This frequent, punctual and cheap train service encouraged
artisans, clerks, and shop and warehouse workers to move out
from the inner belt, and private enterprise provided thousands of
small houses for them to rent in Tottenham, Edmonton and
Walthamstow. In Walthamstow, the population grew from 11,092
in 1871 to 95,131 in 1901, and there were similar increases in

Tottenham, Edmonton and parts of Wood Green.

Prompted by the existence of tube railway schemes for north-east London, electrification of the suburban lines was considered, and powers were taken in 1903. But although the traffic continued to grow, nothing was done, nor were any tube railways built. After the first world war, the suburban problem became more burdensome, as the increasing concentration of the rush hours brought severe overcrowding. From 200,000 passengers a day in 1,250 trains in 1912, Liverpool Street's traffic had grown to 229,073 in 1921, with only fourteen more trains. Between 7.30 and 9.30 am, 66,488 passengers arrived, 68,017 leaving in the evening between 5 and 7.

It was impossible to enlarge the terminus any further without enormous expenditure and disruption; electrification seemed the only way of increasing capacity. A scheme for electric services to Palace Gates, Enfield, Broxbourne, Chingford, Ongar, North Woolwich and Gidea Park was drawn up, but the directors hesitated, appalled at the amount of capital required, money which they knew would be difficult, if not impossible, to raise, in view of the small return that could be expected. Yet something had to be done for the heavily overcrowded Enfield and Chingford services, and it was agreed in 1919 to make the best of the existing equipment by spending £80,000 (less than a fortieth of the cost of electrification) on track and station rearrangements, resignalling and other measures that would permit the steam trains to be run at maximum possible intensity. This scheme was planned by F. V. Russell, the GER superintendent of operation.

Although very successful, this was only an expedient, and everyone in authority knew that they were merely putting off the difficult decision of electrification as long as possible. Known officially as the *Intensive Service*, the new arrangements which came into operation on 12 July 1920 were quickly christened the *Jazz Service* by an evening newspaper. An increase of 50 per cent was achieved in the Monday to Friday service between 5 and 7.30 pm and of 75 per cent in the corresponding up service between 8 and 10 am. At the height of the rush period, there were twenty-four 16-coach trains, each with 848 seats, passing each hour along one track between Liverpool Street and Bethnal Green. (Six ran to Chingford, six to Wood Street [fast to St James Street], nine to Enfield Town [three with Palace Gates connections at Seven Sisters] and three to Palace Gates.)

This was a remarkable achievement with manual signalling and motive power largely consisting of o–6–oT of an 1886 design weighing only 32 tons empty, engines with 4 ft wheels and cylinders 16½ in by 22 in. Off-peak and Sunday services were also improved by the introduction of shorter, faster and more frequent trains which provided a basic 10-minute service on the Enfield and Chingford lines.

Every possible step was taken to cut terminal delays. Independent engine docks and layouts were provided for platforms 1 to 4, allowing incoming engines to be shunted without fouling the other lines beyond platform limits. With these and other alterations, trains could be moved into a platform every ten minutes, staying only four minutes. At the busy hours, trains started in sequence from platforms 4 (Wood Street fast), 3 (Enfield), 2 (Chingford) and 1 (Enfield or Palace Gates), at two-minute intervals, followed by a four-minute gap to accommodate arrivals. Each incoming engine, as released, worked the next departure, and extra men were on duty to assist with the uncoupling and servicing of arriving engines.

Additional circulating space was made on the platform side of the barriers of 2 to 6 by demolishing a bookstall, staff offices and lavatory entrances. This gave passengers a choice of exit gates, thus speeding up the clearance of the platform. Access to platform 1 was made easier by finally closing up the Metropolitan branch tunnel (it had been used for stabling stock), making it possible to reach it on the level. After removal of the tracks, the tunnel was converted to staff recreation and dining rooms. The entrance can still be seen from Metropolitan Line trains entering Liverpool Street on the eastbound line.

To obtain longer headways and provide paths for down main-line trains which might be running late, it was necessary to have 'non-stop' working in various combinations. A code number was allocated to each train according to its stopping pattern, and leaflets explaining the numbers were left on the seats of trains some weeks before the new service started. These numbers were prominently displayed on the side of the brake vans and at the Liverpool Street barriers, together with a list of stations passed. Later, 'pedestal' departure indicators with departure time dials and station name displays were placed at the head of each platform (similar indicators were installed on platforms 11 to 18). Finally, to speed up loading, second and first class compartments were temporarily picked out by yellow and blue coloured bands painted between the windows and the roof.

As a consequence of the Jazz Service track alterations, trains using platforms 1, 2 and 3 now ran on the Local lines only in

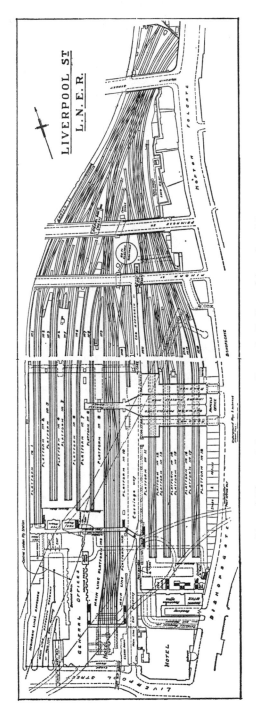

*Plan of Liverpool Street 1924. From the Railway Magazine, May 1924*

H

emergencies, and Enfield and Chingford line trains were confined to platforms 1 to 4. Trains using platform 4 still occasionally ran on the Local lines, but usually on the Suburban lines. Platforms 5 and 6 were connected only with the Local lines. Through services to Palace Gates were reduced to rush hours only, but the branch was worked with a frequent push-pull service, connecting with Enfield line trains, which left Liverpool Street carrying on their smokebox doors the lengthy legend: ENFIELD TOWN CHANGE FOR PALACE GATES AT SEVEN SISTERS.

After a temporary suspension during the 1921 coal strike, the Jazz Service lasted until the 1926 general strike. When that had passed, the slack hour time table was modified, and the pressure on the West Side began to abate. People moved to new houses further out, took up local employment in the expanding Lea Valley industrial area, or used more attractive forms of transport into the centre (until 1925, when the Gresley 'quintuplet' articullated sets were slowly introduced, all trains were composed of gaslit four-wheelers with a very spartan atmosphere in the third class).

Activity at Liverpool Street generally declined. In 1923 244,000 passengers were passing through daily, but this had fallen to 209,000 by 1938 (and was to go down to 171,000 in 1959). The number of ticket collectors decreased from 76 in 1924 to 63 in 1935, and the complement of porters in the same period fell from 134 to 90.

We must now return for a moment to complete the story of the station in the GER years. Liverpool Street was one of the few London termini to suffer serious air raid damage in the first world war. On the night of 8 September 1915 several bombs fell on the approaches, wrecking the Suburban and Through lines, and splitting a water main which flooded the Local tracks. Repairs were quickly effected, and a full service of trains was working by 11 the next morning. During a daylight raid on 13 June 1917, three bombs fell at the outer end of the platforms just before noon, wrecking several carriages of the midday train for Hunstanton, which was standing in No 9. Two carriages in the dock between platforms 8 and 9, in use for medical examinations, were also smashed up. Sixteen people were killed and thirty-six injured. During the war years, the extensive cellars under the station and hotel were fitted up as air raid shelters for the staff and public, and an emergency office provided in them for the staff handling military traffic control.

Almost the last act of the GER at Liverpool Street was to erect a large main-line train indicator on the footbridge above platform 9.

Put into use on 17 December 1922, this showed the times, platform numbers and stopping points of departures in fourteen columns, each with a maximum of twenty indications. Details of arrivals were also displayed.

Nothing of great moment happened to Liverpool Street under the LNER regime. A Continental booking office was added in 1930 and in May 1935 the East Side booking office was modernised and equipped with Westinghouse ticket issue and accounting machines. During 1938-9, after years of neglect and public criticism, some attempts were made to clean and brighten the station. Suburban and East Side booking offices were panelled with vitriolite, a smooth yellow composition that provided an easily-cleaned surface; the steelwork and masonry inside the station lost some of their ingrained dirt; the lighting was improved; and advertisements and notices were regrouped. A new snack bar was provided, together with enlarged waiting and refreshment rooms. The 'backs' had their walls tiled and their lighting brightened up, removing something of their nightmare quality. It was all bits and pieces, good-intentioned perhaps, but it really did not make much difference; the dear old place soon lapsed into its normal grimy, grey state, and the wartime black-out helped no end.

A good deal of damage was suffered by Liverpool Street during the second world war,[6] but at the end, there it was, still looking very much the same. High explosive bombs fell on platforms 1 and 4, the first wrecking a train, which took several days to remove. On the East Side, there was damage to the booking office and platform 18 at the concourse end. A delayed action bomb which landed in the engine sidings beyond platform 10 exploded on the following day and killed two men, even though it had been surrounded by four trucks filled with ballast. A bomb which fell on the Broad Street viaduct whisked an LMSR wagon on to Liverpool Street's roof, where it had to be dismantled before it could be removed. The office blocks were badly mauled; Hamilton House lost a large chunk in January 1941 and in the following May, the West Side block and part of the clock tower were burnt out. The tower remains in decapitated state, now further disfigured with television aerials, but BR did provide a new clock in 1961.

## EASTERN ELECTRICS

Even before the first world war, the suburban traffic of the East Side had shown a vigorous growth following the rapid development of Forest Gate and Ilford between 1880 and 1905. The line from Stratford to Romford was quadrupled between 1895 and 1902, with two new stations in the Ilford area. After 1919, building north and east of Ilford proceeded rapidly, and the pressure of suburban traffic shifted from the West to the East side of Liverpool Street. Overcrowding and the lack of rail transport for the sea of new housing in North Ilford, including the City of London Corporation estates, brought strong pressures on the LNER for electrification and extension, rising to a peak in the 1930s. But the company was financially impotent when it came to expenditure of this order. Quadrupling from Romford to Shenfield was completed in 1934, with Government aid.

A far-reaching plan of co-operation between London Transport and the main-line railways was initiated in 1935 as a result of the London Passenger Transport Act of 1933 and an LPTB–main-line railway pooling scheme, which released the necessary financial support. The 1935 scheme provided for new railway construction in west, north and east London. Designed to relieve unemployment as well as the travel situation, it was to be financed by government guaranteed loans. Included in this plan was the electrification of the Liverpool Street—Shenfield line on the then British standard overhead wire system at 1,500 volts dc and the tapping of the Loughton and Hainault line traffic by an extension of the Central Line tube from Liverpool Street, with cross-platform interchange to the District at Mile End and to the surface lines at Stratford. A great deal of work was done from 1937 onwards, but the demands of war caused operations to be suspended between 1940 and 1945. Central Line trains reached Leytonstone on 5 May 1947 and through workings from Liverpool Street to the Loughton line ceased. A partial electric service between Liverpool Street and Shenfield started on 26 September 1949, and the electric trains took over all local workings from 7 November.

An important part of the Shenfield scheme was the interchange of the positions of the Local and Through lines west of Ilford to permit cross-platform transfers with the tube trains at Stratford and to segregate the types of traffic approaching Liverpool Street. The Through approach tracks therefore became the Electric lines and main-line and Southend trains were transferred to the Local tracks, renamed the Main. Both pairs of tracks were electrified. The long lead from the old Through (now Electric) lines to platforms 7 and 10 was taken out, and the electric trains served only platforms 13 to 18, although 11 and 12 were also wired for emergency use.

A considerable realignment and widening was undertaken on the East Side approaches, including a new retaining wall which provided up to 40 ft more width south of Worship Street. Over-line bridges in the approaches had to be reconstructed to cover the extra width, and to obtain the necessary clearances for electrification.

Extensions of this electrification to Chelmsford and Southend were opened on 11 June and 31 December 1956, but meanwhile further work was announced as part of the British Railways Modernisation Plan of 1955. Under this scheme, some 45 route miles of the Liverpool Street suburban network were to be electrified— Liverpool Street to Enfield Town and Chingford, and a restoration of passenger services over the Churchbury Loop with electric workings over it and beyond to Hertford East and Bishops Stortford. Shortly afterwards it was decided to adopt the 6.25 or 25 kV 50 cycles ac system as standard and to convert to that system the other Liverpool Street electric lines. Platforms 1 to 10 were wired up, and the last steam suburban trains left Liverpool Street on the evening of 20 November 1960. By the end of 1962 all other steam workings had given way to diesel-electrics or diesel multiple-unit sets.

In 1963 express electric working was introduced between Liverpool Street and Clacton, the multiple-unit trains calling at important intermediate stations. Already, some years earlier, London office workers had been encouraged to live at Clacton by the operation of special fast steam services backed with energetic publicity. By the middle 1960s, this Essex seaside town was on the way to becoming as much a London dormitory as Southend or Brighton.

A peak-hour suburban and outer suburban timetable introduced on 9 September 1963 brought the Liverpool Street electrification programme to fulfilment. There were 67 departures between 5 and 6 pm, 27 to the Enfield, Chingford and Bishops Stortford lines and 40 along the Ilford and Romford line. There were fast, semi-fast and stopping trains to most electrically-served stations, the fast trains often leaving after a stopping train and making connections with it further out. To accommodate 12-car trains for the Southend line, platforms 11 to 15 were extended at this time.

British Railways thoroughly cleaned Liverpool Street and installed fluorescent lighting high in the roof. Amongst a number of improvements and alterations in recent years, the most important has been the straightening and widening of platforms 9 and 10 by the removal of the siding known as 9a road, together with one of the two long sidings between these platforms. In 1962-4 the 'backs' were closed in, and a Post Office and a Lost Property Office constructed opposite the end of platforms 9 and 10. The Post Office did not last long—it was closed in 1968. A most successful modernisation of the main-line booking hall was completed in 1965. Except at the end containing the war memorial, the ceiling was lowered, the space above being used for a Continental Travel Office. The well-lit booking hall included a long ticket office with large plate glass windows which afforded an excellent view of the new ticket issuing and printing machines.

Some economies have been effected. The West Side Suburban booking office was closed from 16 October 1967. Beginning on 5 November of the same year, platforms 1 to 9 were closed on winter Sundays.

Few complaints are now heard about Liverpool Street, which is once again London's busiest terminus, although the daily passenger load is still well below the peak reached in the early 1920s. (Waterloo has a larger number of trains, but Liverpool Street has more daily passengers.) Now that the smoke and soot have gone, it is an altogether brighter, smarter place, although to call it clinical, as some steam devotees have done, is to exaggerate. During the 1970s BR was to produce plans for a major reconstruction, and the story is taken up in chapter 16.

### SIGNALLING AND ACCIDENTS

Signalling at the 1874-5 station was interlocked, and controlled from a cabin with 139 levers. After the opening of the East Side in 1894 there were two main boxes, both fitted with Sykes's lock and block apparatus in its most complete form.

The larger of the two cabins, West Side box, had 244 levers in two frames extending the full 70 ft length of the interior, facing east and facing west. This was the largest box on the GER, continuously manned by four men and a boy, and needing five men at peak periods. Sited beyond the end of platform 6, under Primrose Street bridge, it controlled platforms 1 to 10, and all arrivals and departures.

The East Side was provided with a box containing a 136 lever frame, located under the Pindar Street bridge at the end of platform 11. Subsidiary to the West Side box, this controlled the eastern platforms, 11 to 18.

As all the platforms could not be seen from the East and West boxes, there were observation boxes for the platform lines, equipped with electrical plungers and switches. These were East Platform box, at the end of 14 and 15, and West Platform box at the end of platform 5. When a train arrived in a platform road, the Platform box signalman turned over the switch hook on his plunger instrument for that line, maintaining the corresponding block indicator in the main box at danger. On the platform road becoming clear, the Platform box man took off his switch hook and could also then plunge the main box to free the latter's home signal for another train to enter that platform. The main box home signal became front-locked after use, in the normal Sykes's manner, until another plunge was given from the Platform box. These arrangements were necessary because there was no track circuiting or similar device.

In 1919, in connection with the introduction of the Jazz Service, route indicators were installed for incoming trains on the West Side, and 65 signal arms were abolished. Electrically worked banner or repeating signals were also provided at strategic points.

Four-aspect colour-light signalling was installed between Liverpool Street and Gidea Park with the Shenfield electrification. At Liverpool Street, a new signal cabin was built out from the east wall, just south of Worship Street, and carried over the electric lines on cantilevers. This cabin, opened on 25 September 1949, controlled all the approach tracks and station working. Three signalmen operated a three-section route-setting panel, one for each set of approach tracks, controlling 318 routes. Liverpool Street thus became the first London terminus to be completely equipped with relay interlocking controlled signalling.

There have been few serious accidents. On 13 December 1963 the last car of a down rush hour suburban electric train was derailed near the closed Bishopsgate Low Level station by a broken axle. An eighteen-year-old girl was killed in the overturned coach, but there were no serious injuries to other passengers.

# Fenchurch Street

## FIRST IN THE CITY

Tucked away in a side street, the little terminus of Fenchurch Street is one of the least known in London. It has never housed great expresses, and the furthest point reached from its platforms is a mere 39½ miles away. Yet, despite a seeming dullness, it has a long and interesting history, and was the first railway terminus within the City of London. Situated in the midst of the shipping quarter, and serving the docks and the estuary, it naturally acquired a maritime flavour, but nowadays this is less evident.

By the 1830s, steamer services on the Thames were well developed. The acknowledged route from London to Kent was by steamer to Gravesend, thence by road. The river was also the best way to Woolwich, to the pleasure gardens at Rosherville (near Gravesend), and to the seaside resorts of Southend and Thanet. Larger vessels worked passenger services between London and the Continental ports. Almost all these steamers called at Brunswick Wharf, Blackwall, at the entrance to the East India Dock, a long 6½ miles by river from London Bridge round the pendulous Isle of Dogs.

In 1836, a 3½-mile railway was sanctioned between the Minories in the City of London and Blackwall, with the dual object of providing a short cut to river passengers and connecting the principal London docks (the East and West India) with the City. Dissatisfied with a terminus on the extreme eastern edge of the City, the railway's promoters tried in the following year to obtain powers for an extension to Lime Street, but their bill was thrown out on the opposition of the City Corporation, which feared street congestion. However, in 1839, while the railway was being built, approval was given for a terminus at Fenchurch Street, on a ¼-mile extension which was to cost £250,000.

The London & Blackwall Railway was one of the first to be constructed through a built-up area. To minimise demolitions and eliminate the necessity for a large number of level crossings, it was decided to place most of it on a brick viaduct. No fewer than six intermediate stations were to be opened over the $3\frac{1}{2}$ miles completed in 1841, and as it was thought that steam locomotives would be unsuitable for working such closely-spaced stops and might in any case present a fire hazard to the many small houses nestling against the viaduct and the sailing ships in the Limehouse Basin, alternatives were considered. At this time, the only practical ones were horse and cable traction, and the latter was chosen. The gauge of the line was 5 ft or thereabouts, approximately that of the nearby Eastern Counties Railway, to which there was as yet no connection.

When the line first opened on 6 July 1840 it was single track, the second track being added on 3 August. The temporary terminus at the Minories was a simple two-road shed, with an all-over roof. Construction of the extension to Fenchurch Street was completed in the following year, and the terminus came into use on 2 August 1841. It was sited just to the south of its namesake, a little to the east of Mark Lane, and a new street called Railway Place was cut to give access to it. As it was so close to the terminus, Minories quickly lost importance, and after a temporary closure, it was finally shut in October 1853.

Fenchurch Street resembled Minories, with its two platforms and overall wooden roof, but although a little larger, lacked any architectural pretensions. Perhaps its one claim to fame was that it sheltered the first railway bookstall, operated by William Marshall, the founder of Marshall & Son, a firm of newspaper distributors who became close rivals to the famous W. H. Smith & Son.

The stationary engines which moved the continuous cables were at Minories and Blackwall and the extension had no cable. Incoming coaches, released from the rope at Minories, moved forward to the terminus under their momentum, the 1 in 150 upward slope tending to slow them down as they approached the platform, which was convenient. Departing coaches needed only a slight push from the platform staff.

A provision in the 1839 Act excluded trains from Fenchurch Street on Sundays, Christmas Day and Good Friday. Sunday trains left from Minories until this was repealed in 1842. The new Act explained the reason for the relaxation:

  . . . whereas the Company in the construction of the Extension

have caused the same to be completely enclosed so as to prevent
annoyance to the neighbourhood by the noise arising from the
working of the said Railway, which was apprehended at the time
of the passing of the said Act . . .

It seems that as long as the trains could not be seen or heard, their
working on the Sabbath, even if sinful, was permissible—an interesting illustration of Victorian moral attitudes. For the whole distance between the Minories and Fenchurch Street the line was
enclosed by fenestrated walls and roofed with slate (iron on the
Minories bridge).

Although traffic increased by 50 per cent after the opening of
Fenchurch Street, the London & Blackwall was only a moderate
success. Through bookings were offered to the Woolwich and
Gravesend steamers, but whilst some were attracted by the 45-
minute saving in journey time, many remained faithful to the
water. In an attempt to obtain the traffic, the railway purchased
three boats, working an hourly service to Gravesend in competition with the seventeen or so vessels operated by the five river
companies.

On the railway, a 15-minute service was provided all day, each
line being used alternately for up and down trains. Various
patterns of operation were employed, but apart from Stepney, the
intermediate stations were always served by a form of slip working
and travel between any two of them was impossible without going on to the terminus and moving back. Separate coaches were
worked between Blackwall and Stepney in both directions. The
movement of the ropes was controlled by messages passed
through Cook and Wheatstone single needle telegraph apparatus.

### LINKED TO THE OUTSIDE WORLD

As may be imagined, there were many mishaps and muddles,
and with two guard-brakemen on each coach, the system of working was to say the least somewhat staff-expensive. Plans were soon
made to connect the line to the ordinary railway system, with
operation by conventional means.

A turning point in the history of Fenchurch Street came on
2 April 1849 when a 1¾-mile branch was opened from Stepney to
a station alongside the Eastern Counties Railway. At first there
was no junction with the larger company, and the Blackwall was
obliged to operate a shuttle service between Bow and Fenchurch
Street. As the ECR had converted to standard gauge in 1844, the
L & B branch had been built to that gauge and the rest of the

Blackwall Railway was converted to it. From 15 February 1849 cable traction had been discarded and a small stud of 2-2-2 well tanks with 5 ft 6 in driving wheels acquired to take its place.

A physical link with the outside world was finally established on 26 September 1850 when the East & West India Docks and Birmingham Junction Railway opened. This line (North London Railway from 1853) formed a junction with the Blackwall at Bow and ran north and west to Islington. From its opening, a 15-minute service was worked between Fenchurch Street and Islington and the L & BR shuttle to Bow, Eastern Counties, was taken off. The newcomer's trains were extended from Islington to Camden Town (now Camden Road) on 7 December 1850 and to Hampstead Road (near Primrose Hill) on 9 June 1851.

The additional traffic brought by the new service, with the prospect of further business from a proposed London Tilbury & Southend Railway, led the Blackwall Railway to enlarge and re-build Fenchurch Street. This work was undertaken to the designs of the engineer, George Berkeley, and was completed in February 1854.

The new station had a single arch all-over roof with a closed end, a design common enough in America, but virtually unknown in Europe at this date. In the street frontage there were eleven bays of white brick, each with a tall arched window. Above was a pediment, its top revealing the curve of the roof. At street level were five small double doorways, protected by a flat canopy extending the full width of the station and covering the pavement. When this canopy eventually collapsed, it was replaced by a tooth-edged see-saw wooden awning of the pattern used over many GER station platforms. Adjoining the main front, to the north, was a small office building with three floors, coming up to the lower edge of the pediment.

Beyond the street doors were two gloomy booking halls, one allocated to the proposed London Tilbury & Southend Railway. From these halls, passengers ascended stairs at the north and south ends of the building to reach the concourse, which was at the level of the viaduct. A third stairway at the north end provided direct access from street to concourse.

As later at Broad Street and St Paul's, there was no platform access for vehicles; hydraulic lifts were installed to carry parcels and luggage to rail level. The small concourse extended the full width of the station, and was partly over the booking halls. From its north east corner, a passage into the office block led to the L & BR board room, which had a high ornamented ceiling, and was later converted into a waiting room for first class ladies. There were four short platforms under the 300 ft long, 101 ft span of the crescent truss roof. Along the south wall, at platform level, were small rooms for staff use.

All this, together with a third approach track (for up services, completed in 1856) was very largely for the benefit of the London

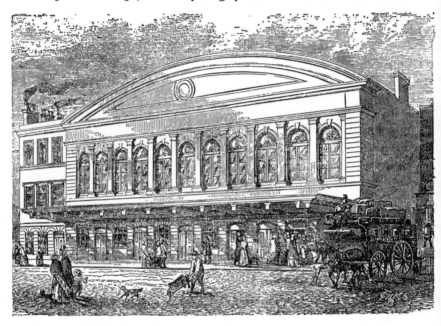

*Fenchurch Street as rebuilt, 1853, to the design of George Berkeley. From a drawing by T. Gilks for the* Illustrated London News, *10 December, 1853*

Tilbury & Southend Railway, a scheme sponsored by the Blackwall and the ECR in an attempt to obtain some of the heavy river traffic between London, Gravesend and Southend. The first section of the LTSR, from Forest Gate to Tilbury (for Gravesend) was opened on 13 April 1854, and on the same day, a connection was at last made between the ECR and the Blackwall Railway at Bow. Eleven LTSR trains each way then worked between Fenchurch Street and Tilbury via Barking, a Bishopsgate portion being attached or detached at Stratford. (The LTSR was leased to the contractors, Peto, Brassey & Betts for 21 years from 3 July 1854, but its train services were operated by the ECR, who provided both engines and stock.) To relieve congestion at Stratford, a more direct line was constructed

for the LTSR between Bow and Barking, and put into use on
31 March 1858. LTSR trains now entered Blackwall territory at
Gas Factory junction, Bow, just north of the junction with the
North London Railway, and the Tilbury company was given per-
petual running powers over the 2¼ miles into Fenchurch Street.

At the beginning of 1866, the Great Eastern Railway, which had
succeeded the ECR in 1862, took over the working of the London
& Blackwall on a 999 year lease, with a rent equivalent to 4½ per
cent on the Blackwall's ordinary capital. It was shortly after this
that the sinecurist Blackwall directors felt able to give up their
board room to the first class ladies. They did however continue to
meet elsewhere twice a year until the 1923 grouping, to receive
their guaranteed rent and declare a dividend, and then, weakened
by these exertions, to dine and wine together.

When Broad Street opened in 1865, the North London Railway
started an almost circular 15-minute service between its old and
new termini via Bow and Hackney, but this did not last for long,
and on 1 August 1866 was altered to run Broad Street—Poplar,
with a 15-minute connecting shuttle service between Bow (NLR)
and Fenchurch Street. This shuttle was taken over by the GER on
1 January 1869 until its termination in 1892, and NLR passenger
trains were seen no more at Fenchurch Street. The terminus was
now virtually owned by the GER, with the LTSR very much the
tolerated lodger.

Until the opening of Liverpool Street in 1874, Fenchurch Street
was the GER suburban line terminus, and apart from the Bow
shuttle already mentioned, that company ran trains to North
Woolwich (from 1 June 1854), and to the Loughton branch
(opened in 1856 and extended to Ongar in 1865). By the late 1860s,
city merchants were moving into sumptuous new villas along the
Loughton line and Fenchurch Street was handling a preliminary
trickle of first class season ticket holders. In the 1900s, the Loughton line trains had a good proportion of first class coaches, altogether a different type of traffic from that handled on the West
Side of Liverpool Street.

In 1872 there were eighteen trains daily to the Loughton branch,
twenty-six to North Woolwich, eighteen to the LTSR (only six to
Southend), as well as the 15-minute services all day to Blackwall
and Bow (NLR).

The LTSR, which had reached Southend via Tilbury on 1 March
1856, became an independent company by an Act of 1862 and
independence was completed by an Act of 1882 which rescinded
the GER and Blackwall powers to appoint directors. It acquired its

own coaches in 1876-7, and locomotives three years later. As early as 1881 a fast business train was started between Fenchurch Street and Southend, taking one hour for the 42 miles via Tilbury. A direct line from Barking to Southend was completed on 1 June 1888, and a suburban business was gradually built up, encouraged by the offer of cheap season tickets. By the end of the century, Fenchurch Street was very busy indeed, but some of the pressure was taken off in 1902, when a connection was opened between the Metropolitan District Railway at Whitechapel and the LTSR at Bow. Traffic from the inner suburban stations of the LTSR was then mopped up by District trains working as far out as East Ham and, after quadrupling, by District electric trains to East Ham (20 August 1905) and Barking (1 April 1908). The Tilbury company contributed electric stock to these trains.

In addition to the growing traffic of the LTSR, the Fenchurch Street approach tracks had to carry an increasing number of freight trains, serving the six goods depots and branches which had been opened within half a mile of the terminus. These were on the north side: *Goodman's Yard* (GER), *Haydon Square* (LNWR), and *Commercial Road* (LTSR); on the south: *Royal Mint Street* (GNR), *Royal Mint Street* (Midland) and the GER London Docks spur. A fourth approach track became a necessity, and this was completed in March 1896.

At the turn of the century, Fenchurch Street had five platforms, of varying lengths. Against the south wall was the 380 ft No 1, the home of the Blackwall trains, still leaving every 15 minutes throughout the day. Patronage was falling off; the first depletion had come with the decline of the steamer traffic (ironically a consequence of the opening of the Thames-side railways); then, after the adoption of the telephone in City offices, the messengers passing between the City and the docks had disappeared (and the ships themselves, now larger, moved to new docks further down the river); and finally, electric trams and motor buses had taken most of what was left. Sunday trains to Blackwall ceased from 1 October 1908 and the weekday service was reduced to three an hour about the same time. In the first world war, a 30-minute service was sufficient, but afterwards the 15-minute frequency was recklessly restored. By then, the trains were running almost empty, and in 1926 the decision was taken to abandon the service. It ceased on 3 May as a result of the General Strike, never to be resumed. Platform 1 was also used by the NLR trains when these were operating to Fenchurch Street, but as mentioned, this had ceased long before, in 1869.

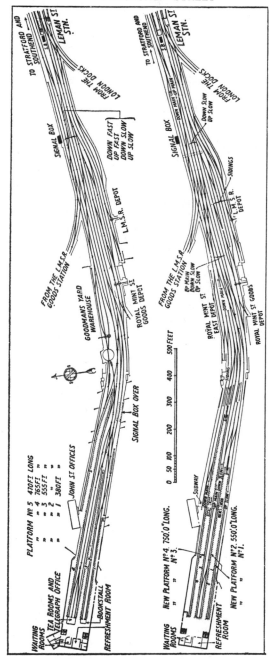

(upper plan) *Old layout at Fenchurch Street before remodelling;* (lower plan) *new layout and station as reconstructed 1935. From the Railway Magazine, July 1935*

Platforms 2 and 3 were on a 555 ft island, protected beyond the overall roof by umbrella awnings. GER trains on the Ilford line used 2, and those to Loughton and Ongar were seen at 3. On Sundays, North Woolwich trains also used 3, and LTSR trains were occasionally seen there. Next came an engine road, with a crossover at the buffer stop end, and then, the pride of Fenchurch Street, the 765 ft platform 4, the only one which could accommodate the bogie stock trains of the LTSR, and exclusively used by that company. This face, which could take 13 coaches and the inevitable Tilbury 4–4–2T, was the busiest in the station. At its far end, on the north side, and entirely beyond the overall roof, was No 5, a 470 ft bay. Here were found the North Woolwich and Gallions trains. (Trains ran from Fenchurch Street to Gallions over the Royal Albert Docks Railway from July 1881 onwards.) A footbridge from the outer end led to the signal cabin on the south side of the station. Stairs from platforms 4 and 5 linked them with a separate entrance and booking hall in John Street (now Crosswall). This was in a five-storey building erected in 1881 to house the offices of the L & BR and the LTSR.

Conditions on platform 4 during the evening peak hour were described by W. Ivey, chairman of the West Ham Tramways and Electric Lighting Committee, in evidence to the Royal Commission on London Traffic in 1904. Ivey thought the most popular train was the 5.58 pm:

> That is a very long train . . . when it draws in there is a great rush of people before it stops, to get seats in the carriages, and I have seen people knocked over; and it is not altogether decent, in fact, to see sixteen or seventeen people inside one compartment . . .

He went on to describe how a fellow councillor had

> counted in a first class carriage as many as twenty-six passengers, among whom were two females (shame).

He added that passengers for the GER trains in the bay were occasionally unable to reach them, owing to the crowded state of platform 4.

Between 1902 and 1909, the LTSR season ticket traffic almost doubled. Fast trains and the exceptionally generous rates—an average of six miles for one penny—encouraged London office workers to live at Westcliff and Southend in increasing numbers. By 1909,

(above) *London Bridge* LBSCR *and forecourt about 1905, the* LBSCR *offices, formerly the Terminus Hotel, are seen at the right;* (below) *Interior, London Bridge (ex* LBSCR*), 4 April 1959, Fairburn 2-6-4T 42103 on 13.27 for Tunbridge Wells*

(above) *Cannon Street at night, an 1891 painting by W. Tuker Jr.;* (below) *London Bridge* SER *approaches c 1864. The 'AB' signal cabin is seen in the foreground. 'CD' cabin is in the background right. An engraving for* The Illustrated London News

seven full train loads were being brought into London from Southend in two hours each morning with an average running time of
59 minutes.

Some hope of relief came in 1912 when the Midland, needing
better access to the docks, succeeded in pulling off a diplomatic
coup, acquiring the LTSR under the very nose of the GER. The new
owners undertook to electrify the Southend line and to apply for
powers to do so by 1914. For their part, the GER agreed to enlarge Fenchurch Street and to electrify the approach tracks to receive the LTSR trains. It did not prove possible to make a start on
these works before the outbreak of the first world war, which
caused a further postponement. After 1918, the financial difficulties of the private railway companies ruled out capital expenditure of the order required on a scheme likely to provide such a
small return, and electrification of the LTSR had to await nationalisation. However, long before that, as we shall see, the other
promise was kept.

## LNER OVERSHADOWED BY LMSR

At the 1923 grouping, the LNER inherited Fenchurch Street, and
the LMSR took over the LTSR services. By the late 1920s when there
were some 50,000 passengers on the 300 trains handled daily, the
LMSR presence was overshadowing that of the rightful owners,
whose Ilford, Ongar and North Woolwich services were but poor
things beside the still burgeoning traffic of the Southend line. Such
was the growth of the latter, and so inconvenient the layout of
Fenchurch Street, that something just had to be done, and a
£250,000 scheme to increase the capacity of the terminus was
started in 1932.

It would have been impossibly expensive to add to the number
of platforms by widening the station site, owing to the high value
of the surrounding property, so the scheme merely tried to make
the best use of the existing area. By far the greatest defect of the
layout was that there was only one platform long enough to take
the Southend trains, and that to reach or leave this and the adjacent
No 5 bay, all trains using the fast road had to share a short stretch
of single track in the immediate approach. It was therefore decided to provide an island platform of suitable length for the
Southend trains, with an independent approach road to each face.
For the LNER, there was another island platform, slightly shorter,
placed between the up and down slow lines. The reconstructed
station thus had two platforms of 750 ft (3 and 4) and two of

I

550 ft (1 and 2), instead of five of assorted lengths, all but one of which had been too short for modern requirements.

To relieve pressure on the main entrance and exit, each island platform was given two sets of stairs to a new subway through the viaduct, linking them with a new Crosswall entrance. Beyond the main roof, both islands were protected for their whole length by umbrella awnings.

In the approaches, the tracks required a considerable amount of rearrangement, and this involved reconstruction and strengthening of the bridges over Minories, Vine Street, Cooper's Row and Crutched Friars. At the far end of the station, the old telegraph office and tea room, backing on to 3 and 4, and the bookstall, backing on to 1 and 2, were demolished to increase the circulating area at the head of the platforms. A combined cafeteria, buffet and waiting room was erected at the back of the concourse. The platform ends were given an elegant wrought-iron barrier, arranged to give alternative exits from all platforms on the plan adopted at Liverpool Street West Side some years before. New indicators, with departure time clocks and station name displays on the Liverpool Street pattern were installed at the barriers. At ground level, the LTSR and GER booking offices were combined in 1932, when the concourse parcels office was moved there.

When the reconstruction, which included signalling modernisation, was completed in April 1935, additional trains were introduced on the Southend line. New Stanier 2–6–4T arrived during the same year to operate all the Southend trains. At the evening peak, departures for the LTSR lines now left at four minute intervals, incoming train engines taking the next train out. In an effort to equalise loading, each train served a different pattern of stations in the Southend area. There were now 370 trains a day, with some 70,000 passengers, most of them on the former LTSR lines.

On the LNER side, it was a different story. For a few more years, things remained much the same, but by 1949, all the services had disappeared, leaving the former LTSR line trains in sole occupation. First to go was the North Woolwich service, which ceased during the bombing of October 1940. When tube trains reached Leytonstone on 5 May 1947 services to the Loughton lines came off, and the remaining Ilford line trains vanished when the Liverpool Street to Shenfield line was fully electrified on 7 November 1949. Platforms 1 and 2 were then taken over by trains to and from Tilbury,

A feature of the Liverpool Street—Shenfield electrification as planned by the LNER had been a shuttle service of electric trains between Fenchurch Street and a terminal bay at Stratford, affording cross-platform interchange at the latter station with down electrics from Liverpool Street and eastbound Central Line tube trains. The 1500 V dc overhead wires were duly erected for this service over all four tracks out of Fenchurch Street, where platforms 1 and 2 were wired up. The bay was built at Stratford. This done, it was decided that whilst the shuttle service would offer some convenience, it would largely duplicate existing Underground facilities, and the project was abandoned. Empty trains ran over the line regularly to keep the wires clean, as it was realised it would have strategic value in an emergency. And so it proved in February 1953, when the LTSR line was cut by floods between Benfleet and Leigh. A special service of electric trains was then worked for five days between Fenchurch Street and Shenfield in connection with steam trains thence to Southend (Victoria).

During the mid 1950s, the LTSR steam services suffered a sad decline. Locomotive breakdowns and mishaps of various kinds became everyday events. As is not unusual with London railway matters, the situation was greatly blown up in the press, especially when, after a period of severe weather in the winter of 1956-7, a Congregational minister was moved to refer to the railway service as 'an illustration of inhuman wickedness'. The difficulties arose largely from an acute shortage of experienced men, especially locomotive fitters and firemen, the consequent lack of proper maintenance playing havoc with the heavily-worked locomotives.

## UNDER THE CATENARY AT LAST

By this time, approval had been given for electrification of the line, under the British Railways modernisation plan. The engineering works associated with electrification were extensive, and another five years were to pass before all was ready for the new trains. In the meantime, by dint of strenuous efforts on the part of management and staff, there had been some improvement in the standards of steam working. At this period, Fenchurch Street was dealing with about 37,800 passengers a day, in some 175 trains.

The LTSR line electrification was carried out to the new British Railways standard of 6.25 or 25 kV 50 cycles ac. The existing 1500 V dc line into Fenchurch Street was converted at the same time as an emergency route, and to provide access to Ilford depot, though there was still no intention of running a public service to Stratford. Some electric trains began to run in steam timings in the slack hours on 6 November 1961, but all services were not worked electrically until 17 June 1962. The new timetable, which has since been modified, provided six trains an hour from Fenchurch Street in the off peak period, four of them via Upminster. Fast trains reached Southend Central in 45 minutes. There were 17 departures between 5 and 6 pm, all of 12-car trains, each offering a total of 57 first class ond 1,032 second class seats.

At Fenchurch Street, platforms 3 and 4 were wired. The track layout was simplified by removing the engine spurs and modifying complicated point formations. From 1 April 1963 Swedish Lloyd boat trains were transferred from St Pancras, as electric trains, covering the 22½-mile run to Tilbury in 30 minutes, could offer a faster run.

As is usual with electrification, traffic soon began to increase. In 1968, 30,728 passengers arrived in the morning peak hours on the October census day, compared with 18,606 in 1959, and the total number of passengers passing through the terminus daily had increased to 67,300 from 43,000 in 1959.

Apart from the introduction of electric services, BR made a number of improvements. Fluorescent lighting was installed throughout the station in 1953; on the whole it was well arranged, but it still left the booking hall rather gloomy. In 1959 new departure indicators were erected at the platform barriers, with linked displays in the two booking halls, controlled either by the train announcer or the ticket collectors. This apparatus did not have a happy life, and in 1967 was modified to work with the standard train describer system.

Fenchurch Street is one of the two London termini that lack Underground connections. The nearest station is Tower Hill (District Line), a few minutes' walk to the south. On 5 February 1967 the London Transport station was resited, providing a more convenient interchange for passengers able to use the Crosswall entrance to the terminus (open only from 6 am to 9.45 pm, Mondays to Fridays). So popular did this prove, that the Crosswall entrance had to be widened in the following year.

A plan for rebuilding Fenchurch Street incorporating an office block above the platforms was put forward by private developers in 1959, but was refused by the City Corporation on the grounds that offices should be restricted to sites already zoned for them. Berkeley's stern frontage therefore still remains, increasingly out of place amidst a forest of modern office blocks and towers.

Further redevelopment schemes came forward in the 1970s and as related in chapter 16, a start was made in 1984. Whilst the rush hour traffic remains at its present level, closure is not likely, but in the longer term, a rebuilt Liverpool Street may be able to take this station's traffic.

## SIGNALLING

The mechanical signalling at Fenchurch Street was controlled from a cabin situated on the south side of the station over the up slow line. This was provided with lock and block instruments and 115 working levers in a Saxby & Farmer frame.

Together with eight other cabins, it was replaced on 14 April 1935 by a new 140-lever box at Fenchurch Street and modernised cabins at Stepney East and Gas Factory junction. These three boxes controlled the Siemens & General Electric Railway Signal Company's four-aspect colour lights and point motors installed in the station area and as far east as Bow Junction.

As part of the electrification scheme of the early 1960s, an SGE NX push-button panel was installed in the 1935 box to provide remote control of the junctions at Stepney East and Gas Factory. At the same time, the 1935 track circuiting was changed from 50 to $83\frac{1}{2}$ cycles/sec ac. No other alterations were made to the LMSR colour light signalling.

# CHAPTER 8

# *London Bridge*

DOYEN OF THEM ALL

Oldest of the permanent termini, London Bridge dates back to the opening of London's first passenger railway in 1836. After this came the development of an untidy sprawl of separate stations, all on arches above street level. The complex underwent two major changes in the 19th century, but after 1902 there were no major structural changes for 70 years. If allowance is made for the bomb damage of the last war, the physical appearance of most parts of the station remained in the late 1960s much as it was in the early years of the present century. It prompted no affection in the heart of the ordinary railway passenger, to whom it offered little comfort or convenience. Thanks to its hybrid origins, subsequent neglect and German bombs, it was indisputably the most hideous of all the termini. All this was to disappear, whilst trains continued to run, in a worthy rebuilding of the 1970s.

In 1831, a 3½-mile railway was proposed between Greenwich and Tooley Street, London Bridge. Some 2,000 people were moving daily over the 5½-mile road between the two places, and it was hoped to attract most of these as well as develop new traffic. The promoters adopted a scheme drawn up by Lt Col G. T. Landmann, a retired Royal Engineer, who had suggested that the line be placed on a brick viaduct of 878 arches. This scheme not only solved the problem of the many roads and lanes intersecting the route in Bermondsey, but also offered the possibility of additional revenue from the letting of the arches as warehouses, stables, or even dwellings.

The first section of this London & Greenwich Railway, the first passenger railway and the first steam railway in London, was opened on 8 February 1836 from Spa Road, Bermondsey, to Deptford. If one really wishes to be pedantic, Spa Road was therefore the first railway terminus in London, but it was a very temporary affair. From 10 October 1836, passengers used London Bridge Station, walking some 300 yards to join trains at Bermondsey Street. On 14 December 1836, the Lord Mayor of London, attended by the sheriffs, the Common Council and some 2,000 other guests, arrived for the formal opening of the London & Greenwich Railway. Trains began to run at midday, and with a band of musicians dressed as Beefeaters riding on the roof of one of the carriages to provide a suitable accompaniment, the Lord Mayor travelled to Deptford and inspected the installations. Two years later, the railway finally reached Greenwich.

Approximately in the space between the present platforms 6 & 7, the station was a very spartan affair with three tracks and two platforms, reached by an incline and steps from the street below. In short, it was the stub end of the long viaduct, entirely unprotected from the weather (tarred canvas was erected in 1840 to give some shelter). The ticket office and the company's offices were in a very plain three-storey block on the south side of the viaduct. A design was prepared for a triumphal arch to stand across the entrance, but this was never erected, no doubt through lack of funds.

It seems that the low platforms caused lady passengers some distress, because the conductors were rather lax in letting down the carriage steps to the fullest extent, thus exacting a display 'of the beauty of their legs and ankles'. It is just possible that this neglect of duty was deliberate, as the same account (in the *Kentish Mercury* for 31 March 1838) relates that when helping the weaker sex into the carriages, these officials were apt to press the ladies' fingers and stare them 'full in the face'.

From the start, the Greenwich Company had dreamed of greater things, aware for some time that other more important railways had their eyes on London Bridge as a terminus. In preparation, they had wisely acquired more land than they needed for immediate requirements, and had spread out the viaduct at the London end to take eight tracks. In 1835 a London & Croydon Railway had been authorised, and this was to enter London over the Greenwich tracks, which it would join at Corbett's Lane, Bermondsey, a privilege which was to cost it 3d for every passenger carried. A year later, the South Eastern Railway obtained its Act. This was to form an extension of the London & Croydon Railway through Coulsdon and Redhill to Tonbridge and Dover, and would also use the Greenwich line on payment of a toll.

When the L & CR opened on 5 June 1839 it ran twelve trains each way daily, using a separate three-track terminus at London

Bridge immediately north of the Greenwich company's premises. All Croydon trains therefore had to cross the Greenwich line on the level, and when questioned about this by a Parliamentary committee, the Greenwich representative confessed that it suited them, as it gave them a hold over the London & Croydon. The Croydon's station was about 300 ft long and 100 ft wide with a train shed 170 ft long by 48 ft wide, supported on one side by fourteen cast-iron columns and on the other by a brick wall with piers and arches. The booking office was in Joiner Street below, and separate stairs were provided for first. and second class passengers. The remaining space on the viaduct was occupied by a small goods station between the train shed and Tooley Street.*

It was first intended that the Croydon's station should accommodate not only the trains of that company and those of the SER, but also give shelter to a third user of the Greenwich Railway, the London & Brighton Railway, incorporated in 1837. Parliament now required extra tracks to be provided into London Bridge, preferring a widening of the existing viaduct to the construction of separate lines, which would have been more destructive of property. The Greenwich accordingly obtained powers to build a second pair of tracks on the south side of the viaduct, and agreed with the Croydon company that it would exchange stations at London Bridge to avoid crossing over by the trains of the user companies. In 1840 the four companies were authorised to make agreements for the apportionment and management of the London Bridge terminal area and to construct new works, while the Greenwich was given powers to build a new station for the three user companies.

### THE JOINT STATION

The first section of the London & Brighton Railway opened on 12 July 1841, and the additional tracks into London Bridge were ready on 10 May 1842. Sixteen days later, the SER trains began to run between London Bridge and Tonbridge (Dover was reached on 7 February 1844). Building of the Joint Station was pressed ahead, and it was possible to open it in February 1844. The Croydon then moved in, and the Greenwich company's own trains began to use the Croydon train shed on the north side of the viaduct.

This new Joint Station, designed by Henry Roberts[1] had a very pleasant two-storey frontage building in the 'Italian palazzo style', with a pretty campanile at the southern end, carrying clock and weather vane. An 80 ft wide approach road came up from Borough High Street, skirting the northern boundary of the St

---

* The lower part of the L & C station still survives beneath the viaduct in Joiner Street.

Thomas's Hospital grounds. In the ground floor of the 250 ft block were booking hall, parcels offices and waiting rooms. To the south, facing Joiner Street, was a smaller, triangular block for the offices of the Brighton, Croydon & Dover Joint Station Committee which had been formed to manage the new terminus, and functioned only in 1844-5. Behind these buildings, the engineer William Cubitt provided three tracks in a new train shed on the site of the old Greenwich station, and departure and arrival sheds, each with a main and subsidiary platform and three tracks. The platform on the south side of the northernmost shed (intended for the North Kent Railway) was 240 ft long, whilst the main departure platform was 338 ft and the main arrival stage 531 ft. At the rear of the triangular office blocks was a four-road carriage shed, connected to the Joint Station by traversers.

This was spendid, but never finished, and very soon to be proved far too small for the rapidly increasing traffic. And there was another cloud on the horizon, for all was not well between the Greenwich and its customers. Ever alert for the quick penny, the Greenwich had raised the toll as soon as the second pair of tracks was ready, obliging the three companies to pay 4½d a passenger, irrespective of class. This was particularly painful for the Croydon, on which journeys were much shorter than those of the Brighton and the SER, and where relatively smaller fares were quite disproportionately inflated by the new toll.

Attempts were made to force the hand of the Greenwich company by starting a bus service between the Croydon's station at New Cross and the West End, with fares cheaper than those to London Bridge. The Croydon also refused to carry third class passengers between New Cross and London Bridge. These measures failed to move the Greenwich.

### BRICKLAYERS ARMS, OR THE WEST END IN BERMONDSEY

As a more dramatic ploy, the Croydon and South Eastern companies conspired to erect their own terminus on the east side of the Old Kent Road, just south of its junction with what is now Tower Bridge Road. This station, laughably referred to as a 'West End terminus' was known as Bricklayers Arms, after a nearby coaching inn, and was opened on 1 May 1844. In just one sense was the wild claim to serve the West End within sight of the truth: the direct roads to the river bridges at Waterloo and Westminster gave a shorter journey time than that from London Bridge.

Although partly fashioned as a rod to beat the Greenwich company, Bricklayers Arms had other uses. It was to provide accommodation for the traffic in sheep, cattle and goods which could not be conveniently handled in the cramped conditions at London Bridge; it offered room for a locomotive yard; and, finally, it projected the South Eastern part of the way towards a *real* West End terminus. Some 26 acres were available for cattle and goods traffic, and the Croydon and South Eastern companies at once deserted the goods facilities on the north side of London Bridge. J. P. Fearon told the Royal Commission on Metropolitan Termini in 1846, 'It is no doubt too far from town for a West End terminus, but it is most efficient and most complete for a goods station'. The approach was made by a 1¾-mile branch from the Croydon's line just before it met the Greenwich viaduct. A third of the cost was contributed by the Croydon, the SER finding the rest, but in 1849, the latter used power given in the authorising Act to purchase the Croydon's share. Thereafter, the Croydon had to pay a toll of 1¼d a passenger over the branch.

Bricklayers Arms was a neat and compact little terminus with a layout and arrangement similar to that of the original Euston. Architectural gloss, in the fashionable Italian villa style, with some Baroque details, was provided by Lewis Cubitt (see Chapter 4, note 1, p 356). His main contribution was a screen across the end, penetrated by 22 ft archways with exaggerated keystones and by doorways protected by pantiled hoods on heavy stone brackets. Above the central arch was a clock, and above that, a little arcaded campanile topped by a weathervane. Contemporary drawings exaggerate the height and dignity of this screen and do not accurately portray the arrangement of the openings.[2] It was a poor thing in comparison with the front of Kings Cross.

Along one side of the station was a tiled colonnade where passengers alighted from their vehicles, passing through to the first and second class booking offices and waiting rooms alongside the departure platform. At the other side of the train shed was an arrival platform and carriage way, and at the outer end, a two-track loading dock for private carriages, with its own waiting room. Between the departure and arrival tracks were two empty carriage lines. Across the end, a narrow platform connected the departure and arrival sides behind the screen. Beyond the offices on the departure side, at the outer end, was a four-track carriage shed. At inner and outer ends of the station tracks were sets of turnplates for moving carriages and vans, the set at the outer end also providing access to the carriage shed and private carriage loading dock. Three parallel iron roofs sheltered the platforms and tracks, but they suffered some basic defect in design, as they collapsed soon after opening, and again in 1850, when a train collided with a supporting pillar.

An hourly service was at once started to and from the Croydon line; this was not only more frequent, but cheaper than the London Bridge—Croydon trains. At last moved from its inflexible attitude, the Greenwich agreed in July 1844 to charge the Croydon varying tolls, based on the same proportion of the overall fare as the length of its viaduct bore to the overall journey mileage. For its part, the Croydon agreed to equalise the fares and train service as between London Bridge and Bricklayers Arms, and at once did so. It was quickly realised that there was little point in terminating half the Croydon trains at the remote Bricklayers Arms station, and the Croydon company gave up serving it in March 1845.

The South Eastern ran about half its main-line trains to Folkestone and Dover from Bricklayers Arms, and from 1845 also ran some excursion trains. Some confusion occurred at first.

> . . . the Dover Railway Company, finding the inconvenience of two stations (namely, the *Bricklayers Arms* and the *London Bridge*), ceased to split the trains at Deptford, and now run alternately, for this very reason, that a man never knew which station he was going to in London; and therefore if he said to his servant, 'You will meet me at the Dover Railway on Friday', he said, 'Which station am I to go to, the Bricklayers Arms or the London Bridge?' . . . the present Dover Company run one train to the Bricklayers Arms and one other to London Bridge on purpose to obviate this difficulty . . . (*B. W. Horne, evidence to the Royal Commission on London Termini, 1846*.)

Despite the omnibuses, arranged to meet all trains and carry passengers to the City for 3d and to the West End for 6d, Bricklayers Arms was a complete failure as a passenger terminus. By May 1846 the SER trains had been reduced to a couple up and down daily, and in October even these disappeared. All that remained was the curious practice of attaching a first class coach to the 11 pm down goods 'at the special request of travellers desirous to reach Folkestone or Dover in time for the morning steamer' as *Bradshaw* stated in January 1846. Who were these 'travellers'? Probably diplomatic couriers and the occasional newspaperman, but what a convenient and inconspicuous means this must have offered of leaving the country in those days of no passports. One likes to imagine that the facility was sometimes used by young bloods escaping from gaming debts or respectable merchants decamping with trembling mistresses.

A brief new life of passenger activity came to Bricklayers Arms in 1849 after a connection had been made between the branch and the new North Kent line of the SER. From 1 September, a 15-minute shuttle service was operated between the terminus and exchange platforms built at this junction, the SER claiming that this provided '. . . a West-end terminus for every train to the North Kent and Greenwich traffic' (report read at the meeting of the SER, 20 September 1849). But once again, the 'West End terminus' was spurned by an ungrateful public, and the service, reduced in March 1850, was withdrawn altogether early in 1852. No more regular passenger trains were seen at Bricklayers Arms, and the train shed was handed over to the goods department. Shortly after the opening of Bricklayers Arms, the Croydon company had to return to the goods station at London Bridge because the SER wanted its site for a locomotive yard, but following an agreement between the two companies in 1847-8, the SER constructed a new five acre goods depot for the LBSCR (the Croydon's successor) at Willow Walk, on the north side of the Bricklayers Arms branch. This was opened in July 1849. The sheds at Bricklayers Arms itself were exclusively used by the SER.

With its direct road access to the West End, Bricklayers Arms was convenient for royal traffic and continued in use for this purpose, suitably cleaned up and decorated, until the even more accessible Charing Cross was opened. One of its last royal patrons was Princess Alexandra of Denmark, who arrived in March 1863 to marry Edward (later Edward VII). In 1913 the royal and first class waiting rooms were converted to offices for the goods invoice clerks and cashiers. A brief revival of passenger activity came between 1932 and 1939, in which years the Southern Railway ran a few summer excursions from the old terminus. Cubitt's frontage was severely damaged in a fire during 1936, and was afterwards demolished.

### PARTITION AT LONDON BRIDGE

We must now return to London Bridge, and the affairs of the little Greenwich company. Like the similar Blackwall line across the river, the Greenwich had much to offer the larger companies, and it was only a matter of time before it fell into more powerful hands. Under the shadow thrown over its business by the construction of goods and passenger facilities at Bricklayers Arms, the London & Greenwich entered into negotiations with a confident SER, and it was soon agreed that the main-line company should take it over on lease from 1 January 1845. It remained a separate undertaking until 1923, when it was absorbed into the Southern Railway.

With Big Brother now that much more firmly established at London Bridge and the new Joint Station already proving too small, squabbles quickly developed between the users, and it was finally decided to divide up the site. So it was that the pretty Joint Station was demolished after a mere five years' use.

*London Bridge, road approach to* SER *station 1851. From the* Illustrated London News, *15 February 1851*

In 1850 the SER erected a boundary wall down the centre of the London Bridge terminal site and set about building its own terminus on the north side. A three-storey frontage was designed by the SER architect, Samuel Beazley.[3] This building had a flat roof and curved inwards to the station at the south end, the last short section being set back a little from the rest. A flat canopy, supported by iron pillars ran along the entire length, curving gracefully at the southern corners. The *Illustrated London News* of 15 February 1851 did not think much of the new block, observing that it was 'of less merit than its predecessor'. Almost the only feature of note was the chiming clock which projected above the cornice, decorated birthday cake fashion with cement 'in a manner by no means advantageous to Mr Beazley'. Sadly mauled by German bombs of world war II, and the necessary demolitions for the Charing Cross extension, a very small part of this building survived until 1970.

Supplementing the frontal block was a 150 ft long three-storey building flanking the Tooley Street side of the inclined approach road. This had a ground floor of shops in Tooley Street, and an arcade of shops and a refreshment room on the incline side. There were offices on the top floor, under a flat roof. Completed in August 1851, the shops in 'London Bridge Arcade' remained empty for some time as the rents were thought too high.

Inside the main block were separate booking offices for the Greenwich, North Kent and Dover lines. Behind, in a narrow shed of their own (the old Croydon terminus) were the three Greenwich lines. Immediately south of these were the North Kent lines, an arrival and departure road, with an empty carriage track between. The southern part of the premises, known as the 'Dover Station' was adjacent, an arrival and a departure track, with empty carriage road between, under a single span roof on the site of the 1836 station. In 1853, two years after the completion of this SER station, there were thirty departures daily on the Greenwich line, and about fifty on the various SER lines (North Kent to Gravesend and Chatham via Woolwich, and to Margate, Ramsgate, Dover, Folkestone and Hastings).

The Croydon and Brighton companies had combined in 1846 to form the London Brighton & South Coast Railway, and in the following year, there had been an important agreement between the LBSCR and the SER. With certain exceptions, the LBSCR was to cease paying tolls over the Greenwich viaduct and Bricklayers Arms lines, and the SER was enabled in return to run free, also with exceptions, over the LBSCR between Corbett's Lane and Croydon. The exceptions related mainly to future lines and effectively marked out the 'legitimate territory' of each company.

Although the SER was prepared to offer its neighbour accommodation, this would obviously have been inadequate, and the new company decided to build its own terminus on the southern side of the wall. In 1850 things were still in a state of flux, but a booking office had been erected, with a temporary screen on each side, that on the left of the gateway to the SER station's carriage road, that on the right forming the entrance to the arrival side carriage road of the new Brighton station. A three-storey 'Italian style' frontage block was erected in 1853-4. This had a flat roof like its neighbour, and was decorated with stone dressings and rusticated pilasters and quoins. A narrow, flat canopy, supported by iron wall brackets, ran along the front over the footway and entrances (after about thirty years this was replaced by a much larger affair which covered part of the cab yard). Behind, the departure and arrival platforms were covered by a 700 ft long train shed of about 100 ft span, glazed with rough plate glass.

The half-finished station had to cope with the heavy traffic arising from the Great Exhibition of 1851, an event not without significance for the LBSCR. Sir Joseph Paxton's remarkable glass exhibition building was purchased in the following year by a company closely associated with the LBSCR and moved from Hyde Park to the 300-acre Penge Park, which had been sold without pain by Leo Schuster, an LBSCR director. A railway station on a new branch was opened for passenger traffic on 10 June 1854, the same day that Queen Victoria opened the re-erected building, now known as the Crystal Palace. Two short platforms were added at London Bridge about the same time to handle local trains, including those serving Crystal Palace. As had been hoped, the Palace proved a useful source of additional traffic for the LBSCR, so much so that the company's stock of locomotives and carriages was often taxed to the limit to meet the demands of the public. On one day in 1859, 112,000 were conveyed up to the Palace, some 70,000 of them from London Bridge. Normal LBSCR service in 1858 at London Bridge comprised fourteen trains daily each way on the main line, and forty-eight on the local routes to Croydon, Crystal Palace and Epsom.

A third pair of approach tracks was added to the Greenwich viaduct to carry the additional traffic created by the opening of the North Kent line in 1849. These were situated on the north side and came into use on 24 February 1850. Another track was built at the same time beyond Corbett's Lane Junction to the point where the North Kent diverged (just south of the Surrey Canal). To avoid crossing the down line on the level at North Kent East Junction, the self-contained Greenwich line was then changed over to right hand running, the six tracks on the viaduct being worked as follows:

    Greenwich up
    North Kent and Greenwich down
    North Kent and Dover up
    SER and LBSCR down
    SER and LBSCR up
    Croydon up local[4]

Three more tracks were provided on the south side of the viaduct for the opening of the South London Line from London Bridge to East Brixton on 13 August 1866. These became:

down South London
up South London
up South London,

and were worked and owned by the LBSCR, whose trains could now for the first time enter London Bridge under the control of the company's own signalmen.

In connection with the opening of the South London line, the LBSCR side of London Bridge was enlarged. A new train shed was

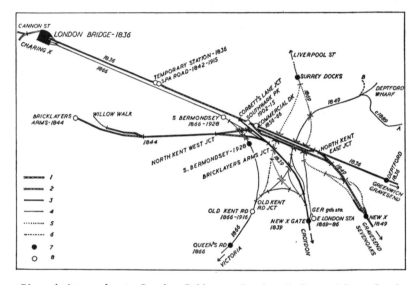

*Plan of Approaches to London Bridge. 1, London & Greenwich. 2, South Eastern. 3, London & Croydon. 4, London Brighton & South Coast. 5, East London. 6, East London (abandoned). 7, Passenger Stations. 8, Docks. The date of the line from Deptford Wharf to the Foreign Cattle Market should be 1899. (Map by H. P. White)*

erected, and a group of additional platforms (latterly 19 to 22) provided on the south side, making a total of nine.

A hotel was built on the Brighton side of the station by private enterprise in 1861. It was placed as near as possible to the station, at its south west corner, against the viaduct, fronting St Thomas and Joiner Streets, with its second floor at platform level. Designed by Henry Currey,[5] the architect and surveyor to St Thomas's Hospital, the Terminus Hotel had about 150 public rooms in seven storeys. It never proved very popular and was purchased in 1893

(above) *The* LCDR *south bank Blackfriars station and river bridge in 1864, an engraving for* The Illustrated London News; *(below) Cannon Street station and approaches, 12 July 1955, before the demolition of the bomb-damaged roof*

(above) *Ludgate Hill*, LCDR *in 1865. A train is seen on the viaduct to the City Widened Lines at the extreme left. An engraving for* The Illustrated London News; *(below)* *Ludgate Hill* LCDR *c 1898.* LCDR *0-4-4T 216 is entering with an Up Local train*

by the LBSCR, which converted it to general offices. After suffering grievous bomb damage, it was demolished in 1941.

## PRESSURE TO GO WEST

Around the middle of the nineteenth century, strong pressures were developing for railway extensions further into the City and West End to accommodate the rapidly increasing passenger traffic of the southern lines. Reporting in 1855, the Commons Select Committee on Metropolitan Communications revealed that the number of people using the London Bridge stations had increased from some 5½ to over 10 millions in the five years 1850-54. Sir Joseph Paxton pointed out in evidence that it took longer to go from London Bridge station to Paddington than to travel from London Bridge to Brighton. Two years later, as the price for refusing the East Kent Railway access into London, a Commons committee extracted a promise from the SER chairman that his company would produce a scheme for a West End terminus for the lines from Kent and the Channel ports. After its secretary, Samuel Smiles, had thoroughly investigated the matter, the SER, working through a subsidiary, obtained powers in 1859 for a terminus at Charing Cross, to be reached by an extension from London Bridge.

Almost as soon as it left the north side of London Bridge, this Charing Cross extension was made to swerve south west by the presence of Southwark Cathedral across its path. In so swerving, the alignment cut across a small corner of the grounds of St Thomas's Hospital, at that time situated immediately east of London Bridge station. Although the amount of land required was a mere one-sixth of an acre, for which the railway company offered £20,000, the governors of the hospital used powers given to them in the Act authorising the extension and compelled the purchase of the whole of the hospital and grounds. For this they coolly demanded £750,000, a sum which represented 90 per cent of the Charing Cross company's capital. After arbitration, the railway paid £296,000, which went a long way towards the £500,000 cost of the new Albert Embankment hospital of 1868-71.

Before it could be converted to a through station, the north side of London Bridge required substantial alterations. The London Bridge Arcade was swept away and a railway viaduct built above. This viaduct carried the extension on to an ugly plate girder bridge over the station approach, which was followed by another similar bridge over Borough High Street. The Greenwich terminus (the original Croydon station) disappeared, and the tracks off the Green-

K

wich viaduct into London Bridge on this side were lifted at 1 in 103 into a high level through station with five platforms (two down and three up). These platforms, alongside and above Tooley Street, came into use with the extension on 11 January 1864. At first only the Greenwich and Mid Kent line trains used the extension, the lines being opened to all traffic on 1 May 1864. The southern part of the SER station became a Continental Goods Depot, with eight roads under an overall roof.

As traffic continued to increase in the 1870s, the LBSCR considered enlargement of its station, but dismissed it as too costly. As an alternative, it was decided to secure the maximum capacity from the existing site by rearranging tracks and improving the signalling. Platforms were extended at the outer ends and in and out roads provided so that they might be used for either departures or arrivals. The new signalling allowed two trains in the same platform simultaneously if desired. By shortening the cab road at its eastern end, room was found for two more short platforms (latterly 17 and 18), making eleven platforms in all, numbered from north to south. This work was finished in 1879.

Pressure from increasing traffic was also felt on the SER side, and in 1893-4 this was rebuilt, with an additional platform face on the north. These platforms were now numbered south to north 1 to 7, omitting 3 (there was a No 3 road between the platform lines of 2 and 4, of which more presently). At the time of this rebuilding, new railway offices were provided for SER staff in the narrow space between platform 7 road and Tooley Street.

Major changes in the London Bridge layout were made at the turn of the century. After many years of intense competition, the South Eastern and the London Chatham & Dover companies had come together, from 1 January 1899, under a managing committee consisting of four directors from each board, using the name South Eastern & Chatham Railway. In 1901, continuing widenings begun by the SER in 1895, the managing committee opened two extra tracks on the north side of the viaduct as far as Spa Road the Greenwich trains resuming normal left hand running as a consequence of this on 26 May. Work on widening continued until 1906.

A vast sweep of eleven parallel tracks, the approaches to London Bridge now formed one of the most impressive stretches of railway in Britain, alive with trains for most of the 24 hours. From north to south the various lines were:

SECR No 1 down
SECR No 2 down
SECR No 3 down
SECR No 2 up
SECR No 1 up
SECR down main (also used by LBSCR)
SECR up main (also used by LBSCR)
SECR up local (also known as up Croydon) (also used by LBSCR)
LBSCR South London down
LBSCR South London up main
LBSCR South London up local

Beyond Spa Road three new roads were laid on the north side of the viaduct, and the working of the first six roads from that side was:

SECR No 1 down
SECR No 2 down
SECR No 3 up
SECR No 2 up
SECR No 3 down
SECR No 1 up

On 19 October 1909, in preparation for electric working, the middle South London line was resignalled for reversible operation as far as South Bermondsey Junction and over the 'Spur' to Bricklayers Arms junction. This was intended to relieve the congested down main, which in 1912 was carrying fourteen LBSCR and five SECR trains between 5 and 6 pm.

Early in 1901 the Continental Goods depot was moved to Ewer Street, Southwark, on the Charing Cross extension (Ewer Street closed in 1960 upon the opening of a new and larger Continental Freight depot at Hither Green). On the Continental depot site four low level terminal platforms (latterly 8 to 11) were constructed; 8 and 9 were 660 ft long, 10 was 510 ft, and 11 only 393 ft. The old wooden overall roof was removed and umbrella canopies provided for the new passenger platforms. Separately numbered 1 to 4 from south to north, these platforms came into use on 2 June 1902, with a covered footbridge joining them to the high level station.

## ELECTRIFICATION

London Bridge now had twenty-one platforms, fifteen terminal, six through, but its capacity was to be vastly increased in later years by electrification and the installation of colour-light signalling.

The first electric trains appeared on the Brighton side on 1 December 1909, providing the service over the South London line to Victoria, via Denmark Hill. They were operated on the 6,600 V single phase ac system with overhead wire distribution and bow collectors on the trains. The six most southerly platforms (latterly 17 to 22) were wired, but 17 was rarely used by the electric trains. In 1912 the electrification was extended to the other services: Crystal Palace (LL) via Tulse Hill (1 March) and Streatham—Victoria via Tulse Hill (1 June). Electric trains also ran to Norwood Junction when working in and out of Selhurst depot. In 1912 the number of trains using the Brighton station daily was 901, compared with 663 before electrification.

No damage was inflicted upon London Bridge during the air raids of the first world war, but precautionary measures included the provision of office accommodation in the Tooley Street arches and under the Brighton station, with special facilities for staff controlling military traffic. The SECR air raid control centre, which gave instructions for the working of traffic during air raids, was also located at London Bridge.

At the grouping of 1923 the London Bridge stations passed to the Southern Railway which at once determined to electrify all the former SER suburban lines, using the 600 V dc third rail system. The services through London Bridge to Bromley North, Orpington, Beckenham Junction, Hayes and Addiscombe were electrically operated from 28 February 1926, and those to Dartford via Blackheath and Charlton, via Bexleyheath and via Sidcup, as well as the Plumstead via Greenwich service, followed on 6 June. Full services on all these routes began on 19 July. The Caterham and Tattenham Corner services were electrified from 25 March 1928, with a full service from 17 June.

On the Brighton side, the overhead wire was replaced by third rail, whilst other services were electrified on the new system, and by the early summer of 1928, all the platform lines in this part of the station were fitted with conductor rails. The first dc electric trains ran on 25 March 1928 to Crystal Palace (LL) via Sydenham, and on 17 June the services to Coulsdon North (peak hours only), to Epsom Downs via West Croydon, South London line to Victoria, to Crystal Palace via Tulse Hill, to Streatham Hill and to London Bridge via Selhurst and Sydenham (and vice versa) were electrified on the dc system. Finally, on 3 March 1929, it was the turn of the services to Dorking North and Effingham Junction via Mitcham, and from the same day, the Streatham Hill trains were extended to Victoria.

After the conversion of the suburban network, electric working was extended to the south coast resorts, whose stations already provided a considerable business traffic to London Bridge. Platforms 14 and 15 were lengthened to 800 ft, and from 1 January 1933, electric trains ran to Brighton and West Worthing (previously, from 17 July 1932, there had been electric working as far as Reigate and Three Bridges). The Seaford, Eastbourne and Hastings services were electrically operated from 7 July 1935, and then from 3 July 1938, the Bognor and Littlehampton rush hour trains.

Long-distance season traffic had been a feature of the Brighton side of London Bridge for many years, and indeed without too much exaggeration, one could say that the whole of the LBSCR was virtually a suburban system. Perhaps the most impressive sight that London Bridge could offer was the nightly departure of 'the Fives' from adjacent platforms. In steam days these were:

5.0 pm  'City Limited', Brighton non stop (a train dating from the 1840s),
5.5 pm  Eastbourne,
5.8 pm  Hove and Worthing,

all using the same main line for a considerable distance. Just before the main-line electrification, the Brighton train would consist of ten corridor coaches and a first class Pullman car (252 first and 224 third class seats), drawn by a handsome Billinton 4–6–4T; the Eastbourne, which included a slip coach for Horley and stations to Forest Row, also had a first class Pullman, and would probably be hauled by a U or U1 2–6–0; and the 5.8 would have a two-coach slip portion for Haywards Heath and stations to Brighton and be headed by another 4–6–4T. Three minutes later, another train would leave for Brighton, semi-fast, and in this eleven minutes seven electric suburban trains would also have left the Brighton station. Translated into electric working 'the Fives' became:

5.00 pm  Brighton (12 cars including buffet)
5.02 pm  Eastbourne and Seaford (12 cars)
5.05 pm  Hove, Worthing and Littlehampton (12 with buffet)
5.11 pm  Brighton and Littlehampton (10 cars).

There have been changes since, but the timetable well into the 1970s still showed four main-line departures between 5 and 5.15 pm.

## CHANGES OF 1928

We must return for a moment to 1928, which was an important year in the history of London Bridge. Perhaps the most momentous change, symbolic of the unification of the southern lines, was the making of an opening in the wall between the two sides of the station, now known as the Eastern Section (ie the former SER) and Central Section (former LBSCR) stations. With the hole in the wall came a second footbridge over the low level and through platforms to facilitate interchange across the station. In part these alterations were designed to make things a little easier for the increased number of rush-hour passengers forced to change trains at London Bridge, an unfortunate consequence of the more frequent service provided by electrification. As early as 1867 some trains from the Brighton side had run through the high-level platforms into Cannon Street; this had not lasted very long, but for many years a few trains on the SER Caterham and Tattenham Corner services had crossed over from the far side to reach Cannon Street and Charing Cross, as had three or four business trains from the Reading—Redhill and Redhill—Tonbridge lines. When intensive electric services were introduced on the Brighton side in 1928 it was clear that such crossing movements, fouling three other lines, could no longer be tolerated in the rush hours. Caterham and Tattenham Corner electric trains were therefore terminated in the Low Level platforms at rush hours and the steam business services mentioned suffered the same fate.

Another important change of 1928 also followed electrification on the Brighton side. This was the conversion of the middle South London road out of London Bridge from reversible to down working, and consequent rearrangement of the approach tracks. The old down South London line became up local, and from 17 June the eleven approach tracks were used as follows: Eastern Section numbers 1, 2 and 3 down, Eastern 2 and 1 up, Central Section down local, Central down main, Central up main, Central up local, South London down, South London up.

Following these changes, on 17 June, the twenty-one platforms were numbered consecutively from north to south, apart from the 'missing' platform 5. There never had been such a platform, but a number 5 (formerly 3) through road existed between the platform roads of 4 and 6. This was used as a light engine line and also as a refuge for freight trains awaiting a path to the northern lines via Ludgate Hill and Farringdon. After the opening of the

Lewisham loops in 1929 the number of these cross-London freights through London Bridge was substantially reduced. The middle road was removed in 1952 to facilitate the extension of platforms 3 and 4 in the 10-car scheme.

## LAYOUT

This is a convenient point to offer a description of this complicated station, as it was in its last years. In the Through, or High Level station were the curved island platforms 1 and 2, 3 and 4, 6 and 7. As well as the connection offered by the footbridges already mentioned, there were subways from the London ends of these platforms to a very cramped circulating area beneath the viaduct of the Charing Cross extension. Here was found a wooden booking office and a buffet, the latter inside the old SER frontage block. Platforms 1, 2 and 3 were served by down trains, and 4 could be used for down working in foggy weather or other special occasions by trains which had terminated in it. Main-line trains serving the Kent coast used platform 3 in the down direction, 6 and 7 when coming up; the sharply curved, uptilted 7 provided steam drivers with many an embarrassing start. The six through platforms varied in length from 602 to 745 ft before they were extended in 1954 at the country end to accommodate ten-car trains. Opposite platform 7, sharing the same road, was a short low platform used for postal traffic. Known as 'the Mount', its surface was shiny from the constant friction of mailbags. A roadway through the old SER building led to a small yard behind this platform which was used by the Post Office vans. Amenities at platform level were few; 1 and 2 boasted bookstalls and 1 had a tiny buffet at the country end where homegoing commuters drowned the day's troubles or prepared to face their wives.

Alongside the Through station were the Low Level terminal platforms 8 to 11, used for parcels traffic and the rush-hour workings already referred to. Platform 11, not electrified and only 393 ft long, was normally used for stabling vans and locomotives, although it saw the occasional slack-hour passenger train in steam days. Its other face, 10, was full length, sheltered at its inner end by the first floor of the long and narrow office block that abutted on to the south end of the old SER frontage.

Passing through the hole in the wall, the passenger reached the concourse of the former LBSCR station opposite the ends of the northernmost platforms, 12 and 13, which were of medium length and used for suburban services. Between 13 and 14 were two non-

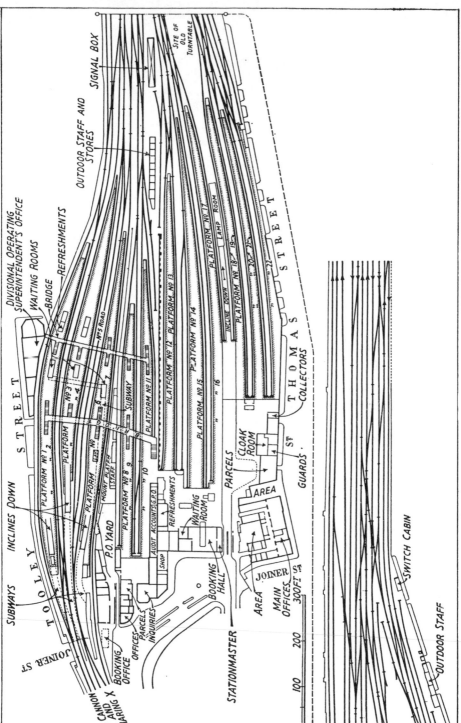

Plan of the 1927 layout of London Bridge station, Southern Railway. From the Railway Magazine, February 1927

electrified sidings, one of which disappeared in a widening and
lengthening of 14 and 15 in 1931. At the buffer stops was a bookstall of which more will be heard.

South Coast main-line trains used the three long platforms 14,
15 and 16, the only ones capable of taking 12-car electric trains, 16
being the longest in the station at 827 ft. On the opposite face of
16 was the shortest platform, the 518 ft No 17. Between 17 and
18, another short platform, there was an incline off the end of the
carriage roadway, leading down to the old lamp room. At the far
side were Nos 19 to 22, usually referred to as the South London
line platforms.

A waiting room and a booking hall were to be found in the
ground floor of the frontage building, and in a passage through it,
on the north side, were some shops. At the north side of the concourse was a buffet, with a tea room above, subsequently a staff
canteen. On the St Thomas Street side, between the old hotel and
the South London platforms, there were a cloakroom, parcels office
and staff rooms; the South London platforms had their own buffet
and bookstall, at the back of 19 and 20. All this was under a three-
section roof, with a central arch of 80 ft span over platforms 15
to 18, carried on elegant fluted iron columns and decorated
brackets, and a series of gambrels, forming horizontal sections
either side, on lattice girder supports.

In 1936, with the reduction in steam operation, the 46 ft 5 in
turntable opposite the ends of 15 and 16 was removed, and the
remaining engines were turned at New Cross Gate sheds. In its
place, the Southern erected a giant nameboard, floodlit at night,
presumably to reassure dazed commuters of their whereabouts.

As may be surmised, this somewhat confused cluster of platforms and stations was not conducive to smooth passenger flow.
At rush hours, the footbridges over the Eastern Section platforms
were the scene of some confusion, and the various currents of
passenger movement on the Central side not only conflicted with
the flow to and from the Eastern Section, but tended to tangle with
the road vans and other impedimenta of a healthy parcels, newspaper and mail traffic centred around the carriage roadway alongside platform 16.

By 1936 the combined stations were handling about 250,000
passengers a day, but only 170,000 passed through the barriers.
There were 2,407 train movements at London Bridge in each 24
hours, and in the busiest morning peak hour, 94 trains arrived,
29 continuing to Cannon Street, 19 to Charing Cross, and 46
terminating. To assist rush-hour crowds and supplement the des-

tination indicators worked from the signal box, the SR experimentally installed loudspeakers on platforms 1 and 2 in 1927, probably the first equipment of its kind on a major London station.[6]

Apart from its predominant suburban and business traffic, London Bridge saw special workings for events at the Crystal Palace, race days at Epsom, and the September picking season in the Kentish hopfields. Over 33,000 travelled each year to and from the hopfields during the 1930s, carried in special trains made up from the oldest available stock. Vans were provided to accommodate the various household accoutrements—a line was drawn at tables and chairs, but most other essential domestic equipment was accepted. These trains usually left very early in the morning or from the Low Level platforms after the Saturday rush hours. Now hop-pickers' traffic has entirely disappeared (the last special train ran in 1960), partly owing to the adoption of machines, but largely because those attracted to a free country holiday now enjoy a vastly improved standard of living. The new generation flies to Majorca for fish and chips in the sun.

In contrast to its treatment in the first world war, London Bridge received severe punishment in the second. On 9 December 1940, the signal box had a narrow escape when a parachute mine, entangled in a signal girder, settling against the wall of the cabin. Whilst the three men inside continued with their work, two sailors defused the mine. In the great fire raid on the City (29/30 December 1940), bombs rained on the station. The large clock on the end wall of the Central Section building stopped at 12.27 as the hotel and the top floors of both frontage buildings were gutted by fire. The Central Section parcels office was destroyed. Parcels work was moved to the booking office and tickets were sold from a wooden hut on the concourse. A quarter of a century later, this splendid piece of wartime improvisation was still there. Another casualty was the Eastern Section buffet at the entrance to platforms 6 and 7, but this was repaired and reopened in May 1948. After the damage to the Central Section side, platforms 18 to 22 shared a common entrance and exit.

Between 1958 and 1964, the remaining steam services disappeared. The Hastings via Tunbridge Wells trains which passed through the Eastern platforms, were worked by diesel-electric multiple-unit sets from 9 June 1958; the remaining steam trains through this side of the station vanished with the completion of the Kent coast electrification in June 1961. The last steam workings at London Bridge, to the Oxted, East Grinstead, Eridge and

Uckfield lines, were replaced by diesel-electric multiple-unit-sets or locomotives, and the final regular steam run was made in 1964. The sole remaining train to the Redhill—Reading line (the 5.25 pm) last ran in February 1963.

After 1945 peak-hour traffic continued to grow, becoming still more concentrated in time. In 1958, 37,000 left London Bridge in the heaviest hour, compared with 24,000 in 1939. There was then a slight decline: the corresponding figure for 1967 was 30,900. (These figures do not of course include those in trains through the Eastern Section platforms.) In the 1967 peak evening hour there were 61 trains through the Eastern Section station, including those not stopping, and 44 left the Central Section platforms. Although this total of 105 was only 14 higher than 1939, it must be remembered that the trains were longer and more capacious than those of the immediate pre-war period. A typical pre-war 8-car suburban electric train offered a total of 652 seats (112 first class), but a modern 8-car electric train as used on the Central Section has 772 seats (an increase of 17 per cent), whilst the 10-car trains introduced on the Eastern Section in 1955-7 had a total of 958 seats (46 per cent increase).

At first, BR did not do a great deal for London Bridge. The war-damaged frontage blocks were left in a semi-ruined state, but part of the remains of the SER frontage was demolished in 1966 to provide a van yard in front of the Low Level station. Wooden platforms were replaced with concrete and asphalt (a job begun by the SR in 1942) and new barriers were erected on platforms 12 to 17 in 1953. The Post Office in the Eastern Section frontage, which had been open for over fifty years, suffered a loss of business, and was closed on 31 August 1963.

When the City and South London tube railway was extended to Moorgate on 25 February 1900, an Underground station was provided near London Bridge station, at the bottom of the approach road. Communications were improved on 2 December 1901 by the opening of a 180 yard subway from the tube station to lifts and a small booking hall at the southern corner of the Brighton station forecourt, but the SER passengers still had a tiresome walk in the open air. In December 1940 this Brighton side tube entrance was damaged by bombs and closed. Reopened on 9 July 1945, it was only available in peak hours from 8 April 1957. A new, larger tube booking hall, with three escalators replacing lifts, and generally more convenient for the main station, was opened by London Transport on 19 November 1967. Construction of a subway from the new tube station to the main concourse was delayed until a decision had been taken on rebuilding the terminus, and this new access was opened in 1975.

In 1967, the old London Bridge was, as it still is today, very much a rush hour station. Some 86,300 passengers arrived daily, 61,400 between 7 and 10 a.m. Then, until the evening rush, there was but a trickle of customers. After 1 October 1966 the Low Level platforms were closed between 10 am and 3 pm and at weekends, and from the same day, apart from platforms 18-22, the Central Section station was closed on Saturday afternoons and Sundays. Mail had been carried from London Bridge since 1837 and was still an important activity, notably at 'The Mount' platform and platform 16 which saw the departure each night at 11.50 pm of the London to Dover Travelling Post Office. Newspaper traffic, especially evenings for south east England, was heavy.

Each weekday morning, between 8 and 9, huge crowds flowed out of the station, forming a human tide which washed into City offices across the river, returning between 5 and 6 in the evening. At the same times thousands more passed through the station on the Eastern Section side, whilst hundreds moved to and from the tube station and the buses which terminate in the forecourt[7]. All these people, forming the vast majority of the station's users, knew their way about, which was just as well, for its untidy, disjointed layout, inherited from the railway politics of the 19th century, and smashed about by wartime bombs, offered many a hazard to the stranger, and cried out for rationalisation and rebuilding.

BR had produced plans for a new station in 1961, only to meet Government opposition to the new offices which were to help pay for it. Fortunately, planning policies changed again, and as described in chapter 16, work was to start at last in the early 1970s.

## SIGNALLING AND ACCIDENTS

Not surprisingly, London Bridge has a varied and interesting signalling history. At first, the Greenwich Railway used hand flags and lamps, but later they installed 15 ft posts carrying square iron plates showing red on one side and green on the other, controlled by hand levers at the base. The London & Croydon used a primitive form of semaphore from about 1842, and a contemporary illustration of the Joint Station shows a double arm signal. The block bell system invented by C. V. Walker, the SER telegraph superintendent, was installed outside London Bridge in 1852.

With the opening of the Charing Cross extension in 1864, an entirely new signalling installation was provided by Saxby & Farmer. Two cabins, AB and CD, were erected over the approach tracks to the south of the station, with semaphore signals in splendid array on their roofs. Each box had three posts carrying three double semaphores, up and down arms for each set of approach tracks. 'Stop' was indicated by the horizontal position, 'caution' by a lowering of the arm, but the 'all clear' indication (arm hidden in a slot in the post), was not given in this busy area. Each arm carried a letter code indicating the route to which it referred. Both boxes were manned by a crew of three; signalman, telegraph clerk and signal lad. At the suggestion of Captain H. Tyler, the block bell signals were replaced by miniature semaphores in the signal boxes.

For the reconstructed through station of 1894, there were three boxes on the SER side; A, with 41 levers, at the west end of the present platforms 1 and 2, B, with 148 levers, an overhead box at the other end of the station, and C, sited at the crossover junction to the Croydon lines, with 47 levers. These boxes had Sykes's lock and block apparatus, and, in common with other boxes in the inner area, were fitted with Walker's clock face train describers.

After the construction of the South London line in 1866, the LBSCR operated its own signals at London Bridge, opening three boxes, South, East and West, a total of 72 levers. All had Saxby & Farmer's 'striking' interlocking, and in 1879 some of this equipment was taken to Epsom Downs station, where it survived in use until quite recent times.

As part of the scheme for increasing the capacity of the Brighton station, the East and West boxes were closed in 1879, and replaced by a large North box situated opposite the ends of what are now platforms 17 and 18. This new cabin, which straddled the turntable siding, was to remain in use until the colour light installation of 1928. It was 71 ft 4 in long and 26 ft 4 in wide, containing 280 levers in two Saxby & Farmer back-to-back frames. The 'grid iron' interlocking initially installed was later replaced by the more conventional tappet system. North was really a yard box, as the Sykes's lock and block working began at South box, situated on the south side of the South London line, just outside the station. This was a mere 9 ft wide and 53 ft long, with 98 levers.

The 1879 installation included route indicators on the signals controlling the six 'in and out' roads (A to C on the South London side, D to F on the main-line side). They were enamelled discs, numbered and lettered, placed on the posts, and illuminated at night by oil lamps. Sheathed when not in use, they were worked by separate levers in the signal box. The discs on the outer home showed the road to which the train would run, those on the inner home the platform it would use, a pattern followed in the later colour-light installation. Starting signals showed the road to be taken to the advanced starters.

Another interesting feature of the 1879 equipment was the use of fish-tailed arms to indicate platform occupation, permitting the working of two trains into one platform when required. If the distant and home arms were both lowered, the platform was fully clear to buffers, but if only the home arm was off, the driver knew he must enter with great caution as the platform was partly occupied. In later years it seems doubtful whether the distant arms were ever pulled off, even when the platform was completely empty, probably because the signalmen could not see the platform ends and preferred to err on the side of safety. During the first world war, the platform distants were replaced with conventional calling-on arms which were pulled off under a level home arm to indicate partial occupation of the platform.

Colour light signalling, with track circuiting and power operated points was introduced by the Southern Railway for the dc electrifications of the 1920s. The tracks in London Bridge station and the approaches, together with the through lines to Borough Market junction, were changed over to the new signalling on 17 June 1928. A power signal box, 113 ft by 14 ft 9 in, containing a Westinghouse & Saxby frame of 311 miniature levers, controlled all the platform lines and approaches.There were two 'spotlight' track diagrams, each 18 ft long. So extensive was the mechanical interlocking of this frame that it rested on the floor below that used by the signalmen.

Four-aspect colour lights were used on the Eastern Section lines between Borough Market and Spa Road, but as there was no freight traffic on the Central side, three aspects were considered sufficient between the Central platforms and Bricklayers Arms junction (main line) and Old Kent Road junction (South London line).

Unfamiliarity with this new signalling was the probable cause of the first serious accident at London Bridge, which occurred just east of the signal box on 9 July 1928. Observing a signal changing to green, the driver of a light engine moved off, ignoring a ground signal at danger, and colliding with the front of the 7.22 pm electric for Epsom Downs, which was proceeding under clear signals. The engine, and two cars of the passenger train left the rails, killing one passenger immediately and fatally injuring another. Twenty years later, on 23 January 1948 at 9.30 am, an up electric from Seaford and Ore over-ran the up inner home signals, to enter platform 14, which was already occupied by an empty train. The motorman of the passenger train and a learner with him were trapped, dying in the arms of a priest from Southwark Cathedral, who had climbed into the wrecked cab. The empty coaches were forced up over the buffers, killing a man on the concourse and wrecking the bookstall. A third accident, fortunately without fatalities, occurred about 8.30 pm on 22 October 1956 under hand signalling during a track circuit failure. A down train was wrongly allowed out of the station, and collided with an incoming train at a crossover about 500 yards outside. Fortunately both motormen saw what was inevitable, and braked hard.

In 1967, in conjunction with a new timetable giving a larger number of trains through the high level stations in peak hours, additional signals were provided between London Bridge (Eastern Section) and Cannon Street and Metropolitan junction.

Subsequent signalling changes are described in chapter 16.

# CHAPTER 9

# Cannon Street

A great train shed yawning over the Thames, high brick walls, proud towers, and a wedding cake hotel across the street frontage combined to give the old Cannon Street a special aura. Now, thanks to German bombs, and the requirements of longer trains, this architectural magic has all but vanished. Only the towers and part of the walls remain in sad, soot-blackened splendour, to form an incongruous frame for the monotonous new office blocks and smart modern concourse at the north end. Opened in 1866 as the City station of the South Eastern Railway, Cannon Street now handles little else but season ticket business, its long-distance services confined to a few rush-hour trains.

At first the SER had been content to serve the City from London Bridge and two proposed intermediate stations on the Charing Cross extension (at the south end of Southwark Bridge and at Blackfriars Road), but in 1860, a year after the Charing Cross Act, the London Chatham & Dover, the SER's great rivals, were authorised to extend into the City as far as Ludgate Hill. Spurred by this, the SER-backed Charing Cross Company decided to complement the West End terminus with a City station on the north bank of the river. There was as yet no Metropolitan District Railway, and street congestion, even in those days, was decidedly tiresome. In 1846 William Hosking told the Royal Commission on Metropolitan Termini that in the summer of 1845 it had taken him $1\frac{1}{2}$ hours to come up from Brighton by train and $\frac{1}{2}$ hr more to reach Trafalgar Square by any road; he added 'I have walked as quickly as I could go by any other mode.' There was every reason to hope then that a useful local traffic might be built up between this City station and Charing Cross, to supplement the suburban and long distance business. An Act was obtained in 1861 for a station in Cannon Street, opposite Walbrook and St Swithin's Lane, just two minutes' walk from the Bank and Mansion House.

This was to be reached by a 60-chain branch from a triangular junction with the Charing Cross line just west of London Bridge. The station, river bridge and viaducts of the approaches were all designed by John Hawkshaw,[1] consulting engineer to the SER. Work began in July 1863.

On its east side, the triangle south of the river had three tracks, one down and two up; a fourth line, for down traffic, was added in 1896. On the west, there were three tracks, two towards Charing Cross, one towards Cannon Street, and across the 'base', only two, one up, one down, because it was planned to run almost all trains between London Bridge and Charing Cross in and out of Cannon Street. All three sides were on a brick viaduct, and at the north end of the layout was an engine shed, turntable and coking stages (space was so tight that engines had to run on to the turntable before they could get in or out of the shed).

### ACROSS THE RIVER TO THE CITY

Carrying the five approach tracks across the river was an 80 ft wide bridge, 706 ft long, supported on four piers, each pier of four cast-iron columns, with cast-iron moulded caps. The two shore spans were each 125 ft long, and the three centre ones 136 ft. At Trinity high water mark, there was a minimum clearance of 24 ft 8 in to the soffit. The columns were filled with concrete below the river bed and with brickwork in cement above. They were 18 ft diameter below low water line, 12 ft above it. In contrast to the Charing Cross bridge, all main girders ran longitudinally, and there were no high girders above rail level. The four running lines and the engine road rested on a plate girder superstructure.

On the north side, the bridge widened out into a 202 ft fan to carry the nine roads into the station, the platform ends and engine sidings. Footways were provided on each side of the bridge between ornamental parapets and the railway. That on the west side was opened to the public, on payment of a ½d toll, between 1872 and 1877, whilst that on the east was used by railway staff to reach the installations on the south shore.

Hawkshaw's station abutted immediately against the bridge. To gain the necessary height, it was built on a substructure of brick piers and arches. Over Upper Thames Street, the rails and platforms were carried on wrought-iron girders, the span being 37 ft.

Over the platforms towered a vast roof of 190 ft span. Surmounted by a 22 ft wide lantern which ran nearly the full length

L

of 680 ft, this roof was 106 ft 6 in above the rails at the apex of
the arch, and was glazed over two-thirds of its surface area. Solid
brick walls, averaging 6 ft 6 in in thickness, and relieved by arched
bays, supported this pretentious canopy. On the inside, these walls
were later disfigured by scores of advertisement panels, including
one which tempted sober City men with the delights of the Bal
Tabarin. At the river, the walls terminated in arcaded towers which
rose to the level of the roof lantern and were surmounted by
weather vanes dutifully marked SER in the tails of their arrows.
These towers, which were relieved by rusticated stone quoins,
contained water tanks providing hydraulic power for the lifts to
and from the station's vaults, and later, water for carriage cleaning. Across the river end, the roof was closed by a gable windscreen glazed in wooden frames made to fit between the iron struts
and ties.

Inside the well-lit train shed, despite the advertisements, there
was an air of spacious dignity. West to east, the arrangement was
as follows:

> single track
> Charing Cross platform (480 ft)
> two tracks
> west arrival platform (721 ft). (Carriage loading dock at north end)
> cab roadway (empty cabs entered from Upper Thames Street via
>     a U ramp at the south end and left with their fares through the
>     frontage block and yard)
> east arrival platform (721 ft)
> three tracks (the middle road for spare stock and standing room,
>     with carriage loading dock at north end)
> general departure platform (665 ft)
> two tracks
> Greenwich platform (522 ft)
> single track.

The Charing Cross and Greenwich platforms were 13 ft 6 in wide,
the overall width of the arrival platforms and cab road was 30 ft,
and the general departure platform was 19 ft wide. The Charing
Cross platform, as the name implies, was used by the shuttle service between the two termini. Greenwich trains terminated at
Cannon Street from its opening day; later, when Greenwich was
linked to Maze Hill, a half-hourly service was operated to Charlton
Junction, extended in peak hours to Plumstead. Mid-Kent, and
some North Kent Line trains, also used the Greenwich platform.

The ends of the general departure platform and the east and
west arrival platforms projected beyond the shelter of the train

shed on to the bridge. Widths of the platforms varied from 12 ft 6 in to 19 ft.

Beyond the buffer stops was a circulating area across the full 187 ft width of the station, and north of this were waiting rooms, booking office, refreshment room, and cloak room. On the street side, steps led down to a 90 ft deep forecourt between the station building and Cannon Street, with further flights of steps at the north west corner and in the centre, and a cab gateway at the north east corner. Before the forecourt was laid out, a tunnel was constructed 28 ft below the surface for the future District Railway.

The frontage block was a five-storey hotel, the City Terminus, opened in May 1867 by an independent company, but later taken over by the SER. A high Victorian jumble of Italianate and French Renaissance styles, it was the work of Edward Middleton Barry.[2] Its north-east and north-west corners, each crowned with a mansard rooflet and a spirelet, were brought forward a little from the main building line; between them, the steeply-pitched main roof was spattered with banks of chimneys and a row of arched-top dormer windows. An Italianate water tower marked out the south-east corner. First, second and third floors had balconies along the front, the two lower ones with flower bowls marking each window division. Much use was made of Blanchard's artificial stone as facing, and of white glazed terracotta.

The Cannon Street Hotel, as it was later renamed, has a small place in history, for it was in these unlikely surroundings that representatives of various revolutionary bodies met in July 1920, to set up the Communist Party of Great Britain. A decline in business led to the closure of the hotel in 1931, but the large licensed public rooms were kept open for meetings and banquets. The remainder was converted to offices and let under the name of Southern House.

Opened on 1 September 1866, Cannon Street was served by almost all trains proceeding to and from Charing Cross, including the Continental boat expresses. In addition, a shuttle service was worked every 20 minutes (later every 10 minutes), providing, with the other trains, an average frequency of 5 minutes between the City and the West End. For the 7-minute run, the SER charged 6d first class, 4d second, and 2d third, compared with 3d for a horse bus ride between Bank and Charing Cross. During 1867, Cannon Street handled some 8 million passengers, of which $3\frac{1}{2}$ million were local between West End and City.

The westernmost track of the river bridge was used exclusively by the inter-terminal service; the neighbouring track was for up trains from both London Bridge and Charing Cross, whilst the centre track was used by up trains from London Bridge; next came the main down line to London Bridge or Charing Cross, and lastly, the engine road, used by locomotives entering or leaving the depot on the south bank, or awaiting their trains. All trains entering Cannon Street had to be supplied with another locomotive for the outward journey, this being called forward from the engine sidings on either bank, or from the engine road. Any available engine was used for taking trains on to Charing Cross, and for bringing trains from there to Cannon Street. In general, main-line locomotives worked to and from Cannon Street, and not to Charing Cross.

### CURIOSITIES OF SERVICES

Local traffic between the two termini slumped badly as soon as the District Railway opened from Westminster to Blackfriars in May 1870, and even more so when it reached Mansion House in July 1871. Upon the completion of the Inner Circle on 6 October 1884, a station was provided under the Cannon Street forecourt. Attempts were made to advertise the 'open air route', but the Underground was more reliable as well as more direct. Even before the opening of the Underground line, one special type of traffic on the City—West End route had largely disappeared. Some ladies of the streets had found that the SER's first class compartments, combined with the uninterrupted seven-minute run, provided ideal conditions for their activities at a rental that represented only a minute proportion of their income. The number of drawn blinds on these trains noticeably decreased after the opening of an intermediate station at Waterloo, at which most trains stopped, on 1 January 1869.

A curious service of the early days was that worked from Cannon Street to Kensington (Addison Road) (with carriages through to Euston), via Waterloo Junction, Latchmere Junction and Battersea. This had begun in July 1865 between London Bridge and Euston, but was diverted to Cannon Street from 1 February 1867. Cut back to Waterloo for the month of January 1868, it was withdrawn from 1 February. Another 'foreign' service was that operated by the LBSCR, two business trains from Brighton to Cannon Street, and back again in the evening, lasting only from 2 September 1867 to 31 July 1868.

However unsuccessful these experiments, and the local service to Charing Cross, the general suburban traffic to and from the City increased steadily, as did that of the main-line services working through to Charing Cross. In 1878 there were 165 trains in the busiest 2½ hr, more than one train a minute. By the middle 1880s it became necessary to increase the capacity of the approaches, and to this end, the bridge was widened to 120 ft, to accommodate ten tracks, including sidings. Two more cast-iron columns were added to each pier on the western side, and the rebuilt bridge was completed on 13 February 1892. The bridge layout now had a siding on each flank, and the remaining eight tracks, west to east, were: No 1 out (Charing Cross), Nos 2 and 3 in, No 4 out (London Bridge or Charing Cross), No 5 (dead end siding), Nos 6 and 7 in, and No 8 out (London Bridge). Engine facilities were provided on each side of the layout on the south bank, with a turntable at each side, and an engine shed and coaling stage on the east side.

In the station, another platform was added by inserting a single track bay between the east and west arrival platforms, in space gained by shortening the cab roadway and blocking up the entrance from Upper Thames Street. The platforms were now numbered 1 to 9 from west to east, with the bay described as No 4 on both its faces. Platforms 3, 4 and 5 were extended on to the bridge as far as the first pier.

Although the weight of locomotives and the volume of traffic had increased considerably since 1866, a thorough examination of the bridge in the 1900s disclosed no signs of settlement in the piers. But it did reveal that the superstructure had received heavy punishment from both the load and the weather, and it was necessary to impose restrictions until it had been strengthened. Carried out without any interruptions to traffic over a period of 4½ years, this work was completed in 1913. Six new main girders, each 443 ft long, were inserted between the existing ones. The flooring was renewed and reinforcing plates were attached to the old girders at the points of greatest strain.

War brought important changes. From 15 November 1914, all the SECR Continental services were transferred to Victoria, and apart from specials to be mentioned later, boat trains were never seen again at Cannon Street. The practice of running Charing Cross trains through Cannon Street ceased almost completely on 31 December 1916, a severely reduced passenger timetable coming into force on the following day. Cannon Street was then closed on Sundays, and from 1 May 1918 it was also shut from 3 pm on Saturdays and between 11 am and 4 pm Mondays to Fridays. These closures allowed the use of the terminus as an engine and crew exchange point for the large number of goods trains which were moving war supplies between the northern lines and the Channel ports via Farringdon and Ludgate Hill. The GNR and Midland trains were dealt with at Cannon Street in alternate weeks; the consequent speedier return of the northern engines and crews to their parent systems and the reduction in the number of

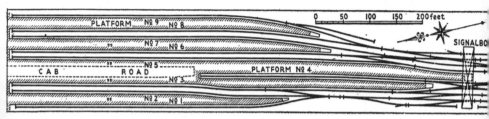

*Layout of Cannon Street station platforms before reorganisation of 1926.
From the* Railway Magazine, *August 1966*

pilotmen provided a welcome increase in productivity. Between May and November 1918, when the normal week-day opening of Cannon Street was resumed, some 175,000 goods wagons and vans in 5,803 trains were worked through Cannon Street under this arrangement.[3]

Air raids provided few problems. Minor damage was inflicted on 7 July 1917, when some 500 panes of glass were smashed and a bomb which fell outside No 2 cabin failed to explode. On 28 January 1918 an empty carriage train leaving the station was damaged by an anti-aircraft shell.

Suburban traffic had grown appreciably in the first years of the new century, becoming an increasing burden to operate. The SECR had obtained powers for electric working as early as 1903, and in 1922 produced a plan which obtained a Treasury guarantee of principal and interest under the Trade Facilities Act, 1921, but this was overtaken by the formation of the Southern Railway. In the meantime, the SECR endeavoured to improve operation by the adoption of parallel working in the rush hours. Introduced on 12 February 1922, in the morning peak, this arrangement involved no track or signalling changes, merely timetable revision to secure the simultaneous passing of up and down trains on the same route at junctions, and parallel running on multiple tracks. In this way, many conflicting movements were eliminated, and the experiment was so successful that similar arrangements were later introduced for the evening business traffic.

## REMODELLING THE TRACK

As mentioned in Chapter 8, the first of the former SER suburban services were electrified on the third rail dc system in 1926. To obtain the best results from electrification, the track layout, platforms, and signalling at Cannon Street were completely remodelled. The old layout was designed to facilitate the reversal of trains proceeding to and from Charing Cross, and allowed trains coming in from London Bridge to cross over on the river bridge and reach a central or western platform where they would be ready to depart for Charing Cross, and vice versa, in the opposite direction. There was little space for light engines, and those waiting to take trains out had often to be held on a running line.

The major aim of the new layout was to allow as many parallel and non-conflicting movements as possible. On the south bank there were four electrified tracks towards London Bridge, down local, down through, up through, up local. On the Charing Cross side of the triangle there were two electric lines, 'Out Met' and 'In Met', and a third track, in the form of a non-electrified loop, known as 'Met Siding'. ('Met' was an abbreviation for Metropolitan Junction, where the lines from Cannon Street towards Charing Cross joined the direct tracks from London Bridge.) At the northern tip of the triangle, Stoney Street junction was abolished, as were the engine sidings, coaling stages and turntable on the eastern side of the line. The small engine shed was demolished and a substation built over its site. Facilities for engines were retained on the western side and the new layout allowed engines to run from the west side of Cannon Street into the Ewer Street depot or to Charing Cross without fouling the running lines from London Bridge. There was no access from the up local line to No 1 platform, but apart from this, all platforms could be reached from all up roads, and all platforms had access to all down roads. A link between No 1 and the up local would have needed very sharp curves, and the balance of advantage was given by omitting this connection. A considerable simplification was effected, and the number of sets of points in the new layout was seventy-seven, twenty-four fewer than in the old.

The new track for the approaches was delivered to a field alongside New Cross Gate goods yard, where it was patiently assembled, adjusted to get the best alignment, and fitted with point locks, point machines, conductor rails and cables. This eliminated all cutting and adjusting of rails on site, but even so, removal of the

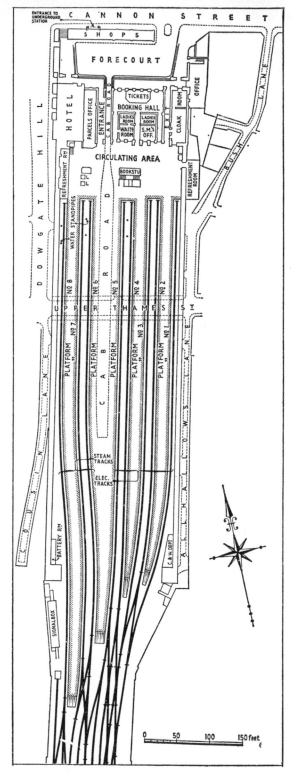

*Cannon Street station as re-arranged in 1926, in connection with electrification. From the Railway Magazine, August 1966*

old track, erection of the new, resignalling, and testing, required the complete closure of Cannon Street station from 3 pm Saturday, 5 June until 4 am Monday, 28 June 1926. Most of the 56,000 passengers who used Cannon Street each day were dealt with at London Bridge under emergency arrangements which must have been somewhat trying for all concerned.

In the station, the bay platform was abolished, and the remaining platforms rearranged to provide a total of eight, all more or less in line at buffers, and numbered from east to west. Each platform was faced with concrete blocks and surfaced with mastic asphalt. As before, there were single tracks against each outer wall, with a platform face on the inner side; all other faces had a pair of tracks between them. Platforms 1 and 2 were 569 and 567 ft long, 3 and 4, 580 and 574 ft; 5 and 6, 675 ft, and 7 and 8 752 and 745 ft. Numbers 1 to 5 were electrified, the others being left for the main-line steam trains, which also used 5. The concourse was enlarged, the booking hall rearranged, and new iron railing barriers and gates provided at the platform entrances in place of the former very ugly timber screens.

A provisional service of electric trains to Orpington, Bromley North, Addiscombe, Hayes and Beckenham Junction had begun from the old platforms 5 to 8 on 28 February 1926, and with the new layout on 28 June, electric trains began to run between Cannon Street and Dartford via all four routes. Full electric services on all nine routes were operated from 19 July.

In a typical slack hour, there were eight electric departures; in the peak hour, seventeen. There were thirty-six steam departures daily, mostly to Chatham and beyond, via the North Kent line, ten of them between 5 and 6 pm. Since 12 July 1925, the whole of the residential service to and from the Kent coast had been concentrated at Cannon Street (previously the best down train, the 5.10 pm, had started from Holborn Viaduct, running non-stop from St Paul's to Margate West).

Further electrification took place on 2 July 1929 when the Gillingham and Maidstone services were converted. At Cannon Street, platforms 6 and 7 were then fitted with conductor rails.

In spite of the sparse traffic on offer, it was decided to reopen the station on Sundays from 6 July 1930. Another facility restored in a very small way was the resumption of a very small number of workings through Cannon Street to Charing Cross from 17 July 1933. Some of these survived unadvertised until 1956. Continental trains were also seen again in the summer of 1936, when some agency specials were diverted on Saturdays to relieve Victoria, a practice which was repeated each summer up to 1939.

From 16 October 1939, the station was again closed outside rush hours (between 10 am and 4 pm and after 7.30 pm on week-days, and at week-ends after 3 pm on Saturdays). Services were re-duced, and by 1944 there were only twenty-four departures be-tween 5 and 6 pm, five of them steam main-line trains. The Kent coast had but one fast train, at 5.45 pm.

German bombs made their mark on this prominent riverside structure, notably on the night of 10/11 May 1941, when South-ern House was burnt out, and both the station roof and the river bridge were hit. As the roof burnt, and blazing timbers and molten glass fell on the platforms, railwaymen bravely hauled trains out on to the bridge in an effort to save them, only to be bombed again in this exposed position. 'Schools' class 4-4-0 St Lawrence re-ceived a direct hit, but was eventually repaired. The bridge was not seriously damaged.[4] Some time later, all the remaining glass in the roof was removed for safety.

## NEVER ON SUNDAYS

After the war, Southern House was patched up, and the two top floors rebuilt. An inspection of the station roof revealed that it was in no state to carry new glass, but would be safe enough in skeleton form for a few years. From 31 May 1948, the station was again open all day, also on Sundays, from 3 October; this lasted until 15 September 1958, when economy measures enforced week-end closure. The doors were closed at 1.45 pm each Satur-day, not to reopen again until 4.35 am on Mondays.

British Railways has wrought great changes at Cannon Street, both in the structure and in the train services. Steam hauled busi-ness trains to Hastings were completely replaced by diesel-electric multiple units on 9 June 1958. The last regular steam train left Cannon Street for Ramsgate a year later, on 13 June. Full electric services to the Kent coast came into operation on 18 June 1962.

As at the other Southern termini, rush-hour traffic became in-creasingly concentrated. In 1939 the heaviest evening peak hour saw about 16,500 passengers leaving, but by 1959 the number had grown to 23,500. It was 26,300 in 1967. One measure to meet this problem was the 10-car train scheme for the Eastern Section. For this, Cannon Street's platforms had to be lengthened, a job which raised a few problems. For operational reasons the eastern platforms could not be further extended on to the bridge, and the only alternative was to push the concourse back under the old hotel. The other platforms, 5 to 8, which could be built out on to the bridge were lengthened to take 12-car trains. In 1955 it was announced that the platform extensions would be undertaken as part of a major reconstruction of the station, including a new concourse in the ground floor of Southern House and the replacement of the old roof by one of the ridge and furrow pattern similar to that at Charing Cross. This scheme, costed at £1,250,000, was started on 17 November. Three of the extended platforms (1, 4 and 5) were ready on 4 March 1957, when the first 10-car trains ran, and the remainder were put into use early in 1958.

## ALL BUT REBUILT

In April 1958 the contractors began to take down the ironwork of Hawkshaw's arched roof whilst passengers sought their way through the various demolitions and temporary buildings below. From 10 April to 30 June, as the major part of the roof dismantling proceeded, the station was closed from 10.45 am to 3.15 pm on weekdays, and on Saturday afternoons and Sundays. By the end of January 1959, the roof had gone, but in response to pleading from the President of the Royal Academy, the Fine Art Commission and others, the walls and towers were left, although they were meaningless and more than a little absurd without the graceful curve of the roof to unite them.

In 1956, soon after the reconstruction work had started at the northern end of the station, structural faults were discovered in Southern House. It was decided to demolish it, and erect new office blocks across the northern part of the terminus. Expensive models were produced and elaborate plans prepared for a 20-storey block with a 14-storey wing, but the City Corporation refused permission on grounds of excessive height (220 ft), alleging that the view of St Paul's would be obscured. Revised plans were then submitted for a 15-storey frontal block, another lower one over the northern ends of the platforms and a third in Bush Lane alongside the station. A flat roof was to be built over the platforms, adaptable as a car park or heliport. This met with approval, but the roof was later omitted on the grounds of cost. At last, in April 1963, work began on the demolition of the old hotel, in preparation for what the Southern Region's publicity leaflets described as 'London's First Big Rail Terminal of the Sixties'.

The Bush Lane building and the podium block over the eastern

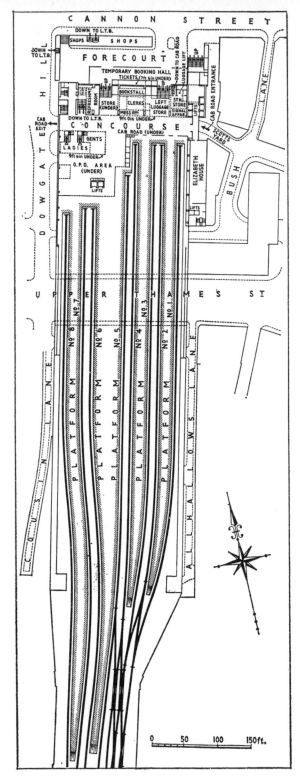

*Layout of Cannon Street station 1966. From the* Railway Magazine, *September 1966*

part of the new concourse and the inner ends of platforms 1 to 5 were completed in 1962. A flat slab roof was extended westwards to shelter the remaining part of the concourse and the inner ends of the other platforms. Across the front of the station a 15-storey block, 220 ft long and 170 ft high, was finished in 1965. Both buildings had the featureless and sterile appearance common to most contemporary office architecture.

A pleasant and spacious concourse, floored entirely in rubber, with a new entrance from Dowgate Hill, came into use on 25 October 1964. A new buffet and stationmaster's office were ready on 2 November 1965, and the left luggage and enquiry offices on 13 December.

In connection with a scheme for a dual carriageway road from Blackfriars to the Tower, the City Corporation proposed to widen Upper Thames Street, which passes beneath the station about one third of the distance between Cannon Street and the river. This entailed the removal of the existing 37 ft span bridge and its replacement by one of 77 ft span, with twin box girders for each line. The work was completed in June 1964, and was followed by the erection of umbrella type canopies over the exposed southern sections of the platforms. At the same time, the old side walls of the station were demolished as far as the southern abutments of the new bridge, to be replaced by metal and glass screens.

Fourteen years after the announcement of the rebuilding scheme, the work was still incomplete. Pending the widening of Cannon Street, and the consequent rebuilding of the Underground station, the two-storey structure planned to form the main entrance and booking hall remained on paper, and the modern ticket issuing facilities introduced in December 1965 were accommodated in a temporary wooden building which projected from the front of the office block into the untidy remnants of the 1866 forecourt. Today's railway engineers and architects must envy their nineteenth-century forebears, who could design a terminus to their own liking and requirements and then get on with it, not needing to wait for the permission and approval of others or for the commencement of non-railway works.

By the end of the 1960s there were 80,000 passengers daily compared with 26,000 in the 1860s, but all this activity was concentrated in a few hours at the mornings and evenings of the five weekdays. In 1967, 40,800 arrived daily, 38,300 between 7 and 10 am. There were 39,200 passengers leaving daily, 38,100 between

4 and 8 pm. At other times, although the trains were not infrequent, the place was dead.

## SIGNALLING AND ACCIDENTS

The first signal box was a fine-looking affair, mounted boldly on a 62 ft girder bridge, 11 ft 6 in wide, spanning all the tracks over the northernmost pier of the river bridge. As with the London Bridge and Charing Cross boxes built at the same time, signal posts sprouted from the roof, and at a distance this must have looked rather like the rigging of a sailing ship. There were eight arms on each of the outer posts, and four on the two inner ones. The cabin itself, 42 ft long and 9 ft wide, contained 30 point and 37 signal levers, the former black, the latter red for up, blue for down and yellow for distants. Two men worked the box on an eight-hour shift, accompanied by a telegraph clerk. All the equipment, including the striking interlocking, with its 32 locking slides and 1,000 locks, was supplied by Saxby & Farmer.

As the signalmen were not given any preliminary practice with the frame, great confusion existed on the opening day, so much so, that the general manager of the SER wanted the interlocking taken out. Fortunately this decision was delayed, and the men soon mastered their work.

When the widening of the bridge was finished, the station was resignalled, and two new boxes, fitted with Sykes's lock and block, were opened on 22 April 1893. No 1 box, 110 ft 6 in by 18 ft 6 in, spanned all the tracks over the second pier from the north bank, occupying almost the full width of the enlarged bridge. It had 244 levers, interlocked on Francis Brady's cam system, and arranged in one row, 100 ft long. Five men and two lads were required for most of the 24 hours. The other box, No 2, replaced the old Stoney Street junction cabin, in the neck of the junction. It was situated on south bank, on the west side of the line, 230 yards beyond No 1, and had 87 levers. This box, together with others in the Charing Cross—Cannon Street—London Bridge complex, was fitted with the rotary train describer instrument devised by C. V. Walker. This apparatus, the earliest example of a multiple aspect visual train describer, was later used elsewhere by the SER and by the SR. It consisted of a dial bearing such indications as: *Main Line Empties, Engine, Greenwich, Empties Maze Hill, Mid Kent, North Kent, Redhill, Tidal or Mail, Cancel last Signal, Blackheath, via Chislehurst, Dartford Loop*, all shown by an electrically-operated needle.

For the working of the suburban electric services and the new track layout in the approaches to Cannon Street and Charing Cross, the Southern Railway installed track-circuited four-aspect colour light signalling between Charing Cross, Cannon Street and Borough Market Junction, just west of London Bridge. This scheme, which included power-operated points at the termini, came into use on 27 June 1926. The Cannon Street approaches and platforms were worked from a 140-lever power box, 45 ft long and 12 ft wide, situated on the west side of the bridge between the end of platform 8 and the parapet. There were 46 running signals, 42 shunt signals, 41 point movements, 1 bolt, 1 slot and 9 spare.

After surviving the ordeals of wartime, this timber box was badly damaged by fire on 5 April 1957, probably as the result of an electrical fault. All trains were diverted from Cannon Street until the following day when a partial electric service was resumed under hand signals. The London Midland Region came to the rescue of the harassed Southern, offering a 227-lever power frame which it had in store against emergency. This was used to make up a 47-lever frame, installed in the remaining part of the old box on 5 May. Full electric service was restored on the following day. Platforms 7 and 8 remained out of use, and the opportunity was taken to get on with the lengthening work. Steam trains were either diverted to other termini, with fast electric connections from Cannon Street, or cut back to Chatham, with similar connections. A new permanent box, in brick and glass, was opened at the east side of the old Stoney Street junction on 16 December 1957. This had a Westinghouse 'C' type electrically-locked frame, also made up from the LMR apparatus. There were 124 working levers, and 43 spare levers reserved for possible future absorption of Borough Market Junction.

Only two serious accidents have occurred at Cannon Street. The first took place on 27 June 1914 when the driver of a down Hastings train missed his route indicator and misread the advance signals. In the resulting collision with an up Plumstead train a passenger with his head out of a window was killed. At 9.16 am on 20 March 1961, at the south end of the bridge, a 6-car up train from Addiscombe, carrying some 600 passengers overran the up home signals and sliced into the side of an empty 12-car diesel-electric multiple-unit train which was leaving the terminus for Grove Park depot. Several coaches of both trains were derailed, and the station was closed for the rest of the day. The driver and 10 passengers were slightly injured, and it was said that the tight packing of the suburban train protected the passengers from serious injuries. Following this accident, rail level repeaters of the inner home signals were installed.

(above) *Holborn Viaduct station and hotel in 1877. Building work is still not quite complete;* (below) *Holborn Viaduct approaches on 21 March 1959. The train at left, a Railtour special, is ascending from the City Widened Lines and the former Snow Hill station*

Page 190

(above) *Nine Elms, 1838;* (below) *Blackfriars* BR *(St Paul's* LCDR*) in February 1954. The 1865 viaduct to Ludgate Hill is seen at the right*

# CHAPTER 10

# Blackfriars, Ludgate Hill and Holborn Viaduct

## THREE-IN-ONE

As they were in a sense one, these three stations can be taken to-gether. They were all owned by the London Chatham & Dover Railway, which secured Parliamentary powers for a deep penetration into the City of London, managing, alone among the southern companies to join hands with the northern lines across the very centre of the metropolis. This great effort made, the LCDR sank into a parlous state, and was never able to afford the luxury of an adequate city terminus. Instead, it made do with three small stations, all nestling together along a quarter of a mile of track.

In 1859, the East Kent Railway, which was building a line from Strood to Dover, changed its name to the London Chatham & Dover. Assuming the role of competitor to the South Eastern Railway, it sought and obtained access to central London, first over other companies' lines, then constructing its own approaches to the central area, as described in more detail in Chapter 13. By its Metropolitan Extension Act of 1860, the Chatham was empowered to build from its existing approach at Beckenham through Dulwich and Herne Hill, and then westwards to Victoria and north-wards over the river to a junction with the Metropolitan Railway at Farringdon Street, in the City. Capital for these costly new lines was raised in an extravagant and reckless fashion, and after the financial panic of 1866, the company was landed in Chancery for five years. Left with a burden of debt, it continued for the rest of its existence in a poverty-stricken state.

The City extension, carried on a brick viaduct through inner South London, reached the south bank of the Thames in 1864. Here, on 1 June, the LCDR opened a station called Blackfriars. Situated on the east side of the southern approach to the new road bridge (then not yet completed), it was designed by the engineer Joseph Cubitt, and was of course a through station, although it

M

had to serve as a terminus for six months pending further progress northwards. There was delay in crossing the river because the City Corporation had dithered over the design of the Thames bridge (they managed to decide that it should have the same number of arches as the new road bridge, but couldn't make up their minds how many arches there should be).

This Blackfriars Bridge station was quite an impressive affair, with a long iron and glass overall roof and high walls which came right up to the edge of the river. On the eastern side was a range of offices and a goods shed, with a riverside wharf. There were only two public entrances, both off the inclined approach road to the City Corporation's bridge. Rows of narrow arched windows, decoration in light coloured bricks, and sheer bulk gave it a certain dignity which contrasted with the squalid surroundings of factories and warehouses.

Cubitt carried the four tracks across the river on a 933 ft lattice girder bridge. The piers of the five spans were in sets of three, each individual pier of stone, supporting a cluster of four iron columns. At each end of the bridge were large decorative features in cast-iron, displaying the arms and full title of the LCDR, the motto *Invicta*, and the royal initial surmounted by rose and crown. Stones from the old Westminster Bridge, demolished in 1861, were used in the abutments. From 21 December 1864 trains terminated in a temporary station at Little Earl Street on the north bank just south of Ludgate Hill. This was the first railway service to the City from south of the river.

A permanent station, Ludgate Hill, was opened in an unfinished state on 1 June 1865. This was on the east side of New Bridge Street, immediately south of Little Bridge Street (now Pilgrim Street). There was a street frontage alongside the viaduct, extending well above rail level to carry the all-over roof. This building was described in the *Illustrated London News* of 10 June 1865 as having 'no great pretensions to dignity of style, but it presents rather a lively appearance, with its turrets at each corner, and its decorations of parti-coloured brickwork above the arched doorways'. A small forecourt in New Bridge Street was accessible to cabs through entrances in Union Street and Little Bridge Street. Placed under the viaduct, the booking hall had a circular ticket office in the centre, one side allocated to suburban passengers, the other to main-line and Continental bookings. Twenty feet above, reached by narrow staircases, were two low and narrow wooden island platforms, the eastern for main-line trains, the other for suburban and local services. Additional staircases, only six feet wide, led from the northern ends of each platform into Little Bridge Street.

In the course of erection, the iron and glass roof had collapsed. Its place was taken by a timber truss roof supported by the high side walls and rough hewn wooden columns on the platforms. This roof spanned all four running lines, the station width being no greater because of the high cost of property in the City. The four tracks extended from Ludgate Hill to a point south of the 1864 Blackfriars station, but quadrupling took place on the west side between there and Loughborough Junction in 1866.

Blackfriars remained open as a passenger station until 30 September 1885 when the whole site was made over to freight both at rail and street levels. There was no space for wagon sorting, and Herne Hill sorting sidings (between Loughborough Junction and Herne Hill) were laid out to supplement Blackfriars. Until 1968 the western side of the 1864 station could still be seen, with the characteristic LCDR parti-coloured bricks much in evidence.

## ACROSS THE CITY

Seven months after the opening of Ludgate Hill, on 1 January 1866 the Metropolitan Extension was completed to its meeting with the Metropolitan Railway at West Street Junction, Farringdon, and Ludgate Hill also became a through station. This final link included a wicked 1 in 39 descent from the viaduct at the north end of Ludgate Hill.

By what G. A. Sekon described as 'the remarkably hypnotic influence of the late James Staats Forbes,[1] who appeared able to induce otherwise shrewd railway officers to support, by financial aid, his schemes for the extension of the LC & DR,' the LSWR had subscribed £310,000 and the GNR £320,000 towards the cost of the Metropolitan Extension in exchange for running powers. These two companies now exercised their rights.

On 1 March 1866 a connection was made between the LSWR at Clapham Junction (Ludgate Junction) and the LCDR at Wandsworth Road (Factory Junction), over which LSWR trains began to work between Kingston and Ludgate Hill on 3 April. This service was replaced on 1 January 1869 by one between Richmond and Ludgate Hill, running via a new line from Richmond to Kensington (Addison Road), and by another between Wimbledon and Ludgate Hill via the Tooting, Merton and Wimbledon line and a new spur opened on that day to connect Herne Hill and Tulse Hill. The LCDR also worked trains between Clapham Junction and the

City. An LCDR service between Herne Hill and Kings Cross had operated from the opening of the connection at Farringdon, and two days later, on 3 January 1866, GNR suburban trains began to run into Ludgate Hill. The north-south services were further developed by LCDR trains running between Herne Hill and Barnet from 1 August 1866 and by GNR trains working on the same route, and on to Hatfield, from the same day. On 1 March 1868, the GNR trains were altered to run Barnet—Victoria and Edgware—Ludgate Hill, the latter extended to Loughborough Junction from 1 June.

A third user was the Midland, running trains to Herne Hill via Ludgate Hill from 1 June 1869 to 30 June 1875, then from 1 July 1875 from South Tottenham or Hendon to Victoria. Reciprocal LCDR workings as far as Finchley Road started on 1 June 1869, extending to Hendon from 1 July 1875.

Finally, the cross-city connection saw GNR trains operating between GNR suburban stations and Woolwich Arsenal, SER, from 1 June 1878, using a new connection between the Metropolitan Extension and the Charing Cross Extension, near Union Street, Southwark. As by this time the rivalry between the SER and the LCDR amounted almost to a state of cold war, the latter refused to allow passengers for SER stations to board these trains at Ludgate Hill and Snow Hill, where stops were made for setting down only. This Woolwich service was worked by the SER from 1 August 1880, terminating on the northern side at Enfield or Muswell Hill (Alexandra Palace when open).

## STATUTORY WORKMEN'S SERVICE

Of the LCDR's own services from Ludgate Hill, the most important of the local workings was that to Victoria via the connection betwen Loughborough Junction and Brixton, opened on 1 May 1863 at the time of the construction of the approach lines to Victoria and Blackfriars. On this route special provision was made for workmen, as required in the Metropolitan Extension Act. When this legislation was before Parliament, it was realised that the approach lines would cut their way through a densely built-up part of South London, destroying hundreds of houses in their path. The newly-developed social consciences of the period were duly pricked, and to meet the opposition on this account, the company had graciously offered to operate a few trains at extremely low fares for the benefit of workmen forced to move further from their place of employment.

Parliament had made sure of this by making both service and fares statutory, the first of many such provisions in railway legislation. At first the procedure was a little fussy. The workmen 'both male and female' were required to give their names, addresses and occupations, and particulars of their employers before they were allowed to purchase a shilling weekly ticket. This was valid for six daily return journeys betwen Ludgate Hill and Victoria, or between any station on the route and one of these termini. Trains left each terminus at 4.55 am, returning at 6.15 pm (2.30 pm on Saturdays). As mentioned in earlier chapters, the vast majority of those displaced did not move any great distance from their old homes, and the immediate effect of urban railway construction was an increase in overcrowding.

On 1 September 1871, after completion of a curve to the east, some LCDR local services ran through to Moorgate Street. By agreement with the Metropolitan Railway, the LCDR was obliged to operate at least eighty trains a day over the new curve, or forfeit £30,000. There was little point in this as for many years the main business area was south of Moorgate Street station, and after stations had been opened at Snow Hill and Holborn Viaduct in 1874, it was usually quicker to walk from them than to stay in the train.

Other local services worked through Ludgate Hill were those to Crystal Palace High Level (after the opening of a curve at Loughborough Junction on 1 July 1872) and to Beckenham and Bromley via Penge. Main-line trains ran to Ramsgate and Dover via Chatham, and to Sevenoaks.

The concentration of all these services on the two island platforms at Ludgate Hill led to a good deal of congestion and inconvenience. Any enlargement of the station was ruled out by the high price of the surrounding property, not to mention the impoverished state of the railway company. The LCDR therefore investigated the cheaper alternative of constructing a small terminus in the new street called Holborn Viaduct. Some land here was already owned by the railway, and use could be made of the space over the lines down to Farringdon. In 1870, when the LCDR telegraphs were sold to the Post Office for £100,000, it was decided to go ahead with this scheme. A puppet, the Holborn Viaduct Station Company, was discreetly created to raise the balance of the capital required.

### A MINI-TERMINUS

This new station, reached by a 264 yard spur off the viaduct, was primarily intended for main-line trains. It was a very modest affair consisting only of four short platforms (six faces), each capable of taking half a train length, the idea being that all mainline trains would have a City and a West End portion, to be split or combined at Herne Hill. The 400 ft platforms were numbered 1 to 6 from east to west, and were sheltered by iron, glass and wood ridge roofs in three sections, abutting against the frontage block at the north end, and extended at the south by individual platform canopies. A carriage roadway entered the station at the west side and ran for a very short distance alongside platform 6, against the west wall.

This mini-terminus was opened on 2 March 1874. As well as the main-line trains, including the City portion of the Dover boat trains, services were worked from it to Maidstone and Ashford when the LCDR reached those towns in 1874 and 1884. Boat trains for the Flushing service began on 26 July 1875, working first to and from Sheerness, and then, from 15 May 1876, to and from Queenborough Pier. Some local trains were also dealt with at Holborn, but most continued to use the line down to Moorgate, on which two low level platforms were opened on 1 August 1874. This subterranean station was first called Snow Hill, but was renamed Holborn Viaduct (Low Level) from 1 May 1912. To the north of it were four sidings connected at the far end by a fan table and used for turnover purposes. From the street, the platforms were reached through a small entrance on the north side of the Viaduct, another in Snow Hill and a third from the main concourse.

An hotel designed by Lewis H. Isaacs was constructed along the front of the main terminus and opened on 17 November 1877. It was let to Spiers & Pond, the LCDR caterers, for 6 per cent of its capital cost and 10 per cent of its profits. After early activities in Australia, this firm had begun their long career as railway caterers with a buffet at Farringdon Street station, opened in 1863. Their association with the LCDR started soon afterwards and lasted until 1905, when they were ousted by Lyons. In 1888 they became the official caterers to the LSWR, and in 1899, to the SER. From January 1924 until December 1930 they acted as caterers to the Southern Railway. Their stores and headquarters were in the arches of the LCDR viaduct immediately south of Ludgate Hill station, with a frontage to Blackfriars Lane, still to be seen today. During the first world war, the Holborn Viaduct Hotel was requisitioned for government purposes and afterwards became the main office of Henley's Wireless Telegraph Works Co Ltd. It was destroyed by German bombs in 1941.

## ST PAUL'S FOR ST PETERSBURG

The final development of the LCDR's cluster of City stations came in the 1880s, when the approach tracks on the south bank of the Thames were widened, and another bridge constructed alongside and to the east of that of 1864. This carried seven tracks and had five arched spans, from south to north, 183 ft, 175 ft, 185 ft, 175 ft and 185 ft. At the northern end, it fanned out to a width of 123 ft to carry the platforms of a terminus fronting the south side of Queen Victoria Street. Opened on 10 May 1886, it was known as St Paul's until 1 February 1937, when the Southern Railway renamed it Blackfriars. (This renaming followed London Transport's decision to change the name of a Central Line tube station from Post Office to St Paul's. The new name of the SR station was not only more accurate but identical to that of the adjacent District Line station.)

St Paul's was another small terminus, and rather mean, but the best the poor Chatham could afford. In pink-red brick, it huddled apologetically against the viaduct, trying hard to look dignified by displaying stumpy towers at each corner, seeking to impress by showing, in incised letters on the stones around the street doors, the names of fifty-four towns and cities which could somehow be reached from its platforms. This catalogue was a curious mixture of the romantic and the mundane, ranging from St Petersburg and Vienna to Westgate-on-Sea and Crystal Palace.[2]

The frontage building straddled the District Railway and the situation made a forecourt and cab access to the platforms a physical impossibility. Fronting the street was a fairly spacious booking hall with a wooden ticket office. From this a wide staircase led up to an intermediate floor where there was a small buffet (against the east wall) and the ticket barriers and stairs to the platform. At rail level were three terminal roads, one against the east wall, with a platform face on the west, the other two with a platform face either side. On the west, a pair of tracks was looped through the station from the original main lines, with a platform face on each track. The four tar-coated wooden platforms were covered at the inner end by a short all-over ridge roof of iron and glass, just adequate to disperse the smoke from the engines of terminating trains. At the outer end, the roofing was extended at a lower level in the form of linked canopies. The terminal roads had hydraulic buffers of an early pattern, which the patentees claimed would stop a 200 ton train at 6 mph 'without inconvenience', whilst at 12 mph 'no harm would happen to the buffers . . .'

Alone among the LCDR's City stations, St Paul's had direct access to the Underground. The District Railway had reached Blackfriars from Westminster Bridge on 30 May 1870 and by this time the Inner Circle was complete. Stairways and passages were opened on 13 November 1886 to connect the District platforms with the intermediate floor at St Paul's.

Most of the main-line trains to and from Holborn Viaduct called at St Paul's, as did all the local trains, except those between Moorgate and Victoria. It was also the terminus for the City portions of the trains using the new Gravesend branch opened on the same day, and for the Greenwich Park service, when that branch was completed on 1 October 1888.

The LSWR trains from Richmond and Wimbledon continued to terminate at Ludgate Hill, working forward to Snow Hill sidings to reverse, and causing a good deal of congestion in the process. Trains routed through St Paul's were obliged to use the main-line platforms at Ludgate Hill, but those using the original lines to and from Snow Hill and Holborn Viaduct could be directed through either the main or the local platforms.

Many passengers continued to use Ludgate Hill, either from habit, or because it was more convenient for their final destination. A very generous and varied train service was still offered, in spite of the opening of the other two stations. In the mornings and evenings the narrow platforms were dangerously overcrowded and the evening congestion was so bad that returning workmen had been made to use Holborn Viaduct since 1875. At most times of the year, a wait on the Ludgate Hill platforms was a distinctly uncomfortable experience, as the all-over roof turned the place into a very effective wind tunnel. Public dissatisfaction with this somewhat primitive station had grown steadily over the years—even the LCDR admitted that it was unsatisfactory.

In April 1903, the chairman of the City Corporation Streets Committee, one Alpheus Cleophas Morton, told the Royal Commission on London Traffic that the Corporation considered Ludgate Hill Station inadequate, inconvenient, and positively dangerous to the large number of people using it, and in 1898 had complained about it to the Board of Trade. The City authorities had also met the railway company, who did not seem either able or willing to enlarge it, although 'they found the money to build the great useless station called Holborn Viaduct'.

Among the many who moaned about Ludgate Hill were the

Fleet Street journalists, for whom it was the nearest station. It is an interesting thought that the anti-railway complex that has long been prevalent among London newspapermen may have its roots in the inadequate railway and Underground facilities of the Fleet Street area. For many years those working on morning papers sought a late train back to the suburbs; their wishes were finally granted in 1910 when they were given a 1.15 am departure from Ludgate Hill, calling at most stations to Beckenham Junction. The *Railway Magazine* recorded (could it have been true?) 'Journalists who live in the outer suburbs on the south side of London are showing their gratitude'.

This late train was eventually supplemented by others providing service through the small hours to Orpington via Catford and via Herne Hill, and to Wimbledon (also to Sutton after the opening of the Wimbledon & Sutton line in 1930). These facilities were also used by market and post office men, but patronage fell off sharply in the 1950s as more night workers bought their own cars. In 1963 the four trains between Holborn Viaduct and Orpington between 1.30 and 3.15 am, and the connecting service from Herne Hill to Sutton were carrying an average of twenty or so passengers each; BR discontinued them as an economy measure from 17 June and a replacement coach service was soon abandoned.

## CAPITAL SPENT IN VAIN

Finally bowing to the criticisms of Ludgate Hill station, the railway company set about a minor reconstruction, which lasted from 1907 until 1912. The main-line island platform, which had become superfluous since the opening of Holborn Viaduct and St Paul's, was taken out, and the resulting space used to slew over the two main lines and the down local line. In turn this made room for a more commodious island platform on the local side, 440 ft long and, at 32 ft maximum, almost twice as wide as its predecessor. This made it possible to broaden the notorious staircases. As some of the roof supports were on the old main-line platform, it was necessary to remove the roof. When this was done, the height of the side walls was reduced, and an umbrella canopy, supported on central columns, was erected on the new platform. The bridges over the booking hall and over Union Street were renewed with steel girders. Tracks in the station area were rearranged so that trains to and from Holborn Viaduct could use the new platform or the main lines; up trains for Snow Hill or beyond could pass through on the main or local lines, but in the

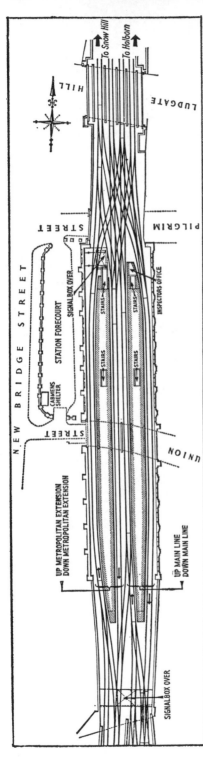

*Ludgate Hill station layout in the 1890s, showing the suburban and main line platforms. From the Railway Magazine, December 1964*

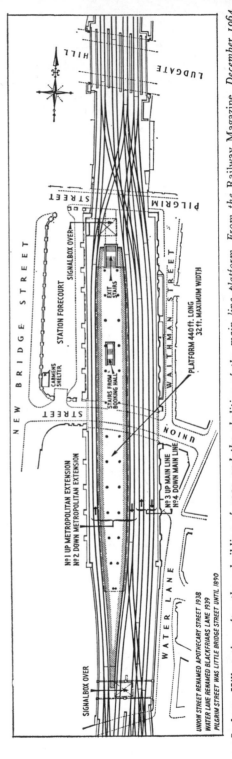

*Ludgate Hill station after the rebuilding of 1910 and the abolition of the main line platform. From the Railway Magazine, December 1964*

UNION STREET RENAMED APOTHECARY STREET 1938
WATER LANE RENAMED BLACKFRIARS LANE 1939
PILGRIM STREET WAS LITTLE BRIDGE STREET UNTIL 1890

opposite direction, they had to use the platform road and cross to the down main south of the station.

As was so often the case with railway works in the early years of the present century, valuable capital had been spent in vain. Traffic trends were already changing. After 1901, the electric tramcar, underground train and motor bus quickly sucked away the cross-city and inner area business, and one by one, the services through Ludgate Hill succumbed. Those to and from the GNR ceased in 1907, the Midland ones in the following year, even as the work on the new station was proceeding. After that, passengers for Farringdon and points west and north had to use the SECR services, changing at Aldersgate. The death blows came with the war, when special demands were made upon the capacity of the north-south link. From 3 April 1916, SECR trains were withdrawn from Moorgate and Aldersgate, a few still going through to Holborn Viaduct Low Level until that station closed on 1 June. Stripped of its regular passenger trains, the Ludgate Hill—Widened Lines connection had a little more room for the constant procession of freight trains that were bringing coal, munitions and military stores south. To facilitate the working of this vital traffic, some signalling improvements had been carried out at the Low Level station during 1915.

## ELECTRIFICATION

The LSWR services from Richmond and Wimbledon to Ludgate Hill also disappeared in 1916, as did the once busy LCDR service to and from Victoria. The lines north of St Paul's were thus left to the trains starting or terminating at Holborn Viaduct, the freight traffic and a few special workings. As almost all the Holborn Viaduct trains called at the through platforms in St Paul's, Ludgate Hill became superfluous, and was opened only in weekday rush hours from 1919. A few trains terminated and started from there and from 27 August 1923, the Wimbledon service was restored in rush hours only (four morning arrivals and three evening departures). After the electrification of the Holborn Viaduct local services in 1925, these seven trains were the only ones to use Ludgate Hill. When the Wimbledon service was also electrified, from 3 March 1929, the doors of Ludgate Hill were closed to passengers for the last time after close of traffic the previous day. It is doubtful if there was any thought of keeping it open any longer, but even if there had been, there was a considerable deterrent, for its platform was 80 ft too short for an 8-car electric train.

Four years before closure, the City Corporation had widened
New Bridge Street. Shops and offices were then erected in the
station forecourt, obscuring the 1865 frontage. An entrance to the
station was left in the centre of this new building, and this continued in use as access to Spiers & Pond's station restaurant, which
had existed in one of the railway arches since 1 January 1866, and
remained open until 1938.

Third-rail electric services from Holborn Viaduct and St Paul's
were inaugurated by the Southern Railway on 12 July 1925. The
basic workings were St Paul's to Crystal Palace High Level, St
Paul's to Shortlands via Catford Loop, and Holborn Viaduct to
Shortlands and Orpington via Herne Hill. At Holborn Viaduct
space restrictions were such that only platforms 4 and 5 could be
lengthened sufficiently to take 8-car electric trains. Tracks at
St Paul's were rearranged to allow Holborn Viaduct trains from
the local lines to run through the loop platforms parallel to trains
entering the terminal platforms at St Paul's from the main line.
These latter platforms were altered so that the middle road had a
face on its eastern side, and the western road a face on its western
side. All platforms were extended to take 8-car trains, providing waiting passengers with some fascinating riverscapes
downstream.

In 1934 the section from Bickley to St Mary Cray was electrified, and the Shortlands service was extended to that station from
1 May. This was only a temporary arrangement, and on 6 January
1935, an electric service was begun between Holborn Viaduct and
Sevenoaks via Swanley and Otford. Nine months later, an entirely
new facility was offered in the peak hours following the electrification of the 1929 connections between the LCDR Greenwich Park
branch (which had been closed from 1 January 1917) and the
former SER lines at Lewisham; these connections had the object of
enabling freight trains to and from the northern lines to avoid the
congested tracks through London Bridge. Now they served a similar purpose for passenger services, carrying, from 30 September
1935, peak-hour electric trains between Dartford and St Paul's via
Sidcup and via Bexleyheath.

A final electrification of the Holborn Viaduct services took place
on 2 July 1939 when the peak-hour trains to and from Gillingham
were changed over from steam. It was necessary to extend another
platform for these trains, and after much head scratching, what
was formerly thought impossible was achieved. By widening the
bridge over Sea Coal Lane, it was found feasible to extend platform 1 to 520 ft. But these platform extensions imposed severe

restrictions on the working of the station: platforms 2 and 3 were blocked if there were an 8-car train in 1 or 4; the electrics had to be coaxed right up to the buffers to keep the outer ends of the platforms clear; and the only parallel working possible with electric trains was a departure from 1 or 4 whilst a train arrived at 5.

No damage of any consequence was inflicted at any of the City stations in the first world war, which was just as well, in view of the great reliance placed on the cross-city connection for the movement of military traffic and coal diverted from the coastal shipping services. In the second world war, German bombs found the Metropolitan extension, and wrought a great deal of havoc. At Holborn Viaduct the old hotel building was hit on 26 October 1940 and then completely gutted by fire on the night of 10/11 May 1941. Such was the damage that no trains could use the station until 1 June. When it reopened, a temporary ticket office was provided in the passage leading from Old Bailey, in a part of the buildings which escaped damage, and this remained in use until 1963 when the new buildings were ready. On the night of 16/17 April 1941 a grievous blow was suffered when the important Blackfriars signal box on the south bank was completely destroyed, together with much of the railway bridge over Southwark Street. With military assistance a temporary bridge carrying two tracks was completed on 29 September, and a permanent structure came into use on 9 October 1942. Makeshift signalling arrangements remained in force until after the war, and the terminal roads at Blackfriars station were locked out of use.

The Dartford rush-hour services via Lewisham, withdrawn from 16 October 1939, were restored on 12 August 1946 with the opening of a new signal box at Blackfriars and the reinstatement of the terminal roads. On that day the platforms at Blackfriars were renumbered 1 to 5 from east to west (formerly only 1 and 2, between the eastern 'bay siding' and the up and down loops had borne numbers). Outside the peak hours, the terminal roads were used for berthing empty rush-hour trains, and in connection with the Eastern Section 10-car train scheme, alterations were made to allow these roads to accommodate 10-car trains, which were worked empty to and from Cannon Street and Charing Cross via the connecting curve from Metropolitan Junction. Additional siding accommodation for these empty rush-hour trains of the Cannon Street and Charing Cross lines was provided in 1967 on the down side of the former Blackfriars goods depot.

### VANISHED STEAM AGE CHARM

Until the end of the 1950s, Holborn Viaduct retained much of its Victorian atmosphere, despite the wounds of war. Its old-fashioned buffet, with long high counter, was one of the last of its kind on any London station, and the calm, unhurried air of the concourse and platforms, even at the height of the rush hour, was very relaxing. To the initiated, a sly push on an unlocked door on the concourse offered a special treat. Descending dark steps, one would arrive in the smoky cavern that was once Snow Hill. Here the ghosts of the nineteenth century still lingered. Daylight somehow penetrated through the ever-present smoke and the deep shadows cast by the high buildings all around, feebly illuminating the station walls, on which soot became encrusted to a depth of almost two inches a year. Here, as late as 1958, one could still see the elegant long-armed signals of the LCDR. Occasionally a J50 tank or an LMSR 'Jinty' would thrust through the gloom, trundling the trucks and vans of a transfer freight. Should it be going south, the train would be banked by a GNR 0–6–2T, and the resultant duet would echo from the narrow confines. The scene could also be glimpsed by peering over walls in Holborn Viaduct and in Snow Hill, but now the hole has been built over and this unique view of London's only cross-city main-line link is no more.

Also now gone is the steam-age charm of Holborn Viaduct station, where British Railways carried out a reconstruction similar to that at Cannon Street. The ugly ruins of the old frontage were removed, and in their place rose a ten-storey office block. Completed in 1963, this building had a 250 ft frontage, and included station facilities and railway offices on the ground and on part of the first floor.

Through the plate-glass doors of a handsome entrance under scoop arches, the trains could be seen from the street. Beyond these doors was a pleasant low-ceilinged concourse area beneath the office block, opened on 9 September 1963. In the centre was a bookstall, on the east side a booking office, and on the west, a combined buffet and waiting room which advertised itself through large windows on to the street. The concourse opened out to a narrow cross-platform overlooked by a balcony serving the staff offices on the first floor of the frontage block. In the spring of 1967 the old train sheds were taken down and replaced with umbrella canopies over platforms 1, 4 and 5. Later the platforms were pushed back into the concourse and equipped with new barriers.

After temporary suspensions in both world wars, the Crystal Palace High Level service was discontinued for good in 1954. Mainline trains from Holborn Viaduct were severely cut in the first world war, and in 1922 there were only eight departures, including the two Kent coast residential trains. The latter were transferred to Cannon Street from 12 July 1925. Thirteen years later, there were but three steam-hauled passenger departures, all in the peak hour, to Chatham and Gillingham, and these were electrified in 1939. There were also one or two early morning trains, primarily for newspapers and parcels, but tolerating passengers, and these continued to run until the Kent Coast electrification of 1959. By that time, Holborn Viaduct was left with but two basic services: to Sevenoaks via Catford and Swanley (connections to Ramsgate, Dover, Ashford, Sheerness and Maidstone), and to Wimbledon, Sutton and West Croydon via Tulse Hill with a connection to Orpington at Herne Hill. At peak hours these were supplemented by trains to Orpington and St Mary Cray via Herne Hill, and to Dartford via Bexleyheath and via Sidcup, plus a small number of semi-fast trains to Gillingham.

After 10 July 1967, the three effective platforms handled twenty-two trains in the busiest hour between 8 and 9 am, an increase of five on the previous service. In 1967 some 30,000 passengers passed through daily, almost all of them in peak hours. Week-end traffic declined so much that after 14 June 1964 the station was closed between 2 pm Saturday and midnight on Sunday. Until June 1965, when it was transferred to other SR termini, parcels, mail and newspaper traffic was quite heavy, and the non-electrified platforms usually stocked a few vans.

In 1968, Blackfriars, with its gloomy, dusty passages and wooden platforms still had a trace of the Victorian aura. True the old buffet, with its frosted glass windows, had been replaced by more commodious premises at street level, but the hydraulic buffers, engineering wonders of 1886, could still be seen, and the walk up to the platforms, with its unexpected glimpse of the District through a dirty window, took one back fifty years, given a little imagination. Apart from a few trains to Sevenoaks, Wimbledon and West Croydon, and Dartford in the peak hours, Blackfriars was largely a through station with the same service as Holborn Viaduct, though of course it became a terminus again when the latter was closed at week-ends. By 1968 very little traffic passed over the 1864 bridge outside the station. In 1961 the engineers decided that this bridge should have its load eased by removing the two outer tracks to eliminate the possibility of four trains crossing at the same time. As the cross-London freight services had been much reduced, this did not cause any serious operating difficulties. Subsequent changes and the rebuilding of Blackfriars are dealt with in chapter 16.

The fate of the Metropolitan Extension north of the river is uncertain. The County of London Plan of 1944 proposed that it be placed in tunnel, but desirable as this might be on aesthetic grounds, such an operation would be fabulously expensive and is unlikely to be undertaken. From time to time consideration is given to the possibility of providing main-line electrified links across the centre of London, and in any such scheme, these lines would play an important part.

SIGNALLING AND ACCIDENTS

There were originally seven boxes on the inner part of the City extension, all equipped with Sykes's lock and block: Holborn Viaduct Low Level, Holborn Viaduct, Ludgate North, Ludgate South, St Paul's Yard, St Paul's Junction, and Blackfriars Junction. Holborn Viaduct was a 62-lever cabin straddling the ramp down to the Metropolitan lines. Ludgate North was over the up local line at the north end of Ludgate Hill platforms and controlled inter alia, a gantry on the bridge over Ludgate Hill which did much to enliven the view of St Paul's Cathedral from Fleet Street. Ludgate South was sited over the main lines at the south end of Ludgate Hill station.

Soon after the first electrification, on 21 March 1926, the Southern Railway resignalled the section between Holborn Viaduct and Elephant & Castle, using four-aspect colour lights for the first time. Siemens-General Electric equipment was employed, and the seven manual boxes were replaced by two power frames. At Holborn Viaduct an 86-lever frame was installed in the old manual cabin, but at Blackfriars Junction, near Southwark Street, the overhead box was dismantled and a new box built on the up side. This contained a 120-lever power frame to control the approaches and platforms at St Paul's.

As related earlier, this cabin was completely destroyed by enemy action in April 1941. Its place was taken by a red-brick hut with a power frame controlling only the main signals, which gave indications restricted to caution and danger. A new permanent box, which allowed restoration of all the original signals and connections, came into use on 11 August 1946. This was situated on the west side of the line, just south of the original south bank Black-

(above) *The Old Waterloo, c 1900, looking across the concourse of the Windsor and North stations, platforms 6-10;* (below) *Waterloo concourse, from the cinema, showing late Summer Bank Holiday traffic 1968*

Page 208

*Summer holiday main line departure, Waterloo about 1922*

friars station. Subsequent signalling changes are described in chapter 16.

A curious accident occurred at Ludgate Hill in 1870. When the Hawthorn 0–6–0 locomotive *Ajax* began to give trouble, the engine crew left the footplate in some panic. With regulator open, the little engine rolled briskly down the 1 in 39 to Farringdon, on through Kings Cross (Metropolitan). Finding her way on to the Midland, she finally came to rest in Haverstock Hill tunnel, no doubt much to the relief of the signalmen clearing the road before her.

# CHAPTER II

# Waterloo

## PRIDE OF PLACE FOR HALF A CENTURY

For almost fifty years, until the reconstruction of Euston, Waterloo held pride of place as the most modern of the termini, the only one built in the twentieth century. Today its extrovert architecture is out of fashion, but many find its warm red bricks and Portland stone kinder to the eye than the harsh concrete of the new Euston, less drab than the grey and yellow stocks of other termini. This is a well-liked station, with a spacious, almost opulent air, commodious and convenient for both passenger and operator.

Curving along the heads of twenty-one platforms, the wide concourse is always animated by a wonderfully assorted selection of travellers. Well-padded widows for Bournemouth avoid sun-tanned soldiers from Aldershot; Pompey-bound sailors mix with the luggage-cluttered cruise passengers that form most of today's boat train traffic; peachy schoolgirls, up for the hols from exclusive establishments deep in Hants, cast sulky glances at red-coated Chelsea pensioners taking wreaths to a comrade's funeral. As the rush hours fade, senior civil servants stride across, black briefcases full of last night's drafting; but the City men avoid the concourse, and are glimpsed only briefly in their impatient transfer from train to 'Drain'. In the night hours, Waterloo gives precarious shelter to London's roofless, who obstinately prefer its draughts and persistent policemen to the free bed which awaits them at the Camberwell Centre. A survey carried out by the National Assistance Board in December 1965 found 247 men and 28 women sleeping out in London, more than half of them in the large railway stations; Waterloo, with 63 on the concourse, was the most favoured refuge.

No more on winter Saturdays do little wooden booking booths appear, surrounded by rugger watchers bound for Twickers; at other times, the same booths dispensed tickets to punters and card sharpers making for Surrey race courses. Through it all, porters and postmen had innocent pleasure from harassing passengers with tractor and truck. (The postmen had some connection with a mysterious beast which lurks at the York Road end of the concourse, its lair marked prominently DO NOT FEED and DANGER KEEP AWAY.)

To enter the concourse after crossing the windy wastes of the South Bank is to experience a dramatic change of scale, to feel human once again. Here, set between the arid office blocks of York Road and the cockney life of Lower Marsh, is an oasis of civilisation, whose continuous interest and activity has been superbly photographed and recorded in the prize-winning British Transport Film Unit documentary, *Terminus*.

Waterloo was preceded by Nine Elms, the metropolitan station of the London & Southampton Railway, first promoted in 1831. A four acre site in Nine Elms Lane, just south of Vauxhall Bridge, was chosen because it could be reached with virtually no disturbance of property and because of its proximity to a convenient berth for the lighters and steamboats that were to link the railway with the City. Seemingly remote, the situation was in fact no further from the centre of London than Euston and a mile nearer than Paddington.

Nine Elms was opened to the public on 21 May 1838 with the first 23 miles of the Southampton Railway, as far as Woking Common. Not until 11 May 1840, almost a year after assuming the grander title of the London & South Western, did the company reach Southampton. On that day, just after 8 am, a party of directors and guests arrived at the beflagged terminus preceded by bands of music. Three hours later, the special train, headed by the locomotive *Venus*, reached Southampton, to be greeted by a salute of 21 guns.

Designed in simple classical style by William Tite,[1] the two-storey building at Nine Elms consisted of a central porch of five arches set between rusticated end blocks. Behind the porch were booking office and waiting room, the former with an open counter over which passengers were issued with paper tickets. (Edmundson card tickets, with the necessary arrangements for one person to appear before the clerk at a time, were introduced in 1846-7.) Beyond the booking office, a cross-platform connected the arrival

stage on the west side with the departure stage on the east. Doorways from the arrival platform opened on to a vehicle yard alongside the station. Over the platforms and the two empty carriage
roads between them was a low wooden roof in three spans, supported on cast-iron columns with ornamental stiffeners. The platforms, only 15 inches above the ground, were completely within
the 290 ft by 74 ft 9 in train shed.

A single track was carried over Nine Elms Lane on the level into
a $\frac{3}{4}$-acre goods yard by the river bank. Wagons were moved into
this yard by horses, and the freight was lifted on and off the
Thames lighters by a crane. Passenger steamboats hired by the
railway company ran between this wharf and the City, leaving
Old Swan Pier, Upper Thames Street, an hour before the departure
of each train, and calling at intermediate piers. Buses worked between the station and various points in the City and West End.
Pack horses were kept so that anyone wishing to take his private
carriage on the train could have it driven home or fetched, the
charge for this service being half a guinea, including driver.

At first there were five trains each way daily, their departure
signalled five minutes before by a bell on the roof of the station.
Life was tranquil enough for the first eight days after the opening, but the ninth day was one the staff were to remember for the
rest of their lives. As 30 May was Derby Day at Epsom racecourse,
the L & SR had advertised eight special trains from Nine Elms to
its station on the Kingston to Epsom road. For one guinea, passengers would be provided with a coach from the station to the
course; the other excursionists, unless they were very fortunate,
would have a walk of six miles to the racecourse after their $10\frac{1}{4}$-
mile rail journey. This last information was not included in the
advertisement. Much to everyone's surprise, a crowd of several
thousands arrived on the appointed day, virtually besieging the
little terminus. As many as possible were despatched, but there
were far more than could be carried, and soon the doors were shut.
The more aggressive members of the crowd then pressed forward
and soon had the doors off their hinges. In swept the angry
throng, through the booking office, on to the platform, and into the
guinea train, which was waiting to leave. A messenger was despatched to the Metropolitan Police, who arrived in due course and
succeeded in clearing the station. About noon calm reigned again,
as a notice went up announcing that no more trains would leave
that day. Not discouraged by this experience, the company advertised a few weeks later that special trains would run to Woking
station for the Ascot Races. This time all went well.

## OVER THE ARCHES TO WATERLOO

Short-distance traffic soon become a feature of the line's business. The original section had stations at Wandsworth (west of the present Clapham Junction), Wimbledon, Kingston (east of the present Surbiton), Ditton Marsh (now Esher), Walton, and Weybridge. A branch, opened from what is now Clapham Junction to Richmond on 27 July 1846, serving Wandsworth, Barnes and Mortlake, quickly provided almost a quarter of the total number of passengers carried in and out of London. Despite its steamboat and omnibus connections, Nine Elms was hardly a convenient station for this local traffic, and the company was well aware of its deficiencies. In 1846, Joseph Locke, its engineer, admitted in evidence to the Metropolitan Termini Commission that its isolated situation discouraged business traffic, pointing out that road coaches were still running between Chertsey and the City even though the railway covered the distance more quickly.

Conscious that passenger traffic was of growing importance, and likely to form a substantial part of its revenue, the LSWR began to make plans for a better terminus. Another stimulant had been the proposal of the initially independent Richmond company to construct a line from near Nine Elms to a 'West End' terminus adjacent to Hungerford and Waterloo bridges. In 1844 the LSWR agreed to work the Richmond line and took over its 'West End' project, obtaining powers in 1845 for an extension to a terminus on a site in York Road, near the south end of Waterloo Bridge, with a supplementary Act in 1847 for two more approach lines and more land at the terminus.

Leaving the original line at Nine Elms junction, a short distance south-west of the L & SR station, the extension crossed an already built-up area, breaking down some 700 houses in its path. To minimise property disturbance, most of its $1\frac{3}{4}$ miles were on a brick viaduct with well over 200 arches, snaking about to avoid a gasworks, Lambeth Palace and the Vauxhall Gardens, and crossing 21 roads on brick arch and cast-iron bridges. The largest bridge, over Westminster Bridge Road, with a skew span of 90 ft, worried the Board of Trade Inspector, who delayed the opening of the line whilst some deflection tests were carried out. There was one intermediate station, at Vauxhall.

At the annual meeting of 1848, W. J. Chaplin, the LSWR chairman, explained why four tracks had been provided :

. ; . in order that we may have no trouble or inconvenience in future in the traffic; and also that, whatever may be the adventurous schemes of the age in future, whatever may be the probability of introducing lines south of London, we may not only have ample means of conducting our traffic, be it what it may, but of ability to let others come and hire, that we may benefit by their enterprise and industry on our property.

'Others' who may have come included the LBSCR. Between 1844 and 1846, the London & Brighton Railway had considered, with the LSWR, the possibility of running into the proposed Waterloo station, via a new line between Croydon and Wandsworth, which would make some use of the course of the old Surrey Iron Railway, but this had come to nothing. An Act sanctioning a line between Croydon and Wandsworth, to enable the Brighton to reach Waterloo, was passed in 1846. In that year the Brighton and the Croydon companies combined to form the London Brighton & South Coast Railway; the Croydon, under W. A. Wilkinson, regarded the Wandsworth connection as a threat to its traffic and when, after the amalgamation, relations between the LBSCR and the LSWR became soured over other matters (thanks to the Croydon), the scheme was dropped. Again in 1853-5, the LBSCR had a chance to get to Waterloo over the projected West End of London & Crystal Palace Railway as recounted in Chapter 13.

In view of the later inadequacies of the LSWR terminus, it is perhaps as well that the Brighton went to Victoria instead. The SER also thought of using Waterloo, and in 1846 had a scheme for an extension towards it from Bricklayers Arms, a Bill that failed to pass through Parliament. In practice, the additional pair of tracks were used from the opening day by the trains of the Richmond line. That railway was extended to Windsor on 1 December 1849, and before long the westernmost pair of tracks acquired the label *Windsor Lines*, which they retain to this day. A third (up) line was provided betwen Nine Elms and Falcon Bridge (Clapham Junction) in August 1848; a fourth (down), in August 1860.

The new terminus, built on arches about 20 ft above street level, occupied an area corresponding approximately to the present platforms 7 to 12. About ten acres of land was taken, not all of it used at first, in an area which had been let out on a building lease in the 1820s, the site of the station containing parts of eight streets, miscellaneous haystalls, cowyards, dungheaps, and a large pond.

As the LSWR had obtained an Act in 1846 for a further extension, to London Bridge, Waterloo was laid out as a through station, with vehicle ramps either side. An iron and glass roof in two

140 ft spans sheltered six tracks and four 300 ft platforms (two arrival, two departure, six faces in all). Soon after the opening, the length of these platforms was doubled. On the west of the site, a spur pointed towards the river and future hopes in that direction.

Waterloo* was opened to the public on 11 July 1848, Nine Elms closing for regular passenger trains after traffic the previous day. The old terminus came back into use temporarily on 13 April 1856, when Tite's timber-built Vauxhall station was destroyed by fire and some up trains were diverted. Apart from this, Nine Elms, like Bricklayers Arms, was convenient for handling royalty and other notabilities. The first royal user of Nine Elms was Queen Adelaide, widow of William IV, who made a return journey to Southampton in June, 1842. Garibaldi arrived from Southampton in 1864, and the station was regularly used by Queen Victoria, whose royal saloons were kept there in readiness. For her convenience, some alterations, including the installation of a movable platform, were made in 1849-50. The Queen found that Nine Elms offered her the privacy of which she was so fond, as well as easy access to and from Buckingham Palace, and when the company wished to use the old station as a carriage shop, they made a new private station for her in Wandsworth Road, south of the main lines. Finished in 1854, this had one covered platform, and survived until the track rearrangements of 1877-78. Edward VII and his successors were content to use Waterloo.

Although Robert Stephenson told the Royal Commission in 1846 that 'there is no point on the south side of the Thames so good for a large railway station, or a combined station, as the south end of Waterloo Bridge', the LSWR was not content with this alone and, as already mentioned, had obtained powers in that year to go on to serve the City. Chaplin explained to the Commission that goods traffic could not be handled at Waterloo, as the way to the water was blocked by Goding's Lion Brewery;[2] a City extension was needed to obtain a better site for a goods station as well as to accommodate the many passengers who wished to go there. The 1846 Act, and another in 1848, provided for a terminus just south west of London Bridge. A considerable amount of property was purchased before the scheme was killed by the financial crisis of 1848-9. The South Western's access to the City was eventually realised only in partial and unsatisfactory forms, firstly by running powers over the LCDR (see Chapter 10), then by an almost useless connection with the SER extension to Charing Cross, and finally, by the construction of a tube railway.

Until 1853, probably owing to the uncertainty about the City

* The station was known as 'Waterloo Bridge' until October 1882.

extension, there were no really adequate buildings at Waterloo. In that year, a block was erected along the east side of what was then platform 1 (on the extreme east side of the station). This had a cab yard outside, served by an incline from York Street (now Leake Street), and an exit into Waterloo Road. Additional timber roofing, which was to survive until the early years of the present century, was put up at the same time. On the west side of the station, a carriage loading dock was built, with turnplates providing access to all tracks in the station. Beyond this, near York Road, was an engine shed, sidings and a turntable on the river-pointing spur already mentioned.

## A ONE-WAY TRAFFIC

A strange one-way traffic started in 1854, when the London Necropolis & National Mausoleum Company[3] opened a cemetery at Brookwood together with a private Necropolis station at Waterloo. The latter had two short sidings and a small building with a single platform; it was situated on the east side of the approach tracks just north of Westminster Bridge Road. A stairway connected the station with the company's office in York Street, opposite All Saints' Church. Funeral trains were operated daily, using specially-built hearse carriages.

Through the remaining years of the nineteenth century, Waterloo was extended piecemeal, in an even more haphazard fashion than Euston. The first additional platforms, opened on 3 August 1860, were on the north-west side of the original station, extending the area of the terminus to the screen wall still to be seen alongside platform 16. Four new platform roads were provided, the centre platform having a track on each face. This extension, intended for the Windsor, and other local traffic, became known as the Windsor Station. It was separated from the original platforms (the Main Station) by its own cab yard, which had an inclined approach from Griffin and York Streets. A direct vehicular approach to the Windsor Station from York Road, running parallel to Mepham Street was opened in 1875. Included in the Windsor Station for working purposes was a dock siding of the Main Station, converted into a running road, with platform, on 17 March 1869.

When the London Bridge—Charing Cross line was opened in 1864, the owning company provided a 5-chain connection into the LSWR at Waterloo, as required by its Act. This single-line spur was an extension of the empty carriage line between platforms 2 and 3 of the Main Station which passed through the end wall, crossing above Waterloo Road to form a junction facing London Bridge. The short-lived through service from Kensington (Addison Road) over it has been mentioned in Chaper 9. After that episode the spur saw no regular passenger workings, but occasional movements of vans, horse boxes and passenger saloons continued to use it. Queen Victoria passed this way when travelling between the LSWR station at Windsor and Channel ports. A part of the Kensington service was resumed from 1 July 1875, from which day about seven LNWR trains each way ran between Willesden Junction and Waterloo, taking thirty minutes. These trains were taken off in January 1893 in response to an LSWR plea that Waterloo was too congested to accommodate them.

Under pressure from the LSWR, the SER opened a station at Waterloo, east of the junction, on 1 January 1869. This offered no great convenience to LSWR passengers, who for a long time were forced to rebook. Later, through season tickets were issued from LSWR suburban stations to Cannon Street. There were also through fares, including a cheap day return from Cannon Street to Windsor. Even so, as we shall presently see, this was not a very satisfactory access to the City for LSWR passengers.

CYPRUS AND KHARTOUM

More platforms were added to Waterloo in 1878. Yet another virtually separate station was opened on 16 December on the south-east side, a double-sided platform on the other side of the cab yard of the original station (now called the Central Station). The two platform faces of what was known as the South or New Station were used by suburban trains. Railwaymen, with their liking for naming new installations after contemporary events, called it 'Cyprus', (that island having been ceded to Britain by the Berlin Congress of 1878). About the same time, some of the tracks in the Central Station were rearranged, and the platforms improved. New booking offices and refreshment rooms were opened, and a 300 ft frontage erected in the Waterloo Road from the outer edge of the South station to the boundary line of the Central. This was supported on columns over the cab yard beneath.

The final addition to the old Waterloo was the North station, erected in continuation of the Windsor Station towards York Road and completed in November 1885. As this was the year of Gordon's murder and of the abandonment of the Sudan, the staff called it 'Khartoum'. There were six new platform faces, making a total of eighteen in the terminus (two in the South, six in the

Central, four in the Windsor, and six in the North). Unlike some of the other termini, all platforms could be used for arrivals or departures.

Outside the terminus, all sixteen platform tracks converged on the four approach lines of 1848. By the 1880s there were some 700 trains a day at Waterloo and there was much delay and congestion until two more running lines were added between the terminus and Nine Elms in 1886-92. An interesting feature of this widening was to be seen at the north end of Carlisle Lane. Here the additional width, mostly on iron girders, had to be carried across the vestibule and entrance to the Canterbury Music Hall. To avoid any interruption to the performances, most of the work was carried out between 1 am and 4 pm, and on Sundays. Several of the old bridges in the viaduct were reconstructed to carry the heavier loads now imposed.

From east to west, the six tracks were worked as down main, up main, up main, down Windsor, down Windsor and up Windsor. A seventh road between the Waterloo A and B signal boxes, the down relief, was added on the east side on 4 July 1900. In 1916 further widenings were completed between Waterloo and Queen's Road East box, giving eight tracks as far as Loco Junction, and seven thence to Queen's Road. (Eight tracks already existed between Queen's Road West and Clapham Junction.) At Vauxhall in 1890 the LSWR provided tenements to rehouse the 1,041 people displaced by the widening work.

As at most other termini, platforms were originally 'open', tickets being collected at a special stop outside. At Westminster Bridge Road an army of ticket collectors would comb each arriving up train, passing rapidly from one compartment to another. To facilitate working, the 1892 widening had included an additional up Windsor road through Vauxhall station, which was entirely rebuilt in the process. The introduction of corridor trains, combined with the construction of closed platforms at the new Waterloo station from 1910 onwards, dispersed the 'Westminster Bridge mob'.

## GETTING TO THE CITY

Mention has been made of the SER insistence on rebooking at Waterloo Junction. This was not the only source of irritation to LSWR passengers. Train service over the heavily-occupied section between Waterloo and Cannon Street left much to be desired, particularly in the foggy weather then frequent in winter months.

Nor was Cannon Street a convenient station for passengers requiring the western side of the City. In 1880, Harris C. L. Saunders of
the Sun Life Office led a group of dissatisfied South Western commuters to form the Metropolitan Express Omnibus Company,
which began to operate horse buses between Waterloo and the
City. A year later this company was purchased by the Railways &
Metropolitan Omnibus Co Ltd. By the middle 1880s it was working eighteen two-horse, twenty-six-seat buses on the route and
carrying some two and a half million passengers a year. These
buses were allowed to terminate in the cab yard at the top of the
incline from York Road.

For its part, the LSWR remained interested in schemes to get its
passengers to the City. Some 50,000 passengers were arriving at
Waterloo daily in 1892, of whom it was estimated about 12,000
continued to the City, half by the SER, the rest by the RMO buses,
by cab, or on foot.[4] Schemes for an overhead railway were considered in 1882 and again in 1891, but dismissed as too costly.
Eventually it was decided to support a proposal for a Waterloo &
City tube railway. This was authorised by an Act of 1893, and the
LSWR, which provided five of the eight directors, undertook to
work the line for not more than fifty-five per cent of the gross receipts, on which the payment of a three per cent dividend was to
be the first charge.

These terms attracted investors, and the line was opened on
8 August 1898, offering a frequent service of electric trains between a station in the basement of Waterloo and another at the
Bank of England. There was no connection with any other line,
and no intermediate station. To this day, the Waterloo & City,
popularly known as 'the Drain', remains independent of London
Transport, the only tube railway operated by British Railways. A
power station and open air carriage sidings were constructed east
of Waterloo station adjacent to Lower Marsh. Coal trucks and
rolling stock were moved in via a hoist in the Windsor line carriage sidings on the York Road side of Waterloo. The LSWR took
over the tube completely in 1907.

Tube railway connection to the West End was attempted in the
1860s. Construction of a pneumatic tube, the Waterloo & Whitehall, was begun, but was abandoned in 1868 when the company
(which was ignored by the LSWR) ran into financial difficulties.
More successful, but also unsupported by the LSWR, was the Baker
Street & Waterloo Railway, opened on 10 March 1906 between
what is now Lambeth North station and Baker Street. Its Waterloo
station was reached by lifts from a small booking hall next to

York Road, at the extreme western end of the subway running under the main-line station. This booking hall was also connected to the end of the North Station concourse by stairs and a subway.

## WHERE THE FRENCH GOT LICKED

At the turn of the century, Waterloo was an untidy and confused collection of platforms, passages, stairways, cab yards and offices, the despair of any stranger. To make confusion worse, the platform numbering system was almost beyond comprehension; the existence of the South station was ignored, and No 1 was the main departure platform in the original or Central station. Beyond this, the other fifteen platform faces had to share the numbers 2 to 10, thus many of the platforms, although bearing a single number, had a track either side, and the unfortunate passenger, having succeeded in finding the correct platform, was still left in doubt as to which was his train.

Reliable information about departures was almost impossible to obtain, especially if one was in a hurry. In *Three Men in a Boat* (1889), Jerome K. Jerome made fun of the difficulties of finding a train to Kingston, telling how the destination was eventually reached only by bribing an engine driver. Two years later, Henry Wheatley, writing in *London Past and Present*[5] thought it 'probably the most perplexing railway station in London'. Another writer remembered 'a jumble of shabby, poverty-stricken buildings . . . quite unique in London, although quite in keeping with the squalid neighbourhood surrounding it'.[6] A story was circulated that an old Devon farmer, turning to his wife on the footbridge after four or five unsuccessful attempts to find his train, had remarked in admiration, 'No wonder the French got licked here, Mary.'

Probably the best way to describe it is to take an imaginary tour of the premises as they were around 1900. A gloomy doorway in Waterloo Road opens on to an equally gloomy flight of steps. At the top of these, we find the small concourse of the South station. Trains leave the double-sided platform for Kingston, Leatherhead and Hampton Court, and the rather cramped accommodation is the scene of some confusion in the rush hours. A passageway on the right leads us to the 1853 cab yard alongside the offices of the Main or Central station. As we face the building, with its pavement steps down to the cab road, cabs are coming up the ramp on our left from York Street after negotiating a dark tunnel under the station 'which in those days of horse traffic, resembled for all the world some evil-smelling sewer'.[7] The pavement steps were known as 'The Bench', a name perpetuated in the title 'bench foreman', which was in use until at least 1946. After depositing or picking up passengers, cabs leave at a smart pace down a steep ramp on the right which takes them into the Waterloo Road. There is never a shortage of cabs at Waterloo as any driver may use the station on payment of a nominal toll of one penny.

Passing through the building, we find the main departure platform, No 1. A handbell is being rung to announce the departure of a train, and the platform presents a scene of great animation—all platforms in the terminus are 'open', and tend to be crowded with see-ers off and lookers-on in addition to the genuine passengers.

At the outer end of this platform, in the angle between the Central and South stations, is a small engine shed and turntable built over the top of the cab incline. The buildings alongside the departure platform contain the booking office, waiting and refreshment rooms, all equally mean and thoroughly grim. Even without looking up, we are conscious of the low roof at the inner end of the platform, supported by heavy timbers. As the three tracks between platforms 2 and 3 extend further into the station than any others, a footbridge is provided to connect the main departure platform with the cab yard that separates the Central station from the Windsor.

Crossing the bridge, we pass above No 2, another departure platform, one face of which shares the No 1 platform road. Between 2 and 3 is the centre road which goes through the end wall of the station and crosses over Waterloo Road to join the SECR. Both platforms 2 and 3 come almost up to the Waterloo Road, and to enable passengers not using the footbridge to get round the ends, the connecting line to Waterloo Junction is spanned by a small opening bridge with two flaps. Outside, the end wall of the old station rises sheer from the pavements of Waterloo Road, with the junction line emerging from its middle.

Back on the footbridge, we can now see No 3, the main arrival platform. Then comes the last of the Central station platforms, No 4, also used for arrivals, sharing a track with the opposite face of No 3. Beyond the buffer stops, is another steep cab exit down to Waterloo Road, and alongside is the cab yard of the Windsor station. At its outer end, this yard is served by an inclined entry from York Street which rivals the other in insalubrity.

Descending from the bridge, we are at the west side of the cab yard, and enter the Windsor station, with its three platforms, 5, 6 and 7, the centre one having a track either side. Along the inner ends of these is a small concourse, well back from the Waterloo Road; between this and the cab yard at the top of the approach from York Road is a block of offices. We can now see the wall carrying the roof of the North station, and proceeding along the concourse, we enter this, the most modern part of the terminus. The roof, with its decorated iron supports, is in elegant contrast to the crude timbers of the Central station. There are six platform roads, the two platforms in the centre (8 and 9) having a track either side. Walking to the end of the last platform, 10, we find seven sidings and a turntable in the space between the station and York Road. Behind the boundary wall of the station is the hoist used to reach the Waterloo & City tube railway. At the other end of 10, in the angle of the cab approach and York Road, are the general offices of the LSWR, with a wing projecting along the north side of the North station concourse. We have now roamed through the whole tangle, but there are many nooks and corners we have not seen, and it would take many such rambles before one could be sure of really knowing the place.

All the military traffic for the South African War of 1899-1902 passed through Southampton, much of it entraining at Waterloo, although cavalry went from Nine Elms. In December 1899 the terminus saw the dramatic departure of Lord Roberts to the front. Waterloo always had a strong military flavour, serving as it did the great army establishments at Aldershot, Bordon and Salisbury Plain, as well as the naval bases at Portsmouth, Portland and Devonport. As Britain's military might expanded in the years before 1914, uniforms became more and more conspicuous on its platforms.

Another speciality was race traffic. The LSWR served the racecourses at Epsom, Windsor, Sandown Park, Hurst Park, Ascot, Kempton Park and Salisbury and the Imber Court Trotting Course, all easily accessible from Waterloo. In the 1900s, on the occasion of a big meeting, as many as 14,000 racegoers would leave the terminus in regular and special trains. Much of this traffic was gradually lost to the motor car and road coach, but in the 1920s and 1930s it was still heavy, and many of the special trains included restaurant cars. As late as 1939 in Ascot week, the concourse offered a fashion parade, attracting suburban housewives, who came up to stand and stare. Horse racing and other sources provided sufficient business in the 1900s to justify five daily departures of trains made up entirely of horse boxes with connections all over the LSWR system.

## A FRESH START

As the nineteenth century drew to a close, directors and management debated what was to be done about their ramshackle terminus. To its lasting credit, the board eventually decided to pull it all down and start again. Powers were obtained from Parliament in 1899 and 1900 and about six and a half more acres were purchased, mostly on the south side. This property included six streets, with parts of two others, a church (All Saints') and church schools. Protestants greeted the disappearance of All Saints' with some elation as the services were among the most ritualistic in Britain, and it was thought that these popish practices could not be restarted in a new church. Six blocks of flats were erected by the LSWR, providing accommodation for some 1,750 people, more than the number displaced. Five of these blocks went up behind the Bakerloo tube station in Westminster Bridge Road, the other in Stangate.

J. W. Jacomb-Hood, who became the LSWR's chief engineer in 1901, went to the USA to study the design of terminal stations. The new Waterloo largely followed the plans he drew up on his return, providing a straightforward and spacious station on this difficult site. There were to be twenty-three platforms in all under a new roof, with a wide passenger concourse across their ends, flanked on its outer side by a long frontage block, containing the amenities and railway offices. In practice this plan was modified, and some economy was achieved by Herbert Walker's[8] decision to retain the relatively modern and quite satisfactory roof over the North station, thus reducing the total number of platforms to twenty-one. Jacomb-Hood died in 1914, when the work was well advanced; he was succeeded by A. W. Szlumper, who completed the task.

Site clearing began in 1900. Among the properties demolished were the disorderly houses which had found much custom from the soldiers and sailors passing through Waterloo. (The squalid neighbourhood around the old station, *Whoreterloo*, is well described in chapters two and three of Michael Sadleir's *Forlorn Sunset* [Constable, 1947].) A healthier, if less exciting haven for the servicemen, the Union Jack Club, was established in the Waterloo Road opposite the terminus in July 1907. This offered 355 clean, but lonely, beds, and a billiard room.

While the preparatory work was going on, other men toiled unseen beneath the platforms, strengthening the arches to carry the new superstructure. New foundations had to be dug as deep as 30 ft to reach the clay beneath the marshy ground. Another ancillary task was the rebuilding of the bridge over Westminster Bridge Road to carry eleven tracks.

Standing in the way of the track rearrangements, the Necropolis station was demolished and replaced by a new structure on the south side of Westminster Bridge Road, opened on 16 February 1902. This had two platforms, one for mourners, the other for coffin-loading, an arrangement which ensured that the operation was carefully screened from the eyes of the funeral party.

Once the site was cleared and the foundations prepared, work began on the roof which was to cover the South station and the area to the south east of it, and this was completed in 1907. A cab road was built alongside and in front of the new station, starting from an entrance in Westminster Bridge Road, and curving under the full width of the approach tracks before climbing at 1 in 25 along the south-eastern boundary. At the top, it was later to turn sharply left along the outer face of the new frontage building, finally reaching an exit in York Road against the Charing Cross Railway viaduct. Two spur roads were made into Lower Marsh. Additional powers were taken in 1911 to buy land on the north side and to abandon the SECR connecting line.

Erection of the steel-framed frontage block began at the south-east corner; some parts of it were ready in time for the opening of the first five platforms in 1909, but the main-line booking hall was not opened until 11 June 1911. This hall was 95 ft long, 45 ft wide and 30 ft high to a curved ceiling carried on pairs of plaster columns. At one side, doors opened to the covered cab yard along the front, at the other, to the new concourse. Some changes were made in 1924, when the plaster columns were replaced with bronze-capped columns of Brèche marble and the original wood block flooring by coloured glass tiles; at the same time, the two doors to the cab yard were converted to windows.

Next to the booking hall, on its south-east side, was a large luggage hall (75 ft by 45 ft) and beyond that a cloakroom (left luggage office) with additional storage space in the basement. This cloakroom was the scene of some macabre incidents in 1924. A certain Patrick Mahon, having murdered and cut up his mistress on the Crumbles at Eastbourne, arrived here on 16 April and deposited a Gladstone bag containing a blood-stained knife and other incriminating items. His suspicious wife, finding the cloakroom ticket in his clothes, persuaded an ex-policeman friend to withdraw the deposit. On seeing the contents, he informed the railway police, who returned the bag to the shelf, and gave Mrs Mahon the ticket to put back in her husband's pocket. A guard was then placed on the cloakroom by the police, who detained Mahon when he foolishly came back to retrieve his bag.[9]

From the concourse a wide flight of steps led to a 'gentlemen's court' beneath the frontage block. This haven of relief, 80 ft long by 40 ft wide, was enthusiastically described in the *Railway Magazine* of December 1910, as 'perhaps the finest in England'. It had the traditional white-tiled walls, relieved by a black and white marble floor, and teak doors and partitions. Supplementing the usual facilities were bathrooms, a boot cleaning room and a hairdressing saloon. 'If desired', the contemporary accounts coyly announced, 'the air could be changed every five minutes by the action of electric fans'. Necessity soon made such desire continuous.

### THE NEW STATION TAKES SHAPE

Above platform level, the frontage building contained railway offices. These were supplied with electricity and hot water from the Waterloo & City Railway power station in Lower Marsh. Between the building and the platform barriers was the first section of the wide concourse that was to run across the full width of the new station. In the end wall, a door opened on to the cab approach alongside the station, an entrance at first reserved for royalty and other notabilities, as it permitted a reasonably private passage to and from the new platform 1.

This initial section of the new station contained five ferro-concrete platforms, the first three of which came into public use on 24 January 1909. Platform 4 was in service on 25 July 1909, and platform 5 on 6 March 1910. (At last there was a number for each platform face.) Nos 1, 2 and 3 were sited on the new land, whilst No 4 was approximately where the first platform of the old South Station had been. The name 'South Station' was perpetuated unofficially and is still in use today for this part of the terminus, where the loudspeakers can occasionally be heard appealing for the 'South Station shunter'.

About one-third of the way down each pair of new platforms was a flight of steps leading to an 18 ft wide subway providing access to the two tube stations beneath the terminus. Below this subway was a second one served by electric lifts from each pair of platforms and intended to facilitate movement of parcels, luggage and mail across the station, or between the platforms and the parcels depot in the basement arches. Claims were made that would bring a hollow chuckle from the present day user of Waterloo: 'Roundabout methods are now eliminated, lost time and congested platforms a thing of the past' (1922 advertisement). . . . 'The station is so designed that very little movement of luggage and parcels can interfere with the passengers' (*Railway Gazette*, June 1922). Alas, methods of handling parcels have changed, and the electric lifts stand almost idle as tractor drivers form up long trains of the appropriately named BRUTES (British Railways Universal Trolley Equipment), setting out to corral as many passengers as they can by making enormous U turns between concourse and platform gate.

Over the next thirteen years the great rebuilding continued, gradually moving across the station site from south east to north west, until the bow-shaped concourse and frontage block were completed along the full width, and all twenty-one new platforms were finished.[10] All platforms up to 15 had access to the tube subway, and all except 16, 18 and 21 had luggage lifts. Each line ended at Ransomes & Rapier hydraulic buffers, impressive beasts of 7 ft stroke, strong enough to arrest a 400 ton train moving at 10 mph. An iron screen with Bostwick collapsible gates separated platforms from concourse.

Not all was perfect at the new Waterloo. A curious short-sightedness was shown in regard to platform lengths, despite longer trains. In steam days it was not unusual for trains into Waterloo to be made up to twelve or more corridor coaches (say 750 ft), and with an engine at each end, even this unremarkable length was troublesome at most platforms.

Platforms 1 to 6, used by the local services to Hampton Court, Leatherhead, Shepperton and Kingston, were 696, 695, 683, 685, 720 and 723 ft long. Bournemouth and West Country trains usually left from 7 (728 ft) and Portsmouth trains from 8 (735 ft). Platforms 9 and 10 (756 and 765 ft) were used by main-line stopping trains, whilst 11, the longest, with the cab yard alongside, was convenient for the Southampton boat trains. This platform was originally 860 ft, but was later extended to 946 ft.* At the south end of the cab yard was an incline for empty cabs entering from Griffin Street (since closed) and above this were loading docks 160 and 175 ft long. At the other side of the cab yard was No 12, 843 ft, used for arrivals and for loading mail, parcels and newspaper trains in view of its location alongside the central roadway. Most main-line trains arrived at 13 (857 ft) or 14 (860 ft). No 15 (635 ft) was also used for arrivals, but in view of its short-

* In 1938 mainly for summer holiday traffic; No 7 was also extended at the same time to 798 ft and 8 to 805 ft. The umbrella roofing over 9-16 was extended in 1937-39.

ness was usually employed for loading and unloading van trains, including the milk and fish traffic still handled at the terminus.

Between platforms 15 and 16 was a two-storey office block completed in 1920 and known as 'the Village'. Erected under the main roof, this building served the station's 450 staff and included the stationmaster's offices, staff dining room, ticket collectors' porters' and guards' rooms and the lost property office. At the concourse end were two escalators, either side of a fixed stairway. They connected the concourse with the subway to the tube stations 26 ft below and were brought into use on 9 April 1919.

At the other side of the Village were the Windsor Line platforms, 16 to 21, all under the original roof of the 1885 North station, but served by the north-western end of the new concourse and thus fully integrated with the rest of the station. Platform 16 (570 ft) was used by electric services to Wimbledon via East Putney and to Shepperton via Richmond. Numbers 17 and 18 (600 and 612 ft) were allocated to the Hounslow loop service via Richmond and via Brentford. At No 19 (605 ft) were found the Kingston 'roundabout' trains, whilst 20 and 21 (625 and 551 ft) were used by the Reading and Windsor steam services. At the outer end of 21, on the opposite side, was a 234 ft dock for loading vans. Between this and York Road, the engine and carriage sidings, turntable and the hoist to the tube railway remained largely unchanged. In the north-west corner of the station site the old general offices were left undisturbed, but were connected to the frontage block by a new wing.

Within the station, all that remained of the old Waterloo was the roof over 16 to 21, with its supporting walls. Over the rest of the station, 560,000 superficial feet of new roofing had been erected. This roof was of the ridge and furrow type, the ridges 60 ft above the platforms. There were nine spans at right angles to the tracks over platforms 1 to 15, and twenty-five spans parallel with the rails over the concourse. The steel roof girders were supported by octagonal steel columns on brick piers.

The vehicle roadway from Westminster Bridge Road had been opened as far as the main-line booking hall on 18 December 1911, and by 1922 had reached York Road. It was roofed over between the south-east corner of the station and the bridge over Waterloo Road, and also for a short distance opposite platforms 12 to 15.

Mention of the bridge over Waterloo Road recalls the fact that, inevitably, the connecting line to Waterloo Junction had disappeared during the reconstruction. It was taken up in March 1911, but on the far side, near the Junction station, a siding re-

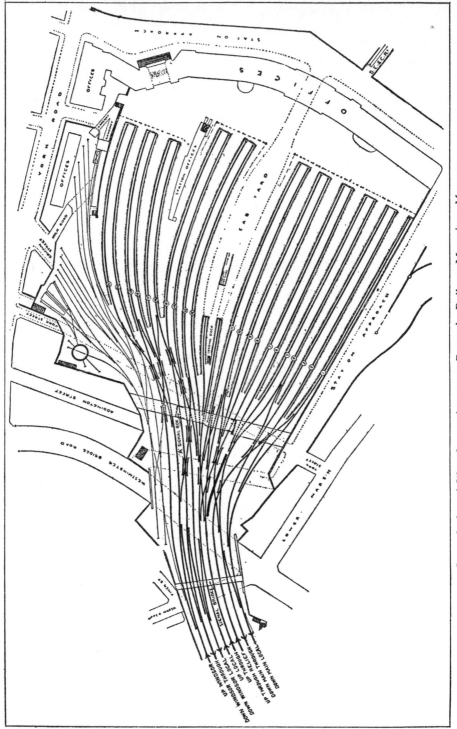

*General plan of Waterloo station 1922. From the Railway Magazine, May 1922*

mained until 3 May 1925, when the connection and ground frame
were removed. The bridge remained for the use of passengers
walking across from one line to the other and it was not until
7 July 1935 that the word 'Junction' was dropped from the title
of the former South Eastern through station, which then became
integrated to some extent, with its platforms lettered A to D.

## FOR THE BENEFIT OF MANKIND IN GENERAL

Free from pillars and other obstructions, the wide and well-lit
concourse was a predominant and successful feature of the new
Waterloo. It curved gracefully from one side of the station to the
other, 120 ft wide and 770 ft long, serving all twenty-one platforms. There were three bookstalls, an inquiry office and a com-
mendably clear departure indicator at platforms 6 and 7 showing
the departure time, platform number and stations served by each
train. A similar, smaller indicator was placed opposite the Windsor
Line platforms. At each end were timetable stands, illuminated in-
ternally. Opposite platform 9 a Bodmin & Wadebridge Railway
four-wheel composite first and second class coach of the 1830s,
stood on a section of the original permanent way with its granite
sleeper blocks. This coach, in use from 1834 to 1886, was brought
to Waterloo from Eastleigh in 1915. It is now in the Transport
Museum at Clapham.

Staircases sited opposite platforms 8 and 12 led down to a wide
subway which opened out on to the Waterloo Road opposite the
Union Jack Club and the then LCC tramway terminus. Next to this
opening was a low level cab yard underneath the main vehicle
roadway. In the north-west corner of the concourse, slopes and
stairs led to the tube stairway and booking hall. Opposite platform 19 an impressive archway and flight of steps led up from the
vehicle roadway near the York Road exit, forming the main
pedestrian entrance to the station.

This was the Victory Arch, so called because it formed the LSWR
war memorial, its walls displaying bronze tablets with the names
of the 585 employees who were killed. The arch, of Portland stone,
held a memorial window and was flanked by sculptural groups
supported on pylons. One of these, '1914', featured Bellona,
goddess of war, astride the world in scaled armour, with flaming
torch and naked sword; the other, '1918', showed Peace enthroned
on Earth, holding symbols of peace and victory. High above, over
the cornice and the legend WATERLOO STATION, sat a rather

masculine Britannia triumphantly holding aloft the torch of liberty 'for the guidance of her children and children's children and the benefit of mankind in general'. This archway, together with the other achitectural features of the new Waterloo, was the work of James Robb Scott.[11] Scott had a great predilection for fasces, heads and swags, and these decorative features were liberally spattered about the station.

The frontage block, of which the Victory Arch was a dominant part, was in the impressively monumental style sometimes called Imperial Baroque, but was hopelessly swamped by the ugly viaduct carrying the railway from London Bridge to Charing Cross. Most people who use Waterloo arrive by taxi, bus or tube, and do not see the frontage at all; of those who come on foot, many would find it difficult to describe the outward appearance of the terminus. It is quite impossible to stand back far enough to take it all in, except at a sharp angle, from the other side of York Road. Were there no foreground clutter, it would present a noble prospect from the other side of the river.

Apart from the centre section, which was higher than the rest, this building was flat roofed. At the south-east end were the luggage and booking halls already described, and the remainder of this first section contained waiting rooms, lavatories for first and third class ladies, and a circular refreshment buffet opposite platforms 10 and 11. This buffet had a crescent-shaped counter at the back and was lined with marbles of various colours. Its floor was of Roman marble mosaic. Under British Railways it was thoroughly brought up to date, becoming the garish, noisy and very popular Horseshoe Bar, with a somewhat battered mural of the RMV *Queen Mary* looking out of place amid the modern décor. Above the buffet, and reached by a staircase and lift opposite platforms 10 and 11, was a tea and luncheon room, and next to it, an oak-panelled dining room seating 150. These three refreshment rooms were opened in 1913, and together with other refreshment facilities on the station, were managed by Spiers & Pond.

Next to the circular buffet was a wide central archway linking the cab yard between platforms 11 and 12 with the vehicle road along the front of the station. Most of the building on the other side of this archway, towards York Road, was completed in 1920-21, whilst the portion already described was largely finished by 1914. Opposite platforms 11 and 12 was another luggage hall, and next to this, a large buffet measuring 79 ft by 39 ft. Here was the most richly decorated room in the station: walls panelled with Greek Cipollino marble; fluted sienna pilasters; bays for statuary; a

'Grinling Gibbons' ornamented plaster ceiling 18 ft high; and a magnificent bar, 65 ft long, at the back, laid out for heavy traffic. At the front of this buffet, a semi-circular booking office projected on to the concourse, matching the similar one outside the main-line booking hall. Adjoining the buffet was a pleasant tea room with oak parquet floor, and cream walls decorated with mirrors. Latterly known as 'The Windsor', this room was a firm favourite with those who cherished the Edwardian atmosphere which still lingered although the American soda fountain had long since disappeared.

The remainder of the block was taken up with waiting rooms, ladies' lavatories, another left luggage office, and a bank. The latter, opened in 1923 by the National Provincial, and the first on a London station, was originally open until 6 pm (2 pm on Saturdays). Another branch was opened by the same bank on Victoria (Eastern Section) at the end of 1928. Below this part of the building was another large lavatory for men (unlike the ladies, they were offered no class distinction). Beyond the Victory Arch, at the extreme end of the concourse, was the entrance to the general offices, now embellished with a small plaque in memory of Sir Herbert Walker unveiled on 27 May 1952.

The upper floors of the frontage block, apart from the tea and dining rooms near the central arch, were occupied by the various railway offices. These included a communications room, in telephonic or telegraphic contact with all the stations on the system. Spread around the new station were some 240 synchronised electric clocks of various sizes, including a 6 ft diameter, four-face turret clock hung above the centre of the concourse, and a sunray clock in the Memorial Window. Waterloo was now the best served of all London termini as regards amenities, with an excellent selection of shops, kiosks and restaurants. Today there are about 30 shops and service points supplementing the railway facilities, offering a range of items from ties and croissants to foreign stamps.

By the beginning of 1922, most of the reconstruction work was completed, and the new station, covering some twenty-four and a half acres, was formally opened on 21 March by Queen Mary, deputising for the King, who was indisposed. After studying the Memorial Arch, the Queen passed along the concourse.

## WATERLOO AT WAR

No doubt the royal visitor was reminded of the important part the station had played in the 1914-18 war, when millions of soldiers and sailors, with their equipment, had passed through the terminus, day and night. As well as the draft and leave movements to and from the many camps and bases served by the LSWR, there was a heavy traffic to Southampton, the port which handled the embarkation of the British Expeditionary Force in 1914, subsequent reinforcements until the spring of 1915, and after that, embarkations for other theatres of war. At certain times during the war the terminus also dealt with ambulance trains and army overseas mail. Station officials had often worked continuously for eighteen hours at a stretch; the numbers of men returning from leave on Sunday nights were so great that up to thirty special trains would have to be organised. Between December 1915 and April 1920 a free buffet, open throughout the twenty-four hours, and staffed by voluntary lady workers, dispensed over eight million meals. The buffet was in the long subway beneath the platforms, where a plaque records this prodigious feat.

Bomb damage in 1914-18 was limited to the night of 29 September 1917, when explosions occurred on the down main line between A Box and Westminster Bridge Road and in No 6 siding north of the station. Track damage was restored in sixteen hours. In the vast warren of arches and subways beneath the station, shelter accommodation was set aside for the railway staff, including the military control office. Elsewhere, the public responded in large numbers to the invitation of the railway company to use the basement at their own risk.

### ELECTRIFICATION AND RE-ARRANGED TRACKS

Stimulated in part by competition from the electric tramcar and motor bus, and also by threats to extend the Central London tube railway into the Thames Valley, the LSWR had electrified some of its suburban services, using the economical and straightforward 600-volt dc third-rail system later adopted for the 'Southern Electric'. The Wimbledon via East Putney service had been electrified on 25 October 1915 and the Kingston Roundabout and Shepperton services had followed on 30 January 1916. Just over a month later, on 12 March, it was the turn of the Hounslow loop, and on 18 June of the Hampton Court service. The 'New Guildford' line was electrified as far as Claygate on 20 November, with a steam push-pull connecting service beyond, but to provide more rolling stock for the other electric services, this Claygate working had been suspended in July 1919. All eight running lines in the terminal approaches were equipped for electric working, but in the terminus itself only platforms 1 to 6 and 16 to 21 could take electric trains.

After the formation of the Southern Railway in 1923, the live rail was extended from Raynes Park to Dorking North and Effingham Junction and from Claygate to Effingham Junction and Guildford. A full public service of electric trains began on these lines on 12 July 1925. Five years later, on 6 July 1930, the Windsor service was electrified. At that date, a total of thirty-two electric trains left Waterloo in the evening peak hour (5 to 6 pm). From 3 January 1937, Windsor electric trains divided at Staines, the rear portion serving Chertsey and Weybridge.

A third tube service was available from 13 September 1926, when the present Northern Line was extended southwards from Charing Cross to Kennington, giving the terminus direct connection with Euston and (with one change) access to Kings Cross and St Pancras. Three escalators linked the tube platforms with a new booking hall beneath the Windsor Side, completed in 1927. Forty years later, rush hour traffic justified the construction of a fourth escalator.

Until 1920 the up main through line into Waterloo ran into platforms 7 to 11 and 12 to 16, but in that year, a new lead was built to provide access to platforms 4 to 6, making it possible for a train to run into one of these platforms parallel with one from the up main relief into 1, 2 or 3.

Further expansion of the electric services into Waterloo was hindered by the inadequacies of the track layout and the limited capacity of the manual signalling. At the beginning of the 1930s, the approach tracks inwards from C Box (just north of Vauxhall station) were worked (south to north):

> down main local (serving platforms 1 to 10)
> down main through (4 to 10)
> up main relief (1 to 6)
> up main through (4 to 16)
> up main local (7 to 16)
> down Windsor local (7 to 16)
> down Windsor through (13 to 21)
> up Windsor (13 to 21)

Although interchange facilities at B Box made it possible to route a train to or from almost any part of the station, all electric trains approaching the electrified platforms 1 to 6 were confined to the up main relief from which they had to cross the down main through immediately outside the station.

Towards the end of 1934, the SR announced that £500,000

would be spent putting this right. At Durnsford Road, Wimbledon (the nearest suitable site), a flyover would be built to carry the up main local over the up and down main through lines so that from that point inwards, the tracks would be:

> down main local
> up main local
> down main through
> up main through,

joined at Clapham Junction by:

> down Windsor local
> down Windsor through
> up Windsor through
> up Windsor local.

From Vauxhall to Waterloo, an additional up main relief road would be sited between the up main through and down Windsor local, but as before, there would be only one up Windsor road on this stretch. At the terminus, platforms 7 to 9 would be electrified, and all electric platforms up to 9 would be available to the up main local. Concurrently with these changes, colour light signalling, with track circuits and power-operated points, would be installed between Waterloo and Hampton Court Junction.

Following the Cannon Street precedent, engineers assembled and tested the new Waterloo layout in a field near Mitcham. On Sunday 17 May 1936, the flyover, new tracks and most of the colour light signalling were brought into use, but the signal changes at the terminus itself were delayed until 18 October, clear of the holiday season. Weekday electric services were rearranged from 5 July, with Dorking North and Effingham via Leatherhead trains running fast between Waterloo and Wimbledon (Motspur Park in peak hours), supplemented by an all-stations service from Waterloo to Motspur Park (extended to Tolworth over a new line, 29 May 1938 and to Chessington South, 28 May 1939). These improvements went some way towards meeting the traffic demands arising from new housing developments in the area south west of Wimbledon.

One little nuisance remained after the layout changes. The two small turntables at Waterloo (B Box sidings, 49 ft 11 in and North sidings, 54 ft 10 in) were inadequate for modern locomotives and engine facilities at the terminus were little used after the 1920s. To reach the 64 ft 10 in turntable at Nine Elms locomotive depot, light engines of main-line trains were obliged to cross the up and down main local lines, which could cause delays to build up on the suburban services. However, if conditions allowed, this awkward movement could be avoided by sending the engine to Clapham Junction, crossing it over there. Engines coming out of Waterloo or Nine Elms loco were often run light to Clapham yard to pick up empty stock which they would haul back to Waterloo over the up main local and (after 17 May 1936) over the up main through. After the departure from Waterloo, they would run out behind, ready to back on to their own train. Outward empties were usually worked over the down Windsor lines to avoid conflicting movements at Clapham yard.

With the new track layout and signalling working smoothly, the way was clear for more electrification. A full service of electric trains to Woking, Guildford and Portsmouth Harbour (connections to the Isle of Wight) started on 4 July 1937, together with a connecting service to Aldershot and Alton. In the coming war, these trains were destined to carry a very heavy military and naval traffic as well as encouraging a strong flow of commuters from the 'stockbroker belt'. From 1 January 1939 electric trains ran between Waterloo and Reading, shedding a portion at Ascot to serve Guildford via Camberley and Aldershot.

Little modification was required to the structure of the rebuilt station. Experience demonstrated that the provision for luggage and waiting rooms was over-generous; part of the luggage hall opposite platforms 12 and 13 was converted in 1937 to a post office, and the waiting room opposite platforms 8 and 9 became an inquiry office. Loudspeakers were installed and used for the first time on 9 March 1932, a memorable day when the University boat race clashed with a rugby football international match at Twickenham. As an experiment, light opera music was interspersed with train announcements in 1937, becoming a regular feature in 1940. During the war, planned programmes of music were broadcast, a welcome diversion in those grey years. In 1948 passengers were questioned about the music; most approved, some suggesting that lively marches should be played in the morning rush hours, with something more soothing for the homeward journey. It was announced that the music would continue, but vocal records would be avoided as they might be confused with train information (!).

At first the train announcer-cum-disc jockey was in a booth over a kiosk opposite platforms 8 and 9, but was later banished to an eyrie on top of the Village.

Another form of entertainment was to be found in the small cinema opened by the entrance to platform 1 on 27 August 1934. Its auditorium, seating 250, was carried on girders over the cab road outside, and its frontage, in the brutal, jazzy style of the 1930s was the work of Alistair MacDonald, son of the famous Ramsay. An hour-long programme of news films, cartoons and 'topical features' was screened continuously from 9.45 am to 11 pm. Announcements of train arrivals would be projected at the side of the screen on request to the cashier. In more recent years the cinema became part of the Classic chain, showing full-length feature films.

In preparation for the expected war, air raid shelters for some 6,500 people were constructed in the arches beneath the station. When the bombing began, those who had lost their homes took up permanent residence, bringing in bits of furniture, even laying linoleum and carpets. There was also accommodation for the station staff and a telephone room for use by the headquarters staff should they be driven out of their wartime home at Dorking by invading armies. Someone had a respect for history. Not without effort, the Bodmin & Wadebridge coach was moved from the concourse to the relative safety of the lower subway.

Waterloo felt the first effects of enemy action on 7 September 1940 when the viaduct at John Street, just outside the station, was opened up by a bomb. All platforms were out of use until 19 September, and despite the assistance of the Royal Engineers, services were not fully restored until 1 October. During the interval, mail piled up until there were around 5,000 unsorted bags. Night newspaper trains were diverted to Clapham yard, bombed out of there, transferred to Wimbledon, and when bombs blocked the road access to that station, moved again, to Surbiton. Following damage by oil and incendiary bombs on the night of 29 December 1940, the station was closed again. It reopened on 5 January 1941, and on that night the old general offices in the York Road corner, already damaged by an earlier air raid, were largely destroyed by a bomb which also badly battered the Underground lifts and booking hall.

During a very heavy raid on 10/11 May 1941, more damage was wrought, by high explosive, delayed action, incendiary and oil bombs, and a furious fire was started in the basement arches where great quantities of spirits fanned flames which burned on until 15 May, when the station was partly reopened. Altogether, some fifty bombs found the station and its approaches, and one, a 2,000 pounder, lay undiscovered until office building operations started along the York Road side in 1959.[12] The Necropolis station was obliterated by a land mine, and Tite's Nine Elms lost its roof and attic.

Waterloo has seen few changes since the war. On the traffic side, the most notable have been the disappearance of steam, which held out here longer than at any other London terminus, and the decline in the transatlantic boat train traffic to and from Southampton following the capture of passengers by the airlines in the 1950s. A number of boat trains still survive at the time of writing, but these are almost all related to cruise and emigrant sailings. Almost gone are the days when Ministers of State, film stars and other notabilities said their helloes and goodbyes in front of press cameras at Waterloo, although such memories did return in December 1968 when Ginger Rogers arrived in her special train.

Largely for the benefit of boat train passengers, the roof over the cab yard opposite platforms 12 to 15 was extended a further 135 ft towards York Road in 1948. An overhead footway, the first to serve any London terminus, was opened on 11 October 1965, linking the concourse to the South Bank walkways, Hungerford Bridge, and Charing Cross. Shortly after leaving the concourse, this walkway penetrated the new office block which was built alongside the station in the early 1960s.

During 1967 accommodation for railway staff was erected over the barrier ends of platforms 1 to 6, partly to replace the main-line booking-on point that disappeared with the closure of Nine Elms locomotive depot in that year. This wooden structure, supported on steel girders, had a communicating gallery overlooking the platforms, a place where guards and drivers could gaze down at the rush-hour crowds with a feeling of superiority. Also accommodated here were the staff of the Thomson Newscaster, a device offering in lights a close mixture of news headlines and advertisements. Installed over the news cinema, this eventually came to life on 4 April 1968. At least it didn't make a noise.

Until the summer of 1962, the throbs and fumes of the diesel were almost unknown at Waterloo. Steam locomotives were to be seen there at all hours of the day; BR 2–6–2T and 2–6–4T had at last replaced the venerable LSWR M7 0–4–4T on the empty stock workings, but on the main-line trains to the west, to Bournemouth and to Weymouth, Bulleid's Pacifics still shared the burden with the more handsome BR rebuilds. Even when the diesels did appear they did not sweep the board—steam survived on the ECS workings and on some main-line trains until the final completion of the Bournemouth electrification on 10 July 1967.

That was the year when the long familiar Southern green finally began to give way to 'rail blue' and yellow front ends, but it was above all the year when Waterloo became the funeral parlour of main-line steam working in southern England. Every day until the changeover on 9 July, a band of mourners gathered at the platform ends, dressed in cameras and tape recorders, pockets bulging with notebooks and stopwatches, in greedy struggle for mementoes. Steam railtour followed steam railtour round the same old circuits. And from the concourse, Mr McKenna's loudspeakers blared out *Colonel Bogey*. A year later, the smoke-blackened roof glass over the central platforms still remained, in memoriam.

### SIGNALLING AND ACCIDENTS

During the time that Nine Elms was open to regular passenger working, trains on the running lines were controlled by the time interval system. On arriving at the approaches to the terminus, they proceded under the instructions of a manually-operated revolving lamp showing red (danger), green (caution), or white (all clear), or flags of the same colours. At the entrance to the station, the locomotive was uncoupled, proceeding to a siding whilst the carriages were hauled inside the train shed by rope.

Waterloo's signalling arrangements grew in the same piecemeal fashion as the station. At first each platform had hand-operated disc signals and the points were controlled by outside hand levers. At a ground hut close to Westminster Bridge Road sat the 'stop signalman' controlling a manual disc signal and an 'auxiliary' or distant signal worked by a wire. He also operated a gong which warned staff of incoming trains, providing a code description. All up trains stopped at a ticket platform south of Westminster Bridge Road (later, at Vauxhall) where a long removable coupling was placed between the locomotive and the first coach. When the train started off again, and a speed of some 10 mph had been reached, this coupling was slipped, the locomotive moving forward into a siding. The points were quickly reset as the coaches rolled on into their appropriate platform, where they were braked by the guard. Time-interval working was the rule until the criticisms of the government inspector investigating a collision between Ascot race specials at Egham in 1864 provoked the introduction of block working. By the beginning of 1866, this system was in use from Waterloo to Woking and Staines.

A signal box was opened at Waterloo in March 1867. Erected by Stevens & Sons, this was on a gantry over all four approach tracks at the entrance to the station. The hook locking frame had 24 main-line levers and another 23 for the Windsor lines. Two tall posts, each with six semaphore arms (three for up and three for down trains, the up and down arms on the same pivot) sprouted from the gantry, one at each end. The post on the south side, by the Necropolis station, controlled the main lines, the other the Windsor lines. Disc signals remained in use for distants and for the engine roads. At first there were no starting signals, but when these were provided, a stirrup frame was fitted to work them.

Saxby & Farmer built a second box alongside the old in 1874, with 'rocker and grid' locking frames for Main and Windsor working—100 levers in a continuous row. It was enlarged four years later by Stevens & Sons, who added 35 levers for the new South station. Another 65 levers were added in 1885 for the North station. By the latter date, the box, which had two parallel frames, back to back, was worked by four men between 7 am and 10 pm, and by two men on the night shift. At busy times each man was pulling over the heavy levers once every fifteen seconds. Hernia was an occupational disease of signalmen in those days.

A new and larger box was required when the approach tracks were widened in 1892. Built alongside, and to the north of the old, this was opened between 1 and 15 May 1892. It had Stevens frames, with a total of 220 levers. As triple working and gear levers were used, the 102 signal levers in this total controlled no fewer than 247 semaphore arms. The gantry which supported the box carried a magnificent display of signals, six sets of triple bracket posts, each controlling one of the six approach lines. High enough to disappear in foggy weather, the gantry had four rows of arms; at the top were the two down Windsor indicating signals, then a row of twenty up and down main-line signals. Beneath these were twenty-seven arms for Windsor line movements in and out of all platform roads, and at the bottom, a row of twelve shunt arms. At the platform ends, thirteen sets of starting signals on wrought iron brackets replaced the old wooden posts.

The box, 74 ft by 30 ft, consisted of two storeys, the upper one containing the lever frames and a mess room. The tappet interlocking supplied by Stevens was very comprehensive; some main signals were controlled by as many as 15 levers. A large amount of auxiliary electrical equipment was installed. When the approach tracks were further widened and the station rebuilt, the number of levers was increased to 250, plus six slides. With the special levers already mentioned, this was equivalent to a total of 410 ordinary levers.

By 1922 the skyline signals over the box had all but disappeared (a photograph taken about this time shows only nineteen arms). They had been replaced by route indicating signals for the up trains and signals at the platform ends for departures. Track circuits had been fitted to all running lines by the early 1920s, and the box equipped with illuminated diagrams showing the occupation of the circuits and the Sykes's electric fouling bars. A tentative trial of a light signal took place in 1920 when a three-position signal of the pattern used on the Pennsylvania Railroad was fixed on the girder of the box opposite platform 16. Rows of yellow-white lights indicated danger at the horizontal, caution at the oblique and clear at the vertical positions.

At this time six men were required to work the box between 6 am and 2 pm, and between 2 pm and 10 pm, while the night shift needed four men. There were also eight booking boys and three telegraph lads. The latter did not survive long into the SR era as the new company made a clean sweep of telegraph instruments, relying entirely on telephones.

Supplementing the main (A) box were B, C and D, and the three yard cabins. One of the latter was in the engine yard near the end of the South station platform, and another on the north side of the station by the turntable near York Road. The third, opened seven years after the first main box, and altered from time to time, was nicknamed the 'Crows' Nest' because it was situated against the gable end of the Central station roof. These yard boxes supervised the admission of trains to the platforms, and Crows' Nest also worked the connecting line to Waterloo junction. This little box at one time controlled the bolt locks of the turnplates which connected the tracks of the original station and were used to marshal trains in the days of four-wheel coaches (and also to turn horseboxes and carriage trucks off trains). Crows' Nest disappeared in 1911, during the rebuilding of Waterloo, as did the other yard boxes.

Box B was another overhead cabin, 462 yards out from A, with a 100-lever Stevens frame. It was worked by three men at busy times, two at night. Boxes C and D were much smaller, and were between B and Vauxhall station; C, with 35 levers, was on the down side 445 yards from B, and D was an overhead box with 23 levers another 522 yards down the line.

All the traffic of this great twenty-one-platform terminus remained controlled by this complex mesh of levers, wires, rods, slots, bolts, bells and fallible human beings without serious accident until 1936. The mental and physical strain on the men had been relieved to some extent by track circuiting and other refinements, but Waterloo A remained one of the most demanding jobs on offer for a railway signalman. As they looked through the window and saw the new concrete box going up, these fine men must have had few regrets at the passing of the old regime.

In the 'Odeon cinema' style favoured by the SR in the 1930s, the new box was built over the cab entrance in Westminster Bridge Road, on the site of the old blacksmiths' shop. It came into use on 18 October 1936, replacing six manual boxes. There were 309 miniature levers and sixteen train and engine describers in three sub-frames, one for the suburban platforms 1 to 4, another for platforms 5 to 15 and the third for 16 to 21. Four track diagrams of the negative type covered all lines between the station and Vauxhall. Four signalmen were required for the early and middle turns, three for the night shift. Three-aspect colour light signals were used between Waterloo and Loco junction, four-aspect beyond to Hampton Court junction. The three-light junction indicator was used for the first time in an SR installation.*

In its short career as a passenger station, Nine Elms suffered one serious accident. On 17 October 1840, in the hours of darkness, a train arrived very much behind time (such behaviour is not new, despite what we read in the papers). Whilst its engines were being detached, the following train came in *early*, and the confused policeman omitted to show a red light to its driver. In the resulting collision, one passenger was killed.

Serious accidents at Waterloo have fortunately been few. Soon after the opening of the new A box, on 21 August 1896, a light engine left the locomotive yard to run into the South station under hand signals. Over-running the clearance point, it collided with a down train just leaving, derailing its engine. This was not serious, but unfortunately the sudden stop of the outgoing train surprised the driver of the light engine following up its rear; he could not stop in time, and ran into the back of the train, injuring five passengers.

On 5 May 1904, a signal linesman carrying out some repairs accidentally stepped on to a signal wire, putting the signal to clear. A train of empty milk vans moved off and collided with a passenger train, killing one passenger.

On 11 April 1961, about 5.20 pm, the motorman of an electric train from Effingham via Leatherhead passed a signal at danger, bringing his train into collision with Bulleid Pacific *Crewkerne*,

---

* Subsequent signalling changes are mentioned in chapter 16.

which was crossing over to reach Nine Elms depot, after working the 1.25 pm from Weymouth. This accident, which occurred about 400 yards out of the terminus, caused the death of the motorman, who was crushed in his cab.

A bizarre incident took place on 13 April 1948. A Drummond M7 tank was propelling four loaded coal wagons on to the Waterloo & City hoist when suddenly the lift began to sink, taking trucks and locomotive with it. Driver and fireman jumped clear as their engine tilted into the shaft. It landed upside down at the bottom, spurting steam, and resting on the smashed coal wagons. Raised piecemeal, its parts were later used as spares.

# CHAPTER 12

# Charing Cross

## IN THE HEART OF THINGS

'Only Charing Cross really puts you down in the heart of things, in an air melodious with the bells of St Martin's', wrote Ronald Knox. And so it is. Although Cannon Street is ideal for the heart of the City, Charing Cross is closer than any other terminus to what is generally accepted as the true centre of London. Without doubt it is the capital's most conveniently situated main-line station. Used daily by some 120,000 passengers, it is so well-placed that many can complete their journey on foot. Yet, for all its convenience and utility, it has long been an irritant to politicians and the less practical town planners and civic designers, who would see it swept away to give place to a new road crossing of the river into an enlarged Trafalgar Square.

Now primarily a commuter station, Charing Cross has a cramped concourse which is the scene of great activity in the rush hours. Most of the time, the miracle is achieved, and as the incoming evening tide advances from the Strand, capacious electric trains suck it away as fast as it comes, but should there be some disruption or delay to slacken the pace of the outgoing trains, the jam-packed mass will quickly solidify. Charing Cross is then no place for the weak.

The SER had promoted an unsuccessful bill for an extension from Bricklayers Arms to Hungerford Bridge as early as 1846, and we have already seen how it had promised Parliament in 1857 that it would establish a West End terminus. After some abortive attempts to get into Victoria, the company obtained the consent of the LBSCR to a westward thrust from London Bridge. In 1857 Samuel Smiles,[1] the SER secretary, investigated possible routes and sites, concluding that the best choice for a terminus was Hungerford Market in West Strand. He also proposed that the approach line should connect with the LSWR at Waterloo. Traffic prospects were, he thought, bright; there would be foreign workings via the Waterloo link, and as well as the obvious demand for a terminus further west (Smiles had found that some three-fifths of the passengers at London Bridge were making for the West End) a healthy local business was expected from the West End to the City (there was then no District Railway, and no Victoria Embankment). Smiles recommended two 'City' stations on the extension, one in what is now Blackfriars Road, the other just west of London Bridge.

An Act of 1859 authorised the separate, but SER-inspired Charing Cross Railway Company to construct one mile, sixty-eight chains of line to the new terminus. The SER agreed to contribute £300,000 of the £800,000 capital, later increasing this to £650,000. On 1 August 1864, seven months after the opening of Charing Cross, the little company was completely absorbed into the SER.

Apart from the thorough milking organised by St Thomas's Hospital (Chapter 8), the line proved to be far more expensive than expected. It passed through a thickly built-up, insalubrious area, and landlords were successful in forcing up prices all round. The cost was further increased when in 1862 the company decided to have three running lines instead of two, and a quadruple rather than double track bridge over the river.

To minimise property disturbance and maintain a reasonably level gradient throughout, the running lines were carried on 190 brick arches (fourteen of them were over streets). There were also seventeen iron bridges and two iron viaducts, including one of 404 ft over the Borough Market, which was rebuilt at the railway's expense. 'Amidst an effusion almost suffocating' well over 7,000 corpses were removed from the College Burial Ground of St Mary, Lambeth, to be reburied at Brookwood.

There were three tracks from Cannon Street West junction (now Metropolitan junction) to the Thames, worked as up, down and up. Between the junction and Borough Market junction, two tracks were thought sufficient as it had been decided to work most of the passenger trains in and out of Cannon Street to accommodate the West End—City traffic already mentioned.

The subsequent decision to build Cannon Street eliminated the need for the intermediate station near London Bridge, and this was not started. The other station was opened with the Charing Cross extension and was sited just north of the junction of Great Surrey Street (now Blackfriars Road) and Charlotte Street (now Union Street). It had a short life, closing on 31 December 1868 in favour of Waterloo junction. There is no sign of it now, apart from a widening on one side of the viaduct. Nearby, from Metropolitan junction, a curve was later put in to the LCDR at Blackfriars junction (1 June 1878). The other link, to the LSWR, has been described in the Waterloo chapter.

### OVER THE RIVER TO WESTMINSTER

Beyond Waterloo, a gradient of 1 in 210 was required to gain sufficient height for the river crossing. The line was carried over the Thames on a lattice girder bridge, 61 ft 3 in wide, with four running lines, one of which was later converted to a siding. The new bridge occupied the site of the Charing Cross Suspension Bridge, designed by I. K. Brunel, and opened on 1 May 1845, in the hope of attracting custom to the Hungerford Market from the Surrey side. After purchase by the railway, the chains and ironwork of the bridge were sold and used for the Clifton Suspension Bridge at Bristol. Much abused by the 'scrap Charing Cross' party in later years, the Charing Cross railway bridge was a straightforward engineering job with little attempt at ornamentation, contributing nothing to the riverscape. Had the Victoria Embankment existed, there is little doubt that Parliament would have insisted on something rather more monumental.

There were six spans of 154 ft, and three of 100 ft, the last on the Westminster shore, carrying the track fan at the entrance to the terminus, as the ground available was somewhat restricted. The superstructure of the longer spans consisted of two main side girders carrying cross girders some 30 ft above the high water mark, and the whole was supported on cast-iron cylinders sunk into the clay beneath the river bed, and also on the two red brick piers and the abutments of the old suspension footbridge. Except at the fan end, the cylinders were 14 ft diameter below ground and 10 ft above. There were four piers, three between the towers of the old bridge and one between the tower and the abutment on the Surrey side. Each consisted of two cylinders 49 ft 4 in apart centre to centre, filled with concrete up to low water level, and brickwork above. At the fan end, there were two piers; that next to the brick tower had seven cylinders, that next to the abutment, nine. The outer cylinders here were 10 ft diameter below ground, 8 ft above, the inner ones 10 ft and 6 ft.

On both sides of the bridge the cross girders were prolonged beyond the main ones to support 7 ft 6 in wide footways which the railway company were required to provide to replace the suspension bridge. This path was reached by wooden stairs from Villiers Street, and on the south side by a wooden ramp from Belvedere Road. The suspension bridge was kept open until the footways were ready, so as not to interrupt pedestrian traffic. A halfpenny toll was exacted for the crossing until 1878 when the Metropolitan Board of Works secured its abolition on payment of £98,000 to the SER. Ten years later, the Board erected an iron staircase to link the footway with the west side of the Victoria Embankment.

Work on the railway bridge began in June 1860 and it was finished in about three years. Charing Cross station was opened for Greenwich and Mid Kent line trains on 11 January 1864, North Kent services using it from 1 April, main-line trains from 1 May. Bridge and station were designed by John Hawkshaw, but the hotel forming the frontage of the terminus was the work of E. M. Barry. From its elevated approach, the line came to an end approximately at ground level, owing to the siting of the station against the gravel terrace. The substructure of the building was composed of arches up to 30 ft high, offering excellent cellarage for wine merchants, a purpose for which it is still used.

Hawkshaw's train shed, 510 ft long, was topped by an all-over arched roof of 164 ft clear span, rising 98 ft above the rails to disperse the smoke and steam. Very shortly after, Hawkshaw built another similar roof at Cannon Street; from the river, both appeared enormous, 'colossal sheds of stations . . . that mar the river's banks, that soar and project like Brobdingnag pokebonnets'.[2]

Inside Charing Cross there were single tracks along each wall, and between them, six platform faces, numbered from west to east. Between platforms 2 and 3 were three tracks, and between 4 and 5, two. The middle road between 2 and 3 and the platform 1 road terminated in loading docks. All platforms were wooden, and all extended some 20 ft beyond the train shed on to the bridge, the longest being about 690 ft. Platforms 1 and 2 were used for mainline arrivals and departures; between them was a cab road with an exit through the front of the station and a ramp for empty cabs coming up from a tiny yard in Villiers Street. Before the station was completed, this ramp served for a while as a passenger entrance. Beyond the cab incline, at the outer end of 1 and 2, was the Customs searching room, waiting rooms and accommodation for Customs officers, with a bedroom and sitting room for the head officer. These latter facilities were required for the boat trains to and from Dover and Folkestone. An engine siding (the

'Gusset') was later provided at the end of platform 1, and another opposite the end of platform 6.

Between the buffer stops and the frontage was a small concourse, overlooked by a large clock on the inner wall of the hotel. 'Under the clock at Charing Cross' became a favourite meeting place, in more ways than one: 'half feminine London used to wait there at night for its young man, and the other half said that was who it was waiting for'.[3] Some of the latter would be those who made such lucrative use of the Cannon Street run.

The ground floor of the frontage building contained a cab exit arch at the Brewers Lane (Craven Street) side, and an exit archway of similar dimensions at the other. Between were three separate booking offices (the main line, near the cab arch, the North Kent, and the Greenwich and Cannon Street) as well as a cloakroom and waiting rooms.

## HOTEL FRONTAGE

Barry's 250-bedroom hotel formed the main 300 ft frontage, also extending a short way down Villiers Street alongside the concourse. It had seven storeys including attics. The architectural style, vaguely French Renaissance, was suitably pompous, but spoilt by too much emphasis on horizontals. The cab archway, and its opposite counterpart, distinctly elegant, were later marred by iron and glass 'conservatories' erected immediately above them.

Inside the hotel were pleasant and richly ornamented public rooms, some with little balconies overlooking the station concourse. The lift was quaintly described in a contemporary account as a 'rising room, fitted with comfortable seats'. Opened on 15 May 1865, the hotel, with its excellent appointments, and central situation, soon became a popular resort, reaping dividends of between 10 and 12 per cent. A ninety-bedroom annexe, connected to the main building by a footbridge over Villiers Street, was completed in 1878.

At the front of the hotel was a cab yard, 120 ft deep, separated from West Strand by iron railings and stone pillars. A gateway at each end was guarded by a police lodge. Later, these two lodges were let, one to a tobacconist, the other to Hands & Co, who operated a *bureau de change* for the benefit of Continental travellers, with side lines in the sale and purchase of Irish and country banknotes, war medals and gold and silver. In the centre of the forecourt was Barry's reproduction of the original Charing Cross. This had marked the last resting place of Queen Eleanor's body before burial in Westminster Abbey and was erected in 1291, probably at the top of Whitehall, where the King Charles statue now stands. It had been demolished by order of Parliament in 1647. Barry completed his work in 1865 with, to quote Walford again, the 'scanty guidance of two or three scarce and indistinct prints'. This 70 ft edifice was carved from Portland stone, Mansfield stone and Aberdeen granite by Thomas Earp of Lambeth. Unfortunately it does not stand out well against the ornate background of the hotel, and many pass by without noticing it.

When opened, the West End terminus of the SER took all the main-line services which had formerly terminated at London Bridge, including the Continental boat trains. It soon assumed an international flavour, and with Victoria, was the main point of departure for travellers from London to Europe and beyond, so much so that Percy Fitzgerald was moved to describe its platform barriers as 'the Gates of the World'. Thomas Cook & Son set up an ornately decorated office (matching the style of the hotel) on the Craven Street side of the forecourt (the premises are now occupied by a wine merchant), and French and German were always to be heard around the station. After the opening of the Sevenoaks cut-off in 1868, the SER route to Dover was one and a half miles shorter than that of its rival at Victoria. By 1913, Paris was within six and a half hours of Charing Cross.

In the winter months, Charing Cross was often wreathed by the fogs, which hung thick and low over the river when the air-was still. In such conditions, working was frequently disrupted; signals blanketed from view, the trains moved very slowly, their progress punctuated by detonators and the crackling braziers of the intrepid fogmen. Viewed from the Embankment on such a night, the station offered a picture to stir the imagination:

> look up at the great half circle of the station roof, and watch the trains thunder along the bridge overhead, the lights flashing through the girders, and the torrents of dull white steam bursting out above, falling again beneath the weight of the fog, and melting into nothingness as they fall.[4]

### UNFULFILLED CONNECTIONS

Not to be outdone by its competitor, the SER supported a scheme for a connection between Charing Cross and the northern lines. The North Western & Charing Cross Railway Act, which proposed a shallow subway line for goods and passengers between Charing Cross and the LNWR just outside Euston, was passed in 1864 soon after the terminus opened. There was a joint guarantee of five per cent from both main-line companies, but the capital could not be raised, and the scheme died in the financial crisis of 1866. A similar proposal, the London Central Railway, which also included a link to the Midland at St Pancras, was authorised in 1871. Parliament imposed obligations to construct new streets above the line and this, together with a severe vibration clause, discouraged investors; despite support from the Midland and the SER, the scheme was abandoned in 1874.

The proposal for a shallow subway between Euston and Charing Cross came up for the last time in 1885. On this occasion it foundered owing to a dispute between Watkin and Moon (the chairmen of the SER and the LNWR) as to where one-third of the capital should rank—the two main-line companies were each ready to put up a third of the £1,500,000 capital, but the outside parties putting up the remainder wanted their investment to rank in front of the other two-thirds. When the connection was eventually established, it was in the form of a deep level tube railway with no physical connections to the main lines. Just as well perhaps, for no one seems to have given much thought to the problem of handling cross-London traffic on the congested fog-ridden line between Charing Cross and London Bridge.

The difficulties of working an expanding business over this line led inevitably to widenings. The river bridge was tackled first, and in 1887 was widened 48 ft 9 in on the upstream side to carry three more tracks. From south west to north east, the order of lines was then:

    up west No 1
    down west
    up west No 2
    engine road
    up main
    down main
    up local.

Between Belvedere Road, Waterloo, and Metropolitan junction, another track was added to the south side of the viaduct and came into full use on 2 June 1901. The two inner roads were then worked as down lines, the outer ones as up, a practice which provided the minor convenience of down trains either side of the island platform at Waterloo Junction. Two sets of scissors crossovers were installed east of Waterloo Junction between the up lines, and between the down lines.

From the 1880s, if not earlier, enlargement of Charing Cross station had been under consideration, and a number of freeholds were purchased either side, in Craven and Villiers Streets. Powers for enlargement of the station, and for a further widening of the bridge (on the City side) were obtained in 1900, but no action was taken, largely because of the uncertainty caused by the Charing Cross Bridge Scheme, a matter which will be considered presently. Eventually, electrification and resignalling created a substantial increase in terminal capacity, rendering physical expansion less urgent.

### UNPREMEDITATED REBUILDING

A rebuilding of sorts did take place in the 1900s, but it was unpremeditated. A programme of roof maintenance work was begun in June 1905, and for the remainder of the year, some thirty or so men toiled away above the trains and passengers. On the afternoon of 5 December, glazing and sash bars were being renewed when, at approximately 3.45, there was a sudden and unusual noise. The repair men were seen trying to escape from their precarious situation, and staff and passengers beat a hasty retreat, fearing that worse was to follow. It did. Twelve minutes later, the physical strains worked themselves out and 70 ft of the roof, two bays, with the huge windscreen at the river end, crashed down into the station with a roar, pushing the side wall outwards until it tipped over on to the Avenue Theatre at the bottom of Craven Street (now the Playhouse). About 100 men were at work on the reconstruction of that building, and three were crushed to death as the avalanche of iron and bricks thundered through its roof. In the station itself, three more men had died as the 3.50 pm train for Hastings was buried in the rubble.

The railway staff closed Charing Cross at once, shutting the forecourt gates and halting incoming trains on the bridge, whilst police sealed off Craven and Villiers Streets; medical staff from Charing Cross Hospital, alerted by the thunderous crash, tended the wounded and dying. Firemen and railwaymen were soon busy shoring up the wreckage.

The formal inquiries established that the cause of the accident was a sudden fracture in a weak wrought-iron tie rod of the main principal next to the windscreen. It was thought that a flaw in welding had occurred at the time of manufacture and that during the next forty-two years the rod had gradually weakened as the metal expanded and contracted with changes in air temperature.

Some additional strain had been imposed by the weight of the repair gang and their staging, and although this was not in any way unreasonable, it was the immediate cause of the final fracture.

Although some engineering witnesses had given the remaining eleven bays of the roof at least forty more years of safe life, the railway company decided to take no chances and brought it all down. The side walls were rebuilt at slightly reduced height and a new ridge and furrow type roof was erected in place of the old single span. This had no end screen, but the girder across the outer end was decorated with a large coat of arms, flanked by the letters SE CR.

During the reconstruction, the station remained closed to traffic, but the various amenities and offices, including the refreshment rooms, were opened towards the end of December. Most trains terminated at Cannon Street, but some boat trains, and all horse and carriage traffic, were dealt with at Victoria. A partial train service was restored on 19 March 1906.

Good came out of evil, not for the SECR, but for the Underground Company, who were building a tube station beneath the forecourt and paying £60,000 for the privilege. Before the accident, the main-line company had insisted that any temporary occupation of the forecourt for this work should be as brief as possible to avoid any interference with the cab traffic in and out of the terminus, and the engineers had therefore planned to work upwards from the tube tunnel, by no means an easy task. When the roof collapsed, the Underground Company suggested the closure of the terminus might have changed the situation. They were told that they could break up the forecourt, provided all was made good within six weeks. Good use was made of this time, and the construction of the tube station was greatly facilitated. The Charing Cross Euston & Hampstead Railway was opened to the public on 22 June 1907, placing the terminus in direct communication with Euston, Highgate and Golders Green. Stairs from the main-line concourse led directly to the tube station booking hall beneath the forecourt, whilst other entrances were available in West Strand and Villiers Street.

Following the completion of the new roof, the amenities of the terminus were rebuilt and improved. The dark and narrow booking offices were demolished and the various waiting and other rooms in the ground floor of the frontage building were entirely rearranged. In the centre a new combined booking hall was built measuring 58 ft by 22 ft. On the eastern side of this was a new general waiting room, 34 ft by 33 ft, panelled in Riga wainscot oak. Between this and the concourse was a new ladies' waiting room 34 ft by 22 ft, its walls covered with scagliola marble; stairs led down from this to the lavatories, bathroom and dressing room constructed in the upper space of the arches under the station. This work was completed in 1913. The general waiting room was converted to an inquiry and reservation office in the 1950s.

As the nearest English railway system to the scene of war, the SECR played an important strategic role during 1914-18. Charing Cross, close to the centre of government and administration, was in the thick of things, and in constant use by ministers, high ranking officials and their staff on their way to and from France. A special train, coded *Imperial A*, consisting of a D or E 4–4–0, a Pullman car partly converted, or saloon, and a bogie brake composite, was held in a constant state of readiness for emergency journeys from Charing Cross to the coast. This train ran non-stop on a cleared path and 283 journeys were made by it during the war period. In addition, a military staff officers' train was despatched daily to Folkestone at 12.20 pm. When a critical situation arose on the Western Front in March 1918, vans of small arms ammunition were attached to this train and flown direct from Folkestone to the beleaguered sections of the front. In the opposite direction, a sad procession of ambulance trains brought back the mutilated bodies of the young men who had left their homeland in such high enthusiasm and patriotic fervour. The reception of sick and wounded was concentrated at the partially completed Dover Marine station from 2 January 1915 and the trains ran from there not only to Charing Cross, but to hospitals all over the country. This ambulance traffic was conducted with great efficiency and speed. An account in *British Medical Journal* for 1 August 1917, recorded that the first wounded of the Battle of Messines, which had begun at dawn on 7 June 1917, were brought into Charing Cross station at 2.15 pm the same day.

Precautions against air attack were taken at a surprisingly early date. At the end of October 1914, following a Zeppelin raid on Antwerp, but before any raids on England, the London district superintendent of the SECR instructed the Charing Cross stationmaster to post a responsible man to keep lookout on the bridge as soon as telephone warning of imminent danger was received from London Bridge. Should danger threaten, no trains were to be allowed on the bridge. But nothing more serious than a few panes of broken glass happened to Charing Cross.

During the war years, civil traffic to Europe was severely restricted. Dover was appropriated entirely for military purposes and there were no public boat services from 3 August 1914. All SECR civil traffic was diverted to Victoria from 15 November, one advantage being that that station provided more space for the rigorous passport and immigration controls that had been introduced. Restrictions were further increased in November 1915 when the SECR ceased to handle civilian boat traffic via Folkestone.

With the ending of the war, the SECR resumed its cross Channel services; Dover—Ostend began again on 18 January 1919; Dover—Boulogne on 3 February 1919 (Folkestone reopened on 1 March); and Dover—Calais on 8 January 1920. As the stringent customs, passport and immigration examinations were continued after the armistice, the SECR made the sensible decision to concentrate all the associated boat train services at the more spacious Victoria from 8 January 1920.[5] The former LCDR terminus also offered the advantage of engine and carriage accommodation conveniently close to the station. (Continental empty carriage stock for Charing Cross was worked up from Rotherhithe Road, taking about twenty-five minutes, including the necessary reversal at Surrey Canal Junction.)

With the transfer of the boat train traffic, Charing Cross lost much of its character and romance. It was never the same again. But before this happened, there was a final blaze of glory, commemorated by a plaque near the entrance to the booking hall. On 26 December 1918, President Woodrow Wilson of the United States arrived at Charing Cross, where he was greeted by King George V and his ministers: 'at a supreme hour in human history. The war over, the future to be fashioned, the two nations significantly met'.

Slowly, the old international atmosphere faded away. The Customs shed was demolished and the cab rank from Villiers Street blocked up; signs reading HERREN, DAMES, or BAGAGES were taken down.

## THE BATTLE OF THE BRIDGES

Some people were hoping that Charing Cross would not only lose its boat trains, but would close altogether. Soon after the formation of the London County Council in 1889 there had developed within that body an entirely commendable and new-found pride in the capital city and its appearance. In the Progressive Party in particular there bubbled a healthy zeal to make London a better place to live in. A leader of this movement was

John Burns,[6] who cherished dreams of a new riverscape, with a graceful road bridge in place of the Charing Cross railway bridge.

Within the LCC, the proposal to demolish the railway bridge and reconstruct the terminus on the south bank met with considerable support, as it would permit the widening of West Strand, and provide a new road bridge over the river at a point where one was said to be urgently required. In 1901 the Council sought the railway company's views, but the SECR was not enthusiastic and the expense of purchasing a new site for the terminus was enough to give the LCC pause. Discussions were held at intervals, but no tangible scheme emerged before the outbreak of the first world war. Meanwhile, the SECR had a problem on their hands.

Designed for the lightweight locomotives of the 1860s, the original bridge had a maximum live load of one ton per foot of track, about half that required for the steam engines of the twentieth century. While the station was closed for the reconstruction of the roof in 1906, the opportunity was taken to make a thorough examination of the bridge. Some new main girders were then put in to strengthen it, but this was not in itself sufficient, and the civil engineer had been obliged to follow the work with load restrictions, to avoid overstressing the girders and foundations. The heavier classes of locomotives were banned from the structure and it was ruled that not more than two of the tracks should be under load at the same time, and then not on adjacent lines. This produced serious delays because trains had to be held at one side or the other whilst another train passed in the contrary direction, and the effect was to reduce the capacity of the bridge by 25-33 per cent.

In 1916 the SECR came to Parliament seeking powers to strengthen the bridge more substantially, so that it could be used to the full extent of its track capacity, postponing indefinitely the need for any further widening or reconstruction. Four new masonry piers were to be built and balanced cantilever brackets erected to take the strain from the cross girders, forming arched spans.

Perhaps the railway company hoped that its Bill would go through on the nod, whilst the war occupied everyone's attention. If so, it was unlucky; the controversy erupted with new force. In Parliament, Burns worked himself into a great froth:

> It violates all the canons of public taste, and it outrages all the amenities of a fine riverside view . . . now is the hour when a

discussion of this problem suggests that all the local authorities concerned, and the railway company, should substitute for the Charing Cross station, which is cabin'd, cribb'd, confin'd on the north, a fine station on the south.

Others opposed on the flimsy grounds that the new arches would impede navigation, and the Permanent Secretary of the Office of Works was quoted as being of the opinion that the proposed works would make the bridge even uglier. This official counselled delay, pointing out that Charing Cross was unlikely to be adequate for future traffic, especially when the Channel Tunnel was built. Someone else inserted the notion that the site of the station might be required after the war for a national monument to Lord Kitchener. Despite Board of Trade support, the Bill was defeated in a thin House of Commons, when railway director MPs were otherwise engaged.

Another attempt was made in the following year. The Bill, which included abandonment of the 1900 powers to widen the bridge, was more successful, thanks to better explanations of the company's needs and intentions and a less emotive reception in Parliament. The Act, passed on 2 August 1917, insisted that the new spans should have curved soffits, firmly imposed a ban on enlarging the *station*, as well as the bridge, and required that no work above water level be started for three years. In the meantime, beginning at the end of October 1916, urgent minor strengthening work was undertaken between 12.30 am and 8.30 am each day, some trains terminating at Cannon Street during those hours.

Burns pressed on, enlisting the aid of other politicians and artists to work for the destruction of 'that ugly red oxide Behemoth which sprawls from the north to the south', but after some meetings and pamphleteering in 1916-17, the fuss subsided. Repainted navy grey by the SR, the Behemoth attracted less attention.

But not for long. Interest in the bridge revived in 1925 when a Royal Commission on Cross River Traffic in London considered various bridge schemes. In May, the LCC and the SR had an informal conference on the future of Charing Cross Bridge, but reached no conclusions. The report of the Commission, published in 1926, included a proposal that the monstrosity be replaced by a monster: a double-decker, 60 ft road above, six rail tracks below, with a new Charing Cross station into the bargain, a little east of the old. To this the SR offered no objection, secure in the knowledge that it would gain improved terminal facilities, backed by adequate compensation. After consulting with the LCC, the Ministry

of Transport then requested Messrs Mott, Hay & Anderson, the
consulting engineers, to investigate and cost the project in detail,
with the assistance of the LCC's chief engineer, Sir George W.
Humphrey, and A. W. Szlumper, the former chief engineer of the
SR.

In May 1928 the engineers reported, finding the double-deck
scheme quite feasible, but once again throwing up the old idea of
a road bridge, with the railway removed to the south bank.
Szlumper naturally refused to endorse the latter proposal. The report alleged that the road bridge scheme would be much cheaper;
£10.77 million against £13.05 million for a satisfactory double-
deck bridge and approaches. Promising a 75 per cent contribution
towards the cost of an agreed scheme, the government favoured
the road bridge, and the Prime Minister (Stanley Baldwin) urged it
upon the SR as a matter of national importance. After achieving a
modification which brought the proposed new terminus from
Waterloo junction to the river bank, the SR waited while the LCC
prepared firm plans. Provisional agreement was reached between
the council and the railway company in 1929; in return for the
railway viaduct beyond York Road, the bridge, and all railway
property at Charing Cross, the LCC offered the SR the eight and a
half acre Lion Brewery site (immediately south of Waterloo
Bridge, bounded by the river, Waterloo Road, and the line of the
railway viaduct), for the new terminus.

In addition to the cost of the new terminus, the SR was to receive £325,000 as compensation for the hotel and other losses. On
30 July 1929, after the directors had recommended these terms as
the best available, and told the shareholders that the plan had been
accepted with reluctance, and only because the government had
said it was of national importance, a substantial majority of the
proprietors voted in favour of the agreement.

An LCC bill was then prepared, seeking the necessary powers for
a 95 ft wide road bridge and approaches, and for railway access
to the new station and hotel site. It was now Parliament's turn to
influence events. No fault was found with the idea of a road bridge
at this site, but the Commons Select Committee, under Sir Henry
Cautley, could not stomach the idea of a railway terminus prominently placed at the bridgehead on the south bank, and the Bill was
rejected on 6 May 1930. After this, the LCC exhaustively examined
a number of alternative proposals including the construction of a
terminus below street level, out of sight from across the river. Still
hoping for the 75 per cent grant, the Council was ready in July
1931 to promote another Bill, but the Government had second

(above) *Waterloo 'A' Box, looking outwards 1911. The skyline signals have already been pruned;* (below) *Charing Cross signals and river bridge c 1864*

Page 258

(above) *Charing Cross interior in 1864. The cab ramp from Villiers Street is seen in the centre; (below) Charing Cross with its new roof c 1911.* SECR 4-4-0 No 165 *is about to leave with a Dover Boat train*

thoughts, and the Minister of Transport announced that in view of the controversial nature of the south bank terminus proposal, the changes stemming from railway electrification, and the serious economic situation, he was not prepared to renew the offer of a 75 per cent grant. That killed the scheme stone dead.

In 1936 the problem was examined by the London & Home Counties Traffic Advisory Committee, which concluded that pruning back the railway to the south side was no longer a practical proposition; a tunnel was out of the question from the engineering point of view, and the double-deck bridge scheme of 1926 seemed the only answer. The SR announced that it was willing to co-operate, and was anxious for a decision, as it wished to rebuild both the station and the hotel. The Westminster City Council and the Metropolitan Police Commissioner also expressed support for retaining the terminus on the north side. Further moves in the game were effectively stifled by the outbreak of war, and since 1945, apart from the occasional newspaper article, there has been no revival. It would be unwise to assume that the issue is dead.


### BENEFITS OF ELECTRIFICATION

In spite of all the expenditure on legislation, nothing more was done to strengthen the bridge, and the working restrictions continued until 1926 when electrification of the Eastern Section suburban services presented a neat solution to the problem. With a uniformly distributed load of only 0.7 ton per foot, multiple-unit electric trains imposed no strains on the old bridge; it was therefore decided to route all the electric services over this part of the structure, reserving the stronger 1887 section for the main-line steam trains. The load on the original bridge was further relieved by reducing the running roads to two (up and down local) and using the rest of the space for sidings arranged in such a way that there could be no possibility of lines being simultaneously loaded side by side except over the short section resting on the masonry pier nearest the Surrey side. These arrangements gave the old bridge a lower level of stresses than those in Hawkshaw's calculations—the mildly alarming shudder that one experiences on the footway as a train rumbles across is no more significant than the movement of a skyscraper in a strong wind.

With the rearrangement of tracks on the bridge, the order of the lines between Belvedere Road and Metropolitan junction, north to south, became:

Q

down local
up local
down through
up through.

At the south-east corner of the bridge, near Belvedere Road, the old turntable, water crane and coaling stage were retained, connections being provided to the up and down local lines so that steam engines could be worked to the electrified side in emergency.

Other changes were made in Charing Cross station. The numbering of the platforms was reversed so that 1 was against Villiers Street, and 6 by Craven Street. All platforms were lengthened, 1 and 2 to 610 ft and 640 ft, 2 and 3 to 750 ft and 5 and 6 to 690 ft and 748 ft. Numbers 1 to 3 were electrified. With the removal of the middle road between 4 and 5, a useful widening of platform 4 was achieved. Between the outer end of platform 6 road and the edge of the bridge, there was a short loop siding for standing engines. As engine movements from one platform to another across the width of the station were no longer necessary, it was possible to simplify the track layout at the outer ends of the platforms.

The final changeover, including the rearrangement of tracks, was made on 22/24 August 1925 and on Sunday 23 August a skeleton service of local trains ran on a single line from London Bridge, hand signalled into Charing Cross. All work was not completed until November. Electric services to Orpington, Bromley North, Addiscombe, Hayes and Beckenham junction started on 28 February 1926, and those to Dartford by all four routes began on 6 June. Electrification encouraged the usual traffic increase: the terminus was handling 71,200 passengers daily in 1930, compared with 48,800 in 1925.

A gruesome discovery was made in the cloakroom in 1927. Their suspicions aroused by a foul odour issuing from a trunk, the attendants summoned the police. The case was found to contain five separate pieces of a woman, later identified as a Mrs Bonati. She had been killed in Rochester Row by a man called John Robinson, who was eventually traced and convicted.

During the 1930s some modest improvements were made to the terminus. The circulating area was enlarged in 1930 by setting forward the buffers of platforms 2 and 3 some 65 ft, bringing them into line with those of platform 1, which had been set back slightly to the eastern side of the Villiers Street steps. In 1934 the ugly and crude wooden platform gates were replaced by metal barriers; two years later, these were rearranged to provide direct access across the ends of 1 to 3. Suburban traffic increased steadily

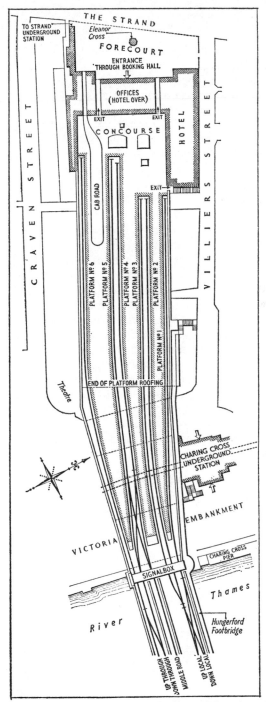

*Plan of Charing Cross 1964. From the* Railway Magazine, *January 1964*

at Charing Cross, as more offices opened in the West End. To accommodate this growth, additional rush-hour trains were provided to and from Charing Cross in 1932.

Although no longer possessing the strategic importance it had in 1914-18, Charing Cross received its share of attention in the air attacks of the second world war. A train standing in the station was badly damaged during a daylight raid in the Whitehall area on the morning of 8 October 1940, but the worst onslaught came on the night of 16/17 April 1941, when the hotel was severely damaged by fire and high explosive and many fires were started on the bridge. Four trains were set alight, three within the station, another on the bridge, and whilst these were being dealt with, a porter discovered that a land mine had come to rest near the signal cabin, its parachute gear entangled in the girders of the bridge. A fire under No 4 platform was creeping towards this 28 cwt mine, but was brought under control when within 12 ft of the canister, which the heat of the fires had fused to the conductor rail. Throughout 17 April the station remained closed whilst the fires were extinguished in the hotel, the mine defused and debris cleared. Another bad night was experienced on 10/11 May, and the terminus was again closed for a while.

After the excitements of Spring 1941, things remained quiet until 18 June 1944 when a flying bomb blew out a span of the 1864 bridge near the south side. The site of this damage is still marked by a missing section of the original ornamental balustrade in the footway. Access to the station was still available via the tracks on the upstream side, and trains were running over them by 11.30 am. Normal working over the bridge was not resumed until 4 December.

Repairs to the hotel were deferred until after the war, but by 1951 everything had been restored and a new top storey added. Little or no attempt was made to match the new work with Barry's style, and its rather plain appearance tended to spoil the whole, though the incongruity has been less obvious since BR completed a thorough cleaning of the masonry and brickwork of the hotel and Cross in the early 1960s.

### TEN-CAR TRAIN SCHEME

As at the other Eastern Section stations, platform lengthening was necessary for the ten-car train scheme. This involved a new track layout for the approaches to platforms 1 to 3. Once again this was laid out and tested at New Cross before being placed in its final position on 2/3 April 1954. Ten-car trains worked on the Bexleyheath line from 14 June 1954, and on the Dartford loop from 13 June 1955, but the full service of the long trains did not operate until 17 June 1957.

The widening of West Strand, planned by the LCC at the turn of the century, was at last realised in the late 1950s. The work entailed a reduction in the size of Charing Cross forecourt with the consequent disappearance of the boundary pillars and lodges (demolished in 1958). The entrance to the tube station needed no alteration as it had been sited on the new building line in 1906!

A scheme for a pedestrian subway under the Strand to divert the rush-hour tide from the roadway was announced in 1956, but was not completed until 23 years later. In abeyance is a 1963 proposal to link the station concourse with the Hungerford footbridge. When these works are finally achieved, there will be a safe footway from Trafalgar Square to the concourse of Waterloo station.

To meet the requirements of the 1951 Festival of Britain, the 54 ft turntable at Belvedere Road was removed, after which steam engines had to run back to Ewer Street depot to turn. Steam working into Charing Cross came to an end in June 1961 upon the completion of the Kent Coast electrification scheme. Before that, in June 1958, multiple-unit diesel-electric trains had taken over the service to Hastings via Tunbridge Wells.

With remarkable ingenuity, the Southern timetable men succeeded in introducing six more trains into the rush hour at Charing Cross from 10 July 1967, making thirty arrivals between 8 and 9 am. This was achieved by closer signalling at London Bridge, by running some trains through that station without stopping, and by reducing the number of trains travelling south over Borough Market junction in the peak hour (empty trains from Charing Cross were diverted to new sidings at Southwark depot and Blackfriars). To celebrate the occasion, BR redecorated Charing Cross with new signs, and erected bright modern barrier screens in blue and white, with departure information over each platform entrance. These platform indicators, together with a combined departure indicator on the hotel wall on the Villiers Street side of the concourse, were of the flap type, electrically controlled from a console in the train announcer's room above the concourse. The indications were transmitted by the agency of punched cards, or by manual switch operation if required.

In addition to its important suburban traffic, and the Hastings service already mentioned, Charing Cross remains the terminus for main-line trains to Folkestone and Dover via Tonbridge. These leave from platform 6 (748 ft), the only platform usable by a 12-car corridor train (even then, one car is off the end).

A big question mark still hangs over the future of this station. A plan for 'development', including offices, shops and showrooms, and an extension of the hotel over the platform, was produced in May 1963, but failed to obtain planning permission. The abolition of the railway from the Westminster bank is still advocated from time to time by people who never use the station and choose to ignore the convenience of the thousands who do. Meanwhile Charing Cross is a clean and efficiently run little terminus handling a traffic out of all proportion to its size, and together with its popular hotel, it continues to play a lively part in the life of central London.

## SIGNALLING AND ACCIDENTS

The first signal cabin sat on a gantry over the tracks just beyond the platform ends, on the same alignment as the present one. It contained a small Saxby & Farmer frame with an early form of interlocking. Like the similar cabins at Cannon Street and London Bridge, it had an array of signals on its roof, three posts, each with two sets of double arms, each set controlling one of the six platform roads in both directions. This arrangement eliminated wire runs, and its operating rods were easy to install and maintain, but there were no set stopping places and the engine drivers had to be trusted to pull up clear of the fouling points. In the foggy weather that was a frequent hazard on this riparian site, these high signals were worse than useless, and groundmen were busy. Despite these disadvantages, they continued in use for many years, and in due course four more arms were installed above the central set, making the display even more impressive.

To work the new layout which followed the widening of the bridge, a new box was erected in the same position and opened in February 1888. This cabin began life with 119 levers, but eventually had 130, all cam-interlocked, in one row across the tracks. Walker's miniature semaphore block instruments were fitted, as in the old box, but were eventually replaced by Sykes's lock and block and Walker's dial type train describers. Safe working was ensured by Sykes's electric fouling bars, locking bolts and bars, and rod-worked scotch blocks. Three men were required in this box during the day shifts.

At Belvedere Road, the end of the first block section, the box was on the south-west side of the line. Around the turn of the century this was replaced by an overhead box, erected above the newly-widened approach tracks at the south-east end of the river bridge. This cabin had 129 levers, tappet and spring catch interlocked.

For the electric suburban services of 1926 a colour-light signalling installation was provided. In August 1924 the old manual box at Charing Cross was disconnected and the layout in the station area was worked manually from a temporary box on the up side of the old bridge, at the station end. This enabled the old box to be demolished, and new power frame, light signals and relays to be placed in position and introduced as an entity, without interruption to traffic. Four-aspect colour lights and electrically-operated points were brought into use between Charing Cross and Borough Market junction (exclusive) during a six-hour possession on Sunday 27 June 1926. The new box at Charing Cross, in the same position as its predecessors, had a 100-lever power frame (thirty-two running signals, thirty-six shunt, twenty-five points, one bolt, six spare) with an illuminated track circuit diagram at the back. Constructed of wood and glass, this signal box was no thing of beauty, the style being of the garden shed school. Its crude appearance, emphasised by its prominent position, provided good bait for the anti-railway bridge party.

There were two other boxes in the 1926 scheme, a 60-lever mechanical frame at Metropolitan junction, and the existing 43-lever mechanical frame at Borough Market junction. Both were given illuminated signal diagrams. Borough Market received a 35-lever power frame in 1928 with the resignalling of London Bridge. The Charing Cross area resignalling, by the Westinghouse Brake & Saxby Signal Company achieved a 50 per cent increase in line capacity, and eliminated the manual boxes at Belvedere Road, Waterloo station and Union Street (the other box at Waterloo, 'Waterloo Junction Signals' had been closed about 1914, after the removal of the LSWR connection). *

Despite the strain and difficulty of working manual signals in fog conditions, and the intensity of its traffic, no serious train accident has ever occurred at Charing Cross, but on 25 October 1913 a Blackheath and a Mid Kent line train collided in dense fog at Waterloo junction, killing three passengers. The Inspecting Officer decided that hasty and incautious use of the release key by the signalman at the Junction Box had enabled his colleague in the Station Box to admit the second train into the station.

*Subsequent signalling changes are dealt with in chapter 16.

At 2.15 pm on 31 July 1925 there was a side-on collision between two H Class tanks both moving towards No 2 platform at
Charing Cross. This revealed that some movements at the terminus
were still being made without shunting signals. The incident
caused a great deal of disorganisation of train services and until
matters were restored, some trains were terminated at London
Bridge.

# CHAPTER 13

# Victoria

## WEST END TWINS

The first truly West End terminus available to the southern lines, Victoria was for many years two quite separate stations, a fact which Lady Bracknell, at any rate, found immaterial. With an interesting mix of continental, air feeder, suburban, and short distance main-line traffic, present day Victoria is a characterful if dowdy station, still retaining two distinct flavours. The Central Section side is redolent of the soft, leisured southern counties, with its theatre and racing types, its ageing *nouveau riche*, and its adulterous couples; nowadays this is increasingly overborne by the bustle of the constantly growing traffic to and from Gatwick Airport. Next door, the Eastern section station, that British fag-end of Railway Europe, has the faded grandeur of past glories; the scene of many distinguished arrivals and departures in the last fifty years, it is still the gateway to London for many foreign visitors, and is thronged by those who prefer to *travel* into Europe rather than to *fly* there.

The greater bustle is usually to be found on the Central Side, with its heavy suburban traffic and popular fast electric trains to the thriving inland and coastal towns of Sussex. In summer, the other station is busy enough, with well-filled holiday trains to the Kent coast adding to the weight of the continental traffic, but its suburban load is less heavy.

Pullman is a word to be associated with Victoria. More Pullman cars were to be seen here than at any other terminus before 1914, and the Southern carried on the tradition. First class Pullmans came to the Brighton line on 1 November 1875 and the first all-Pullman train ran on 1 December 1881. The SECR inaugurated Pullman service on continental boat trains on 21 April 1910, and on the Kent Coast lines on 16 June 1919. An all-Pullman boat train, later called the 'Golden Arrow', was started in 1924; this survived until 30 September 1972 but ordinary coaches took the place of some of the Pullman cars in later years.

In the early 1850s, the southern lines had but three London termini: the overcrowded and cramped sheds of London Bridge, the remote and unloved Bricklayers Arms, and Waterloo. Only the last was anywhere near the burgeoning West End. Dissatisfied with its situation at London Bridge, and interested in obtaining a foothold further west, the LBSCR had already made approaches to the LSWR. When the latter company spurned the 1853 promotion of the West End of London & Crystal Palace Railway, the Brighton gave the newcomer every encouragement. This new line was to extend from an end-on junction with the LBSCR'S proposed Crystal Palace branch (sanctioned in the same year) and from its main line at Norwood, to a junction with the LSWR main line in Wandsworth. The 'West End' part of its title was to be a branch from the LSWR main line nearer Waterloo to a riverside terminus on the *south* bank, opposite Pimlico. The WEL & CPR, which opened on 1 December 1856 from Crystal Palace to a temporary terminus at the north end of Wandsworth Common, was worked from the start by the LBSCR, which operated a service between London Bridge and Wandsworth. It was nevertheless an independent and speculative promotion, looking beyond the avuncular interest of the Brighton Company, and obtaining powers in 1854 for an extension eastwards to Farnborough, where it hoped to meet new lines coming up from Kent. The connection with the Brighton main line at Norwood Junction was established on 1 October 1857 and public traffic to and from the riverside terminus at 'Pimlico' began on 29 March 1858, with LBSCR trains serving Brighton and London Bridge. From the new terminus there was direct road access to the West End over the Chelsea Suspension Bridge, completed three days earlier.

From Crystal Palace this substantially built line passed through Streatham Hill and Balham, and on meeting the LSWR main line near what is now Clapham Junction ran parallel with it, without a physical junction, as far as Stewarts Lane. Here it turned north to pass under the LSWR, continuing almost due north towards the river.

### PIMLICO IN BATTERSEA

Some twenty-two acres of land were bought for the so-called Pimlico terminus in Battersea New Town, but the station itself was of wooden construction, and quite clearly of a temporary character. It was next to what is now Queenstown Road, on the east side of Chelsea Bridge, just south of the river bank, and approximately where Battersea Goods Depot now stands. Its precise location was determined by the position of the road bridge and the Southwark Water Works, immediately to the east.

The temporary character of the terminus building was explained by the existence of schemes to push on over the river to a more credible West End location. A Westminster Terminus Railway, which proposed connection with the West End of London and Crystal Palace, and a terminus near the Greycoat School (at the Victoria Street end of Horseferry Road) had been authorised in 1854, but three years later, an even healthier newcomer, the Victoria Station & Pimlico Railway, had appeared on the scene. This was strongly backed by the LBSCR, and obtained its Act in 1858.

The VS & PR proposed a bridge over the river from a junction with the West End of London and Crystal Palace at Stewarts Lane, and a short line built over the course of the obsolescent Grosvenor Canal to a terminus at the western end of Victoria Street, using the site of the Canal basin. Here, next door to the newly-laid-out Belgravia and Pimlico, and within a few hundred yards of Buckingham Palace, the terminus really was in the *West End*, without fear of contradiction.

Construction was begun in 1859, and to ensure security of access to the new terminus, the LBSCR took over the Crystal Palace—Battersea portion of the WEL & CPR from 1 July of that year.

The prospectus of the Pimlico Railway had suggested that the new terminus might be used by the LBSCR, the SER,[1] the LSWR, and the East Kent Railway. The latter was a line authorised in 1853 from Strood, on the SER, to Canterbury (thence to Dover, by an Act of 1855). At first this railway was regarded as a feeder to the SER, the proposal being that its London traffic should pass over that company's North Kent line. Then, in 1856, the East Kent began to look around for a surer means of access to the capital, and found the West End of London and Crystal Palace in suitable attitude. Two years later, the East Kent had obtained an Act for a line inwards from Strood to St Mary Cray, where it proposed to join the Farnborough extension of the WEL & CPR, which it arranged to purchase. Puffed with self importance after attaining this tenuous foothold, the East Kent changed its name in August 1859 to the London Chatham & Dover Railway.

Meanwhile the West End of London had extended from Norwood to Bromley (now Shortlands) on 3 May 1858, and a line eastwards from there to Southborough Road (now Bickley) had been

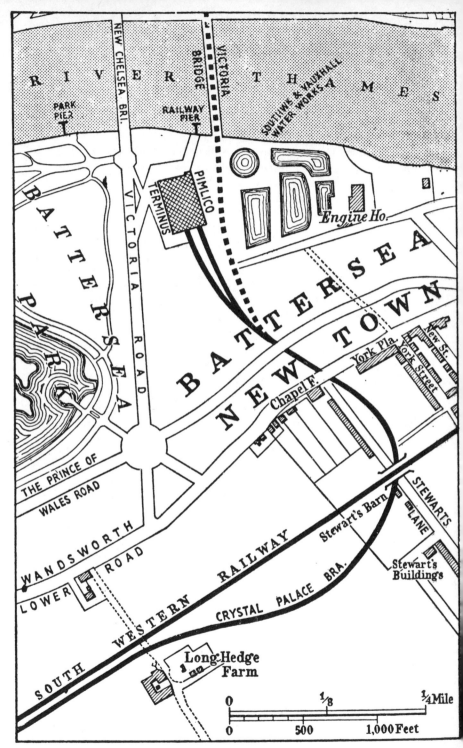

*Pimlico terminus, as shown on Crutchley's 'New Plan of London', 1859 indicating the extension to Victoria, then under construction. From the Railway Magazine, March 1958*

opened by the Mid Kent (Bromley to St Mary Cray) Railway on
5 July. This last section was at first leased to, and worked by, the
SER as an extension of its Mid Kent line from Lewisham to Beckenham, but from 1 September 1863 the lease was transferred to
the LCDR. The Chatham Company reached the eastern end of this
line on 3 December 1860, and as Victoria was now open, it was
able to operate a through service between Canterbury and London.

Realising that it would have to charge fares competitive with
those of the SER, and yet at the same time have to pay tolls to
get into London over other companies' lines, the LCDR determined
to have its own freehold approaches to the centre, and obtained
powers in 1860 to construct lines to Victoria and the City. This
ambitious project, which nearly brought the company to financial
disaster, involved a line from Beckenham to the WEL & CPR at
Stewarts Lane, Battersea, via Herne Hill, with a connection from
Herne Hill to the Metropolitan Railway right across the City, as
described in Chapter 10.

But this is jumping ahead. We must now return to the construction of Victoria station and the arrangements for its use.
Various agreements were made between the Victoria Station &
Pimlico company, the LBSCR and the LCDR regarding the terminus
and its approaches. As a result, the LBSCR, which had subscribed
two-thirds of the VS & PR capital, obtained its own section of the
terminus and use of the access line. The eastern side of the station
was to be leased jointly to the LCDR and the Great Western Railway for 999 years, and in return for the rent, the VS & PR undertook to charge no tolls for the use of its line. As the GWR was still
using 7 ft 0¼ in gauge rolling stock, mixed gauge track was to be
laid from Longhedge Junction, Battersea (the GWR was to reach
Victoria via the West London Extension Railway, opened in 1863)
to the eastern side of Victoria, the work to be done at GWR expense.

Grosvenor (or Victoria) Bridge was the first railway bridge to
cross the Thames in the London area. To reach it, the VS & PR had
to climb at 1 in 50 from its junction with the WEL & CPR (which
in turn had a gradient of 1 in 53 and a fifteen-chain curve in its
passage under the LSWR main line). The 930 ft long river bridge,
which had to be high enough to clear all river traffic that was even
remotely likely to appear, was designed by John Fowler,[2] who,
with the assistance of Benjamin Baker and W. Wilson, was the
engineer of the VS & PR. It carried a mixed-gauge double track and
was 30 ft 9 in wide between parapets. At the southern end was a
land arch of 65 ft span over the eastern end of the old Pimlico

premises, then followed four segmental wrought-iron arches of 175 ft span rising to 22 ft above high water line, and finally, a land arch of 70 ft span over the Grosvenor Road. The position of the faces of the abutments was determined by the line of the river walls and that of two of the piers by the piers of the Suspension Bridge 150 yards upstream. Work on the bridge began on 9 June 1859 and the first train passed over it exactly one year later.

## ON RUBBER, BENEATH GLASS

Immediately on leaving the bridge, the line fell steeply (1 in 57) to reach the level of the canal. It then ran due north for a little way before curving slightly north east over the canal alignment to reach the terminus. Although it would have been possible to avoid the awkward descent from the bridge by constructing a viaduct to an elevated terminus, this would not only have presented engineering difficulties (the subsoil was made ground), it would have offended the influential and aristocratic landowners, who whilst pocketing the compensation, wished to pretend that the railway wasn't there. It was in deference to their wishes that the tracks were covered for most of the distance beyond the bridge by a glazed roof supported on iron columns and arcaded brick walls. They also required the longitudinal sleepers to be cushioned with rubber. It is interesting to speculate what delightful restrictions these gentlemen would have imposed had they been faced with the obscene row of modern jet aircraft.

Of the fourteen acres taken for the terminus, the Brighton's premises, completed first, took up eight and a half. Designed by its resident engineer, Robert Jacomb Hood, this part of the station was opened on 1 October 1860, 'Pimlico' closing the previous day.

Extending from the southern side of the present Terminus Place to Eccleston Bridge, the station was 800 ft long by 230 ft wide, with six platform faces and ten tracks under a 40 ft high ridge and furrow roof in 50 ft spans. This roof was supported on two sets of transverse wrought-iron lattice girders, each of 120 ft span and 50 ft apart and resting on the west wall and two rows of iron columns. As a precaution against a train collision causing the roof to collapse, one row, with foliated capitals and bases, stood in the middle of a 40 ft cab road which ran down the centre of the station between two platform faces; the other row ran along the east side.

Cabs entered by inclined approach from Eccleston Bridge, leaving at the Victoria Street end. Next to the platform roads either

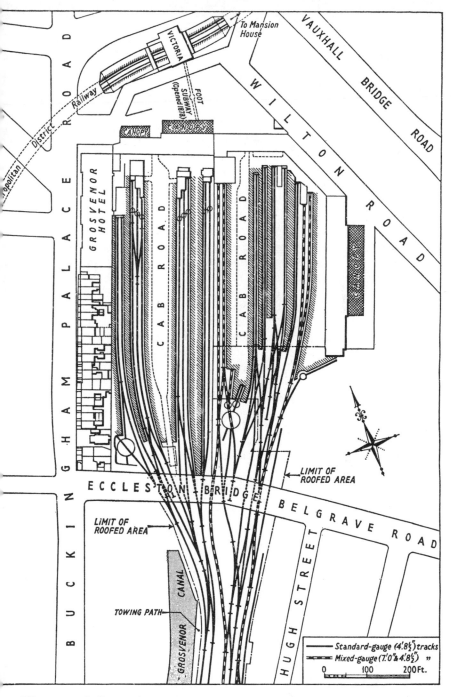

*The two main-line stations at Victoria, from a survey of 1869. The* Railway
Magazine, *September 1960*

side of the central roadway were middle roads with loading docks for horse and carriage traffic at their northern ends. By Eccleston Bridge, at the south-west corner of the station, was a 46 ft engine turntable, whilst the usual turnplates were provided at the inner ends of the main platform roads. Suburban trains used the west side of the station.

At the north end, the cross-platform was narrow and the single storey frontage building distinctly unpretentious. Discreetly hidden by a large canopy, it was dominated by the huge bulk of the 150 ft high Grosvenor Hotel at the west corner. This massively-built edifice, 75 ft wide, extended 262 ft down Buckingham Palace Road along the west side of the station. Designed by J. T. Knowles,[3] its frontage abounded in rusticated stone blocks and crinkly-carved stonework, later to prove perfect resting places for soot. Completed in 1861, the 300-room hotel was owned by an independent company attracted to the site by the presence of the railway.

Two years after the opening of the Brighton station, on 25 August 1862, the LCDR and GWR terminus came into use (the LCDR had been using temporary accommodation at Victoria since its arrival in London in December 1860). This second station occupied six acres along the eastern side of the Brighton terminus, with a main entrance and offices on the east, in a turning off Wilton Road. The latter building in yellow brick, with stone facings, was plain, even severe, in appearance. By 1869 the Chatham station had nine tracks, four of mixed gauge, with nine platform faces. Between the two westernmost faces was a cab road, and the south end of these platforms terminated in horse and carriage docks, with a locomotive turntable just beyond. The 740 ft long iron roof, designed by John Fowler, was in the form of two tied lattice arch spans of 124 ft and 117 ft.

### GREAT WESTERN SERVICES

Whoever had sold a part share in the lease to the GWR had a very persuasive manner, for Victoria could not have brought that company much income. The GWR service began appropriately on 1 April 1863, providing connections to the main line trains at Southall. Later, some trains ran through to Uxbridge, Reading, Slough and even Windsor. In addition to the basic service there were occasional oddities: a slip coach off trains from Bristol and Birmingham in 1864, a Sunday train for river pleasures at Henley between 1904 and 1913. Sunday railcars from Victoria or Clapham

Battersea Park

New Chelsea Bridge

River Thames

PIMLICO TERMINUS

Nine Elms

W.R.

*A drawing from The Illustrated London News 1859, showing the situation of the Pimlico terminus and the construction of the line inwards to Victoria over the Grosvenor Railway Bridge. The LSWR line out of Waterloo is seen at the left, lower, and the old Nine Elms passenger terminus can be distinguished just below the Pimlico station*

(above) *Interior of the old* LBSCR *Victoria station, looking outwards;* (below) *the inelegant northern frontages of the original* LCDR *and* LBSCR *stations at Victoria. The latter, with the Grosvenor Hotel, is in the background, centre*

Junction to the Wycombe line via Greenford from 1905 to 1915, and, from October 1910, as a counterblast to the 'City to City' express of the LNWR, one train each way daily between Birmingham and Wolverhampton and Victoria via the new Bicester route. This latter service had a very short life, and was withdrawn for lack of patronage early in 1912. Although largely rendered redundant by the opening of the underground line between Victoria and Paddington in 1868, the GWR trains to Southall etc continued to run from Victoria until 1915. All rights were relinquished by the GWR in 1932.

On the Chatham side were the trains of the Midland and the Great Northern companies. The GNR started a service from Barnet via Ludgate Hill on 1 March 1868, and Midland trains worked the same way from South Tottenham or Hendon from 1 July 1875 (LCDR trains from Victoria ran on to the Midland from 1 June 1869, at first to Finchley Road, and from 1 July 1875 to Hendon). In the Brighton station, the only foreign colours seen were those of the LNWR, which operated to Broad Street via Willesden Junction and the West London Railway from 1 January 1869. This had begun as Broad Street—Kensington on 1 September 1867 and was diverted to Mansion House, District Railway, from 1 February 1872. It was replaced by an irregular service between Willesden Junction and Victoria which lasted until 1917.

### COMPLICATING THE APPROACHES

Before long the approaches to Victoria became more complicated. On 1 December 1862 the LBSCR opened its cut-off line between Balham and Windmill Bridge junction, East Croydon, roughly equalising the distance between Croydon and the two London termini. The Chatham's own approach lines, mentioned earlier, were opened in two sections, Stewarts Lane—Herne Hill on 25 August 1862, and Herne Hill—Penge Junction (Beckenham) on 1 July 1863. After that, the West End of London between Beckenham and Balham was reduced to the status of a local line.

With steadily increasing traffic, the narrow and tortuous approaches between Stewarts Lane and the terminus were revealed as a serious bottleneck. Sir Charles Fox, the eminent consulting engineer, was engaged to look at the problem. He produced designs for a complicated series of new lines and junctions. These included extra tracks over the river and into the station, and new high-level approach lines to the south end of the river bridge for both the

R

LBSCR and the LCDR, enabling them to bypass the sharp curves and steep gradients of the original line from Longhedge to the river. In addition it was proposed to complete the South London Line between Brixton and the new LCDR high-level line, provide new low-level lines for the LCDR from the bridge to Stewarts Lane, and to link the LCDR and the LSWR (the Longhedge junction railway).

Fox's plans were adopted, and authorised by Parliament. On the two existing approach tracks between the bridge and Victoria, the broad-gauge rails were removed. An additional standard-gauge line for the LBSCR was laid alongside. For the other two companies, three new mixed-gauge and one standard-gauge track were built. As the existing tracks were between retaining walls, the work involved demolition of one of these as well as extension of the statutory covered way to close in all the new tracks with a roof of iron, glass and zinc, the gables being left open to allow the smoke to escape.

On Grosvenor Bridge, the broad-gauge rails were removed and the space used to provide a third line for the LBSCR. A new bridge was constructed alongside, to the east of the old. This bridge had wrought-iron arches with fixed bearings corresponding to the earlier ones, and over the four arches between the abutments was placed a continuous deck, linking the new and old bridges. The piers of the new bridge were faced with Portland stone and Bramley Fall ashlar.

The bridge now had two standard-gauge and two mixed-gauge tracks for the LCDR and GWR, and three standard-gauge for the Brighton, the combined width now being 132 ft 3¼ in between parapets. Work began on 22 February 1865; the first locomotive passed over on 1 August 1866 and the new tracks were opened for public traffic on 20 December.

Provision was made for a station at each end, each with two island platforms, one 25 ft 10 in wide between the LBSCR and LCDR, and the other 12 ft 8 in wide between the two easternmost LCDR tracks. The northern one, known as Grosvenor Road, was opened on 1 November 1867 for LCDR trains. At the south end was the LBSCR station known as Battersea Park and Steamboat Pier, which had originally opened on 1 October 1860 as a substitute for the old Pimlico terminus. This was now rebuilt and survived until 1 November 1870, when the LBSCR opened its own platforms at Grosvenor Road (it had previously only used the one platform for ticket collection). This northern station was very largely used for collecting tickets from up trains, but some local trains called in

either direction. The LBSCR withdrew its services from it from
1 April 1907, and these windswept inhospitable platforms were
finally abandoned from 1 October 1911 when the LCDR also withdrew. Thereafter tickets were collected at Victoria or Herne Hill.

The LCDR high-level line, one mile long, with three tracks,
mainly on a brick viaduct, was opened on 1 January 1867 be-

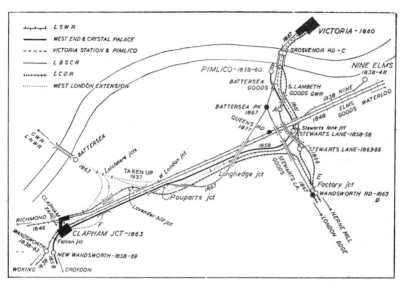

*Approaches to Victoria: A, Battersea Park Road 1867-1916. B, Batter-*
*sea Park and Steamboat Pier, 1860-70. C, Opened 1870. LBSCR side closed*
*1907; LCDR side closed 1911. D, LCDR side closed 1916. E, Wandsworth*
*Road Goods (Midland). F, Falcon Lane Goods (LNWR)*

tween Battersea Pier junction at the south end of the river bridge
and Wandsworth Road. It had a ruling gradient of 1 in 120 and a
minimum curve of twenty chains and crossed over the LSWR just
west of the original underline crossing of the WEL & CPR. The one
and a quarter mile LBSCR line was also mainly on a brick viaduct,
with three tracks, one fast up, one local up and one down. It
crossed the LSWR main line on a lattice girder bridge with a central
span of 149 ft supported on 3 ft 6 in diameter cast-iron columns
14 ft 6 in high. This bridge offered a fine railscape towards Clapham junction as it crossed the Waterloo lines at an angle of fifty-
one degrees. A double-track branch from just north west of Wandsworth Road linked the LBSCR high-level line with the South London
Line, crossing the LSWR on a separate 120 ft span bridge. The

LBSCR new line between the river bridge and Wandsworth Road came into use on 1 May 1867, and the remainder, from York Road station (now Battersea Park) to Pouparts junction (just east of Clapham Junction) on 1 December. The year 1867 also saw the completion of the South London Line, enabling a service to be worked from 1 May between Victoria and London Bridge through the densely populated inner areas of South London.

From the front, the original Victoria stations presented a shabby and unworthy appearance to the arriving passenger. Exhausted by the effort of reaching the West End and building their train sheds, neither the Brighton nor the Chatham had bothered to give any architectural treatment to the northern frontage and the ends of the train sheds were closed off with 'untidy wooden structures . . . in appearance more in keeping with those of some new town of mushroom growth in the wilds of Canada or Australia than with that of the leading railway stations of London.'[4]

Of the two, the Chatham's buildings were by far the worst. It is true that the main office block was round the corner, off Wilton Road, but most people got their first impression of the station coming in from Victoria Street. Facing them, and along Wilton Road, were a shoddy pair of wooden shacks cringing under a wooden hoarding, which though huge, left the tops of the train sheds exposed. This hoarding and other notices exhibited the company's title in full, together with a confusion of destinations ranging from the High-Level station at Crystal Palace to Paris and India. Above the central doorway, a modest board announced with an air of surprise, *Great Western Railway Trains From and To this Station*. The only other features of any prominence were a motley collection of homely chimney stacks topped by giant tin flue extensions. Next door, the Brighton concealed its low frontage building behind a generous canopy of iron and glass.

Inside, the Brighton's premises were not inelegant, though the Fenian Brotherhood had done its best to wreck them in February 1885 by leaving a home-made dynamite bomb in a Gladstone bag. The explosion demolished the cloakroom and ticket office, but the police reacted in time to whisk away similar deposits at Paddington and Charing Cross.

Outside the disreputable frontages was a large cab yard shared by both companies, bounded by a 5 ft high fence of wooden palings. On the northern side of this yard, between it and Victoria Street, was the District Railway station opened on 24 December 1868, connected to both main-line stations by a subway beneath the yard, opened on 12 August 1878.

In the 1890s, the Brighton company was enjoying a period of mild prosperity, its dividend on ordinary stock fluctuating between six and seven per cent. The directors decided that the time had come to widen the approach tracks to Victoria and build a station large enough to meet all requirements. Powers for the quadrupling of the Clapham Junction—Victoria line were obtained in 1898 and the work was completed in July 1907, including two more tracks on the upstream side of Grosvenor Bridge, making a total of nine and increasing the width to 178 ft. Each mild steel arch of the new river bridge supported its own deck. Grosvenor Bridge now consisted of what were in effect three separate bridges on common piers with differing foundations, and arches of similiar profile but disparate design.

### LENGTHWAYS STRETCH FOR THE BRIGHTON

At Victoria, the first steps towards reconstruction of the Brighton station were taken in 1892-9 when the houses on the west side, in Buckingham Palace Road, were purchased, together with the freehold of the Grosvenor Hotel. This last move was undertaken with existing statutory powers as the owners of the hotel proved unco-operative in disposing of houses owned by them. The hotel was then let to Gordon Hotels Ltd for fifty years, and the re-decorated and refurnished building was opened under the new management on 10 December 1900. As part of the arrangements, the LBSCR promised that a new 150-room wing for the hotel would be incorporated in the frontage of the rebuilt station.

Although the purchased property in Buckingham Palace Road provided another 90 ft width between Eccleston Bridge and the Hotel, and more room could be obtained south of Eccleston Bridge by taking in the remains of the canal, this was not in itself adequate for the size of station required. Hemmed in as it was by Buckingham Palace Road on the one hand, and the Chatham's premises on the other, the station could not expand sideways, so Charles L. Morgan, the LBSCR chief engineer, drew up plans for lengthening, as the only practicable alternative. His proposals envisaged two stations end to end, the North and the South, the latter between Eccleston and Elizabeth Bridges. In its final form, the 1860 station had ten roads with eight platform faces. The new one was to have thirteen roads and nine faces.

The necessary powers were obtained in 1899 and work began in 1901. After the old roof had been removed, five new louvred ridge roofs were erected side by side, parallel with the tracks, and another similar set was to cover the South station. Trusses of 50 ft span rested on trussed girders spanning 125 ft and 118 ft, supported on cast-iron columns 1 ft 6 in in diameter. The ridges of the roof were 64 ft above rail level.

Across the front, a nine-storey hotel block was built, 240 ft long and 70 ft wide, set back 56 ft from the old building line. This confident chunk of Edwardian monumental was in the so-called free Renaissance style and blended well enough with the Grosvenor. Its red brick frontage, with Portland stone dressings, was dominated by an illuminated clock flanked by recumbent figures. Below, over the cab yard, an ugly iron and glass canopy supported on iron pillars displayed on its fascia the names of the principal towns served.

The first part of the rebuilt station was opened on 10 June 1906; the five western platforms and a new cab exit to Buckingham Palace Road followed on 10 February 1907. The Grosvenor Hotel annexe in the frontage block was finished by the end of 1907, and the reconstruction was finally completed in 1908 when the four eastern platforms came into use, with a formal opening on 1 July.

Passing from the front cab yard, the passenger entered an impressive booking hall, 120 ft long and 70 ft wide, with a square-shaped ticket office panelled in dark fumed oak. The hall was tiled in pale green and off-white, with small *art nouveau* motifs in green and gold mosaic.

Latterly it was spoiled by a self-defeating muddle of advertisements, a lining of telephone booths, overall dirt and unsuitable lighting. On the east wall was the entrance to the main waiting room, flanked by tile maps of the main line and suburban networks of the LBSCR. Along the west wall was the excess luggage and baggage registration office with two lifts to the luggage subway which connected platforms 1 to 7 (now 9 to 15).

Openings either side of the ticket office led out to a 25,000 sq ft concourse across the heads of platforms 1 to 7, alongside the top end of 7, and across the ends of 8 and 9. Facing the passenger, opposite the ends of platforms 4 and 5, was a departure indicator of Howell's patent, displaying departure times, platforms and stopping stations of eighteen trains simultaneously. Replaced by a larger one of the 'card and key' type in 1927 (another was then erected on the Eastern Section side), this indicator went to Brighton. Behind the indicator was a telegraph office, which backed on to the entrance to the underground 'gentlemen's court', with its hairdressing saloon.

This cramped little telegraph office became a post office on

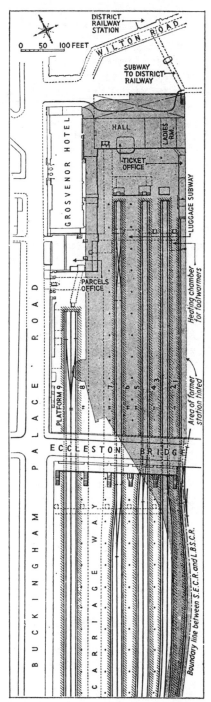

*The 'Brighton' station 1908. From the* Railway Magazine, *October 1960*

2 October 1911, one of the first on a London terminus. Although all London termini had telegraph offices from which the public could despatch private telegrams, and the telegraph office at Kings Cross sold stamps, there was at this time only one post office on a terminus—at Euston. In 1910 the Post Office authorities approached the railway companies about the operation of post offices on their terminal stations. The LBSCR and the GER responded, and post offices opened at Victoria, London Bridge (1912) and Liverpool Street. Later, this facility was also provided at Paddington and Waterloo. At Paddington a fully equipped Crown Post Office was opened on platform 1 on 22 May 1935, said to be the first such on any British railway station. The Victoria post office was closed from 1 November 1967.

In the buildings around the concourse were a tea room, a buffet, waiting rooms, a chemist shop, cloak room, and a parcels office, the last three against the ground floor of the old Grosvenor Hotel, which had an entrance from the concourse. Alongside the eastern wall, at the head of platform 1, was a large suburban booking office and a refreshment room. Each platform was entered through a gate with a pretty arch in cast-iron displaying the platform number in its 'keystone'.

Middle roads, with suitably placed crossovers were provided between the outer halves of platforms 2 and 3, 4 and 5, 6 and 7, and throughout 8 and 9. These roads could be used to allow trains from the North station to overtake those standing in the South station; in other words, one long platform face could take two trains at the same time. Platform 1 could also be used in two sections. Thus the combined North and South stations could accommodate up to eighteen trains at a time. The usual method of working was as follows: the first train would run into the North station, the second into the South, at the same platform; then the engine from train two backed on to train one, taking it out via the middle road; lastly the engine of train one followed over the middle road, reversed, backed on to train two, pushing it into the North station and leaving with it via the middle road whilst train three was already unloading in the South station; and so on. In the slack hours the South station was not normally used for passengers. Before long train lengths became such that they restricted the use which could be made of these facilities, but it was and is still possible for two 8-car electric trains to use the same platform face. At Eccleston Bridge, an interchange footway between the platforms of the South station provided access to exits to the bridge.

Platforms 1 to 4 (now 9 to 12) were allocated to local trains, 5 and 6 (13 and 14) were used by main-line departures, 7 and 8 (15 and 18) for main line arrivals, and No 9 was used as an excursion platform. Platform 7, the longest in the station, together with 8, its opposite face, extended some 400 ft south of Elizabeth Bridge, and platform 9 also extended some way beyond the bridge. A cab road ran into the station from Buckingham Palace Road just south of the Grosvenor Hotel, across the heads of platforms 8 and 9 (18 and 19), and then through the station to Elizabeth Bridge between platforms 7 and 8 (15 and 18).

Coaling stages were built at the ends of platforms 3 and 4 (11 and 12) and 5 and 6 (13 and 14). Two loading docks were available at the outer ends of 7 and 8 (15 and 18). Beyond the station, there were five tracks; down local on the east, up local, down main, up main and a reversible carriage road. The latter was originally worked by Sykes's non-token instruments. At the south end of the station, on the west side, were locomotive and carriage sidings and a 60 ft turntable.

Outside, along Buckingham Palace Road, Parliament had insisted upon an ornamental screen wall. This was duly designed by C. L. Morgan and constructed of Portland stone and red hand-made sand-faced Reading bricks. The niches in this wall still await their busts (who is worthy?). The cab entrance at the north end of this wall took the form of a massive archway, providing a suitably dignified welcome for royalty using the station. A curious consequence of the rebuilding were the artifical humps made in Buckingham Palace Road to meet the increased height of the Eccleston and Elizabeth Bridges.

In size the new station was impressive; 320 ft wide, and 1,500 ft long, its platforms together totalled two and a quarter miles (it feels all of that to the passenger alighting from the end car of a train terminating in the South station). Altogether the Brighton's new Victoria covered sixteen acres compared with the eight and a half of the original. It was a commodious and comfortable terminus, with a vaguely old-fashioned air. This was particularly noticeable at night, when Sugg's patent high-pressure gas lights bathed everything in a gentle glow, a feature which remained, despite the presence of electric trains, until 1927. Another backward-looking amenity (which soon fell into disuse) was a furnace room heating water for carriage footwarmers, a comfort which might be welcomed by today's commuters on those winter mornings when the Southern's electric carriage heating mysteriously goes cold.

More up-to-date than footwarmers and gas lighting were the electric trains, worked regularly into the new station from 1 December 1909 and serving the South London Line to London Bridge. Platforms 1 to 5 (now 9 to 13) were electrified, together with the middle roads between 3 and 4, and between 5 and 6. This was the Brighton's 'Elevated Electric', operating at 6,600 V ac, single-phase, with bow collectors and overhead wires. Following the success of the South London electrification, the Victoria—Crystal Palace (LL) via Streatham Hill service was electrified from 12 May 1911. Next came the London Bridge—Streatham Hill—Victoria and Victoria—Norwood junction trains, on 1 June 1912. The overhead wire electric system was extended by the Southern Railway on 1 April 1925 from Balham to Coulsdon North, and to Sutton via Selhurst.

### SECR REBUILDING

Not to be outdone, the SECR decided that the time had come to replace its ugly and tatty frontage buildings with something rather better. In 1907 the wooden huts were demolished, and in their stead a handsome four-storey masonry block rose up. The style was French Second Empire, with a maritime flavour bestowed by four mermaids contemplating their well-parted bosoms. Finished in 1908, the new block projected a little from the Brighton's establishment, but was rather dwarfed by it. The main feature of the 170 ft frontage was a large central archway for the cab road, flanked by an elegant canopy (since removed) which formed a pleasing contrast to that of the Brighton station.

To the west of the cab arch was a third class refreshment room, to the east, a first class refreshment room and tea room. Upstairs, on the east, was the Pillar Hall Restaurant (appropriately re-named *The Chatham* by BR). All these establishments were originally managed by J. Lyons & Co. The new building, which extended for 200 ft down Wilton Road until it met the old station block, contained on the ground floor a local booking office, cloakroom, lavatories, and yet another refreshment room. The architects were the SECR's Alfred W. Blomfield[5] and W. J. Ancell[6]; the sculpture was by Henry C. Fehr.

Under its double arch roof, the remainder of the Chatham station was virtually unchanged. In the old building off Wilton

Road were the booking hall, baggage office and waiting rooms, including accommodation for royalty. This royal suite was furnished in white and gold and decorated with pictures of various royalty, no doubt discreetly reduced in number during the violent years after August 1914.

These waiting rooms were conveniently situated alongside the main departure platform, which was at the other side of the booking hall block. At this time (1908) the Chatham station had ten platform faces, arranged as follows:

```
wall of the Brighton station
two tracks
platform 1 (main-line arrivals)
cab road
platform 2 (main-line arrivals)
single track
platforms 3 & 4 (short)
single track
platforms 5 & 6 (short)
three tracks
platforms 7 & 8 (short)
three tracks
platform 9 (main-line departures) (900 ft)
platform 10 (a short opposite face to 9 at outer end) (600 ft)
single track (alongside 10).
```

Between the station and the river were one down line, two up lines, and a siding, with an empty carriage or engine road over the bridge on the down side. On the eastern side of these Chatham approach tracks were carriage sidings (roofed over by the SR in 1928) and a 54 ft 10 in engine turntable.

Victoria had handled the LCDR boat trains ever since they had started in the summer of 1862, but it was not until the rebuilding of the Chatham station in 1907-8 that the passenger amenities compared with those available at the rival establishments of Charing Cross and Cannon Street. After the reconstruction, Victoria, with its more spacious platforms and less intrusive local traffic, took pride of place as a Continental terminus. There were not only the boat trains connecting with the Dover—Calais and Dover—Ostend services, but also those of the Gravesend—Rotterdam route, and in the Brighton station, those for the Newhaven—Dieppe.

The canopies of the new Chatham station proudly announced: SHORTEST AND QUICKEST ROUTE TO PARIS & THE CONTINENT SEA PASSAGE ONE HOUR. The Brighton's canopy countered: TO PARIS AND THE CONTINENT VIA NEWHAVEN AND DIEPPE SHORTEST AND CHEAPEST ROUTE, but the LBSCR's

Continental service was little more than a side-show; the three and a half hours' sea journey made it less popular than the Dover and Folkestone routes—the little packet boats of the cross-channel services were often tossed about violently and most people preferred to get that part of the journey over as quickly as possible, even if it did cost a little more to do so.

As elsewhere, the cross-London services working into Victoria succumbed to the improvements in street and underground railway transport. The GNR trains, the first to go, were withdrawn from 1 October 1907; the Midland workings went at the end of June 1908, and those of the LNWR in September 1917. (Until about 1939, the LMSR ran trains into the Central Section station at Victoria, but did not carry passengers beyond the West London line, such trains as continued to Victoria being for parcels traffic only.) Although they remained part lessees of the Chatham station until 1933, the GWR ran no regular services from Victoria after 21 March 1915. The SECR Victoria—Holborn Viaduct trains ceased in April 1916, but the South London electrics continued to serve stations between Victoria and Brixton.

Victoria was worked very hard during the first world war. Troop traffic was heavy, as it was the main London station for leave and draft movements to and from France. Special trains between Victoria and Folkestone for leave traffic began in November 1914, increasing until there were as many as twelve a day each way. Later there were also two daily leave trains between Victoria and Dover. By October 1918 some 7,500 men were travelling each way daily to and from leave. At the cab arch of the Chatham station, almost every day, pathetic little groups of soldiers, families and girl-friends could be seen making their farewells (relatives and friends were not allowed on the platforms for fear this might delay departures). Many, too many, of these men were never to see London again. The scene was captured for all time by F. J. Mortimer's superb photograph, *The Gate of Goodbye*.

Much was done for the welfare of the soldiers continuously moving through the station. From 15 February 1915 to 30 June 1919 a free buffet, staffed by lady voluntary workers, served up to 4,000 men every twenty-four hours, never shutting its doors. Voluntary bodies in profusion, from the YMCA to the Ladies' Vigilance Society (was the vigilance for the ladies or the men?) attended upon the sad procession of khaki to and from the carnage across the Channel. Money exchange offices, manned by off-duty booking clerks, were set up along the arrival platform to change francs to pounds as soon as the men jumped off the trains.

Outward mails for the Western Front were also dealt with at the Chatham station, a train of some thirty vans remaining in the station from 11 am to 11 pm whilst letters and parcels were loaded. Inward mail from France was received at Charing Cross and Cannon Street as well as at Victoria.

The only air raid damage to the terminus was a shell case which returned to earth through the roof, but on 1 October 1917 about 100 ft of Grosvenor Bridge was set alight when an anti-aircraft shell pierced a gas main under the old ticket platform.

At the outbreak of war, Dover was taken over by the military, and all SECR Continental boat trains for the remaining Folkestone service ran from Victoria from 15 November 1914. On 14 October the Germans were in Ostend, bringing to an abrupt end the service to that port. Civil traffic between Folkestone and Boulogne was stopped from 29 November 1915, but the Dieppe service, which had been diverted from Newhaven on 12 August 1914 continued until 13 April 1916. Any civilian passengers for France then had to travel via Waterloo—Southampton—Le Havre.

The war over, memorial plaques were erected on the north walls of both stations. That on the Chatham side listed names of 556 SECR men lost. In contrast, the much larger Southern Railway lost 626 employees in 1939-45.

## CONTINENTAL CONCENTRATION

From 8 January 1920, as mentioned in the Charing Cross chapter, all SECR French services were concentrated at Victoria. There was not only more room than at Charing Cross and Cannon Street, but the locomotive and empty carriage facilities were much closer to the platforms. It is true that the approaches to Victoria were bedevilled with heavy gradients and speed restrictions, but the other factors were more important. The Dover—Ostend service was restored on 18 January 1919, when the public were able to use the new Marine station at Dover for the first time. Civilian traffic between Folkestone and Boulogne was re-established on 3 February 1919 and a Victoria—Dover—Calais—Paris service began on 8 January 1920. The Newhaven boat trains resumed on 1 June 1919, with connections to Paris from 15 July and a night service from 1 March 1920. Enterprising ex-servicemen had begun the first London—Paris air services in August 1919, but as yet they offered no serious competition to the rail-served Channel ferries.

During 1921, the SECR altered the main arrival platforms 1 and 2 (now 8 and 7), lengthening them to 764 ft and 735 ft. A year

later, the stumpy little platforms 3/4 and 5/6, 380 ft and 410 ft
long and only 12 ft wide at maximum, were demolished and replaced by a new platform numbered 3 and 4, 550 ft long and 37 ft
wide. The Chatham side platforms were then renumbered, and
across the station from west to east the arrangement became:

> single track against the wall of the Brighton station
> platform 1
> cab road
> platform 2
> two tracks
> platform 3
> platform 4
> two tracks
> platform 5
> platform 6
> three tracks
> platform 8
> platform 9 (opposite face, outer end)
> single track (alongside platform 9).

Under the Railways Act, 1921, the Victoria Station & Pimlico
Railway Company was taken over by the newly-formed Southern
Railway, which became the sole owner of both Victorias, apart
from the continuing rights of the GWR. The Chatham side was then
known as 'Victoria (Eastern Section)' and the remainder as 'Victoria (Central Section)', but the Southern Railway soon took steps
to integrate the two stations.

Early in 1924 a start was made by breaking open a hole in the
wall between the two termini. At the same time one stationmaster
was appointed to look after both stations, with their combined
staff of 1,016. A second hole was made, to connect the two concourses, later in the year. This necessitated the setting back of
platform 1, Eastern Section (now 8) by 30 ft. The concourse was
then enlarged by bringing all the other platform ends into line
with No 1, and extra width was given to 6 and 8 (now 2 and 3) by
eliminating the middle road between them. A cab incline was constructed to Eccleston Bridge to remove the congestion caused at
the arch by two directions of vehicular traffic. This work was completed in 1925, and on 21 September the platforms of both sides
of Victoria were renumbered east to west in sequence, 1 to 17.

Then the early enthusiasm waned, and life went on much the
same as before, as if the two separate companies still existed. Until
1938 there was no running connection between the two sides of
the station (a transfer siding had existed for many years between

the outer ends of platforms 8 and 9 near Eccleston Bridge). In that year, a direct link was laid between the Eastern Section and the Central Section down local line.

The hiatus in co-ordination at Victoria may have been due in part to the Southern Railway's preoccupation with electrification. In 1926 it was announced that the third rail 600 V dc system would be adopted as standard, and in the next decade, the SR filled Victoria with electric trains. The station's first regular third rail service started on 12 July 1925 when trains for Herne Hill and Orpington began to use platforms 3, 4 and 6 on the Eastern side. 'Elevated Electrics' on the South London line were replaced by dc trains on 17 June 1928, and those on the Crystal Palace (LL) service on 3 March 1929 (the third rail trains worked beyond Crystal Palace to West Croydon and Beckenham Junction). Also on 3 March 1929, electric services were started between Victoria and Epsom via Mitcham junction.

The last overhead wire electric train left Victoria for Coulsdon North at 12.30 am on Sunday, 22 September 1929; third rail trains had begun to take over the service on the previous day. By the summer of 1930, the busiest evening peak hour saw twenty-six electric departures from Victoria.

Main-line electric services to Brighton and Worthing began on 1 January 1933 (some electric trains had run to Reigate and Three Bridges since 17 July 1932). There were four trains every hour throughout the day down the main line from Victoria, including a train every hour, on the hour, reaching Brighton in fifty-eight minutes non-stop. Electric trains between Victoria and Eastbourne, Hastings and Seaford started on 7 July 1935, and Littlehampton, Bognor and Portsmouth were served, via Horsham, from 3 July 1938. The last electrification before the outbreak of war was that to Gillingham and Maidstone East, from 2 July 1939. Electrification almost doubled the rush-hour traffic at Victoria: the number of passengers arriving ·in the busiest hour rose from 10,200 in 1927 to 17,200 in 1937 (today it is over 35,000).

Until 1930 the Customs facilities on platform 8, the main Continental arrival platform, were somewhat primitive, passengers being obliged to wait in the open before examination. In that year, the whole of the platform was roofed over, and heated accommodation provided for the examination area. Other changes of the 1930s included a news cinema similar to that at Waterloo. Erected over the cab gateway by platform 17, this was opened on 12 September 1933 and was also designed by A. MacDonald.

An increasing clientele of newly rich, and, later, some competi-

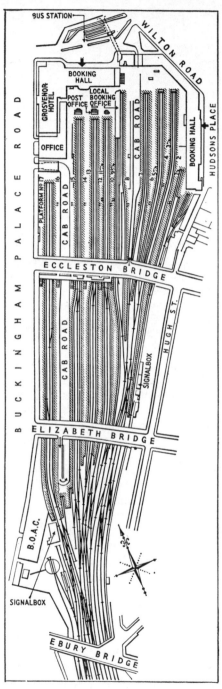

*Victoria station in January 1960. From the* Railway Magazine, *October* 1960

tion from air transport, led to improvements in the Continental services. Pullman cars had been included in these trains since 1910, and in 1924 an all-Pullman boat train was started between Victoria and Dover. Four years later, on 15 May 1929, the all-Pullman 'Golden Arrow' was inaugurated, connecting with the Calais—Paris Pullman of the same name which had run since 12 September 1926. A train of sleeping cars, working between Victoria and Paris Nord via the Dover—Dunkerque train ferry, the 'Night Ferry', was introduced on 14 October 1936. Its cars, of European pattern, and owned by the International Sleeping Car Company, imparted a distinctly cosmopolitan air to Victoria.

The remaining changes of note in the inter-war years relate to Victoria's associations with other forms of transport. Motor buses had followed their horse-drawn predecessors into the large cab yard, although they had not been allowed in until about 1909. The main user was the London General Omnibus Company, which set up a pioneer bus station in the yard in July 1926. In the following year, on 28 August, this was embellished with a control tower of steel and glass, a kind of bus signal box, from which the controller had a clear view of all five 'platforms' as he signalled the movements of the twenty-one terminating services by means of lights. This bus station still survives, but the control tower was removed in 1950 (the light signals had been out of use for some time before that).

Imperial Airways inaugurated its London terminal in Buckingham Palace Road, near Ebury Bridge, in 1939. From an extension of platform 19 below this, Flying Boat trains ran to the Southampton Empire Air Base. The first of this new type of boat train left Victoria on 6 June 1939 and consisted of a composite coach, a Pullman car and a van drawn by a Drummond 4–4–0 (a distinctly old fashioned looking engine for such a train, but the weight restrictions of the route precluded the use of heavier modern locomotives). After spending the night at the South Western Hotel, Southampton, the passengers left early the next morning for the Far East, Australia, the Middle East, and Africa. These specials went out from Victoria via Balham, Tooting and Wimbledon, but in the up direction ran via East Putney, Clapham Junction (Windsor Side), and Longhedge junction. During the second world war, 'Air Specials' left Victoria in the evening to connect with air services from Poole Harbour to Baltimore (USA) and for Bournemouth West for other flights from Hurn. The latter were the first trains ever to run between Victoria and Bournemouth.

s

Victoria had its share of bombs in 1940 and 1941, but although closed through damage to the approaches, it was not itself put out of action. On 15 September 1940 a shot-up Dornier bomber plane crashed against the Eastern Section after its crew had parachuted into Kennington Oval. A flying bomb hit the station on 27 June 1944, removing part of the offices alongside the Eastern Section departure platform, and damaging the booking office.

As the train ferries were required for military use, the 'Night Ferry' ceased to run on 4 September 1939, the cars running back to France empty from Victoria on that day. Boat trains from Victoria were rudely interrupted in May 1940 following the German invasion of northern France. After D-day, military traffic began to move across the short sea routes again, and from January 1945 there were daily leave trains, with buffets in converted Pullmans, between Victoria and Folkestone and Dover. Later in 1945, limited public facilities were made available via Newhaven—Dieppe, and a Folkestone—Ostend service started in October. Regular working of the Victoria—Dover—Calais—Paris route, with connections to other European destinations, began again on 15 April 1946, with a daily boat train and a restored 'Golden Arrow'. From the same day, Newhaven boat trains used the eastern side of Victoria, crossing over to the Central Section local line just outside the station, and to the down main at Balham. The Victoria—Folkestone—Boulogne—Paris service started again in the summer of 1947, and the 'Night Ferry' came back on the following 14 December.

### POST-WAR SCHEMES

These post-war Continental services soon built up a healthy traffic, although the number of destinations bookable from London was at first a mere 173 compared with over 400 in 1939. A new Continental enquiry, reservation and ticket office, with a staff of forty-four, was opened on 14 June 1948. This was on the opposite side of the road to the Eastern Section booking office block. It underwent considerable internal refurbishing and rearrangement in 1962 after an O & M study.

The Eastern Section booking hall was reconstructed and opened in its new form on 5 February 1951. The booking office had six large windows on to the northern side of the hall, and was fitted with four Bellmatic ticket issuing machines. With its travertine wall linings and terrazzo floor, the hall looked very much like a hangover from the 1930s, despite decorative attempts with white and orange cold cathode lighting tubes formed into squares and circles on the ceiling. It became a period piece. A large list of station names over the booking windows contained many deletions of stations subsequently closed, forming an interesting guessing game for the railway student finding himself at Victoria with a few minutes to spare.

Other post-war changes on this side of the station included the 1960 extension of platforms 1 to 8 in connection with the Kent coast electrification and the operation of 14-car electric boat trains. Lavatories and powder rooms to a new standard of luxury, with a 500 per cent increase in entrance fee, were added to the Eastern side in 1965.

The platform extensions caused the reconstruction in single span of Eccleston Bridge, which crossed the outer ends of the lengthened 1 to 7. The little-used southern part of platform 9 disappeared in the consequent slewing over of tracks. At the same time, the siding alongside the Eastern Section tracks between the station and the river was converted to a running line, giving four roads between Victoria Eastern and Battersea Pier junction. Another of the 1960 works was the electrification of the Eastern Section carriage sidings and the conversion of the carriage shed at Grosvenor Bridge to house the new electric trains. Full electric working to Sheerness, Margate, Ramsgate and Dover via Canterbury began on 15 June 1959. The 'Night Ferry', which since 3 June 1957 had also included a Brussels portion, was hauled by electric locomotives from 8 June.

At the height of the London office building boom of the 1950s, a number of schemes were put forward for the 'redevelopment' of Victoria Station, which formed an attractive site for such proposals owing to its excellent transport facilities and proximity to the air terminal. No fewer than five separate plans were put to the LCC in 1956, involving the construction of offices, hotels, air terminals and helicopter stations over or alongside the railway station. At that time any scheme for using railway property for commercial purposes would have required special legislation, but in view of the profits to be made, this was regarded as a minor hurdle. All these schemes were in the event held over, as the planning authorities had doubts about increasing the road traffic congestion in the area. In 1963, exercising its new freedom to develop its property on a commercial basis, the British Railways Board produced its own plan for an office block over a reconstructed station. This too was rejected.

In the face of this lack of encouragement by the authorities, BR allowed a notable piece of private development within the existing

station. On 1 May 1962, London's first rail-air terminal opened at
Victoria. Designed by Clive Pascall, the British United Airways
Terminal was a steel and glass building on a concrete base, held
15 ft above the cab road at the north end of platforms 15 and 18.
by reinforced concrete stilts. It was some 13,400 sq ft in area and
contained an air ticket office, passenger lounge and buffet, reached
by an escalator and staircases from the ground level. Outgoing
passengers used a light footbridge spanning platforms 11 to 18 to
reach trains for London Airport (Gatwick), forty minutes journey
down the Brighton main line. (London Airport [Gatwick] was
opened in 1958, with its own station on the Brighton main line.
There were special train services on a modest scale from 28 May
1958). By 1968 trains calling at Gatwick left every fifteen minutes
throughout the day and in the summer an hourly non-stop all-
night service was provided. In 1962 some 40,000 BUA passengers
used the rail-air facility and by 1965 this number had increased to
230,000. Another 450,000 users were servicemen and passengers for
other air lines using Gatwick. These numbers included those
travelling by the unique rail-air-rail 'Silver Arrow' service from
Victoria to Paris Nord in four and a quarter hours, via Gatwick
and le Touquet.

In 1963 the former Imperial Airways terminal, now operated by
the British Overseas Airways Corporation, was extended by the
construction of an eight-storey block on a 3 ft concrete slab over
the ends of platforms 15 to 19 incorporating a new cab exit from
platforms 15 and 18.

As at the other London termini, steam traction gradually disappeared in the early 1960s. With the electrification of the Continental station at Newhaven Harbour, most Newhaven boat trains
were electrically hauled from 15 May 1949. It was the Kent Coast
electrification that removed most of the remaining steam locomotives from Victoria, but some lingered on until 8 January 1964
when diesel-electric multiple-units and locomotives completely
took over the services on the Oxted, Uckfield and East Grinstead
lines.

Although Grosvenor Bridge had been strengthened in 1920 by
reinforcement of the steelwork and the construction of relieving
arches, it was in poor condition by the 1960s, and beyond
economic repair. A decision was taken to rebuild it to carry twice
the load, by inserting new sections over a period of some four
years whilst the traffic of around 1,000 trains a day continued
with virtually no interruption. Work began in mid 1963. The new
bridge, completed late in 1967, consisted of ten separate arch sec-

tions in each of the four 164 ft spans, each arch carrying one line of rails, making ten tracks in all, one more than the old bridge. The approach spans were 70 ft and 64 ft 4 in, the new piers, larger than the old, 215 ft by 45 ft.

During the greater part of the rebuilding period, only one track was out of action at a time, but for a while two tracks on the Eastern Section side were closed. After the new pier and abutment foundations had been prepared, the prefabricated, all-welded half-arch and single-track deck units were towed up the river in barges, lifted into position and connected up to the existing tracks until all the old work was replaced.

The marked difference in the traffic patterns of the two sides of Victoria has already been noted. In the slack hours of 1967, the Central side had twenty-three trains an hour, including one diesel-electric, rising to thirty-four (three diesel) in the peak; comparable totals on the Eastern side were six and thirteen. The Central not only has four main routes compared with the Eastern's one, but the outlets for the suburban traffic are much greater on the former LBSCR lines. Brighton is Britain's largest coastal resort, generating an all year-round traffic, which is fostered by the excellent electric train service. There is also the heavy Gatwick traffic. The Kent Coast and boat train traffic of the Eastern Section is much more seasonal in character; in 1967 there were eleven booked Kent Coast trains between nine and twelve noon on an August Saturday, compared with three on a winter Saturday. In the same periods, booked boat trains were eleven and six.

With the rebuilding of its cross-river approaches completed, Victoria awaited reconstruction as a combined terminal for rail, air and cross-Channel traffic, including the Channel Tunnel rail service. A rail link between Victoria and London Airport (Heathrow), had been talked about, planned, and re-planned since 1948. Parliament approved the rail connection in 1967, including junctions between the former LBSCR lines and the Windsor fast lines just south of Battersea Park station.

'It is intended that the rebuilt Victoria shall absorb a greater share of the West End traffic from the south-east suburban and outer areas, including that from planned building development at Kidbrooke and the new town of Thamesmead on the Plumstead and Erith marshes. To achieve this it will be necessary to construct some new connections in the Peckham Rye—Nunhead area.

'There are to be twenty platforms, handling international, airport and main-line trains on the west side and suburban traffic on the east. On Grosvenor Bridge, the western pair of tracks will take the Heathrow airport trains; the second pair the Brighton line fasts; the third the fast trains on the Eastern Section, including those using the Channel Tunnel; the fourth, the Central Section slow trains; and the fifth, or easternmost pair, the Eastern Section suburban trains.

'A development study, commissioned by the Greater London Council, Westminster City Council, British Railways and London Transport has prepared an outline plan for the new terminus, which will include a 1,000-bed hotel and airways offices. Work is likely to begin about 1970. Meanwhile, the station's value as a West End terminus was much enhanced by the opening on 7 March 1969 of the Victoria Line tube railway, providing a direct link to the heart of the West End and the northern termini, with connections to all other Underground lines.

'The new Victoria, with trains to European capitals, including through sleeping cars to Moscow and with its continual flow of air passengers arriving and departing for journeys all over the world, presents an exciting prospect. Night and day, it will be one of the busiest and most interesting railway stations anywhere.'

The above four paragraphs reflect the situation when the first edition was being written. Plans were changed and the new developments are described in chapter 16.

### SIGNALLING AND ACCIDENTS

The original stations of 1860-62 were signalled from a small platform set in the eastern wall of the covered way just south of the passenger platforms. This twenty-three lever frame, which was fully open to view in its 'hole in the wall', was completed in 1861, and operated on the interlocking system patented by John Saxby in 1860. There were separate levers for points and signals, the locking between them being set in motion immediately one was moved; no releasing could be effected until the determining lever had been moved through its entire stroke. The levers themselves acted directly on swinging pieces, pushing them to one side; these pieces were connected by bars to others forming obstacles in the path of any lever it was necessary to lock. The box also controlled some curious semaphore route-indicating signals suspended from the roof of the covered way nearby, with two, four and six spectacle glasses set in a revolving disc.

All the signalling was rearranged with the opening of the additional tracks into both stations in 1866-7. There were then five boxes, 235 levers in all, with Saxby & Farmer equipment. The Hole in the Wall disappeared, but another of the same design was erected on the Chatham side and remained in use, together with the Chatham's Yard box, until 1920. When it became necessary to adopt shunting signals on the LCDR side the cramped accommodation in these two boxes did not allow the installation of additional levers. W. R. Sykes's electric shunting signals were therefore adopted in November 1883. These were worked by small switches in the Yard box. In 1887 a similar set was provided for the Hole in the Wall box. These signals had a circular disc, red at front, white at back, and were operated by energising an electric magnet. As the disc turned on edge, it moved a small frame carrying the coloured glass between the gas jet and a bullseye.

A complete resignalling of the Brighton side was undertaken in connection with the rebuilding of 1908. Sykes's electro-mechanical system was chosen, with lower-quadrant semaphore and banner signals controlled and worked electrically and interlocked with the points, which, together with the bolts, were operated mechanically by normal type levers in one long frame. The small 'slides' for the electrically-operated signals were placed above the point levers, providing a useful saving in cabin space. The banner signals controlled not only the shunting and siding movements, but also some on the running lines. They consisted of a centrally-pivoted semaphore arm of red cloth on a wire frame, enclosed in a drum type case with clear glass in front and white glass behind, illuminated by a gas jet at the back. Indications were given in the upper and lower quadrants, to the right as well as to the left, thus distinguishing a variety of movements.

Extensive use was made of Sykes's electric fouling bars, indicated by plates carrying a blue star on a white ground. There was also an interesting arrangement of signal lamps over the platform barriers. The lamp over each gate was covered by a shade which contained a purple and a red bullseye, the latter showing along the platform as long as the barrier was open. When the collector closed the barrier, he turned the shade to show the purple light along the platform as an indication that the train could be started if the starting signal was off. The shade was rotated through the necessary quarter circle by a cord working around the bullseye and reaching to hand level at the gate. This 'passenger signalling' system gradually fell into disuse.

In the station yard were three boxes, the most important of which was South box, with 106 mechanical levers and 163 slides. This was between the dock lines at the south end of platforms 7 and 8 (now 15 and 16) and was 60 ft long by 14 ft wide. North box, 28 ft long and only 10 ft wide, was centrally sited on plat-forms 5 and 6 (now 13 and 14), near Eccleston Bridge. It had twenty-three mechanical levers and eighty-three slides, controlling all platform movements in the North station.

The third box, Shunting Box, was on the south side of Ebury Bridge, on the up side of the line. With eleven levers and eleven slides, it was 16 ft long and 12 ft wide, and dealt with shunting movements to and from the carriage road and within the carriage sidings, which were laid out on the level alongside the main lines at the point where they were climbing to meet the river bridge. Beyond South box were Grosvenor Road (six levers, twenty-seven slides), Battersea Pier junction (eleven and twenty-nine) and Batter-sea Park junction (twenty-three and fifty).

With traffic grown to some 650 movements every twenty-four hours, the need for better signalling on the Chatham side had be-come urgent by the end of the 1900s. The existing equipment was hopelessly inadequate, in particular, Hole in the Wall box, with its glorious jumble of levers made up from frames of different dates, some still with wooden quadrant plates. A scheme for work-ing the whole station from one mechanical box was prepared and discarded; eventually, the decision was taken to resignal the platforms and the lines to Grosvenor Road with the American system of electrically-worked three-position upper quadrant sema-phores, in combination with dwarf ground signals for shunting and local movements, and electrically-worked points. The contract was let to the British Power Railway Signal Company, which ordered all the necessary equipment from the General Railway Signal Company of Rochester, NY. Delays and troubles associated with the 1914-18 war (not least the loss of the locking frame in a torpedoed merchantman) meant that it was not until 4 January 1920 that the new signals came into operation.

It was a notable brace of firsts—the first large scale installation of upper quadrant signals on any British main-line railway, and the first London terminus to be power signalled. The indications were the normal ones viz:

horizontal and red light=danger
45 deg upward and yellow light=clear to next signal
vertical and green light=all clear; next signal off.

In their 45 degree and 90 degree positions, all signals were con-trolled by dc track circuits and by the signal in advance. Ground signals could be moved to 45 degrees regardless of track circuits, the 90 degree indication following automatically after the opening of the circuit. Illuminated theatre type indicators for routes were also provided. Point locking by track circuits replaced facing point lock bars.

The two manual boxes gave way to Victoria A, on the down side, just beyond the end of platform 1 and next to Hole in the Wall. This box had 200 horizontal pull-out slides of standard GRS pattern (107 signal and release, forty-seven points, two Scotch blocks, one bolt block and forty-three spares). Near the carriage sidings was Victoria B, with forty-two levers, and beyond that, Grosvenor Road (fourteen levers), and Battersea Pier junction (twenty-two levers), both all-mechanical boxes.

In 1924 the SR distinguished between the two Battersea Pier junction and Grosvenor Road boxes by designating the former LBSCR ones A and the Chatham ones B, in each case.

These two quite advanced signalling installations worked well for many years. In accordance with the Southern Railway's policy, they became due for conversion to colour-light signalling in the late 1930s, a change accelerated after a collision at Battersea Park in 1937, caused by a serious irregularity on the part of the signalman. The colour-light scheme was carried through with commendable speed, and the first section, south of Victoria to Pouparts junction, was brought into use on 16 October 1938. The remaining Central Section lines were changed over on 4 June 1939, when a new box at Victoria replaced, North, South and Battersea Pier junction A. Conversion of the Eastern Section lines was completed on 25 June 1939, when Victoria B, Grosvenor Road B and Battersea Pier junction B went out of use. Much of the existing GRS apparatus, including the Victoria A power frame, was adapted for use with the colour-light signals.

The new box, situated on the west side of the approaches, near Ebury Bridge, had a 225-lever all-electric frame in three sections, each with its own track circuit diagram. Under the roof of the station over platforms 9 to 17, certain colour lights were two-aspect, but elsewhere there were three and four aspects. Theatre type route indicators and floodlit plate ground discs, together with 'on' and 'off' platform indicators, were included in the installation. Subsequent signalling changes are mentioned in chapter 16.

No serious accident has occurred in the immediate vicinity of Victoria, but on 27 August 1910, a 14-car empty stock train and steam engine, moving out of the Brighton station on the down main line, derailed at a crossing, colliding with part of the 9.30 pm

West Croydon to Victoria, in which three passengers were injured. The enquiry established that following a movement out of the platform which had been signalled by a handlamp (the starting signal was not used), the signalman had pulled the wrong lever.

# CHAPTER 14

# Paddington

## SUNSET ELEGANCE

Paddington's rails go out towards the sunset, reaching the deep peace still to be found in the rural heartlands, stretching on to the relaxing West Country beyond; that they also serve industrial Bristol and the South Wales coalfield is a mere anomaly. From this favoured territory, the terminus gathers a distinguished clientele, which dispenses tips said to be the best of any London station.

This place epitomised *The Great Western Railway*, a belief you either accepted or rejected—there was no room for indifference. But few would deny that the Great Western's London terminus displayed a certain dignity. Brunel's graceful roof, Wyatt's elegant decoration, the spaciousness inherited from the broad gauge, all these contribute, but the indefinable atmosphere owes more to association with the long traditions of the only major railway company to survive the 1921 grouping, the only one which did its damnedest to survive nationalisation. Standing on the hallowed ground of platform 1, or, better still, on the balcony of Brunel's office, it is still not difficult to accept that the Great Western goes on for ever.

Various sites were considered for the terminus of the Bristol line—on the river bank at the south-west corner of Vauxhall Bridge; at Grosvenor Road, south east of where Victoria was later built; and at Euston Square, sharing with the London & Birmingham Railway, after making a junction with it near what is now Kensal Green Cemetery. This last received statutory sanction in 1835.

To the Great Western's brilliant young engineer, Isambard Kingdom Brunel,[1] the Euston plan must have seemed a humiliating second best. A man of powerful drive and imagination combined with great practical ability, Brunel had conceived a railway on the grand scale, and it is certain that he could have had no heart for sharing a London terminus with another line. When he put his plans to the directors, he told them that the Euston arrangement was the only valid argument against the adoption of a broad gauge. On 29 October 1835, the GWR board agreed the line should be built to broad gauge (7 ft o¼ in as laid), setting aside for the moment Brunel's misgivings about Euston. Then the negotiations with the L & BR over the terms of GWR tenure at Euston Square turned sour, and it must have been with considerable relief that Brunel heard, at the end of the year, that he could plan a separate entry into London.

By arrangement with landowners, some work was begun before Parliament had sanctioned the approach line. Authorised by an Act of 1837, this followed the alignment of the Paddington branch of the Grand Union Canal, coming in from Kensal Green through clay cuttings. The terminus was to be at Paddington, north of the Bishops Walk (later Bishops Road, now Bishops Bridge Road), and alongside the canal. This was then the very western edge of London.

Land belonging to the Bishop of London on both sides of the Walk, was leased. Brunel had a long-term plan for a permanent station a little to the south, but lack of capital precluded an immediate start on this. Some twelve years were to pass before he was to have the satisfaction of designing a terminus worthy of his magnificent broad-gauge railway.

### THE FIRST PADDINGTON

The provisional terminus was opened on 4 June 1838 with the first twenty-two and a half miles of the Bristol line as far as a temporary station at Maidenhead, east of the Thames. Reading was reached on 30 March 1840 and through communication between London and Bristol was established on 30 June 1841. This first Paddington station was mostly of timber construction, but the various passenger amenities and offices were in the arches of the bridge under Bishops Road, which were given a simple classical treatment to form the frontage of the terminus. Inside, there was an arrival platform on the north, separated from the departure platform by a wide vehicle roadway. This was quite sufficient for the traffic—a dozen or so trains each way daily. But with the opening through to Bristol, more space was needed, and by 1845 there were seven tracks, with three arrival platform faces and two departure. At the outer end was a carriage shed, with engine shed and workshops beyond.

It was at this station that Queen Victoria arrived on completing her first railway journey (from Slough, then the nearest station to Windsor), on 13 June 1842. Daniel Gooch[2] drove the engine *Phlegethon* at an average speed of 44 mph, which was far faster than HM had ever moved before. That she was a little shaken by the experience was evident in the Prince Consort's request that next time the train be run less quickly. Thereafter her royal progress on the railways was always sedate, until her funeral

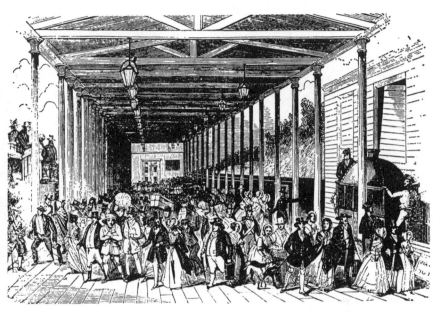

*The first Paddington station, 1843. From the* Illustrated London News

trains, of 2 February 1901, which Edward VII ordered to be driven at a fair lick from Gosport to Victoria and again from Paddington to Windsor. The funeral trains of King Edward VII (20 May 1910), King George V (28 January 1936) and King George VI (15 February 1952) also went from Paddington to Windsor.

Pending the construction of the permanent terminus, a wooden goods shed and offices had been erected on part of the land south of Bishops Road. When, at the end of 1850, the directors finally authorised a start on the work, it was the demolition of these facilities and their replacement that caused irksome delays in the programme. Spurred into activity by the imminent completion of lines to Birmingham and South Wales, the board at first agreed only to a 'departure shed', hoping that the original premises would be able to cope with arrivals for a few more years. In February 1853 they considered the matter again, and sanctioned the remainder of the permanent terminus.

### BRUNEL'S TERMINUS

Brunel was excited at the prospect, and had no lack of ideas. He believed himself competent to design a railway station, especially

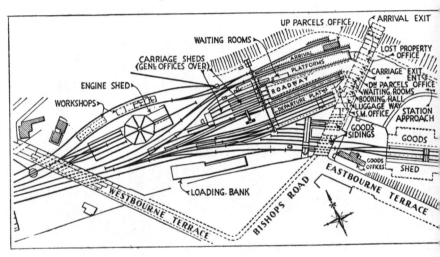

*Layout of the temporary Paddington station, north of Bishops Road, in 1845. From the* Railway Magazine, *June 1954*

one largely of ironwork, but did nevertheless call in an eminent architect, Matthew Digby Wyatt,[3] to provide ornamentation. It was not in Brunel's character to take anything but the major role in a project of this kind, and he made it quite clear to Wyatt that he would act as assistant.

As it was in a cutting, the main visual impact of the new Paddington was to be concentrated in the interior. Inspired by Paxton's Crystal Palace (he had served on the Building Committee) and also by the main station in Munich, Brunel produced the first of the large station roofs in metal. Wyatt contributed new patterns contrived from traditional Moorish motifs, rearranging the old forms in lively manner to decorate the supporting columns, end screens and walls. On the wind screens his metal tracery strangely anticipated *art nouveau*; on the interior walls his work in cement

deceived the eye, seeming for all the world like iron. Perhaps the
most outstanding features of Wyatt's work were the two sets of
delightful oriel windows looking out across the station from the
first floor of the side block.

Covering an area 700 ft by 238 ft, the terminus was about
twenty chains south east of the original station. Its principal building, between the main departure platform and Spring Street (now
Eastbourne Terrace) was 580 ft long. Served on the outer side by

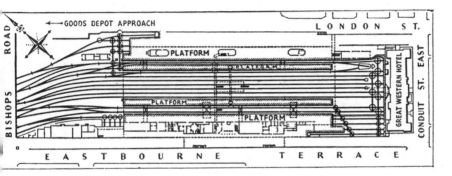

*The new Paddington station in 1854. From the* Railway Magazine,
*June 1954*

a cab road, it contained the main offices and amenities. An additional storey was provided in the early 1900s.

A private entrance to the departure platform was provided
through this building for the convenience of royalty. This corridor
was flanked by a royal waiting room, discreetly lit by a barred,
ground glass window, and filled with stuffy French furniture. Its
walls were enamelled in a salmon tint, inlaid with gilt mould-
ing and relieved by grey silk panels. Above the door of the entrance, Wyatt placed a crown design in relief, but on the platform
side, one doorway was decorated with the royal coat of arms, its
twin by the arms of the GWR.

Light and elegant, the roof of the station was of Paxton glass
and corrugated iron, supported on wrought-iron arched ribs. At its
highest points it was 55 ft above the platforms, and it covered the
station in three spans, 70 ft, 102 ft 6 in and 68 ft, interrupted in
two places by 50 ft transepts. These openings were intended to
accommodate large traversers, to be used for moving carriages
from one track to another, but the machines were never brought

into use. Fortuitously, the spaces provided for them greatly enhanced the visual riches of the roof.

Next to the single face of the 27 ft wide departure platform were two tracks, flanked on the other side by a double-sided subsidiary departure platform, 24 ft 6 in wide. Beyond this were seven tracks, the five centre ones used for storing carriages. Next came a double-sided arrival platform 21 ft wide, a tenth track, and a single-faced arrival platform and cab road, together 47 ft wide. On this last platform was the up parcels office, and on the far side, parallel to the tracks, the approach road to the new goods depot on the site of the temporary passenger terminus.

Beyond the platform ends, the tracks were extended and provided with nineteen turnplates, this portion of the station being designed for the horse and carriage traffic. As the subsidiary platforms were thus true islands, it was necessary to provide some form of passenger access. Brunel solved the problem with ingenious movable bridges; each of these rested on a truck, and by means of hydraulic power, could be lowered and withdrawn under the main platforms when through rail access was required. The bridge between platforms 1 and 2, opposite the main booking office, remained in use until about 1920, but did not finally disappear until the scrap metal drive of 1944, when someone remembered it.

Although the roof was unfinished, the departure side of the new terminus was opened for public use on 16 January 1854, the arrival side following on 29 May. When the new engine sheds at Westbourne Park were completed in 1855, the old roundhouse and remaining parts of the temporary station were demolished to make room for the new goods depot.

Before 1850, the Prince of Wales Hotel, a 'Commercial Inn for Families and Gentlemen', had been opened on the south side of the line next to the temporary terminus. Observing this to be a profitable enterprise, the GWR decided to construct a much larger establishment across one end of the new Paddington. The Great Western Hotel (later the Great Western Royal Hotel) was designed by Philip Hardwick, and opened on 9 June 1854. Obscuring the train sheds, which lay quite separate behind it at a lower level, this stucco building contained 103 bedrooms and 15 sitting rooms, some in suites. The somewhat dreary frontage was finished at each corner with towers, each two storeys higher than the five-storey main block. As for the style, it was a mixture of classical and French-chateau, the latter evident mostly in the roof lines. Above the pediment, John Thomas contributed an allegorical sculpture, described

Page 309

(above) *Continental splendour; the rebuilt* SECR *frontage at Victoria c 1910. Note the legend 'GREAT WESTERN RAILWAY' over the arch, the spot where so many last goodbyes were said in the First World War;* (below) *Brighton ebullience; the rebuilt* LBSCR *Victoria and Grosvenor Hotel c 1911. A solitary motor bus is surrounded by horse buses and cabs*

Page 310

*Brunel's Paddington, looking through the 'transept' from the balcony above platform 1, 31 July 1959*

by George Measom, in his *Official Illustrated Guide to the Great Western Railway* of 1861 as 'Britannia, surrounded by personations of the six parts of the world, and of their arts and commerce'. Thomas's hand is also seen in minor decorations elsewhere.

Managed until 1896 by a company formed of GWR shareholders and officers, after which the GWR took over direct control, this was the precursor of London's large hotels. It was of course eminently respectable; less so were the many small private hotels which later flourished in Eastbourne Terrace, alongside the terminus, and were finally demolished after the second world war.

The graceful roof lines of Paddington were well displayed in W. P. Frith's narrative painting, 'The Railway Station', completed in 1862. Illustrating the varied human life and incident of a large railway terminus, the 10 ft long picture was so popular that no fewer than 21,150 people paid a shilling to see it during the seven weeks it was first on show in London. It is now in the Royal Holloway College, Egham.

## PENETRATING TO THE CITY

Shortly before the opening of the new Paddington, the GWR, conscious of its far-flung isolation from the heart of London, agreed to subscribe £175,000 to the proposed North Metropolitan Railway. Arrangements were made for this underground line to be built to mixed standard and broad gauge, and to be connected to the GWR just outside Paddington. Lack of capital delayed a start on the Metropolitan Railway (so renamed in 1854), but when the work did begin, the junction with the GWR was constructed at an early stage and used for the removal of spoil and the transfer of materials. As the connecting line curved sharply away to the east to join the Metropolitan, it was not possible to use the existing station, and separate premises, known as Bishops Road were erected just outside. Passenger traffic to Farringdon Street started on 10 January 1863, the whole of the fifteen minute service being worked by the GWR, but following a quarrel over money and other matters, this arrangement was terminated by the main-line company after 10 August. Until its own stock was ready at the end of 1864, the Metropolitan made do with locomotives borrowed from the GNR, and LNWR coaches, surviving with sufficient success to find the means of buying out the GWR interest.

In the following year, on 13 June, a public service began on the Hammersmith & City Railway from Bishops Road to a terminus in Hammersmith, leaving the GWR main line at Westbourne Park.

T

This railway was designed as a feeder to the Metropolitan, and was backed by that company and the GWR (from 1867 it was operated by a joint committee of both companies). At first it was worked by GWR broad-gauge trains, running to and from Farringdon, but on 1 April 1865 Metropolitan standard gauge trains began to run through Bishops Road to Hammersmith.

Great Western suburban trains ran on and off the Metropolitan from the opening day of that line, eventually penetrating on mixed-gauge tracks as far as Moorgate. In March 1869, broad-gauge working over the Metropolitan ceased, but after the delivery of standard-gauge stock, GWR trains continued to share the Bishops Road connection with the Hammersmith & City service, eventually reaching as far east as Liverpool Street. There were also the Kensington and 'Middle Circle' services, worked via a connection off the Hammersmith & City line at Latimer Road to Uxbridge Road on the West London Railway.

Hammersmith & City, Kensington and Middle Circle trains used the GWR main lines from Bishops Road to Green Lane Junction, Westbourne Park, until 30 October 1871, when separate suburban lines were brought into use with stations at Royal Oak and Westbourne Park. These trains continued to cross the main line on the level until the subway between Royal Oak and Westbourne Park (H & C) was brought into use on 12 May 1878.

On the Metropolitan, a station was opened in Praed Street, opposite the Great Western Hotel, when that railway was extended round to Gloucester Road on 1 October 1868. Passenger connections between the two services were not easy in the early days. It is true that slip coaches were released into the GWR terminus off trains from Windsor to the Metropolitan from 1866-8, but there was no footbridge between the main station and Bishops Road until around 1878, and no adequate subway between the terminus and Praed Street until 1887. Indeed Bishops Road, and its successor, 'Paddington (Suburban)', have always been out of the public eye, badly signposted. Even today, many users of the main-line terminus are unaware of the existence of this part of the station and its frequent service of electric trains to Hammersmith and the City.

Electric trains appeared at Bishops Road on 5 November 1906 with the electrification of the Hammersmith & City. After electrification of the Metropolitan, GWR suburban trains were hauled to the City by Metropolitan electric locomotives.

A tube railway station at Paddington was proposed as early as 1899, but it was not until 1911 that a firm arrangement was reached. To entice the Bakerloo out to Paddington, the GWR eventually had to offer a subsidy, much to the annoyance of the Metropolitan, which had enjoyed a similar sweetener over forty years earlier. The Bakerloo arrived from Edgware Road on 1 December 1913, went on to Willesden Junction two years later, and ran through trains to Watford in 1917.

The tube railway booking hall was beneath the cab road on the arrival side, with stairs from London Street and subways from the arrival platforms. Another subway joined the booking hall with the 1887 passage to Praed Street station. Two escalators linked the hall with the platforms 40 ft below. So much for the connections to the urban network. We must now return to the main story.

Brunel's broad gauge was a fine concept, but it came too late. The Great Western had to live with the rest of the British railway system, as much as it would have liked to have pretended the rest did not exist. In 1861, when an agreement was made for an amalgamation between the GWR and the standard-gauge West Midland Railway mixed-gauge track into London became an unavoidable necessity. The work was promptly executed, the thirty-seven miles between Paddington and Reading West Junction being relaid in time to carry a standard-gauge train into the London station on 14 August 1861 (public service began on 1 October). From September 1870, most local trains to and from London were of standard-gauge stock, but as no mixed-gauge track was ever laid into the far west, broad-gauge trains to Plymouth and beyond were worked from Paddington for many more years. It was not until the early hours of 21 May 1892 that the last of the giants left the terminus.

## EXPANSION AND CHANGE

By the 1870s, two tracks were insufficient to handle all the traffic in the terminal approaches, and quadrupling was begun. Four tracks were available out to Westbourne Park from 30 October 1871, to Slough in June 1879, and as far as the west end of Maidenhead bridge in September 1884. The fast lines (renamed the 'main' in 1880) were on the south side of the slow roads (renamed the 'relief').

Traffic growth also required more platform space in the terminus. In June 1878 another arrival platform (later No 9) was brought into use, together with a cab road carried in over a bridge from the goods depot approach. Platform and roadway were sheltered by a 50 ft 6 in wide ridge and furrow roof. A new departure platform (later 4 and 5) was added in 1885. As this reduced the amount of space available for carriage sidings in the train shed, the West London Carriage Sidings (on the south side of the main line, by Scrubbs Lane) were opened shortly afterwards.

During 1893 one of the three lines between the platforms corresponding to the present 5 and 7 was removed, to allow what is now platform 7 to be resited in a more southerly position. This made room for a second line between 7 and 8, and the new arrival platform was double sided (now 6 and 7). Apart from the 1878 platform, all this work was completed under Brunel's original roof, in space made available by the abandonment of carriage sidings and broad-gauge track.

In 1881 the station buildings alongside the main departure platform were extended towards the hotel over the site of the old horse dock. This marked the beginning of the disappearance of the tracks at the head of the platforms, a process completed within another decade or so.

One does not associate the post-Brunel GWR with the very latest in technical developments, but there were occasional spasms of daring, of which the most notable was probably the large scale introduction of diesel railcars in the 1930s. Less well-known, perhaps, is the fact that the GWR was a pioneer in the field of electric lighting. At Christmas 1880 Paddington was bathed in the uncertain glow of thirty-four electric lamps installed by the Anglo-American Brush Electric Light Corporation, and supplied from plant at the east end of the down platform at Bishops Road. Although this system proved unreliable, the GWR was sufficiently impressed to embark upon a more ambitious scheme, a move perhaps not unconnected with the fact that Daniel Gooch also happened to be chairman of the Telegraph Construction & Maintenance Company, which was exploiting the electric generators patented by J. E. H. Gordon.*

By April 1886 all was ready. Three generators installed on the south side of the main line near Westbourne Bridge began to supply a nominal 145 V ac for lighting the terminus, offices, goods station, goods yards and the stations at Royal Oak and Westbourne Park. It was recorded in the *Great Western Railway Magazine* of December 1906 that the voltage fell to 105 at Westbourne Park and 120 at Paddington. *The Electrician* (May 1886) saluted it as 'the first effort to be made in England to give a continuous supply of electric light on a very large scale analagous to the rival illuminant, gas'. When the site of the power station was needed in 1906 for an extension of platform 1, the GWR, which had purchased the TC & M installation in 1887, erected a new power station at Park Royal. This not only supplied lighting current to Padding-

---

* Liverpool Street was the first London terminus to have electric light, in 1879. Charing Cross was electrically lit from 10 January 1881.

ton station and area, but produced traction current for the newly-electrified Hammersmith & City Railway. During 1907 the arc lamps in Paddington station were replaced by a larger number of filament lamps.

Serving as it did the rich dairylands of the west, Paddington had for many years an important traffic in milk. A milk arrival dock was built in 1881 at the back of the outer end of the 1878 platform and accommodation for milk traffic was also available on the departure side. By 1900, milk trains were to be seen in the terminus day and night, and over 3,000 churns were handled daily. Paddington also dealt with a variety of other traffics: special daily trains for meat and fish, newspapers and horses and flowers, in season.

Only one 'foreign' working was ever allowed to penetrate the sacred halls of Paddington, and even this was only a flash in the pan. In the 1900s, the northern and the southern companies collaborated in arranging through trains between northern and midland cities and the south coast resorts, enabling passengers to avoid the tiresome transfers between London termini. The GWR reacted by persuading the LBSCR to work a return run between Paddington and Brighton daily, using the latter's engines and stock. This train reached Brighton in 100 minutes, running via the Latimer Road spur and the West London Railway. Starting on 2 July 1906, it failed to attract much custom and was withdrawn in the following June. Just over three years later, another attempt was made, this time by operating a service between Wolverhampton and Birmingham and Victoria; but, as related in the Victoria chapter, this too was a flop.

Despite these minor setbacks, passenger traffic in general continued to grow; trains were getting longer, and a new direct main line to Birmingham was in prospect. The Edwardian years were the last period of real prosperity for the larger British railway companies, and in common with others, the GWR decided that it could afford improvements to its London terminal facilities, not only to relieve existing pressure, but to provide some additional capacity for future expansion. No clouds could be seen on the railway horizon in the early 1900s.

Some preparatory moves were necessary to clear the way. In March 1906 a new locomotive depot was opened at Old Oak Common, replacing that at Westbourne Park; new carriage sheds were erected at Old Oak. In 1906-7 the stationery store was moved from Paddington to Royal Oak. An extension to the main departure platform was completed in 1908. Numbered 1A, this was used for down excursion trains, and, after further extension beyond Westbourne Bridge in 1912-13, for down milk traffic. After 1923, when the milk traffic was moved to Paddington Goods, 1A became a convenient berth for stock awaiting its place in the main departure platform. Ten years later, it was converted to a double-sided parcels platform, serving the new parcels depot in Bishops Road. Other minor works in the mid-1900s included the extension of platforms 2 and 3 to about 1,000 ft and the construction of a luggage subway and lifts to serve platforms 1 to 5.

A major programme for the enlargement of Paddington was approved in 1906. This provided for the extension of the arrival side by the addition of three new platforms under a 700 ft long steel and glass roof of 109 ft span, which was to match the original Brunel roofs as closely as possible. Platform 9 was to be extended to 950 ft, and the Bishops Road platforms were also to be extended and widened. Between Bishops Road and Old Oak Common, the old brick arch overbridges were to be replaced by long span steel structures which would give room for a rearrangement of the tracks. Lastly, a new goods depot would be built in Battersea ('South Lambeth') to relieve Paddington Goods.

### APPROACHES REBUILT

The replacement of the overbridges was not finished until 1914, but before that, work had begun on the rest of the scheme. The rearrangement of the approach tracks was much needed. Separate up and down engine and carriage roads had been provided on the north side of the running lines to serve the new locomotive and carriage depots at Old Oak, but they ran only from Old Oak to Kensal Green box, and inwards from Ladbroke Bridge (up) and Portobello junction (down). Elsewhere, all empty carriage trains and light engines had to occupy running lines, and on a busy day there could be a hundred or more of each. Worse, up empties using the E & C line from Ladbroke Bridge had to cross all the running lines except the down main at Subway junction (a mile from Paddington and midway from Westbourne Park to Royal Oak), before gaining the departure side of the terminus. These arrangements proved a fruitful source of delays and unpunctual departures. Another difficulty was that between Old Oak Common and Westbourne Park, goods trains to and from Paddington depot were obliged to use the main or relief lines. And yet another; that between Paddington and Westbourne Park there was only one down line apart from the Hammersmith & City. The operating and signalling headaches can be imagined.

Work began in 1911 on a scheme to segregate all empty carriage and light engine traffic from the running lines over the whole three miles between Paddington and Old Oak Common. In the following year an independent double line was completed from Old Oak to Ladbroke Bridge box, crossing to the south side of the running lines just west of Kensal Green box by means of a skew girder bridge. Work between Ladbroke Bridge box and Paddington continued slowly, hampered by the necessity to rebuild Westbourne Park station. Under the stress of war, it petered out in 1916.

Ten years later, the task was taken up again. Good progress was made, all the new lines being completed by the end of 1927. There was now a down empty carriage line north of the relief lines all the way to the Old Oak depots, shared with goods trains beyond Westbourne Park, and provided with a junction into the down relief line at Old Oak Common East. The former up E & C line was converted into an up goods running line with a direct junction from the up relief at Old Oak Common East. On the south side of the running lines were the new up and down roads connected to the skew bridge. (The down carriage line over the skew bridge was disconnected during the changes of winter 1967). Down light engines or ECS trains could use this route from Portobello junction box (just west of Westbourne Park), whilst up carriages and engines had an independent through run on this side all the way to platforms 1 to 4 at the terminus. From Subway junction there was a second up empty carriage road into Paddington. After these changes, the last threequarters of a mile into the terminus, from just west of Royal Oak station, was worked as follows:

    up City
    down City
    down carriage
    up relief
    up main
    up carriage
    down main
    up carriage.

During 1936-7, further operating flexibility was obtained by re-signalling the up main and up relief lines between the terminus and Subway junction to allow their being used as required to relieve congestion on the single down carriage line. As related later, the down and one of the up carriage lines eventually became running lines.

At Paddington itself, work began in 1910. A new up parcels

office was constructed, and the immediate approach tracks were levelled and remodelled to provide new and better connections to the Hammersmith & City lines and the Ranelagh engine yard. (On the south side of the line at Royal Oak station, this yard was used for turning engines from provincial depots.) Following extensive excavations on the arrival side, the old high-level goods yard and its approach disappeared, giving place to three new platforms and a roadway. A portion of the new platform 12 came into use on 10 November 1913; the remainder, and platform 11, were ready by December 1915. The new arch roof, the only part of Paddington station that can be seen from Praed Street, and platform 10, were not finished until 1916.

Platform 10 was 800 ft long and 18 ft wide, 11 was 830 ft by 18 ft, whilst 12 was 750 ft long with a width varying from 15 to 35 ft. All three had Ransomes & Rapier hydraulic buffers, a new feature on the GWR. A second arrival cab road was constructed between 10 and 11, and brought into the station at the country end on a bridge over 11 and 12. Cabs queued alongside the new roof before crossing this bridge. Apart from the main enlargement work, there were improvements to amenities. In 1910 a space was hollowed out beneath platform 1 for lavatories, bathrooms and a hairdressing saloon.

After the completion of the extension, platforms were normally used as follows: 1 to 4 main-line departures, 5 to 7 outer suburban trains, 8 to 11 main-line arrivals. Platform 12 was mainly concerned with inwards milk (until 1923), fish, mails and parcels; on its opposite face, a sunken roadway allowed a level transfer of goods between rail and road vehicles. During the 1930s, after the resignalling of the up main and relief roads already mentioned, it became possible to use platforms 5 and 6 for arrivals or departures; 7 was also occasionally used for departures via the down engine and carriage line.

Paddington suffered no air raid damage in 1914-18 other than a few panes of glass broken by shrapnel. Although troop movements were not as heavy as at the southern termini, they were sufficient to justify a twenty-four-hour free buffet, manned by lady voluntary workers. Some ambulance trains were dealt with, a total of 351 arriving during the war period. T. S. Tait gave the station the most impressive of all the London termini war memorials. This was placed between the doors of the royal suite on the main departure platform, and featured an infantryman heavily clad in greatcoat, sheepskin, and woollen scarf, apparently reading a letter from home; naval and RAF symbols were carved either side.

Between 1922 and 1924, the cast-iron columns supporting Brunel's roof on platforms 2 and 3, and between 7 and 8, were removed and replaced by steel ones with broadly similar, but not exact, reproductions of Digby Wyatt's decorations. The original columns in the roadway between platforms 8 and 9 had been renewed with steel when the new roof was erected in 1915.

The Post Office tube railway, opened in December 1927, terminated alongside the station beneath the Paddington District Office in London Street. Chutes for incoming mail were installed at the head of platforms 8, 9 and 10, and a bank of eight chutes along platform 11. Conveyors carried the mailbags to the tube railway platforms. Outgoing mail was brought up from the Post Office Railway by a conveyor which debouched on the departure side, just behind the hotel. Some 10,000 mailbags are handled daily.

## ANOTHER REBUILDING

A second major rebuilding of Paddington was made possible by the passage of the Development (Loan Guarantees and Grants) Act of 1929. This government measure was designed to encourage major works to relieve unemployment, and enabled the Treasury to guarantee loans and make grants towards interest on capital. A £1 million GWR scheme for Paddington was approved by the Treasury, and the work, which began in May 1930, was concluded in 1934.

The project comprised the extension of platforms 2 to 11 to beyond Bishops Road bridge; the construction of a new parcels depot in Bishops Road, releasing the space behind the hotel to form a new passenger concourse; the provision of two new office blocks and other amenities either side of this space; the construction of new cab and goods depot approach roadways; the reconstruction of all tracks for threequarters of a mile out of the station, including the addition of a parcels line on the down side; and the improvement of the Ranelagh engine yard.

The platform extensions, which were covered with veranda type roofing, brought the ends to the westward bend of the line by the original station, producing some very sharp curves at this point. When the work was concluded, main-line platform lengths varied from 1,200 ft (8 and 9) to 980 ft (10 and 11).

An important part of the scheme was the rearrangement of the suburban station. Suburban traffic on the GWR had always been easy, leisurely and comfortable by the standards of other lines. Uncouth expressions such as 'rush hours' were rarely if ever heard on Great Western tongues. When Paddington first opened, there was no station before West Drayton, thirteen miles out, although Ealing and Hanwell were added on 1 December 1838. Southall followed on 1 May 1839; Uxbridge on 8 September 1856; Hayes, 1 May 1864; Acton, 1 February 1868; Castle Hill (now West Ealing), 1 March 1871; and Westbourne Park on 30 October 1871. For many years, tickets were collected from up trains at a ticket platform on the site of Westbourne Park station, and the practice continued for over thirty years after the opening of that station.

In 1903 there were only eight suburban trains arriving at Paddington between 5 and 10 am, compared with 136 at Liverpool Street (the daily total was around forty each way). But as the rush of speculative building spread over Middlesex and south Buckinghamshire in the 1920s and 1930s, the pace of suburban traffic quickened a little (there had already been some additional traffic from the new Birmingham line's suburban halts and stations). With further building expected, it was deemed prudent to enlarge Bishops Road station so that it could be used for terminating and starting suburban trains as well as those to and from the Metropolitan. The old up and down platforms, with their middle road, were taken out, giving way to two 600 ft islands, one with two up faces, the other with two down. Each had luggage lifts linked to the subway across the station. A layby siding was added to the eastern end, by the canal wall, to serve as a stand for the electric locomotives which hauled the GWR suburban trains over the Metropolitan. A passimeter booking office on the Bishops Road bridge was supplemented by a ticket office over platform 8 on a new steel footbridge linking the suburban platforms with the rest of the station.

These works, completed in 1933, involved some difficult engineering. Part of the tunnel to the Metropolitan had to be opened out and rebuilt as a covered way carrying the diverted goods approach and cab roadways over the eastern end of the enlarged Bishops Road station.

From 11 September 1933 the name *Bishops Road* went out of use, the new platforms becoming numbers 13 to 16 of the main station, and collectively known as *Paddington (Suburban)*. Normally the electric trains to and from Hammersmith and Kensington (Addison Road) used the outside tracks (platforms 13 and 16), the centre ones being reserved for terminating GWR steam trains. As all roads were electrified and the standing steam locomotives had a corrosive effect on the live rails, occasional electric trains were run through the centre roads to keep them usable in case of emergency.

In accordance with its later policy of isolationism, London Transport removed the junction to the centre roads in 1966, making platforms 14 and 15 dead ends from 20 August. Later still, as we shall see, the use of these platforms was changed yet again.

At the Praed Street end of the main station, the site of the track ends and turnplates of the 1854 layout was euphemistically known as the *Lawn*.[4] In latter years it had been used for mails and overflow parcels traffic as well as serving as a van approach to the hotel. Sheltered by short-span low steel and glass roofs, supported on numerous cast-iron columns, it was an unattractive spot, cluttered with barrows and reeking of cart horses and their waste products. Passengers were obliged to pass along either side of it when moving to and from the Praed Street underground station. At the platform end, it was crossed by a footbridge, with steps on platform 1 and platform 8, affording access to an elevated corridor passing over it into the back of the hotel.

All this was now swept away, to give place to an airy concourse under a higher, three-bay steel and glass roof. The buffers of platforms 1 to 8 were brought into line and set back a little to provide more space. A new central entrance to the underground station replaced the old side passages, and passengers arriving this way received an altogether improved first impression of the GWR.

Either side of the Lawn, new steel-framed railway office blocks were completed in 1933. That on the arrival side was in modernistic style, with emphasis on the verticals, and faced with Victoria patent stone. On the departure side, the new block had classical elevations to match the older buildings along platform 1. Linking the two office blocks was a low building parallel to Praed Street, incorporating a hotel lounge on its first floor and designed to support a new hotel wing. This extension of the hotel, containing 52 bedrooms and increasing the total accommodation to 250, was eventually completed in the summer of 1936. The hotel itself underwent substantial internal reconstruction in 1936-38. Bathrooms were provided for most of the bedrooms, the entrance hall was much enlarged, a new entrance canopy and drive constructed, and the exterior refaced and redecorated.

The lower floors of the new buildings on the eastern and southern sides of the Lawn contained refreshment rooms and an enquiry and reservation office. As a finishing touch, an electrically-operated train indicator was installed on the Lawn in 1934. The inevitable public address system, with twenty-three loudspeakers, came into use two years later.

All parcels traffic was transferred to a new depot beyond the end of the 1,150 ft platform 1, on the site of the old 1A. This depot had two platforms, 930 ft and 580 ft, its own entrance in Bishops Road and a subway connection to platforms 1 to 8.

## WARTIME WORRIES

Upon the outbreak of war in 1939, the through working of suburban trains on to the Metropolitan was abandoned, the last journeys being made on 16 September. This service was not resumed after the war. Bomb damage at Paddington was severe, but by no means disruptive of traffic. In 1941 a parachute mine demolished a section of the departure side building; three years later, a flying bomb damaged the roof and platforms 6 and 7 below.

There were other wartime worries. Those who could afford to move out of London chose the West Country as the safest refuge; at the peak of the bombing attacks others spent their nights in the comparative quiet of the Thames Valley. Civilian traffic was very heavy throughout the war, notably at holiday times. With the east and much of the south coast taken over by the military, the West Country resorts were a natural objective for civilian holidays, the more expensive fares offering no discouragement in a period of high wages. In 1944 the Government imposed restrictions on the operation of additional trains and the lengthening of scheduled ones, the object being to keep the railways at peak efficiency for military traffic both before and immediately after the Anglo-American invasion of France.

Matters came to a head on Saturday 29 July, when for the first time in its history, the terminus was closed for three hours because no more passengers could be accommodated; the concourse and platforms were jammed tight, and all Underground bookings to Paddington had to be temporarily suspended. After this chaotic morning, some relaxation in the Government restrictions on extra coaches and trains was obtained, but this was not enough, and on the August bank holiday week-end, gigantic queues were organised in Eastbourne Terrace, under the control of mounted police.

British Railways has made a number of changes at Paddington, not all of them attended with success. Brunel's booking hall and ticket office on the departure side were rebuilt in 1952-3, and the new ticket office, in use from March 1953, was half as large again as the original. It possessed eleven windows, and was plastic panelled under a mahogany veneer—a combination appropriately symbolic of the new age.

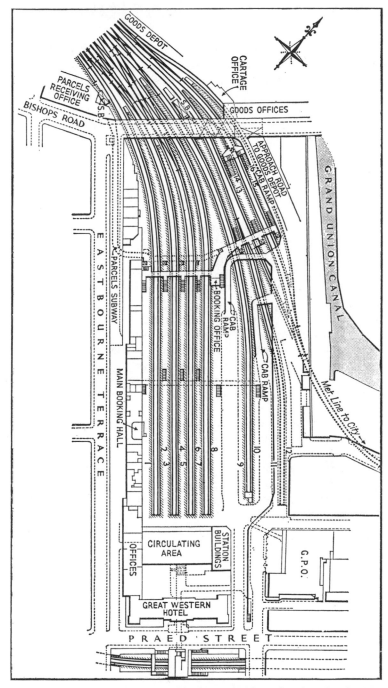

*Plan of Paddington station 1954. The former Bishops Road station for Metropolitan Line trains was incorporated as platforms 13 to 16 of the main-line station in the 1933 reconstruction. From the* Railway Magazine, *June 1954*

To mark the centenary of the station, a bronze plaque of Brunel was unveiled on platform 1 on 29 May 1954. Four years later, the appearance of the master's station was sadly marred by a distracting and restless barrier screen bearing the arms of counties served from Paddington. This screen was placed across the heads of platforms 1 to 8, and was not only ugly in itself, but successful in damaging the precious vista of the roof from the back of the station. In 1963, in slight penance for this desecration, the roof was repainted in what were thought to be the original colours—terracotta and grey; at any rate, it was a much more pleasing combination than the somewhat dreary chocolate and cream of the GWR.

### RETREAT OF STEAM

Steam working into Paddington began to retreat before the diesel advance in the late 1950s. Between 1959 and 1961, the suburban services were changed over entirely to multiple-unit diesel cars, an exercise that proved all but disastrous. Despite the modest service (a mere ten departures in the busiest hour), a batch of troubles (rolling stock difficulties, staff shortages, overburdening of the main line with traffic diverted from Euston) caused late running and serious overcrowding. There were even allegations that the bodies of the cars had been distorted by the mass of humanity packed within, making it impossible to shut the doors properly. Barely had all this been overcome, when in September 1964 a new suburban timetable was bravely introduced. This made maximum use of rolling stock, provided more trains, and gave a regular pattern of departures, offering a fifteen-minute peak service to most stations between Reading and Paddington. Conscious that they were still operating the lightest-loaded of all the London suburban networks, the Western Region men sought more customers with a publicity campaign for their *Western Commuteroutes*, but they were to be harassed by troubles and delays for another two years or so. Meanwhile, regular steam working of main-line and ECS trains ceased on 11 June 1965.

During 1961 the No 2 up carriage road between the terminus and Subway junction was converted to a fully-signalled running line, and the down carriage road was similarly dealt with in 1963. Although this provided four tracks with in and out signalling between those points, the restrictions on the approach tracks still hampered punctuality and efficient working.

## TRACK CHANGES

With the object of providing greater turn-round flexibility by abolishing the traditional division of the station into arrival and departure sides, a £2 million scheme for track rearrangement and resignalling was begun in September 1967. The tracks between Subway junction and the terminus were then set out as follows:

Hammersmith & City eastbound
Hammersmith & City westbound
down relief No 2
up relief
down relief No 1
up main
down main
up engine and carriage.

The four engine and carriage sidings in the yard between the up and down lines were removed, apart from a small dead end section which was retained for holding locomotives. Three new sidings were built south of the line beyond Royal Oak. The sharp curves at the platform approaches were eased, and the general speed limit in the immediate vicinity of the terminus raised from 10 to 25 mph as a result.

From 12 November 1967, Hammersmith & City electric services used platforms 15 and 16 instead of 13 and 16, Royal Oak station was confined to these trains, and all connections between the electric lines and the Western Region were removed. Concurrently with the track alterations and resignalling, the engineers undertook partial rebuilding and resurfacing of platforms 1, 4 and 5, and installed ninety-six point heaters in the station approaches.

Between 15 October and 19 November 1967, whilst the major part of this work was going on, Birmingham trains were diverted to Marylebone, and about half the West Country, Hereford and Worcester services were worked from Kensington (Olympia), where LT provided a shuttle service to and from Earls Court. Some suburban trains were terminated at Ealing Broadway.

These improvements were followed in 1970 by an enlargement of the concourse, achieved by replacing the unlovely barrier screen with a lighter one, incorporating a train indicator, set 40 ft back across the new heads of platforms 1-8. A rebuilt ticket office and hall were opened on 11 May 1970 with stairs to the enquiry office on the first floor.

Adjoining the booking hall, a somewhat cramped travel centre came into use on 17 July 1973. The 1970 work included new lighting for the interior of the station from some well-designed high power lamps. Care was taken in all this work to ensure it would not detract from the splendour achieved by Brunel and Wyatt. For that we must be grateful, as Paddington is a most precious inheritance from the proud age of iron and steam.

### SIGNALLING AND ACCIDENTS

The first signals at Paddington were of the disc and crossbar type, set on revolving posts. Semaphores did not appear until 1 April 1865. A year later, block working was in operation as far as Ealing, using Spagnoletti's instruments.

Eventually there were two large station boxes, one for the arrival side, with seventy levers, one for the departure side, with sixty-five levers, and a twenty-six lever box at Bishops Road station. Beyond there was a fifty-three-lever cabin at Westbourne Bridge, and another box at Royal Oak station.

Arrival box was situated at the end of platforms 8 and 9, and when these were extended, it had to be moved to a new site. Opened on 19 April 1914, the replacement box had horizontal tappet locking and a seventy-lever frame. Platform home signals for the up main and relief lines installed at the same time were of the route indicator type, with four and six positions respectively.

Between 1929 and 1932 the semaphore signals on all lines between Paddington to Southall West junction were replaced by ac electric power signals, mostly in the same locations; dc electric motors were installed for point operation, and there were track circuits throughout. On the running lines, the coloured spectacles of the new signals, moving in front of searchlights, gave the same indications as the old semaphores, but on the engine and carriage roads, three aspects were displayed (green, yellow and red). On the Hammersmith & City lines, two-aspect colour lights were provided. Most of the existing signal boxes and block telegraphs remained in use, but at Paddington three new power boxes were built, and equipped with specially-designed miniature block instruments. The new Arrival and Departure boxes had 184 and 96 slides in General Railway Signal Company mechanical interlocking frames, all slides being approach locked, and all signals detecting each set of points in the route. Illuminated spot diagrams were placed above the frames, two red lights indicating the occupation of each track circuit.

**Page 327**

*Paddington as many like to remember it. No 6005 King George II just arrived at platform 10, 31 July 1959*

(above) *Opening ceremony at Marylebone, 9 March 1899;* (below) *Marylebone exterior, 26 August 1967. The original Baker Street & Waterloo Railway tube station is seen on the extreme left, the Great Central Hotel is out of view, beyond the canopy, right*

Arrival box opened on 13 August 1933, replacing Bishops Road and Royal Oak station mechanical boxes, as well as its namesake. It was worked by two men, one on the main locking frame, the other on the Suburban Lines frame. Departure box was in use from 2 July 1933. At Westbourne Bridge, the new box, with its 88-slide all-electric locking frame, was opened on 10 January 1932, controlling the parcels depot, Ranelagh yard, the down main, and Nos 1 and 2 carriage roads.

Not long after its installation, this equipment was partially destroyed by two fires. The first started at 2 am on 25 November 1938 in the Arrival box, putting it completely out of action. Great difficulty was encountered in improvising signalling arrangements, and the Suburban station was closed. Until the opening of a new box on 2 July 1939, traffic was worked from a makeshift 141-lever frame composed of spare equipment supplied by London Transport and erected on the roof of the old battery house. Suburban services were resumed when this temporary frame came into operation on 13 December 1938, but the City through trains were not restored until 3 July 1939. Main-line signals were worked from the temporary frame from 18 December 1938.

No sooner had this frame been set up than a second fire broke out, this time in the Westbourne Bridge box, putting it out of action from 5 am on 23 December 1938. The new boxes and others at Bristol and Cardiff, were wisely fitted with carbon dioxide fire control and master switches to cut out the entire frame in an emergency. One wonders why these simple and inexpensive precautions were not taken in the first place.

Normal multiple-aspect colour-light signalling was installed in the Paddington approaches as far in as Ladbroke Grove during the 1950s. This scheme was planned on economical lines, and most of the existing boxes and equipment were retained. Train approaching indications were given by audible warning as well as on the illuminated diagrams. Through working could be made automatic when circumstances permitted.

The signalling on the section between Paddington and Ladbroke Grove remained basically as installed in 1933. Although it offered many advantages over the traditional manual-semaphore system, it was nevertheless ill-suited to modern traffic requirements, and served as a monument to the cautious conservatism of the GWR signals department. With the expectation of an increase in suburban traffic, and in conjunction with the major rearrangement of approach tracks planned for the winter of 1967-8, a revolutionary change was decided upon. Paddington was to be the first

U

London terminus remotely signalled from a power cabin several miles away.

This installation, completed in May 1968, placed all operations between Paddington and Hayes under the surveillance of five men standing at a 40 ft entrance-exit route-setting console in Old Oak Common box, three miles out of the terminus. Designed by the Western Region's chief signal engineer, A. A. Cardani, this panel was accommodated in a 50 ft by 25 ft operating room, served by a relay room measuring 45 ft by 25 ft. The Paddington area interlocking provided 228 routes, embracing seventy-seven point machines, ninety-six ac track circuits, forty-five position light and thirty-four multiple aspect signals (four aspects on running lines) and four-character train describers. Old Oak Common box then controlled all eleven miles between Paddington and Hayes.

Concurrently with the resignalling, the signalling of the Hammersmith & City line between Paddington and Westbourne Park was converted to automatic operation and came under LT control. (The signalling between Westbourne Park and Hammersmith had been transferred from GWR to Metropolitan control on 1 January 1913.)

A spectacular accident occurred on 9 May 1864, when a GNR 0–6–0 locomotive suffered a boiler explosion on starting from Bishops Road with the 9.5 am to Farringdon Street. Several persons were injured, two seriously; severe damage was inflicted on the station, and to a train in the opposite platform. Debris fell up to 250 yards away, one piece penetrating the roof of the main-line station.

An engine hauling a down empty carriage train was derailed outside the station, near the parcels depot, on 16 October 1944. Shortly afterwards, two coaches of the down 'Cornish Riviera' express were derailed at the same point. There were no casualties, but blockage here was bound to cause great difficulties, and it was not possible to resume normal working until the following morning.

An accident, costly in the disruption and physical damage to track it caused, but fortunately not attended with loss of life or serious injury, occurred on 23 November 1983 when the *Night Riviera* approached the terminus at well above the 15 mph speed limit which applies at the entrance to the platforms. Its locomotive and 11 of its 13 sleeping cars were derailed, blocking access to all the main platforms. Train services were not restored to normal until 2 December and track and signalling reconstruction was not concluded until two days later.

# CHAPTER 15

# Marylebone

## THE LAST MAIN LINE

There is a touch of romance about Marylebone, the terminus of the last main line to enter London. A bold, if irrational venture, the London extension of the Great Central was almost the swan-song of unrestricted railway competition in Britain. Optimistically arranged to allow for future expansion, the half-finished terminus had little difficulty in accommodating in its four platforms all the traffic on offer; indeed, three would have been enough. Even after the rapid suburban growth of the 1930s and the post-1950 building boom beyond the Green Belt, there is still ample capacity, and the rush hours are rest cures compared with those of Charing Cross and Liverpool Street.

Marylebone has always been a quiet place, with a strong provincial flavour, a station where the twittering of birds in the roof is heard as often as train noises. Only on Cup Final Day, when there were departures every few minutes for Wembley Stadium did it really come to life.

This terminus, and the whole concept of the owning company's assault on London came to fruition through the drive of one man. Sir Edward William Watkin,[1] a dominant influence in the nineteenth century railway scene, was a railway administrator and politician who manoeuvred the affairs of a number of railway companies. One of these was the Manchester Sheffield & Lincolnshire Railway, of which he became chairman in 1864. A straggling cross-country system, its main line ran from Grimsby through Retford and Sheffield to Manchester. Very much a second rate affair, it gave up its London traffic to the Midland and the GNR, with which it had working agreements. This was not enough for Watkin, and after he had become chairman of the Metropolitan Railway in 1872, he determined that if he could not get the MS & LR amalgamated with the GNR or the Midland, he would carry it to

London, using the Metropolitan for the final approach. At the back of his mind were further links, first with the SER, later with the proposed Channel Tunnel, in which he also had an interest.

But the MS & LR was not rich, and for all his drive, Watkin was no company doctor; its highest dividend, three and a half per cent, occurred in the year he took the chair. There was little hope of attracting capital for large schemes, nor did anything emerge from negotiations with other companies, including a move to get the Lancashire & Yorkshire Railway interested in a shared line to London. At the close of the 1880s, Watkin was trying to persuade his fellow directors to go on alone, tempting them with the suggestion that dividends as high as six per cent might appear as soon as London was reached. He persuaded them; a survey was ordered, and a Bill deposited for the 1891 session.

From the southernmost point of the authorised MS & LR (Annesley, north of Nottingham), the line was to run ninety-two and a quarter miles to a junction with the Aylesbury & Buckingham Railway, passing through Nottingham, Leicester and Rugby on the way. The A & BR had opened in 1868 from Verney Junction, on the LNWR Oxford to Bletchley line, to Aylesbury, and had been worked by the GWR until shortly after its transfer to the Metropolitan Railway on 1 July 1891. The latter company was pushing up towards Aylesbury, and arrived there on 1 September 1892. After using the Metropolitan for forty-two miles, the MS & LR trains were to reach their London terminus over a new two-mile line from Canfield Place, near Finchley Road station.

Both the Midland and the GNR were in fierce opposition, as were the artists and other occupants of the pretty villas in London's St John's Wood. But most formidable of all was the wrath of the cricketing interests, which rose as one, scarlet with anger at the imagined threat to the sacred turf of Lords. Not surprisingly, the Bill was thrown out.

A year later Watkin tried again, having softened up the other main-line companies with running powers and other arrangements. By now Watkin was well aware of the almost religious fervour generated among the English middle and upper classes by the cricket game—it is surprising that he could have overlooked it before—and realised that if he was to get his railway beneath the Temple, the homage must be substantial. His proposals (of which more in a moment) proved acceptable. Alongside cricketers, artists hardly mattered, but even they were given a promise that everything would be decently covered in and that no spoil would be carried through the dainty streets of St John's Wood. These manoeuvres accomplished, Watkin achieved his victory, and after a delay caused by the dissolution of Parliament, the Act was passed on 28 March 1893. With the assistance of a subscription from the Metropolitan and of the financier Alexander Henderson, the necessary capital was mustered, and work began in 1894.

In that year, possibly as a result of the strain of getting the extension moving, Watkin had a stroke and was forced to resign his chairmanships. His successor on the Metropolitan was John Bell, who took a strongly independent line, refusing to allow the MS & LR its own way. It was clear that the Met, with its busy suburban traffic, could not accept the newcomer without more tracks, and although it was not quite as Watkin had planned, powers were obtained in 1895 and 1896 for a second pair of lines, for the exclusive use of the new arrival between Harrow South junction and the beginning of the terminal spur at Canfield Place, Finchley Road.

With the London extension well under way, something had to be done about the company's name. After some deliberation, the title was changed to the more resounding *Great Central Railway* from 1 August 1897.

The London terminus was to be constructed on the site of Blandford and Harewood Squares, just west of the south-west corner of Regent's Park, a good half mile further from Charing Cross than Euston, but a little more convenient than Paddington for the residential West End north of Oxford Street. Some fifty-one acres south of St John's Wood Road were purchased for the passenger terminus, goods and coal depots. Not all of it was occupied by pretty villas; these came to an end just south of the Regent's Canal, and much of the rest of the area consisted of some of the most insanitary and overcrowded of London's tenements. From these warrens a total of 4,448 'persons of the labouring class' were evicted. Some were found homes in existing property, but for the 2,690 remaining, the GCR, in the form of the Wharncliffe Dwellings Company, erected six five-storey apartment blocks (Wharncliffe Gardens) off St John's Wood Road. (Lord Wharncliffe had succeeded Watkin in the chair.) Near the passenger terminus, two new 60 ft roads, Harewood Avenue and Rossmore Road, were cut through the demolished property. A school and vicarage were rebuilt for St Paul's Church.

Sir Douglas and Francis Fox were the engineers for the two miles of terminal approach. A large part of it was in tunnel or covered way threaded under the St John's Wood streets. Despite difficulties, the ruling gradient was kept down to 1 in 100. Soon after its junction with the Metropolitan Railway 200 ft north of Canfield Gardens, the double track line entered Hampstead tunnel, a 691 yard covered way which took it to the south side of Hilgrove Road. At first it was quite close to the Metropolitan, at a lower level, but shortly it curved due south although still remaining roughly parallel to the older line. To avoid disturbance should the line later be quadrupled, a second double track tunnel was built beneath Hampstead Baths. Emerging from the tunnel, the line was then in the open for 125 yards whilst it crossed the LNWR main line at the western end of Primrose Hill tunnels, above the south end of Loudoun Road (now South Hampstead) station. The bridge here was 118 ft long in three girder spans.

Beyond the bridge, the double track passed under St John's Wood in a 450 yard covered way, a 723 yard tunnel through London clay, and a 67 yard covered way. At Wellington Place there was an open area, 240 ft long by 121 ft 6 in wide, between massive retaining walls 35 ft 10 in high. This space was large enough to accommodate seven parallel tracks and became the terminus of the slow lines out of Marylebone and of two shunting necks.

Next came the three parallel Lords tunnels, 213 yards, the easternmost of 40 ft span for three tracks, the two double track ones of 26 ft 3 in span. The MCC did well. All that the railway required was a strip 42 yards wide and 110 yards long, none of it used for cricket purposes. To the south was the Clergy orphan Asylum, which was purchased by the GCR, demolished, and rebuilt at Bushey, releasing one and threequarter acres. All this land was given to the MCC, allowing them to extend Lords ground right up to Wellington Road. On the original strip, the turfs and soil were laid aside (one hopes with due reverence), to be replaced as soon as the tunnel arches beneath were finished, supplemented by new turf from Morley's cricket ground at Neasden (purchased by the GCR to form part of a locomotive depot and carriage yard). This delicate operation was begun on 1 September 1896 and completed with commendable speed. The strip was handed back to the cricket club on 8 May 1897 together with the free gift of one and threequarter acres. Not a day's cricket had been lost.

After passing under St John's Wood Road and Lodge Road, the seven tracks fanned out to a fourteen-track bridge over the Regent's Canal. This structure included a second span of 26 ft to accommodate the proposed Regent's Canal, City & Docks Railway. (Authorised in 1882 and kept alive by subsequent Acts for extension of time, this sixteen and three-eighths mile line was to run from

Royal Oak, GWR, to the City and to Royal Albert Docks along the course of the Regent's Canal. The scheme was revived in 1903 when F. B. Behr proposed a monorail line along the same route under the title of the North Metropolitan & Regent's Canal Railway.) Beyond the canal, lines curved away to the west to serve the extensive goods and coal depots on both sides of Lisson Grove. Continuing in a southerly direction to the terminus, on a slight gradient to allow platforms at street level, were the down slow, up slow, down main, up main, and, on the east side, a siding road. Also on the east, just before Rossmore Road bridge, were carriage sheds, a locomotive yard and a fish and milk wharf. Provision was made in Rossmore Road bridge for sixteen tracks and five double-faced platform ends, but, as will be seen, only part of this layout was built.

## THE MODEST TERMINUS

So impoverished was the GCR after its great effort to get to London that the extra locomotives and rolling stock required could only be obtained by setting up a Rolling Stock Trust Company which sold them to the railway company under a hire purchase agreement. Small wonder then that the passenger station was a modest affair, not in the least monumental, and hidden behind a vast hotel, the responsibility for which was gladly handed to other parties. No architect was employed. With proper regard to economy, the 'architectural details' were allotted to H. W. Braddock of the engineer's staff. The result would have been creditable as council offices for a minor provincial town, but was hardly worthy as the London terminus of a railway that aspired to be in the first rank.

Two new 60 ft approach roads were constructed either side of the hotel to serve the 341 ft, three-storey frontage block of the terminus. Dominated by gables in a vaguely Flemish style, the roof was well broken up, and even had a feeble tower. The initials 'GCR' appeared everywhere; in the railings, and in the Doulton buff terracotta dressings that relieved the Redbank pressed bricks. A vast *porte-cochère* of iron and glass spanned the 90 ft road joining the main doorway of the station with the hotel. With its delicate ironwork, this was really rather elegant and pretty, quite the best of any London terminus. BR has enhanced its appearance by painting it white.

Inside the main doors was a booking hall, 63 ft by 40 ft 6 in, its walls lined with Doulton terracotta to 12 ft, cream enamel bricks above, all under a white-panelled plaster ceiling (now gone, the girders exposed). Oil-polished wainscot oak clad the ticket office, with its four booking windows (one window now suffices, a sad indication of declining traffic). Teak blocks covered the floor. To the east were waiting rooms and cloak room, on the west, restaurants and parcels office. Above were committee and board rooms surrounded by railway offices which were occupied by the headquarters staff when they moved from Manchester in 1905. Provision was made for more storeys if required.

Beyond the booking hall was a concourse 100 ft wide by 289 ft long, over twice the width of the platforms and tracks, which were at the eastern end. Each of the five tracks terminated in hydraulic buffer stops. Against the east wall were two tracks, then came platforms 1 and 2, each 25 ft wide and separated by a 30 ft carriage roadway. The latter was fed from a 1 in 20 U-shaped ramp from Rossmore Road bridge, the cabs leaving through an arch in the frontage block. Two more tracks followed, with the departure platforms 3 and 4, 35 ft wide, beyond. Alongside 4 was a single track. That was all. The platforms were 950 ft long, covered for 495 ft by a ridge type roof in three spans (east to west these were 50 ft 4 in, 50 ft 4 in and 40 ft 9 in). The height to the apex of this roof varied from 37 to 40 ft and it was supported by columns at 33 ft intervals along each platform. A 'temporary' cantilever roof, 16 ft 6 in wide, sheltered platform 4 pending completion of the station.

The remaining land westwards from platform 4 as far as Harewood Avenue, enough for another ten tracks, with six platform faces, is now partly occupied by a modern office block (Melbury House) accommodating the British Waterways Board and some British Railways Board staffs.

Over the concourse was a roof with ridges parallel to the frontage in five equal spans carried by rows of girders. The general effect of the low roof, with its profusion of steelwork, was rather depressing, detracting from the appearance of the spacious concourse and platforms.

Quite separate from the station, but built on railway land, was Sir Blundell Maple's red brick Hotel Great Central. Surmounted by a be-turreted clock tower, it dwarfed and successfully obscured the station. Designed in Jacobean style by Robert William Edis,[2] the hotel had a main frontage of 215 ft set back 50 ft from Marylebone Road, seven storeys, and 700 bedrooms. Edis used that favourite nineteenth century material, terracotta, to decorate this tall, steeply-gabled building. Over the main entrance he placed reliefs portraying two females, one with helmet and iron brassière, the other hatless and draped, one breast negligently exposed. Goodness knows what should be read into this little bit of symbolism, or what lessons it may hold for the present occupants of the building. A further touch of the bizarre was the cycle track on the roof. Presumably this was intended as a spectator diversion, not as an exercise ground for overweight executives (for in 1899 a large belly was still the sign of successful maturity).

Hotel Great Central was opened to the public on 1 July 1899. It is doubtful whether it ever paid more than a small dividend—certainly those 700 bedrooms could not have been filled by the GCR's regular London clientele. In 1916 it was requisitioned by a grateful Government to be used as a convalescent home for wounded officers. It was again taken over for Government use in the second world war. Just before nationalisation, an optimistic LNER purchased it for central offices, but with the arrival of nationalisation in 1948 it became the headquarters of the Railway Executive. In 1953 the British Transport Commission and British Road Services moved in. After the dissolution of the BTC, the British Railways Board filled up the converted rooms.

A connection between the terminus and the Metropolitan Railway had been authorised in the 1893 Act. This would have passed beneath the hotel, carrying passengers and freight to the City and the southern lines. Exercising its new-found independence under Bell, the Metropolitan made difficulties about the number of GCR trains it could take and the times when they could be run. There was also strong opposition from the hotel company. Beneath all this the impoverished GCR gladly gave in, and the connection was never started.

Traffic on the London extension began on 26 July 1898 when the first coal train left for Neasden. Marylebone goods yard opened on the following 10 April. A ceremonial inauguration of the extension and passenger terminus was performed on 9 March 1899 by C. T. Ritchie, President of the Board of Trade, who aptly remarked that it was an event London was not likely to see again. Among the 700 guests who sat down to luncheon in the decorated train shed was the ailing Watkin. Three special trains brought notabilities from Manchester, Sheffield and Nottingham. Public traffic started on 15 March 1899, the first train leaving at 5.15 am with but four passengers. The heaviest loading that day was on the 1.15 pm, which carried away thirty-four fare-paying customers. During the first few weeks only two platforms were in use.

From 1 July 1899 there were eleven trains each way on weekdays, seven of them expresses to and from Manchester. Until the track had settled down, and for some time afterwards, running times were leisurely (five hours for the 212 miles to Manchester), but the GCR set new standards of comfort from the first. All the expresses were composed of electrically-lit corridor coaches, and all but the first and last trains of the day had buffet or restaurant cars.

## FAY ARRIVES

In these early days many tales were told of the porters out-numbering the passengers or of the booking clerks dozing or playing cards among piles of unwanted tickets. Things began to change in 1902 when the energetic Sam Fay[3] was appointed general manager of the GCR. Fay inaugurated successful and continuous publicity, backing it up with a high standard of passenger service. Hard work was needed to attract traffic from the older lines. The GCR route to Manchester was twenty-three and a quarter miles longer than that of the LNWR, and the GNR offered a quicker service to Sheffield. Only for Leicester and Nottingham was the GCR really competitive. By 1904 the Manchester time was down to three hours, fifty minutes, Sheffield was reached in three hours, and Leicester in 105 minutes. Through services were operating to Huddersfield and Bradford via the Lancashire & Yorkshire Railway, and to Stratford-upon-Avon via the Stratford-upon-Avon & Midland Junction Railway. At Marylebone, Fay had buses waiting to take his passengers on to the West End and City. But despite all this, it was freight that mattered to the GCR, and after the excitements of the early 1900s the passenger services eventually settled down to a less dramatic level of performance.

The quadrupling of the Metropolitan Railway between Canfield Place and Harrow was finished in 1900. Whilst the old line was rebuilt, there was a short period of mixed use, but from 31 March 1901 the GCR had a double track to itself all the way from Marylebone to Harrow. In 1906 the new line between Canfield Place and Harrow was leased to the GCR, and the Metropolitan lines north of Harrow, including the branches to Chesham, Brill and Verney Junction (but not that to Uxbridge) were leased to a joint committee of the Great Central and Metropolitan Railways, the two companies taking turns every five years to manage and staff the line. The Metropolitan stipulated that the GCR must not seek local traffic between Marylebone and Harrow, but the agreement allowed the main-line company to develop suburban traffic on the joint lines. This it proceeded to do without delay, working local trains as far as Chesham and Aylesbury from 1 March 1906, using John G. Robinson's 4–4–2T and new four-coach bogie sets. For its part, the Metropolitan retained GCR receipts it might otherwise have lost, because the latter now had a second string to its bow.

### ANOTHER WAY IN

Even before the opening of the London extension, the GCR had not been happy to have the Metropolitan route as its sole entry to London. This line presented great difficulties to express trains; compared to the GCR's own new main line, with its ruling gradient of 1 in 176, it was a nightmare. Not only was there the severe reverse curve at Aylesbury (which derailed a GCR express taking it too fast on 23 December 1904), but south of that station came a long climb of 1 in 117 to Dutchlands summit; after Amersham, there was a six-mile descent at 1 in 105, but no advantage could be taken of it as another severe curve lay in wait at Rickmansworth. Onwards to London, the line was a series of undulations with a climax of 1 in 90 and 95 up for one and a quarter miles east of Neasden.

A healthy interest was therefore aroused by the Great Western's proposed new main line to Birmingham via High Wycombe. Approaches were made, and acceptable arrangements reached. By the simple device of constructing link lines from Grendon Underwood (north of Quainton Road) to Ashendon (between Brill and Princes Risborough), and from Neasden to Northolt, the GCR obtained a much more easily graded route at the expense of only four and a half more miles running. The shared section of the new main line was transferred to a joint committee of the Great Western and Great Central Railways. As a *douceur*, the Great Western secured the abandonment of GCR schemes to reach Birmingham.

On the six and a quarter mile line between Neasden and Northolt, three suburban stations were opened, served by a steam railcar working between Marylebone and South Harrow from 1 March 1906. The remainder of the new route was opened to passenger traffic on 2 April 1906 when a second group of suburban services was inaugurated, between Marylebone and High Wycombe.

It was these suburban services which provided a justification for Marylebone. New five-coach sets in varnished teak, with shoulder lights and foot stools in the first class, hauled by Robinson's excellent 4–6–2T, came into use in 1911. A vigorous publicity campaign was conducted from Fay's office, and discerning business-men were soon buying villas in the lovely hill country of south Buckinghamshire. By the 1920s a fair traffic had been established.

The isolation of Marylebone was somewhat alleviated when the Bakerloo tube was extended from Baker Street on 27 March 1907. The booking hall of the Bakerloo station, below street level, and entered from Harewood Terrace, was connected to the main-line concourse by a subway opened on the following day. In deference to the wishes of the railway company, the tube station was named Great Central, but this was changed to Marylebone on 15 April 1917. From 1 February 1943, the lifts to the Bakerloo platforms were replaced by two escalators from the concourse.

The events of the first world war made little mark on Maryle-bone, where the motto was 'business as usual', or even 'more busi-ness than usual'. It was a popular station for journeys north be-cause the GCR retained restaurant cars after the GNR and LNWR had withdrawn them, nor did it decelerate its services to anything like the extent its rivals did.

Towards the end of the war, LSWR engines and stock were seen when the Army overseas mail trains were diverted from Nine Elms to Marylebone at the request of the War Office. As the Army Mail Office was in Regent's Park, these workings, which lasted from early 1917 until 1918, offered greater convenience coupled with the opportunity to economise in petrol.

## LNER DAYS

After the grouping, Marylebone passed to the LNER, which, having acquired a West End terminus, did little to change the station's character or appearance. In GCR days, most of the best trains had taken the Great Western and Great Central Joint route, but the LNER restored many to the older line. In general the pattern of services remained very much the same, the suburban traffic continuing to grow.

From 1923 onwards, heavy crowds were handled at Marylebone on the occasion of sporting events at Wembley Stadium, which was opened for the Cup Final on 28 April that year. Special ser-vices were arranged for the British Empire Exhibition at Wembley Park in 1924 and 1925, and the working of this traffic prompted a limited modernisation of the signalling between Marylebone and Wembley. During the Exhibition season of 1924, a ten-minute service of non-stop trains was operated, each consisting of a 4–6–2T and a five-coach bogie set, offering a much more comfortable journey than the Metropolitan. The less frequent service of 1925 was worked by N7 0-6-2T.

With the opening of the joint Metropolitan and LNER branch to Watford on 2 November 1925, half the service was worked from Marylebone. These Watford trains ceased in the General Strike (from 4 May 1926) and were not resumed.

During 1939-45, there were no direct hits on Marylebone, which was troubled only by a few incendiary bombs, soon brought under control. But the rest of the old GCR's London complex was not so fortunate. The vast goods depot was severely damaged on 16 April 1941, and the tunnel approaches through St John's Wood proved vulnerable. When Carlton Hill tunnel was breached, Marylebone had to close (5 October to 26 November 1940). After the lines had been cleared, this section was left as open cutting. Until permanent repairs were completed in August 1942, single-line working was in operation. Later a flying bomb damaged Marylebone signal box, killing two men.

### SHAVED TO A SLITHER

One of the first moves of British Railways was to concentrate all the High Wycombe and Princes Risborough services at Marylebone. From 4 July 1949 a time-interval basic service was introduced, with a slow and a fast train each hour. This lasted only until 24 January 1951 when the slow push and pull trains to West Ruislip were taken off, leaving virtually no off-peak service for the stations inward from Northolt.

Diesel multiple-units were introduced gradually during 1961, restoring first class to the suburban service. After the completion of a diesel depot at Marylebone in 1962, the diesel multiple-unit sets took over completely (from 18 June). An hourly service was worked betwen Aylesbury and Marylebone (fifteen minutes in peak hours), the journey taking fifty-nine minutes, thirty-one less than the slowest steam trains. On the High Wycombe line, the diesel cars also ran hourly with peak-hour additions, again providing a slack hour service to Wembley Hill, Sudbury & Harrow Road, Sudbury Hill and Northolt Park, although this lasted only until 1964.

On the main line, BR made a brave start by introducing two named trains, the 'Master Cutler' (to Sheffield, from 6 October 1947), and the 'South Yorkshireman' (to Bradford, from 31 May 1948), but after a decade or so of slumber, the economists and accountants began to stir. In January 1960 the Sheffield, Manchester and Bradford services disappeared, leaving only three semi-fast trains each way daily to Leicester and Nottingham, shorn of refreshment facilities, and single night trains to and from Manchester. This move led to speculation that Marylebone, the last London terminus to be constructed, would be the first to close, but this BR sternly denied. Patronage of the Nottingham service slowly declined, not surprisingly, as punctuality was poor and breakdowns were frequent, circumstances which took no turn for the better when diesel traction was introduced for some workings in 1963. At last the brutal but logical decision was taken; the line between Aylesbury and Rugby had to close. Steam working survived until the very end, the engines seeping at all joints, rusty and begrimed, and loved by none but the lineside observers. Marylebone ceased to be a main-line station at 5.23 am on 4 September 1966, with the arrival of the 10.50 pm passenger and parcels train from Manchester Central.

But not quite. In the winter of 1967, during the signalling and layout alterations at Paddington, the Western Region's trains to and from Birmingham were briefly diverted to the old GCR terminus, in truth a preparation for its own funeral.

Few changes were made to the station in 1948-70. The dining room was modernised to form a pleasant self-service cafeteria, but next door, the charming little Victorian buffet still survived. With its mirrors, dark varnished wood, and old fashioned light bowls, it offered a cosy retreat at the end of a busy day.

A wasted asset, Marylebone was left to sleep indolently through the 1960s and 1970s, awaiting its seemingly inevitable closure.*

### SIGNALLING AND ACCIDENTS

When the line opened, three cabins were provided in Marylebone yard—Platform box, Station box, and Goods junction box. At first the line inwards to Goods junction was signalled by the Metropolitan Railway's Spagnoletti lock and block instruments, but after the transfer to the Joint Committee in 1906, GCR block instruments of the three-wire needle type were installed between Marylebone station and Harrow South junction.

Platform box, with 31 levers, was at the outer end of Nos 3 and 4, controlling the starting signals. Station box was between the milk wharf and the running lines, just north of Rossmore Road bridge. It was 54 ft long by 12 ft wide, with 100 levers in its tappet locking frame. This was the beginning of block working and communication with Platform box was by ringing code.

* See chapter 16.

Goods junction box, just north of the Lodge Road overbridge, on the east side of the line, marked the end of the first block section. It was one of the largest cabins on the GCR, 56 ft by 11 ft, with provision for 110 levers, and controlled the junction of the fast and slow lines as well as the entry into the goods yard.

Beyond Goods junction, the second block section ended at Canfield Place box (a Metropolitan cabin until the Joint Line agreement), but in the early years there was an intermediate box at Hilgrove Road.

When the construction of Wembley Stadium and preparations for the British Empire Exhibition began at Wembley Park in 1922, the GCR decided that the special traffic would warrant headways as close as three minutes, with a running time of twelve minutes for the six and a half miles from Marylebone. To work such a service it was necessary to resignal the line between Marylebone Goods junction (inner home and advance starters) and Wembley Hill station and loop. The Westinghouse Brake & Saxby Signal Company was asked to install the automatic and semi-automatic colour light signals and selective illuminated speed indicators. The latter, indicating 10 and 35 mph, replaced splitting distants at Marylebone Goods junction and normally displayed the lower speed, changing when the inner home to fast-line signal showed yellow or green.

This installation, which included ac track circuiting throughout, came into use on 8 April 1923, and was the first daylight and three-aspect colour light signalling on a British main line. The single lens signals were of Hall's pattern; those with two and three lenses were Westinghouse. Platform, Canfield Place and Willesden boxes were all closed, but Canfield Place was available in an emergency. Marylebone Goods junction box had an illuminated diagram controlled by the track circuits, and track-block working was instituted. At Marylebone station, the semaphore signals were retained, but the running lines were track circuited.

With the removal of the down slow running lines and the closure of the goods yards, a great deal of the signalling became redundant. The installation was therefore considerably simplified in 1967, when a new box was built to replace Goods junction and Station boxes. Opened on 8 October, and situated just south of the Station box, this new cabin contained fifty-five working levers and five spares, controlling the station, the diesel depot and power station sidings. It had an illuminated diagram showing the up lines from Neasden South and the down lines to Canfield Place. The only semaphores remaining were the platform starters.

A fatal accident occurred outside Marylebone in the afternoon of 28 March 1913. As a train from Leicester was crossing from the up main to enter platform 4, a High Wycombe train left platform 3, where the intermediate starter, controlled from the Platform box, was off. The driver of the local train was under the impression that his fireman was looking out for the starter, which was seventy-five yards away on Rossmore Road bridge and obscured by the smoke of the Leicester engine. Realising his situation at the last moment, the driver slipped as he went to apply the brake, and his engine collided with the last coach of the up train, killing one passenger and injuring twenty-three others. Five passengers in the local train were also slightly hurt. The Inspecting Officer made the rather obvious comment that the company might consider whether the intermediate starter should not be lowered until the starter was off; certainly the existing procedure, which allowed a down train to draw up to the starter, did not appear to save any useful amount of time for the risk involved.

# Modernisation and Decline 1969–84

Some general comments on the developments and changes since the original work was published in 1969 have been made in the preface to this Second Edition. This chapter brings together the detailed accounts for each station, taking them in the same order as in the main body of the book.

## EUSTON

The great new terminus of 1968, owing as much to the architecture of airports as that of railways, has worked well, requiring little alteration. Since its opening, in a period when most of the termini have lost traffic, the number of passengers using it on weekdays has increased from 40,000 to 67,200. In one small matter the designers overlooked the ways of the Great British Public; seeing no seats on the vast concourse (they had been omitted to discourage vagrants and loafers), the public wrongly assumed there were none anywhere, and complained. British Rail capitulated, and in 1970 fibreglass seats appeared in blocks of four around the concourse pillars, arranged to make the horizontal position uncomfortable, though some do attempt it.

Visually the greatest change was the completion in 1979 of some 405,000 sq ft of office accommodation (architects Richard Seifert & Partners). This was built across the front, effectively screening the station from the Euston Road. On the west side, two towers, one of eight, and one of 14 storeys, faced Melton Street, the westernmost, *Rail House*, sheltering the BR Chairman and his headquarters staff. On the Eversholt Street side there was a ten storey block, and linking them, across the south side of the piazza, a three storey raised block with the platform of a new bus station, serving several routes, beneath it. Exploitation of the site value continues; the next project is a 595-bedroom hotel over the station itself and along Cardington Street.

Within the station, the cessation of general parcels traffic on BR made platforms 18-20 available for stabling empty rolling stock in 1981 and in the following year, after the closure of the facilities at Kensington (Olympia), these platforms accommodated the West Coast Motorail services. As we shall see throughout this chapter, catering facilities have proved very susceptible to the whim of fashion; the *Lancastrian Grill* at first floor level on the east side of the concourse became *Carriages* in 1983, one of the two remaining table-served restaurants at BR stations.

Greater flexibility in the working of the station and approaches became possible after the upgrading of the Up and Down Carriage Lines for passenger working in 1973-74 and with the installation in 1972 of a micro-computer based train describer with LED displays. The 'modern' signalbox of 1952, overtaken by advancing technology, was not demolished until 1969. The electric services to the outer suburbs have prospered, becoming major contributors to the traffic increase. On the Watford service, conductor rail current collection still survives, although since August 1970 the four rail system in the station and approaches has become third rail only, with the return current passing through the running rails.

## ST PANCRAS

This station remains much as it ever was. Its architectural unity and integrity, carefully monitored by the guardians of our building heritage, render modernisation and major structural changes almost impossible. BR sought to ignore this, to their cost. Plans for rebuilding the magnificent booking hall in airline style, banishing the linenfold panelling, were optimistically drawn up, only to be condemned by the Victorian Society as 'unnecessarily aggressive alterations' and then refused listed building consent by the Secretary of State. Scott's work therefore lives on in the refurbished booking hall of May 1983, but the ticket office has been moved to the west side of the hall and the ugly clock of the 1957 restoration has gone.

Modern platform barriers incorporating an electronic train indicator were installed in 1982, doing some damage to the scale of the concourse. The palatial Gentlemen's Conveniences alongside platform 1 were closed in 1978 and in the same year, in preparation for the new booking hall, the penultimate counter-type W. H. Smith bookstall on a London terminus was swept away; its walk-in replacement, with popular 'free-read' magazine racks, found a home alongside the inner wall of the old hotel.

An anomalous vestige of the old Midland Railway, the station's Anglo-Scottish services, vanished in May 1976, with the trains starting and terminating for a while at Nottingham (the sleeping car trains to and from Scotland had ceased in January 1969). Some kind of main line glamour was restored on 4 October 1982 with the introduction of High Speed Inter-City 125 train sets on the Nottingham and Sheffield services. By the following year these had replaced all but two of the locomotive-hauled long distance trains.

Another Midland relic, the 11 acre Somers Town freight depot to the west of the passenger terminus, closed in June 1972. Its site is to accommodate the new British Library building, on which work has started. The low-level goods depot last saw use in June 1967, the coal depot in April 1968, and the St Pancras Goods Depot was closed in June 1975. The steep connnection up from the latter to the North London line (St Pancras Junction to North London Incline Junction) was taken out at the end of 1975.

Electric services at 25kV 50 Hz over the 53 route miles between St Pancras/Moorgate and Bedford, with associated track changes and resignalling, were delayed by a long industrial dispute over single-manning of the new trains. The first electric trains for public service appeared in the terminus on 28 March 1983, but as the ageing diesel units were almost replaced, it became apparent that the new stock required modifications, and it was not until 23 January 1984, two years late, that the full electric service was finally established. This change diverted most of the suburban traffic to and from Moorgate through the new Kings Cross (Midland) station on the site of the old City Widened Lines platforms, where subway connections are available for long distance walkers to all four London Transport Underground lines at Kings Cross.

Resignalling, with four-aspect colour-lights and power-operated, winter-heated points, extended from Moorgate and St Pancras to Sharnbrook, north of Bedford, the whole under the control of a single new power box at West Hampstead. The new signals came into operation in stages, the last on 4 July 1982. At St Pancras, the old platform 1 was disconnected, the remaining six were wired up for electric working, and the approaches from south of Kentish Town simplified from four tracks to Up and Down Fast and a single bi-directional Local line, the latter an arrangement which appears to cause delays at busy times. As a result of these changes, St Pancras signalbox was closed on 2 July 1982 and demolished a year later.

To greet the electrics and the HSTs, and the traffic increase they have brought, the whole of the interior of the station was thoroughly cleaned in 1980-83 and fitted with 122 roof floodlights giving an equivalent of daylight through the roof at night. To ease subsequent maintenance tasks, a three-section self-powered platform was installed. With the aid of Government and GLC grants, a start was made in 1977 with cleaning the soot-blackened exterior, beginning on the west side, but sadly, in 1981, long before it was finished, this work ground to a halt through lack of funds. During 1983 Travellers Fare staff vacated the old hotel, which has been leased for conversion to commercial offices. Alas, it is all a little too large and too costly for the Victorian Society.

KINGS CROSS

Kings Cross is a much better and more efficient station than it was in the late 1960s. Its two major deficiencies, the muddle of approach tracks and inadequate outdated concourse and booking facilities, have been remedied, the first more satisfactorily than the second.

After a good deal of hard work in the midst of normal traffic, a simplified and rationalised track layout between the terminus and Finsbury Park was in full use on 3 April 1977. By reconstructing the old freight flyover just north of the Copenhagen Tunnels at Holloway to carry Up suburban trains to the western side of Kings Cross, conflict with main line movements was minimised. It was at first intended that the flyover should continue to carry trains into the Kings Cross Freight Terminal, but this was closed in March 1973. In these changes, the number of tracks through the Copenhagen and Gas Works Tunnels was reduced from six to four, usage then becoming (west to east):— Down Slow, Up Slow, Down Fast, and Up Fast, all four tracks being signalled for two-way working to maximise use through the Gas Works Tunnels. North of the flyover, the sequence became (west to east): Down Slow, Down Fast, Up Fast, Up Slow. Planning allowed for the vacated eastern bore of the Copenhagen Tunnels to carry lines to a new high level terminal on the west side of Kings Cross to serve the projected Maplin Airport near Shoeburyness, an ambitious scheme scrapped by the Labour Government in 1974.

In the terminus itself, platforms were renumbered consecutively 1 to 14, east to west, on 1 May 1972, but with the track changes of 1976-77 and the more recent diversion of many suburban trains to Moorgate, two of the former seven suburban platforms were sufficient. Numbers 11-13 went out of use on 5 December 1976 (11 was later filled in to widen 10) whilst 14 and the Up Suburban platform at York Road were last used by the public on 4 March

1977. Some of the vacated space on the west side has been used for a staff car park but the western track of the old Milk Dock in Cheney Road remains available for Motorail traffic. With the advent of High Speed Train sets, locomotive servicing and refuelling, which had been continuous at the terminus since 1862, ceased on 13 May 1979, after which the small number of locomotives still using Kings Cross were dealt with at Finsbury Park.

Signalling changes were radical. On 26 September 1971 the former LNER box at Kings Cross was closed, replaced by a power panel at the north end of York Road platform. This eventually became part of a three-storey signalling centre with relay room, telecommunications centre, and an 80 ft panel with computer-controlled train describer systems, all of which finally came into full operation on 13 March 1977, supervising all track signalling over the 83½ route miles between Moorgate/Kings Cross and Sandy/Royston, including the Hertford loop.

Complementary to all this work was the introduction of 25kV 50Hz overhead wire multiple-unit electric trains on the inner and outer suburban services. The former (stations to Welwyn Garden City and Hertford North) started on 8 November 1976, diverted from Kings Cross to Moorgate via the old Great Northern & City tube railway (over which power was taken at 750V dc from a third rail) and new connections at Drayton Park. The notorious tunnels connecting Kings Cross to the City Widened Lines on each side of the terminus saw their last public trains on 6 November 1976. All outer suburban services, to Stevenage, Hitchin, Letchworth and Royston were electrically operated in and out of Kings Cross from 6 February 1978.

Meanwhile the jumble of buildings between the station frontage and Euston Road had been cleared away and replaced with a 16,000 sq ft single-storey structure forming a concourse and travel centre. Opened on 3 June 1973, this had shops on the street side and an electronic train indicator (controlled from the signalling centre) along the old station frontage. Outside, sheltered by a generous canopy, there was a new taxi turning circle and loading bay. Within, on the west side, the travel centre, with its 110 ft counter dispensing tickets, reservations and information, was reached through automatic sliding doors. There was direct access by stairs and an escalator (which hardly ever worked) to the Underground concourse. Although this structure is an improvement on what it replaced, it is inadequate and unworthy of the fine architecture of the 1852 station it serves; with intensive use, it soon acquired a tatty and tired appearance and by 1984 was already undergoing modification. The dead escalator to the Underground ticket hall was removed 'to provide more space' on the concourse where the 1973 rubber tiles were replaced by the currently fashionable white terrazzo tiles installed earlier at Waterloo, Charing Cross and Victoria. Two new information displays and an enquiry kiosk were added at the same time.

Without warning, an Irish bomb was thrown into the old booking hall on 10 September 1973, injuring five people (on the same day another in the Euston Railbar injured eight). Ten years later, on 21 March 1983, thieves used smoke bombs in the travel centre, setting off the fire alarms and causing the staff to move out, thus facilitating the removal of some £65,000.

Apart from the suburban electrics, there is now only one basic type of train to be seen at Kings Cross. After 4 October 1982, with the exception of overnight parcels and sleeper services and some Peterborough commuter workings, all main line services were operated by Inter-City 125 HSTs. Whilst something of a bore for the residual train spotters, these proved such great generators of passenger business that their seating accommodation was often inadequate; queues for them formed right across the modest concourse. Before many more years have passed, Kings Cross will become an all-electric terminus, perhaps with the necessary further improvements to its passenger facilities.

## BROAD STREET

This is a sad tale for the sentimental. Following a lengthy public enquiry in 1976-77, BR received planning permission in 1979 for commercial redevelopment of the combined Broad Street and Liverpool Street station sites, the associated planning gain to be used in reconstruction of the latter, which would accommodate such of the Broad Street services as remained, using a new connecting curve to be built at Hackney. These plans, which involve the complete removal of the present Broad Street terminus and its approaches, have been gestating since the early 1970s, so it is understandable that since 1969 the Broad Street story has been one of almost continuous neglect and decline. The station, which had 633 trains a day in 1902, now has but 127, carrying a mere 4,880 passengers.

After the closure of the goods station on 27 January 1969 the approach tracks were reduced to two with the elimination of No 1 Down from Dalston Junction on 3 November that year. From the same day platforms 1, 2 3 and 9 were closed, leaving only the electrified 4 to 8 which were renumbered 1 to 5 (east to west) from 15 February 1970. On 2 August of that year maintenance was simplified by the removal of the centre earth return rail from the tracks between Broad Street and Gunnersbury.

With the ending of freight services, closure of the east side and the end of locomotive working, it became possible to operate all the signalling from No 2 box so No 1, New Inn Yard and Skinner Street Junction cabins were closed on 3 November 1969, 11 April 1969 and 15 February 1970 respectively. From 2 December 1976, following the elimination of Dunloe Street box, there remained only one block section between the terminus and Dalston Western Junction. On that day, platform 1 and the stabling siding leading out of it were taken out of use and from this time platform 2, although capable of taking a train in an emergency, was used only for stabling.

The through workings to former Great Northern suburban stations which had been wholly operated by diesel multiple-units since May 1969, and numbered eight up and 14 down Mondays to Fridays (two each way on Saturdays) were reduced in October 1971, but survived until the GN electrification, running for the last time on Saturday 6 November 1976. After that, passengers for Dalston and Broad Street from the Hertford North and Welwyn Garden City lines were obliged to change at Highbury. BR also wished to reduce the remaining services in March 1976, but although some Watford peak hour workings were taken off at this time, the Richmond line frequencies were maintained by a grant from the GLC. Most, if not all the Richmond Line trains are expected to be diverted to North Woolwich with the electrification of the Dalston-North Woolwich section in 1985.

A visitor to the concourse today will find it even more destitute than in 1969. The model engine has found a better home in the National Railway Museum and since 12 July 1971 the ticket office has been replaced by self-service ticket machines and a 'ticket control point' worked by the duty railman.

Pending the redevelopment of the site, the superstructure of the old goods station was dismantled and the space converted to a car park. Much of the formerly busy railway area around the entrance to the station is now occupied by parked cars or by grass and bushes, making a strange sight so near the centre of the City of London as Broad Street continues to wait for the redevelopment that has seemed inevitable for so long.

## LIVERPOOL STREET

With the passing of more than a decade of planning and controversy over its rebuilding, Liverpool Street is still essentially the station it was 15 years ago. The knock-it-all-down-and-start-

again scheme announced in 1975, with its office blocks in what
the Victorian Society described as 'an overpowering scale' above
and around a 22-platform terminus, and an hotel and shops, horri-
fied the conservation lobby, determined as they are never to see
another Euston disaster. A 'Liverpool Street Action Campaign' was
formed by some very persistent young men in late 1974 and so
successful were they that within a year the Secretary of State for
the Environment had listed the West Side train sheds and offices
as buildings of special architectural and historical interest. This
new group, backed by the Victorian Society, gave BR a very difficult planning enquiry in 1976-77 and the outline planning permission granted by the Minister in 1979 required the preservation
of the West Side train sheds, which had been described by the
campaigners as 'a cast iron cathedral of the railway age', the
Abercorn Rooms and the Great Eastern Hotel. Returning from a
second design attempt, BR announced in 1981 that it would proceed with a suitably modified plan incorporating 1.25 million sq
ft of offices and 30,000 sq ft of shops. An Act of Parliament was
secured in 1983, but subsequently commercial funding proved a
problem, and it was not until 1985, more than ten years after the
intention to rebuild was first announced, that the new scheme, in
partnership with Rosehaugh Stanhope Developments got under
way. Work will take at least nine years, whilst BR endeavours to
run a normal train service in the middle of it all. Current plans
include two more approach tracks from Bethnal Green, and a
common platform barrier line alongside level concourses for BR
and the Underground, with escalators linking these to street
entrances and a new bus station on the west side.

Given all this, changes in the station's fabric have been relatively minor. The Bishopsgate side booking hall was modernised in
1978, and in 1981 a new Continental Travel Office was opened
on the site of the old. The 1922 arrival and departure indicator
across platform 9, together with the even more antiquated
manually-operated barrier indicators, disappeared in 1980, to be
replaced between August and November by two sets of 62 ft long
electronically-controlled flap indicators on the East and West Sides
and 19 barrier indicators, all worked through a central computer
and communications centre in the former tea room overlooking
the East Side platforms. A new clock system, with remote adjust-
ment facility, embracing 17 double dial clocks fitted with electric
drive was installed in 1983.

On 12 October 1980 the overhead electric traction supply into
the platform roads from Bethnal Green was converted from 6.25
to 25kV ac, allowing the first of the new class 315 inner suburban

electric multiple-unit trains to enter the terminus. Faced with the realisation that much of its Victorian engineering inheritance must live on, BR started a five-year renovation of the West Side roof in November 1982.

Catering facilities were brought up to trend. From September 1974 the West Side footbridge tea room became a 'bistro' with 'a genuine Continental atmosphere' exemplified by a 'Congo Brown' and warm red decor, a genuine Swiss manager and Continental *musak*. Alas, the view from the leaded light windows was sadly marred by the new train indicator. Further gastronomic delights arrived in September 1981 when *The Rainbow* on platform 9 reappeared as the *Jazz Buffet*, after the Jazz Service of 1920, photographs of which were to be seen on the walls. In combination with the brewers Ind Coope Taylor Walker, Travellers Fare provided a 'Victorian Public House' named *The Apples & Pears* on the site of the former *East End Bar* in August 1983.

Since 1968 Liverpool Street has lost almost 27 per cent of its daily traffic load, ceding to Waterloo its place as London's busiest terminus. Much of the 54,700 loss in daily passengers has been sustained on the commuter services; particularly those on the West Side where there has been a substantial diversion to the Victoria tube line. One begins to wonder whether that expensive additional pair of approach tracks will really be necessary, despite the need to accommodate the residual Broad Street traffic.

## FENCHURCH STREET

After several false starts, the exploitation of the air space above the platforms and concourse at Fenchurch Street was secured when the Norwich Insurance Group took a long lease with the intention of erecting 94,000 sq ft of pyramid-shaped offices for its own use, retaining the existing concourse and George Berkeley's frontage of 1853. Work on this scheme, which includes escalators to street level, a setting back of the platform barriers to enlarge the concourse and new platform canopies at the outer ends, started late in 1983 for completion in 1987.

The Docklands Light Railway is to have its own separate terminus nearby at Minories, regrettably with no easy interchange with the Underground, but it is planned to run over two of the four Fenchurch Street approach tracks as far as Stepney East, thence taking the old London & Blackwall Railway as far as the West India Dock.

Whilst there has been a small and general decline in passenger use at Fenchurch Street, it still remains busier than either Paddington, St Pancras or Kings Cross.

Facilitated by government grants and a property deal, complete rebuilding at London Bridge, so long overdue, necessarily took a considerable time; indeed virtually all the 1970s. Finally a workmanlike new station emerged, making the best of an awkward site, with the approach tracks rearranged and resignalled for efficient operation. After all this, the station now has less traffic than the muddle it replaces, particularly on the terminal side, where significant reductions in services were made in May 1984, including complete closure on Sundays. This reduction in the loading of the terminal side has enabled more capacity to be given to the still very busy through lines.

In the rebuilding, one main concourse was provided for the through and terminal portions of the station, its roof extending outside over the forecourt to shelter a rebuilt bus station. On the concourse were a ticket office, travel centre, parcels block, shops, kiosks, lavatories and a buffet-bar called *The Oast House*. At last this station was given the order and unity it had always lacked, a major contributor to this being a new wide covered footbridge across the whole site, linking all the through and terminal platforms. The design was produced by the BR architect N. D. T. Wikely, and the project was executed by a team of architects working with him.

Clearance of the remains of the buildings which accumulated on the site since the middle of the 19th century started in 1970. In that year, although the 270 ft, 155,000 sq ft Oldham Estates office tower erected in the forecourt in the mid 1960s was still empty, BR concluded a redevelopment deal with Peachey Properties. A ground lease was granted and in the early 1970s Peachey erected a 230,000 sq ft office tower at the old LBSCR terminus, letting most of it to the accountants Price Waterhouse. Rebuilding of the station started in earnest in 1972 with the closure of the old platforms 17-22 and their replacement with new ones numbered 16-19. The following year saw the disappearance of old platforms 8 and 10, replaced by a new 10 and 11, and the new footbridge came into use on 21 December 1974. Platforms 6 and 7 were renumbered 5 and 6 on 5 May 1975 and the terminal platforms 10-19 became 7-16 on the following 20 July. That year was also marked by the completion of a new subway between the forecourt and the London Transport Northern Line ticket hall. The new main line and suburban ticket office, travel centre, part of the concourse and a new barrier line were ready in April and May 1978. With work on the through platforms 1 to 6 far from complete, the new station was formally 'opened' by the Bishop of Southwark in December 1978. It was not until the end of 1979 that all the works were finished.

Outside the station, the approach tracks were rearranged in 1972-78, the object being to minimise conflicting movements and to make the best use of capacity. As far as possible Charing Cross trains were now to run on the south side of the viaduct from New Cross inwards, and Cannon Street trains on the north side. To achieve this, two lightly-loaded tracks (the Up and Down Local) into the terminal platforms were slewed into the through lines during 1973. Certain sections of the approach tracks totalling about five track miles were converted to two-way working and a new flyover created at St Johns utilising the existing bridge carrying Lewisham-Nunhead tracks over the main lines and a new spur down to the up Charing Cross line.

When all this was finished there were four roads leading into the terminal platforms instead of six: (south to north) Up and Down South London, Up and Down; and seven on the through side: (south to north) Up Through, Up, Down, Down, mainly for Charing Cross, and Up, Reversible, Down, mainly for Cannon Street services. In the process of track rearrangement, as already suggested above, the former 15 terminal platforms were reduced to ten.

Whilst track alterations were going on, the signalling of the 148 track and 47 route miles between Charing Cross/Cannon Street/London Bridge and Woolwich, Eltham Park, New Eltham, Elmstead Woods, Bromley North, Hayes, Anerley, East Dulwich and Clapham was replaced and put under the control of a new box on the south west side of London Bridge station. This large building, its stark rectangular white masses punctuated by a narrow line of fenestration, came into commission between 20 July 1975 and 20 April 1976. It housed an impressive signalling centre with two illuminated track diagram panels: one 60ft long for the former SER lines, controlling 357 signals and 342 sets of points and a smaller one for the terminating London Bridge services, controlling 190 signals and 114 points. Sixteen existing signal boxes were closed, reducing staff by over 80. At peak periods, nine men in the new centre were supervising the movement of up to 240 trains an hour. A computer-based train reporting system indicated from the panel any lateness in the working of individual trains and by means of television screens, this information reached station staff at the three termini. Centralisation of signalling necessarily renders operations vulnerable to interruption over a wide area, as was demonstrated when a fire broke out on 16 August 1983 on the down side of the main lines near London Bridge station following arcing in the traction supply cable from South Bermondsey substation. The resultant damage to signalling and traction current cabling virtually closed Cannon Street, Waterloo East, Charing Cross and London Bridge stations; normal services could not be restored until 22 August.

Many of the benefits of the new works became available from 20 April 1976, with platforms on the through side of the station re--allocated as follows:

1 : services from Cannon Street
2 : reversible road, used by through non-stopping trains
3 : services to Cannon Street
4 : and 5 : services from Charing Cross, with reversible working facility for trains terminating at London Bridge
6 : services to Charing Cross

By this date, all platforms were fitted with Solari automatic train indicators showing the next departure, complemented by comprehensive indicator displays at the entrances to the terminal and the through platforms and also on the new footbridge. Thanks to the new layout, it was also possible on 20 April 1976 to introduce a time table providing a more reliable service with more regular spacing of trains, a better balance between morning and evening peaks and between the City and West End termini. In response to the increasing use of 'flexitime' in offices, improved service was given at the early part of both morning and evening peak hours and slack hour services were arranged so that on all routes served from London Bridge, up to 30 miles from London, there were two or three trains an hour at even intervals. But as already mentioned, patronage of the terminating services at London Bridge fell off steeply in the 1970s causing substantial reductions to be made in May 1984. The fall since 1967 amounts to almost 26,000 a day, or just over 27 per cent, virtually all of it at peak hours.

### CANNON STREET

Very much a commuter station, Cannon Street has in recent years seen a reduction in services consistent with changes in their use. The modernisation of the 1960s was rounded off in the early 1970s by reconstruction of the underground station and the forecourt area.

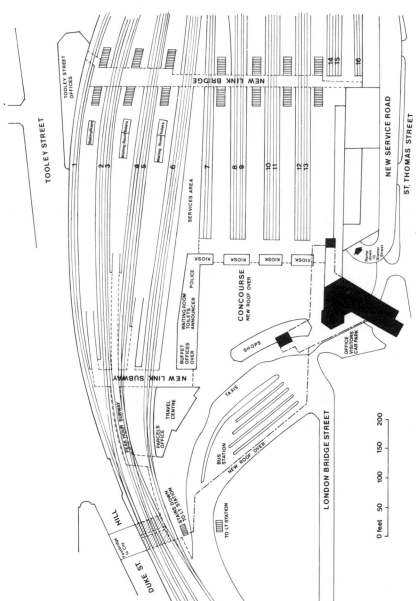

*The new London Bridge station from the late 1970s.*

Derelict since the rebuilding of the 1960s owing to indecision on road widening, the old shops in front of the station were demolished in 1969. Rebuilding of the Underground ticket hall and platforms with regirdering over the District Line tracks to accommodate road widening followed, until all the works were completed in 1973. These included a new lower concourse for the main line station at street level over the Underground booking hall, reached by stairs from the BR platform level. This area contains a five-window ticket office, six shops and the City Travel Centre, opened in March 1974. There are stairs to the Underground station, which is also accessible by stairs direct from the upper concourse.

The windswept platforms, bereft of the war-damaged overall roof, have only the crude corrugated asbestos cement and steel girder canopies erected in the late 1960s; towering above them, the gaunt masses of the old side walls survive to give an impression of past grandeur.

With the end of Saturday morning attendance at City offices, the Underground station was closed completely on that day from 31 January 1970 and Saturday trains ran into the main station for the last time on Saturday 2 May 1970. By 1980 evening traffic had tailed off so sharply that the 14 departures after 19.30 carried an average of only ten passengers each. Despite some protests in Parliament, BR closed the station after that time from 1 June 1981. London Transport followed suit and from 5 October the doors of the Underground station were closed at 19.30 instead of 22.30. In belated recognition of a decline in off peak movements which had begun some 20 years earlier, services were drastically reduced in 1984 leaving the terminus to be served during the slack hours only by a shuttle working to and from London Bridge. At the peak period there were only suburban services.

The station approaches were rearranged in connection with the London Bridge track layout changes mentioned above, and to facilitate the work, the terminus was completely closed from 5 August to 6 September 1974. When services resumed on Monday 9 September, the order of tracks into the terminus, west to east, became: Up, Reversible, Reversible, Up, Down. Between 1977 and 1983 some very costly repairs and renewals were made to the river bridge including complete replacement of the decking. The sensible thing to do now would be to recoup some of this capital outlay by exploiting the site value of the space above the platforms. There never was much to be said for preserving the pathetic relics of the old train shed and sooner or later they will require expensive maintenance.

In its first attempt at direct development of its own property at London termini for commercial gain, BR reconstructed Blackfriars during 1971-79. On the south bank of the river, this was complemented by the erection of over 500,000 sq ft of offices for Lloyds Bank, which, together with a new open space, some council flats and a public house, was partly on the site of the former Blackfriars Bridge station and goods depot. This too was completed in 1979.

For the rebuilding at Blackfriars terminus, BR was in partnership with King's College, Cambridge, owners of the adjacent plot. Work began in 1971 on erection of 150,000 sq ft of offices designed to include a new station entrance hall and a larger high level concourse reached by escalators from street level. The architects were Richard Seifert & Partners, and instead of giving a ground lease to a developer who produced the finance and allowed the railway freeholder a share in growth of income as hitherto, BR financed its part of the scheme. Serious problems were encountered with the foundations, as the arches of the old station building rested on an extensive cold store which in its 80-odd year life had frozen the ground around it to a depth of 20ft. To secure a stable subsoil, the defrosting had perforce to be done slowly. The roof of the District Line tunnel had then to be removed and replaced with a supporting structure to carry the weight of the new building. Platforms and train shed roof were rebuilt, the buffer stops replaced, and a new barrier line with flap indicators and Bostwick gates erected.

The concourse and entrance hall were officially 'opened' (the station had never in fact closed) by the Lord Mayor on 30 November 1977. A pleasing feature was the preservation of the 54 stone blocks listing 19th century destinations from Blackfriars, grouped together on the west wall of the small concourse opposite the two-window ticket office. A single escalator and separate staircase led down to the street level entrance hall, where there was access to the rebuilt Underground ticket hall, finished in 1978. The builders finally left the site in 1979, the accountants Peat, Marwick, Mitchell & Co taking up most of the office space. The new station lacked refreshment facilities.

Through traffic between the City Widened Lines at Farringdon and Blackfriars effectively came to an end when the last daily parcels train ran between Holloway and London Bridge on 23

March 1969 but the line was not formally declared closed until
3 May 1971. On 27 June that year all traffic ceased over the
original river bridge with the closure on that day of the last of
its tracks, the Up Through Reversible. The bridge was removed
early in 1985 using the crane that raised the warship *Mary Rose*
from the Solent in 1982.

In the early part of 1973 the remains of Ludgate Hill's island
platform were levelled and the old subway access to it was filled
in. By the end of 1974 the viaduct between Blackfriars and Holborn Viaduct station had been tidied up and reduced to two tracks,
with a single electrified siding on the site of Ludgate Hill station.
A new concrete bridge carrying the double track over Queen
Victoria Street, far less pleasing to the eye than its decorated cast
iron predecessor, but in harmony with the mostly dreary modern
architecture around it, was completed in November 1974.

At Holborn Viaduct, as at Broad Street, recent years have wit-
nessed little but economies and reductions in service, portents of
future closure in both cases. For Holborn Viaduct, the most likely
fate appears to be replacement by low level platforms on the old
Snow Hill site with through north to south London services via
the City Widened Lines, costs met by the development gains from
the land occupied by the existing surface platforms and
approaches.

Disused since the withdrawal of parcels traffic at the terminus,
Holborn Viaduct's non-electrified platforms 2 and 3 were removed
in 1973 and the site levelled. From 6 May that year platforms 4
and 5 were renumbered 2 and 3, the rearrangement leaving the
station with three eight-car length electrified platforms. The track
rationalisation was followed by a modest signalling modernisation
and in 1974 the signalbox was closed and demolished after transfer of control to Blackfriars. When that box in turn was closed
from 14 February 1982, the station and its approaches, together
with those at Blackfriars itself, came under the supervision of the
Victoria signalling centre at Falcon Lane, Clapham Junction.

Reflecting changes in passenger flow, the Holborn Viaduct terminus was closed on Saturdays after Saturday 2 May 1970, and
on weekday evenings after 19.30 from 1 June 1981. Blackfriars last
saw Saturday trains on 2 October 1976 and Sunday trains ceased
after Sunday 3 October 1976.

To the customer, *The Fusilier* buffet had appeared friendly,
pleasant and efficient, but it apparently could not meet its financial
targets and so was closed in December 1979 to be converted to a
W. H. Smith bookshop. For a short time a small refreshment kiosk
was provided, but early in 1981 this too disappeared, and Holborn

Viaduct joined Broad Street and Blackfriars as London termini without refreshment facilities.

Still one of London's most pleasing termini for the passenger, Waterloo has seen a number of minor improvements combined with some impressive sprucing-up. There have been suggestions of plans for commercial development above the concourse, but it is to be hoped this temptation will be resisted, for however carefully it were to be done, such an addition would inevitably damage the special and stately atmosphere of this fine interior space.

There was no inclination to seek renewal of the cinema lease after a period of declining patronage, so it was closed in April 1970, remaining intact behind a large advertisement hoarding. Higher rentals demanded by BR ousted two other useful services in 1976: the chemists' shop closed in February and the post office in March, leaving the needy traveller to make awkward and time-consuming forays into York Road and Waterloo Road.

A thorough programme of rehabilitation and refurbishment started with the installation of new lighting in 1970-71. Then the *Long Bar* was closed to provide the site for a new ticket office with 16 issuing windows (three for First Class and Season Tickets). Opposite platforms 13 to 15, this was conveniently apparent to passengers coming up the escalator from the Underground. It opened on 6 December 1970 and very shortly after this, the separate Main Line, Windsor Lines and Main Line Suburban offices it had replaced were demolished. Next to the new facilities, on the site of the much-loved and delightfully old-fashioned *Windsor Tea Room*, a travel centre was opened in January 1977. As a sop to the sentimental, the ornamental pay kiosks of the Edwardian Tea Room were retained, looking rather forlorn, with their artificial flowers replacing pretty lady cashiers.

New barrier lines, extending right across the concourse from platform 1 to 21, with staff accommodation above the southern section, new sales kiosks and barrier departure indicators were completed in autumn 1977. With them came a large Solari train indicator above platforms 12 to 15, complemented by satellite indicators over the suburban platforms at the north and south ends of the station. Departure indicators connected to the same system were also placed above the entrances to the platforms from the subway from the Underground and York Road, which runs across the centre of the station.

1978 saw a cleaning of the stone and brickwork on the offices side of the concourse and two years later, 'pneumonia corner', the large but draughty entrance from the street at the top of the war memorial steps, was glazed over at platform level and fitted with a range of swing doors. Almost the last relics of the LSWR's interior fittings, the decorative ironwork around the stairs to the Waterloo Road subway, had been replaced by tiled walls by the end of 1980. The comfortable wooden seats on the concourse gave way to small tip up seats attached to concrete blocks, modern equivalents of misericordes to discourage layabouts. As a finishing touch to these changes, the whole of the concourse was repaved in 1980-83 with white terrazzo tiling. The bright cheerfulness this imparted, with its attendant discouragement to the dropping of litter were of course dependent on regular cleaning, always a feature at Waterloo.

Between 1978 and 1984 the track layout in the approaches to platforms 1-4 was simplified, shortening these platforms to 8-car length.

Those responsible for expenditure on catering facilities have shown a quite remarkable restlessness at Waterloo. The *Horseshoe Bar* was replaced on 25 January 1972 by a self-service cafeteria and bar named *The Drum*, 'a far cry from the traditional station buffet', but this was rebuilt after less than three years, acquiring a juke box in the process. It was completely replaced in October 1980 by BR's first 'fast food' eating place, *The Casey Jones*, serving beefburgers and fishburgers in sesame seed buns, potato chips and various hot and cold soft drinks. Similar installations subsequently appeared at Victoria, Kings Cross, Charing Cross, Liverpool Street and Euston, their 'take-away' debris adding new scents and litter to trains and station premises.

In the old main line ticket hall, a waitress service restaurant with 119 seats, *The Great Express*, took the place of *The Surrey Room* and *The Windsor* in May 1973. Subsequently rebuilt as *The Trafalgar Buffet and Bar*, it was gutted yet again, to reappear in 1982 as *The Trips* restaurant.

Across Waterloo Road, platforms A to D (now 1-4) officially known as Waterloo East from 8 May 1978, have seen modernisation of the buffet and of the booking office in the wall of the access ramp. Solari train indicators were installed on the bridge and platforms in connection with the London Bridge resignalling of 1976. Financial assistance from the GLC enabled the station to be re-lit and refurbished, and this work, which included some cutting back of the platform awnings, was completed in 1984. Lambeth Council provided financial aid for a refurbishment of the long-neglected and grim Waterloo Road colonnade and subway on the north east side of the main station in 1985.

By the end of the 1970s, the wiring and equipment of the 1936 signalbox had reached the end of its useful life. A new panel was installed and came into use on 5 February 1984, controlling a relay room on the site of the old North Side turntable. The new equipment is designed to be incorporated in the future major resignalling scheme for the lines out of Waterloo.

Despite a slight drop in the total number of passengers handled on weekdays since 1967, Waterloo is now London's busiest terminus, both as regards the daily total and rush hour traffic. This fact appears to be known to television and film cameramen, as they are frequently to be seen with their equipment and numerous supporters, both on the concourse and in the gallery behind the platform barriers.

### CHARING CROSS

Like Waterloo, this station benefited in the 1970s from a number of improvements which brightened but did not alter its essential atmosphere and appearance. Its somewhat cramped concourse, under severe pressure at rush hours, still remains obstructed by a very large bookstall and other obstacles.

No doubt essential, but hardly adding to the elegance of the interior, a range of staff rooms was erected above the buffer stop ends in 1970. Modernisation of the booking hall and ticket offices was completed on 1 December 1974, but under constant punishment of very heavy passenger usage, the entrance and hall soon became rather tatty, forming another example of the false economy of low cost alterations of this type. An 'Agiticket' multifunctional (and multi-lingual) electronic ticket printing, accounting and issue machine for public use was placed in the booking hall in August 1983 on a trial basis. The old enquiry office, a cosy relic of the 1950s, was transformed to a travel centre in October 1975, with a new entrance from the forecourt.

A very noticeable improvement to the interior was achieved by cleaning of the brickwork in 1973-74 and installation of new lighting shortly afterwards. This was further enhanced in 1983 when the floor of the concourse was paved with the same bright terrazzo tiling as had been used at Waterloo. When the station was built, the wooden piling supporting the main structure had been embedded in wet ballast but changes in the level of the water table dried out the timbers, rendering them vulnerable to rot. Over the years this caused the piling to collapse, with settlement of the main structure and cracking of the brickwork. A major programme of underpinning the foundations was undertaken in 1977-78 to prevent further deterioration.

The tube station beneath the forecourt underwent complete reconstruction during which it was linked with a new system of spacious public subways connecting the two stations to the north side of the Strand, Duncannon Street, William IV Street and Adelaide Street. Generations of confusion were ended by renaming the station Charing Cross in line with the main station it served and it was reopened on 1 May 1979, now serving the first stage of the Jubilee tube line as well as the Northern and Bakerloo Lines. The pedestrian subways, which have proved a popular free pitch for itinerant musicians, classical and otherwise, were finished by the end of 1979. Already outdated with its 'pop-art' blue, green and yellow moulded plastic decor, the tube booking hall strove to attain a relaxed atmosphere with recessed lighting and lavish use of sound-absorbent materials.

When a new buffet and bar was opened on the main station concourse in August 1972 a smartly-uniformed doorman was employed to throw out the vagrants and loafers who had favoured the old premises. Ten years later he had gone when part of the area was rebuilt yet again, reopening as *Casey Jones* on 5 August 1982.

Hungerford Bridge, maligned and attacked as it has been, remains as it ever was, but still attracts planners, the latest proposal being to add a top deck of shops and entertainment centres. Meanwhile, in 1979-80, it underwent substantial repair and renovation, a process which restricted train services for some time and included the provision of an alarmingly shaky temporary footbridge on the upstream side whilst the permanent footway was rebuilt.

Although rush hour traffic has declined slightly, Charing Cross is one of the four termini to show an overall traffic increase since 1967-68. London's fourth busiest terminus, it now sees just under 4,000 more passengers a day than in 1967, a fact which underlines the continuing convenience of its location.

## VICTORIA

Pity Poor Victoria. Journalists in the 1970s found it easy to castigate: 'a gloomy, grimy goldmine' (Simon Jenkins, 1971); 'unloved gateway of the South' (Arthur Sandles, 1978). 'Victoria tries valiantly, but she cannot cope with the custom' was the conclusion of the Transport Users' Consultative Committee for London's report of 1980, which doubted whether the rebuilding would do more than 'nibble at the edges of that major issue'. Bruised by the burden of a lusty traffic growth in its airport feeder role and hampered by the irrelevance of its 19th and early 20th century layout to modern requirements, this station cried out for total replacement, just as much as Euston and London Bridge had done. But unlike them, it received only piecemeal modernisation which rendered it barely more attractive or more efficient than before. Despite costly resignalling and track rearrangement, the promised improvement in operating performance seemed elusive. Regular passengers have come not to trust it, and when things go awry, feel insecure and irked as they are left to stare at an almost blank train indicator and given no information on what can be expected. Combined with an often sleazy appearance, and a chaotic, cluttered forecourt, this all added up to something less than appropriate for London's third busiest terminus, constantly crowded with the still healthy rail-sea traffic and the ever-mounting flow to and from Gatwick Airport, which make it the first London terminus most foreign visitors see, and the one they see most of.

With several proposals for complete rebuilding discarded in the face of planning problems and lack of decisions on the Channel Tunnel and a rail link to London Airport (Heathrow), BR was left to do what it could afford with the existing structures. Thus the 1970s saw modernisation by degrees, steady as you go: for no-one, from the station staff to the highest in the land ever seems able to say what will happen next at Victoria. Bolder decisions came with the 1980s, when work began on rafting over the platforms to carry a new rail-air terminal and huge office complexes, the former at last to segregate the Gatwick traffic in a station-within-a-station. But the rest of the place, it seemed, would have to muddle along much as before.

No longer was the Eastern side quiet in winter. Rail-sea traffic if not increased, at least spread itself more evenly through the year, and the suburban and medium distance traffic on this side of the station remained buoyant through the 1970s, profiting from the attraction of much easier access to the businesses and shops of the West End after the opening of the Victoria line tube, with its large booking hall under the forecourt, on 7 March 1969. But, encouraged by rail strikes and the Conservatives' Transport Act of 1980, road coach operators, paying nothing to encumber the surrounding streets, began to make a hole in the Kent commuter traffic. There was a fall of just under 20 per cent (36,100 daily) in the total number of daily passengers at Victoria as a whole between 1967 and 1983, much of it rush hour movement.

January 1971 brought a first taste of modernisation with the installation of two 120ft long Solari electronic train indicators, one for each side of the station. These were placed over the platform barrier lines, with separate next train indicators at each gate. The electric impulse clocks on the main displays replaced the old station clocks, including the four-dial LBSCR clock of 1860, which found a new home in a San Francisco restaurant.

The next major item was a stainless steel ticket office erected on the Brighton side concourse, its back projecting into the old LBSCR booking hall. This came into use on 16 May 1976 and those of its 14 windows (one for First Class and Season tickets) which were manned were soon endeavouring to cope with the work of the three former ticket offices, long queues forming back across the concourse in the process. Sometimes these queues are longer than they need be owing to confusion over which windows are open. Much of the rest of the old main line booking hall was consumed by a travel centre opened on 25 October the same year, which dealt with all enquiries except those relating to the cross-Channel services. The associated rebuilding brought to full light of day the LBSCR tile wall maps, which were incorporated in the decoration of a passageway from the forecourt to the concourse.

When the old local lines booking office of the LBSCR had been demolished, the east wall of the Brighton station was clothed with offices for railway staff including a gazebo for the station announcer. Beneath this was a new buffet, a fruit shop and hotel enquiry kiosk. A London Transport travel information centre appeared alongside the old SECR arch in 1982.

In order to provide more space on the old LBSCR concourse, the barrier line for platforms 10-13 was moved 60ft south in line with the head of platform 9. At the same time, the heads of platforms 14 and 15 were moved even further south to line up with those of 16 and 17, thus giving a wide circulation space between platform 13 and the west wall. The former parcels office (retaining its inscription) became a bureau de change. Large enquiry offices for the National and London Tourist Boards were built on the west side of the forecourt in 1983. Fluorescent lighting, fitted throughout the station shortly before, was extended over the enlarged circulating areas and the departure indicator was moved back to the new barrier line of platforms 10-13; all the work just described was finished by the end of 1979. There was certainly more room to move when the station was crowded, and it was easier to dodge the reclining bodies on the floor, but now everyone had much further to walk to and from the trains.

A Gatwick 'Rail-Air Reception Centre' with dedicated ticket office and entry to the platform was opened alongside platform 13 (from which Gatwick trains normally departed) in September 1980, flanked with small offices for British Airways and the British Council. As a final touch, the two concourses with their passageways to the forecourt were paved in 1984-85 with the terrazzo tiling first seen at Waterloo. Other improvements were also made to give them an impression of greater unity and space.

Last of the new facilities planned for the 1970s (though not fully completed until early in 1981) was a large Sealink Travel and Car Ferry Centre alongside platform 2. It had 16 counters for advance ticket and reservations issue, with a number queueing system, seven counters for 'day of use' ticket issue, an information desk, a waiting lounge, and car ferry and European Motorail booking point. This impressive complex occupied the site of the old LCDR booking hall.

The busy bus station in the forecourt, handling over half a million passengers a week, was roofed over with 12,000 sq yd of translucent plastic in 1971, ·but the space between it and. the station canopy was left unprotected owing to current uncertainties about the future of the station building. This uncertainty more or less resolved, the internal and external fabric of the station was cleaned and renovated in 1979-80 bringing to light much hitherto unnoticed detail in the Edwardian décor. At the same time, the original LCDR frontage in Hudson's Place, scene of State Visitor arrivals by rail, was given a new canopy and generally renovated. In 1983 the forecourt in front of the SECR arch was closed to road traffic, paved, and provided with red brick enclosures for plants, shrubs and litter. A few globe light standards of the type favoured by shopping centre architects were scattered about. The total effect was somewhat incongruous against Blomfield's elaborate elevations, nor was it enhanced by discarded luggage trolleys and use of the area for parking railway police cars.

As at London Bridge, the approaches to the terminus have undergone drastic track rationalisation and signalling modernisation. Between 1977 and 1983 a new signalling centre named Victoria but in reality at Falcon Lane, Clapham Junction, took over supervision of all movements over the 267 track miles between Victoria (and Holborn Viaduct/Blackfriars) and Sutton, Epsom Downs, West Croydon, Thornton Heath, Otford and Longfield, replacing 35 signal boxes, including Victoria Eastern, which closed on 13 May 1979, and Victoria Central, which closed on 9 May 1981.

In the feverish rush to keep up with eating fashions, catering facilities have changed and changed again. *The Golden Arrow* bar on the east side reopened as the *Europa Bistro Bar* on 12 December 1972 dispensing 'French-style' food and wines in a simulated Continental atmosphere. It is again being rebuilt at the time of writing. The *Chatham Rooms* and *Garden Buffet* gave way to the *Medway Restaurant* and *Victoria's Pantry* in the early 1970s, only to be rebuilt ten years later as the *Belgravia Bar* and *Casey Jones*. On the west side, the *Brighton Belle* was refurbished as the *Downs* in 1977. Despite all this frenzied activity, some stand-up comics still joke about railway sandwiches.

As for the trains, much glamour has departed. The famous Pullman 'Brighton Belle' favourite of Brighton's thespian community, and immortalised by Olivier's outburst at the withdrawal of kippers from its menu, ran for the last time on 30 April 1972, its stock worn out and BR pleading lack of funds to replace it. The Southern Region's last Pullman service, the 'Golden Arrow', ran no more after 30 September 1972 for the same reason. Another famous train working to and from Victoria, the 'Night Ferry' with its sleeping cars working through to Paris and Brussels, suffered the same fate, leaving the terminus for the last time at 21.25 on Friday 31 October 1980. With all its famous trains gone, a little bit of Victoria died that night. No more was there a civilised alternative to air travel to Europe. But railway glamour did return on 25 May 1982 when a train as splendid as the old 'Golden Arrow', if not more so, the 'Venice-Simplon-Orient Express', with its beautifully-restored Pullman cars, made its first run; but alas it is not a daily all-year-round working.

Excitement of a more sordid kind came to the station when an Irish bomb exploded in the old LBSCR booking hall on 8 September 1973, injuring five people.

Hardly had the 1980s begun when major accretions to Victoria were under way. First of these, completed by the end of 1984, was the Victoria Plaza, a six-storey office block of 220,000 sq ft. Jointly promoted by BR, Greycoat London Estates and Norwich Union, this confection of glass and metal, designed by Elsom, Pack & Roberts, sat on a steel raft erected across platforms 14 to 19 as far as Eccleston Bridge, its frontage to Buckingham Palace Road. The entrance forecourt, behind graceful masonry arches built into the old LBSCR wall, occupies the site of the former parcels depot and van loading bay next to the cab exit arch. Construction of the raft required the demolition of the news cinema, which closed on 27 August 1981. The 1962 air terminal within the station had also to be demolished and was temporarily replaced by a building on the concourse occupying the site of the 1908 post office. Pending installation of forced ventilation in the restricted space between the rail platforms and the new raft, Oxted line diesel trains were banished to London Bridge.

During 1984 the raft was extended eastwards as far as platform

8. It is to carry a rail-air terminal for the Gatwick traffic, linked by escalators to the dedicated platforms beneath (as these were to be numbered 16 and 17, those platforms were renumbered 18 and 19 on 3 February 1980). Non-stop Gatwick trains with specially-rebuilt rolling stock, to work into this new facility every 15 minutes, started to run on 14 May 1984, well before it was ready, using platforms 13 and 14. By this time platforms 9 to 19 had been refurbished with blue and white pillars, white ceiling panels carrying strips of fluorescent lighting and a continuous yellow trim, and white terrazzo floor tiling. There were new clocks and LONDON VICTORIA signs in white letters on a blue ground. When finished, there will be air travel check-in desks, short term car parking and cab access from Eccleston Bridge, all at the elevated level. More offices are also proposed, resting on an extension of the raft southwards to Elizabeth Bridge, this development to incorporate a covered public way linking the main line and Underground stations with the Green Line coach loading points and the Victoria coach terminal. There will however be no connection with the former Imperial Airways building of 1939 since this closed in 1980 as an air terminal and was put up for sale by British Airways two years later.

## PADDINGTON

As at St Pancras, the interior of Paddington is so fine that any alterations require the most careful thought. Fortunately the modernisation of the 1970s and mid 1980s, has only been small-scale and it remains essentially the rather special place it has always been, redolent of the GWR, holidays and the relaxation of the West Country. Both suburban and main line traffic have held up well in the last 15 years (an overall increase in daily loadings of 5000, or 11.6 per cent) and a recent suggestion in a railway journal that it could be closed and its services diverted elsewhere seems a little far-fetched. Shortly after celebrating its 125th birthday, Western Region headquarters staff heard they were to be moved from the old GWR offices to Swindon, and this historic change was completed early in 1984. That year also saw the start of a £1.8m GLC-funded scheme to provide about 65 per cent more space on the main concourse by setting back the platform barriers, with links to a new Underground (LT) booking hall.

Brunel, who since 1982 has been celebrated by a bronze statue on the concourse, sculpted by John Doubleday and donated by the Bristol & West Building Society, would have been pleased with the 125th anniversary celebrations on 1 March 1979. For the first time since 1965, steam locomotives were seen again in the train shed in the form of *King George V* (GWR 4-6-0 No 6000) which worked a special train to Didcot, and *Hinderton Hall* (GWR 4-6-0 No 5900), which with two GWR coaches, formed a static display. More steam was seen on 20 September 1981 on the occasion of the 75th anniversary of the Old Oak Common depot, which serves Paddington. A special service was worked between the terminus and the depot with the GWR 4-6-0 *Drysl1wyn Castle* at the London end of the train and BR 2-10-0 *Evening Star* at the other.

The remaining freight facilities, at Paddington New Yard, were closed on 29 December 1972. At the terminus itself, the Bishops Bridge Road passenger entrance was shut from 4 June 1969.

Alongside platform 1, the refreshment facilities, where silver-plated GWR teapots and GWR plates were still to be seen ten years or more after nationalisation, were refurbished as the *Castle Buffet & Bar* in March 1973. A new *Heralds' Bar* and *Knights' Bar* appeared later that year along two sides of the Lawn, whilst the *Westward Bar and Cafeteria* (what a forties/fifties flavour that word has!) opposite platform 8 was rebuilt as *The Tournament* self-service buffet (108 seats) and waitress-service *Roundhouse Restaurant* (92 seats). There have been some minor improvements to these latter since, and they must be the only railway refreshment rooms in London which have fresh flowers on the tables.

### MARYLEBONE

Transferred from the Western Region to the London Division of the London Midland Region of BR in 1973, Marylebone spent the 1970s and early 1980s awaiting its long-deferred sentence of death. Property developers cast greedy eyes as BR, London Transport and the Ministry discussed ad nauseum what best to do. To be fair to BR, it had tried to close it in 1970, but permission was refused by the Minister. Finally, in 1983, BR announced it would be closed within five more years, with diversion of the High Wycombe services to Paddington. What to do with the Aylesbury operation was slightly more difficult. Whether it will be diesel unit shuttle to and from Amersham or return to London Transport, with extended electric service remains to be seen. National Bus wanted to convert Marylebone to a coach terminus, using the approach tracks to get the coaches in and out of the central area, but this seemed likely not only to produce some engineering problems and operational hazards for the coach services, but also to be less profitable for BR.

With activity limited to the drab comings and goings of the ageing Class 115 diesel multiple units on London's most lightly-used suburban services, Marylebone now comes to life only upon the occasional diversion of main line trains into its quiet portals when things have gone awry on the Euston and Paddington lines. So much spare capacity exists that it is an ideal place for making cinema and television films requiring large railway station locations. Understandably, no money has been spent on it in recent years, although after the 1970 decision to keep it open, the indefatigable controllers of the catering coffers rebuilt the refreshment facilities. These reopened as the *Regency Buffet* and *Victoria Bar*, with appropriate décor, on 14 December 1971. On the 28 acres of the former GCR goods depot Westminster City Council erected its 1500-dwelling Lisson Green development in the early 1970s.

It is interesting to note that despite motorway construction and some road coach competition stimulated by the 1980 Act, Marylebone's daily traffic has dropped only 400 a day since 1968, or just over 2.5 per cent. The remaining patrons of the Great Central are nothing if not loyal.

# Appendixes

## Opening Dates

| | |
|---|---|
| LONDON  BRIDGE | 14 December 1836 |
| EUSTON | 20 July 1837 |
| Nine Elms (Vauxhall) | 21 May 1838 |
| Paddington I | 4 June 1838 |
| Shoreditch | 1 July 1840 |
| Minories | 6 July 1840 |
| FENCHURCH STREET | 2 August 1841 |
| Bricklayers Arms | 1 May 1844 |
| WATERLOO | 11 July 1848 |
| Maiden Lane | 7 August 1850 |
| KINGS CROSS | 14 October 1852 |
| PADDINGTON  II | 16 January 1854 |
| Pimlico (Battersea Pier) | 29 March 1858 |
| VICTORIA | 1 October 1860 |
| CHARING  CROSS | 11 January 1864 |
| Blackfriars (Bridge) | 1 June 1864 |
| LUDGATE HILL | 1 June 1865* |
| BROAD STREET | 1 November 1865 |
| CANNON STREET | 1 September 1866 |
| ST PANCRAS | 1 October 1868 |
| LIVERPOOL  STREET | 2 February 1874 |
| HOLBORN  VIADUCT | 2 March 1874 |
| ST  PAUL'S  (now  BLACK-FRIARS) | 10 May 1886 |
| MARYLEBONE | 15 March 1899 |

* Temporary station in Little Earl Street 21 December 1864.

x

*APPENDIX  II*

*Traffic Statistics 1903 (1)*
*Trains arriving daily (Weekdays)*

|  | *Suburban* | *Total* |
|---|---|---|
| LIVERPOOL STREET | 380 | 416 |
| BROAD STREET | 322 | 322 |
| VICTORIA | 306 | 370 |
| WATERLOO | 256 | 303 |
| LONDON BRIDGE | 243 | 293 |
| FENCHURCH STREET | 232 | 233 |
| CANNON STREET | 211 | 249* |
| ST PAUL'S AND LUDGATE HILL | 171 | 171 |
| CHARING CROSS | 152 | 187 |
| KINGS CROSS | 60 | 101 |
| HOLBORN VIADUCT | 50 | 71 |
| PADDINGTON | 39 | 103 |
| ST PANCRAS | 38 | 66 |
| EUSTON | 36 | 78 |
| MARYLEBONE | — | 13 |

*Source:* Royal Commission on London Traffic, 1905, Volume III
Appendices, Appendix 6, Table 33.

* Includes trains going on to Charing Cross.

*APPENDIX III*

*Traffic Statistics 1903 (2)*

| Season ticket journeys in year (millions) | | Total journeys in year (millions) | |
|---|---|---|---|
| Liverpool Street | 20.0 | Liverpool Street | 65.3 |
| London Bridge (both) | 11.7 | Waterloo | 31.0 |
| Broad Street | 9.8 | London Bridge (both) | 29.8 |
| Victoria (both) | 9.4 | Victoria (both) | 29.4 |
| Waterloo | 8.7 | Broad Street | 26.7 |
| Kings Cross | 8.3 | Fenchurch Street | 23.9 |
| St Pancras | 7.3 | Kings Cross | 15.4 |
| Fenchurch Street | 5.5 | Cannon Street | 13.5 |
| Cannon Street | 4.3 | Holborn Viaduct | 10.7 |
| Holborn Viaduct | 3.5 | Charing Cross | 10.2 |
| Charing Cross | 3.3 | St Pancras | 9.8 |
| Paddington | 2.7 | Paddington | 9.2 |
| Euston | 1.9 | Ludgate Hill | 4.8 |
| Ludgate Hill | 1.5 | Euston | 4.5 |
| St Paul's | 1.2 | St Paul's | 3.8 |
| Marylebone | 0.1 | Marylebone | 0.5 |

*Source:* Royal Commission on London Traffic, 1905, Vol I, para 133.

## APPENDIX IV

*Traffic Statistics 1967-8 (1)*

|  | Trains in and out daily | Passengers daily (weekdays, nearest 100) |
|---|---|---|
| LIVERPOOL STREET | 1,001 | 204,700 |
| WATERLOO | 1,214 | 195,900 |
| VICTORIA | 1,031 | 182,900 |
| CHARING CROSS | 729 | 119,900 |
| LONDON BRIDGE | 645* | 94,400* |
| CANNON STREET | 261 | 80,000 |
| FENCHURCH STREET | 253 | 67,300 |
| PADDINGTON | 287 | 43,000 |
| EUSTON | 410 | 40,000 |
| KINGS CROSS | 297 | 39,900 |
| ST PANCRAS | 187 | 30,000 |
| MARYLEBONE | 126 | 15,000 |
| BROAD STREET | 146 | 9,000 |

## APPENDIX V

*Traffic Statistics 1967-8 (2)*

Passengers and trains arriving 7 to 10 am at the busiest stations.

|  | Passengers | Trains |
|---|---|---|
| LIVERPOOL STREET | 79,904 | 167 |
| WATERLOO | 70,108 | 152 |
| VICTORIA | 57,669 | 107 |
| LONDON BRIDGE | 42,305* | 105 |
| CHARING CROSS | 42,230 | 71 |
| CANNON STREET | 38,320 | 63 |
| FENCHURCH STREET | 30,728 | 41 |
| PADDINGTON | 10,500 | 42 |
| ST PANCRAS | 8,326 | 37 |

* terminating trains only

*Source:* British Railways Regions (Southern Region figures are for October 1967, all others for October 1968)

*APPENDIX VI*

*Traffic Statistics 1983 (1)*

|  | Trains in and out daily | Passengers daily (weekdays nearest 100) |
|---|---|---|
| WATERLOO | 1,129 | 177,700 |
| LIVERPOOL STREET | 985 | 150,000 |
| VICTORIA | 1,008 | 146,800 |
| CHARING CROSS | 635 | 123,700 |
| CANNON STREET | 276 | 68,800 |
| LONDON BRIDGE | 527* | 68,700* |
| EUSTON | 400 | 67,200 |
| FENCHURCH STREET | 269 | 62,000 |
| PADDINGTON | 380 | 48,000 |
| ST PANCRAS | 170 | 36,000 |
| KINGS CROSS | 252 | 35,000 |
| HOLBORN VIADUCT | 162 | 17,900 |
| MARYLEBONE | 110 | 14,600 |
| BLACKFRIARS | 45* | 13,100 |
| BROAD STREET | 127 | 4,900 |

*Traffic Statistics 1983 (2)*

Passengers arriving 7 to 10 am at the busiest stations (nearest 100)

| | |
|---|---|
| WATERLOO | 61,200 |
| LIVERPOOL STREET | 57,800 |
| VICTORIA | 45,100 |
| CHARING CROSS | 39,700 |
| CANNON STREET | 33,800 |
| LONDON BRIDGE | 29,900* |
| FENCHURCH STREET | 28,300 |
| EUSTON | 14,700 |
| PADDINGTON | 9,500** |
| ST PANCRAS | 9,300 |

* Terminating trains only
** Figure relates to 8 am to 9 am only
*Source:* British Rail regions.

## SOURCES AND SELECT BIBLIOGRAPHY

A fully annotated reference for each of the many hundreds of facts and dates in this book would fill almost as many pages as the text itself, pages which would be of value to only a small minority of readers. The following notes and bibliography should provide an indication of sources as well as serving as a guide to further reading.

Much basic information is given in the Acts of Parliament for the works concerned, and in the unsuccessful Bills, with their deposited plans (adequately indexed in the London and Middlesex County Record Offices). Detail is available in the minutes and reports of the various railway companies (Public Record Office, Kew), in contemporary public timetables and travel guides, working timetables and their appendices, and in contemporary maps and plans (notably the large scale Ordnance Survey and the invaluable Railway Clearing House Junction Diagrams). Of major importance as a source are the contemporary accounts and comments in the daily and periodical press, especially: *The Times, The Daily Telegraph, Illustrated London News, Railway Times, Railway News, Railway Engineer, Railway Magazine, Railway & Travel Monthly, Railway Gazette, Railway Club Journal, Railway World, Trains Illustrated, Modern Railways* and *Modern Transport*. Of the various company magazines, the *Great Western Railway Magazine* is particularly useful on Paddington, the *Southern Railway Magazine* on the southern termini; the others are less rewarding. Architectural detail is to be found in *The Builder, Building News*, and *The Architect*. Much is to be gained from magnification of old drawings and photographs, not forgetting the picture postcards of the 1900-14 period.

Some statements in the text are derived from the author's own observations and field work in the past thirty years, and that of friends, particularly the late G. T. Moody, whose notebooks were begun about 1920.

The following books, magazine articles, and reports are suggested to those seeking further background and detail:

## 1. General

Acworth, W. M., *The Railways of England*, various editions from 1889, John Murray.

Clunn, H., *London Rebuilt 1897-1927*, John Murray, 1927.

Clunn, H., *The Face of London*, Spring Books, 1956.

Course, E. A., *London Railways*, B. T. Batsford, 1962.

Crump, N., *By Rail to Victory, the story of the LNER in wartime*, LNER, 1947.

Darwin, B., *War on the Line: the story of the Southern Railway in wartime*, SR, 1946.

Dyos, H. J., *Railways and Housing in Victorian London*, Journal of Transport History, 2 (1955-6).

John, E., *Time table for Victory: a brief and popular account of the railways and railway-owned dockyards of Great Britain and Northern Ireland, during the six years' war, 1939-45*, The British Railways, 1946.

Knight, C. (ed), *London*, Henry G. Bohn, 1851 (chapter by Saunders, J.).

London County Council, *Survey of London*, vols 21, 23, 24.

Nash, G. G., *The LMS at War*, LMSR, 1946

Pratt, E. A., *British Railways and the Great War* (two vols), Selwyn & Blount, 1921.

Sekon, G. A., *Locomotion in Victorian London*, Oxford University Press, 1938.

Thornbury, W. and Walford, E., *Old and New London* (six vols), Cassell & Co, 1897.

Wheatley, H. B., *London Past and Present*, John Murray, 1891.

White, H. P., *A Regional History of the Railways of Great Britain, Vol 3, Greater London*, Phoenix House, David & Charles, 1963.

## State Publications

*Report of the Commissioners on Railway Termini within or in the immediate vicinity of the Metropolis*, and *Evidence*, 1846.

*Report of the Select Committee of the House of Commons on Metropolitan Communications*, 1855, and *Evidence*.

*Report of the Select Committee on Metropolitan Railway Communication*, 1863, and *Evidence*.

*Report of the Joint Committee on Railway Schemes (Metropolis)*, 1864, and *Evidence*.

*Royal Commission on the Housing of the Working Classes*, and *Evidence*, 1885.

*Report of the Joint Select Committee on the Housing of the Working Classes* and *Evidence*, 1902.
*Royal Commission on London Traffic*, 1905, *Report, Evidence, Appendices* (eight vols).


## 2.  Architecture

Hitchcock, H. R., *Early Victorian Architecture in Great Britain* (two vols), Architectural Press, 1954.
Hitchcock, H. R., *Architecture: 19th and 20th centuries*, Penguin Books (Pelican History of Art), 1958.
Meeks, C. L. V., *The Railway Station: An Architectural History*, Architectural Press, 1957.


## 3.  The Stations (order as in text)

EUSTON
Barrie, D. S., *The Story of Euston*, Railway Magazine, July and September, 1937.
Head, F. B., *Stokers and Pokers*, John Murray, 1849.
Smith, G. R., *Old Euston*, Country Life/LMSR, 1938.

ST PANCRAS
Barlow, W. H., Proceedings, Institution of Civil Engineers, vol 30.
Barnes, E. G., *The Midland Drive for London*, Railway World, September 1962.
Scott, Sir C. G., *Personal & Professional Recollections*, Sampson Low, Marston, Searle & Rivington, 1879.
Lee, C. E., *St Pancras Station, 1868-1968*, Railway Magazine, September and October 1968.
Simmons, J., *St Pancras Station*, George Allen & Unwin, 1968.
Williams, F. S., *The Midland Railway, Its Rise and Progress*, Bemrose & Co, 1877.
KINGS CROSS
Gairns, J. F., *Notable Railway Stations and their Traffic: Kings Cross*, Railway Magazine, August 1914.
Grinling, C. H., *The History of the Great Northern Railway, 1845-1902*, 1903.
Johns, C. A., *One Hundred Years at Kings Cross*, Railway Magazine, October and November 1952.
BISHOPSGATE
Evill, W., Proceedings, Institution of Civil Engineers, vol 3.
LIVERPOOL STREET
Gairns, J. F., *Jubilee of a Great London Terminus*, Railway Magazine, May 1924.

FENCHURCH STREET

Gairns, J. F., *Notable Railway Stations and their Traffic: Fenchurch Street*, Railway Magazine, June 1919.

BRICKLAYERS ARMS

Fellows, R. B., *The Failure of Bricklayers Arms as a Passenger Station*, Railway Magazine, July/August and September/October 1944.

LONDON BRIDGE

Reed, B. A. and Lee, C. E., *London Bridge, the Oldest Terminus*, Railway Magazine, December 1936, February 1937.

CANNON STREET

Ellson, G., Proceedings, Institution of Civil Engineers, vol 223.

Lee, C. E., *Cannon Street Station 1866-1966*, Railway Magazine, August and September, 1966.

Wolfe Barry, J., Proceedings, Institution of Civil Engineers, vol 27.

LUDGATE HILL

Lee, C. E., *Useful but Unloved, the story of Ludgate Hill Station*, Railway Magazine, December 1964.

WATERLOO AND NINE ELMS

Anon, *The New Waterloo Station, LSWR*, reprinted from the Railway Gazette, 9 June 1922.

Davis, H. G., *Waterloo Station Centenary, 1848-1948*, British Railways, 1948.

Fay, Sam, *A Royal Road*, W. L. Drewett, 1883.

Gairns, J. F., *The Largest Railway Terminus in Great Britain*, Railway Magazine, May 1922.

Szlumper, A. W., Proceedings, Institution of Civil Engineers, vols 107, 111.

CHARING CROSS

Ellson, G., Proceedings, Institution of Civil Engineers, vol 223.

Hayter, H., Proceedings, Institution of Civil Engineers, vol 22.

Lee, C. E., *Charing Cross Station 1864-1964*, Railway Magazine, January 1964.

Wolfe Barry, J., Proceedings, Institution of Civil Engineers, vol 27.

VICTORIA AND PIMLICO

Fox, C. W., Proceedings, Institution of Civil Engineers, vol 27.

Gairns, J. F., *Notable Railway Stations and their traffic: Victoria (London)*, Railway Magazine, April 1927.

Lee, C. E., *The First West End Terminus*, Railway Magazine, March 1958.

Lee, C. E., *Victoria Station London in the 19th century*, Railway Magazine, September 1960.

Y

Lee, C. E., *Victoria Station London in the 20th century*, Railway Magazine, October 1960.

MacDermot, E. T., *History of the Great Western Railway*, GWR, 1927.

Wilson, W., Proceedings, Institution of Civil Engineers, vol 27.

PADDINGTON

MacDermot, E. T., *History of the Great Western Railway*, GWR, 1927.

Lee, C. E., *The Centenary of Paddington Station*, Railway Magazine, June 1954.

MARYLEBONE

Hobson, G. A. and Wragge, E., Proceedings, Institution of Civil Engineers, vol 143.

*Second Edition Addenda*

## 1. General

Anon., *Your Station in Life*, Transport Users' Consultative Committee for London, 1980

Anon., *Termini Revisited*, ditto, 1982

Anon., *Channel Tunnel London Passenger Terminal*, Greater London Council, 1972

Betjeman, Sir John, *London's Historic Railway Stations*, John Murray, 1972

Garlinge, Bruce, *Waiting Rooms at London Railway Termini*, Railway and Travel Monthly, December 1912

Kellett, J. R., *The Impact of Railways on Victorian Cities*, Routledge & Kegan Paul, 1969

Kemman, G., *Der Verkehr Londons*, 1892

Rannie, Alan, *Empty Stock Working at London Termini*, Railway Magazine, November and December, 1958

Young, J. N., *London's City Trains*, Railway Magazine, January 1971

## 2. Architecture

Biddle, Gordon, *Victorian Stations*, David & Charles, 1973

Richardson, A. E., *Railway Stations*, Proceedings, Royal Institute of British Architects, 1939

## 3. The Stations

EUSTON

Anon., *The New Euston Station, 1968*, British Rail, 1968

Dickens, Charles, *Dombey & Son*, chapters VI and XV

Kichenside, G. M., *Resignalling is Complete from Euston*, Modern

Railways, March 1966

Phillp, S. M., *Notable Railway Stations, No 3*, Railway Magazine, January 1900

ST PANCRAS

Scott, James, *The Fascination of Railway Stations, No. 5*, Railway & Travel Monthly, February 1912

Timins, D. T., *Notable Railway Stations No 19*, Railway Magazine, June 1902

KINGS CROSS

Anon., *Recent Developments at Kings Cross*, Railway Magazine, March 1925

Kichenside, G. M., *Kings Cross Area Resignalling*, Modern Railways, April 1978

Medcalf, J., *Railway Goods Depots IV*, Railway Magazine, April 1900

Perren, Brian, *Kings Cross Today*, Railway World, March 1969

Thrower, W. R., *Kings Cross in the Twenties*, Oakwood Press, 1978

BROAD STREET

Anon., *How Trains are Controlled IX*, Railway Magazine, September 1906

Binney, Marcus, etc., *Save Broad Street*, SAVE Britain's Heritage, 1982

LIVERPOOL STREET

Jackson, Alan A., *The First Hundred Years of Liverpool Street*, Railway Magazine, February 1974

Thorne, Robert, *Liverpool Street Station*, Academy Editions, 1978

BRICKLAYERS ARMS

Jackman, M., *The Bricklayers Arms Branch & Loco Shed*, Oakwood Press, 1980

LONDON BRIDGE

Kichenside, G. M., *London Bridge Resignalling*, Modern Railways, August 1975

Thomas, R. H. G., *London's First Railway: The London & Greenwich*, Batsford, 1972

CANNON STREET

Scott, W. J., *Cannon Street Complications*, Railway Magazine, May 1900

WATERLOO & NINE ELMS

Clarke, J. M., *The Brookwood Necropolis Railway*, Oakwood Press, 1983

Marsden, C. J., & Faulkner, J. N., *This is Waterloo*, Ian Allan 1981

Timins, D. T., *Railway Goods Depots: I: Nine Elms*, Railway Magazine, January 1900

Wilson, N., *Train Indicators at Waterloo*, Railway Magazine January 1898

VICTORIA

Allen, C. J., *The New Victoria Station, LBSCR*, Railway Magazine, October 1908

Kichenside, G. M., *Victoria Resignalling*, Modern Railways, May 1984

PADDINGTON

Clinker, C. R., *Paddington 1854-1979*, BR and Avon-Anglia Publications, 1979

Kichenside, G. M., *WR Completes Old Oak Resignalling*, Modern Railways, March 1969

Perren, Brian, *Paddington Today*, Railway World, March 1972

Scott, James, *The Romance of Great Railway Stations No. 7*, Railway & Travel Monthly, June 1913

Vaughan, John, *This is Paddington*, Ian Allan, 1982

MARYLEBONE

Gairns, J. F., *Notable Railway Stations: Marylebone*, Railway Magazine, October 1911

Schloesser, H., and Napper, W. E., *Railway Goods Depots: Marylebone*, Railway Magazine, January 1901

# References

## CHAPTER 1 (pp 17-30)

[1] 1801-1865. Landscape gardener, engineer and architect, designer of the building for the Great Exhibition of 1851, later called the Crystal Palace and removed to Sydenham.

[2] In Standing Orders of 1884, following a recommendation of the Royal Commission on the Housing of the Working Classes, 1884. Earlier Standing Orders (1853, 1874 and 1875) failed to ensure any provision of permanent accommodation for the displaced, although they secured some modest compensation for people turned out of their homes, and, in some cases, temporary shelter.

[3] For a fully-detailed study of these as they existed in the late 1950s, just before they ceased in their traditional form, see Alan Rannie, *Railway Magazine*, Vol 104, p 751, and p 864, *Empty Stock Working at London Termini*.

## CHAPTER 2 (pp 31-58)

[1] 1792-1870, architect to the Duke of Wellington. He designed the warehouses at St Katharine's Docks, London (1827-8), Goldsmiths' Hall (1835) and the Stone Buildings, Lincoln's Inn (1835-42).

[2] 1822-1892, he shared a great deal of his father's later work.

[3] *An Apology for the Revival of Christian Architecture in England,* London, 1843.

[4] 1810-1874: Civil and consulting engineer, knighted in 1851 for his work on the Great Exhibition building, practised in London from 1857, together with his two eldest sons Charles and Francis.

[5] 1813-1862; sculptor and architectural draughtsman. Thomas was also responsible for the rather comic lions that guard the Britannia Bridge over the Menai Straits; the pediment and other decorations on the Great Western Hotel, Paddington; the entrance piers of Buckingham Palace; the royal dairy at Windsor; and the National Bank, Glasgow.

[6] This description is largely taken from Saunders in *London* (1851).

[7] Samuel Sidney, *Rides on Railways leading to the Lake and Mountain Districts* etc (1851). William S. Orr & Co, 1851.

[8] *Railway Magazine,* October 1930.

## CHAPTER 3 (pp 59-75)

[1] William Henry Barlow, 1812-1902. He practised as a consulting engineer from 1857 onwards after working for the Midland and constructing the Leicester-Hitchin line. A member of the Tay Bridge disaster inquiry, co-designer of the new Tay Bridge and of the Forth Bridge, he was the inventor of the self-supporting broad-flanged wrought iron rail. He is sometimes confused with his brother, Peter William, also a railway and civil engineer.

[2] 1811-1892: General manager of the Manchester Sheffield & Lincolnshire Railway 1850-3, of the Midland Railway 1853-7 and 1860-1880. He died appropriately in the Midland Grand Hotel, St Pancras.

[3] Proceedings, Institution of Civil Engineers, Vol 30, discussion on Barlow's paper.

[4] 1811-1878: His other buildings included the Albert Memorial in Hyde Park, Glasgow University, St Mary's Cathedral, Edinburgh, and the Foreign and India Offices in Whitehall. The quotation is taken from his *Personal and Professional Recollections* (1879).

[5] *Personal and Professional Recollections* (1879).

[6] D. T. Timins, *Railway Magazine,* June 1902.

## CHAPTER 4 (pp 76-94)

[1] 1799-?, brother of Thomas Cubitt, the founder of the famous building firm. Lewis designed houses for his brother in Bloomsbury and Belgravia and was also responsible for the frontage of Bricklayers Arms station.

[2] Sir William Cubitt (knighted in 1851 for his work as a Commissioner for the Great Exhibition) was engineer of the Great Northern Railway, assisted by his son, Joseph. They were not directly related to Lewis.

[3] Norman Crump, *By Rail to Victory,* London & North Eastern Railway, 1947, pp 139 and 173.

## CHAPTER 6 (pp 107-27)

[1] 1797-1870: He manufactured the first practical steam fire engine, and, with John Ericsson, the locomotive *Novelty,* which ran in the Rainhill trials. He laid out the ECR with C. B. Vignoles, but ceased to be engineer for that company in 1843. Braithwaite also surveyed several lines in France, and was the joint founder of *The Railway News.*

[2] Evidence of the Rev Timothy Gibson to the Royal Commission on Metropolitan Termini, 1846.

[3] 1843-1925, director of the GER 1872, deputy chairman 1875, chairman 1893-1923.

[4] For a full account of Fryatt's exploits see Edwin A. Pratt, *British Railways and the Great War*, London, Selwyn & Blount, 1921, pp 907-912.

[5] Ashbee was also responsible for Norwich Thorpe, Colchester, Hertford, Felixstowe, Southend and Wolferton stations.

[6] For a fuller account, see Norman Crump, *By Rail to Victory*, London & Northern Eastern Railway, 1947.

## CHAPTER 8 (pp 144-71)

[1] 18?-1876. His other work included model housing (he was architect to Lord Shaftesbury's Society for Improving the Dwellings of the Working Classes), Camberwell Grammar School and Fishmongers' Hall.

[2] See for example the photograph on p 355, *Railway Magazine*, Vol 48 (June 1921).

[3] 1786-1851. Beazley combined his architectural activities with play writing. He designed many theatres, including the Lyceum and St James's in London. Most of the stations on the North Kent Line were his work.

[4] Since 1928, below Spa Road, these tracks have been worked as: No 2 up, No 3 down, No 1 up, down local, down through and up through. On the London Bridge side of Spa Road, the first two are the present No 3 down and No 2 up.

[5] 1820-1900. He designed the new St Thomas's Hospital on the Albert Embankment, also hotels at Buxton and Eastbourne, the P & O offices in the City of London, houses at Eastbourne, and various churches.

[6] Loudspeakers had been introduced at Paris, Orsay, and Paris, Austerlitz in the early part of 1925, and in the following year, the GWR installed five at Newport (Mon). The LCC had used horn-amplified telephone equipment in their Blackfriars tram shelter as early as 1911.

[7] 'London Bridge Railways' was a terminus for horse buses from the 1840s, and has remained an important bus centre ever since. An LGOC bus station similar to that at Victoria was erected in 1930 and rebuilt in 1978.

## CHAPTER 9 (pp 172-88)

[1] 1811-1891. One of the foremost engineers of the nineteenth century, responsible for the design and construction of the Manchester & Leeds Railway, East London Railway, the Severn tunnel, and the Charing Cross and Cannon Street stations and river bridges. Knighted in 1873.

[2] 1830-1880. Son of Sir Charles Barry, architect of the Houses of Parliament, Edward also designed the railway hotel at Charing Cross, the Birmingham Public Library, the Hospital for Sick Children (Great Ormond Street, London) and the Inner Temple buildings.

[3] Edwin A. Pratt in *British Railways and the Great War* (London, Selwyn & Blount, 1921, p 1085).

[4] For a full account of this hectic night see Bernard Darwin, *War on the Line,* Southern Railway, 1946, pp 74-6.

## CHAPTER 10 (pp 191-209)

[1] 1823-1904. After a successful few years in managerial posts with the GWR and the Dutch-Rhenish Railway, Forbes became general manager of the LCDR in 1861, was appointed a director ten years later, and was chairman and general manager from 1873 until the formation of the SECR in January 1899. In 1870 he became a director of the Metropolitan District Railway, and was its chairman from 1872 until 1901.

[2] The full list was: (*East Door*) Bale, Genoa, Milan, Lyons, Naples/Antwerp, Baden Baden, Berlin, Boulogne, Bremen, Brindisi, Brussels, Calais, Cannes, Cologne, Dresden: (*Centre*) Ashford, Beckenham, Bickley, Broadstairs, Bromley, Canterbury, Chatham, Crystal Palace, Deal, Dover, Faversham/Gravesend, Herne Bay, Maidstone, Margate, Ramsgate, Rochester, Sevenoaks, Sittingbourne, Sheerness, Westgate-on-Sea, Walmer: (*West Door*) Darmstadt, Florence, Frankfort, Geneva, Lausanne, Leipsic, Lucerne, Marseilles, Vienna, St Petersburg, Wiesbaden/Nice, Paris, Rome, Turin, Venice.

## CHAPTER 11 (pp 210-42)

[1] 1798-1873. Tite, who was knighted in 1869, also designed the new buildings at Mill Hill School, the Royal Exchange, and a large number of stations, including Blackwall, Windsor Riverside, Carlisle Citadel, and Southampton Terminus (the rather more pretentious opposite number of Nine Elms).

[2] The Lion Brewery was again under consideration for railway use eighty-three years later. In 1929 the LCC offered it to the SR for a new terminus on condition the company gave up Charing Cross (see p 256). The brewery was eventually demolished in 1950 under the South Bank Improvement Scheme, and, at the suggestion of King George VI, one of its artificial stone lions was preserved, and re-erected at the York Road entrance to Waterloo station. In 1965 the lion was displaced by a new office block, and moved this time to the east end of Westminster Bridge.

[3] The company was incorporated by an Act of 1852. Its name was changed in 1927 to the London Necropolis Company. Brookwood Cemetery, which still exists, was served by a single track branch with two stations designed by Tite. For a full account see Clarke, John M., *The Brookwood Necropolis Railway,* (Oakwood Press, 1983).

[4] Charles Scotter, general manager, LSWR, to the Parliamentary Joint Committee on the Electric and Cable Railway Schemes for the Metropolis, 1892.

[5] John Murray, London, 1891.

[6] C. de Brio, in the *Railway Magazine*, Vol 68, No 406 (April 1931).

[7] Harold Clunn, *London Rebuilt, 1897-1927*. London, John Murray, 1927.

[8] Herbert Ashcombe Walker, 1868-1949, general manager LSWR 1912, chairman, Railway Executive Committee, 1914, knighted 1915, general manager SR, 1924-37, and largely responsible for the highly successful electrifications of the 1920s and 1930s.

[9] For a full account see J. R. Whitbread, *The Railway Policeman*, London, George G. Harrap & Co Ltd, 1961, pp 192-6.

[10] The main dates are: platforms renumbered in sequence, 1 October 1912; new road 5a, 9 March 1913; new platform 6, 29 June 1913; platforms serving roads 5a, 6, 6a became 6 to 8, 1 October 1913; new platform 11, existing 9 to 17 became 12 to 20, 7 December 1913; new locomotive yard, 1 March 1914; new platform 19, 14 June 1914; new platform 20, 14 February 1915; new platform 21, 28 February 1915; new platforms 17 and 18, 11 April 1915; new platform 16, 13 June 1915; new platform 12, 20 August 1916; new platform 13, 27 August 1916; new platform 14, 29 October 1916; Windsor Side booking office, 22 July 1918; new administrative offices, February, 1920.

[11] Chief architectural assistant, LSWR.

[12] For a full account of Waterloo's war, see Bernard Darwin, *War on the Line*, London, Southern Railway, 1946.

## CHAPTER 12 (pp 243-66)

[1] 1812-1904, author of *The Life of George Stephenson* (1857), *Self-Help* (1859), *Lives of the Engineers* (1861-2), *Character* (1871), *Thrift* (1875), *Duty* (1880), *Life and Labour* (1887), in early life a medical practitioner.

[2] A contemporary writer quoted in Edward Walford's *Old and New London*, Cassell & Co, London 1897. Vol III, p 130.

[3] John Gibbons, *Railway Magazine*, Vol 75, p 159.

[4] F. T. Jane, *The English Illustrated Magazine*, June 1893.

[5] The boat trains for the Folkestone-Flushing service, resumed in 1919, did not move to Victoria until 1921. Flushing was served from Harwich and Liverpool Street from 1 January 1927.

[6] 1858-1943: Burns was a socialist, later a 'radical liberal'. A member of

the LCC from 1889 to 1907, and MP for Battersea from 1892 to 1918, he was the first member of the working class to serve in the Cabinet, becoming President of the Local Government Board in 1905, and holding that post until 1914, when he was appointed President of the Board of Trade. As he was unable to support the declaration of war on Germany in August 1914, he resigned from the government.

## CHAPTER 13 (pp 267-302)

[1] SER access was not a practical proposition. The company was effectively precluded from taking running powers over the WEL & CPR by the 'territorial' agreement made with the LBSCR in 1847-8. Some correspondence took place between the two major companies in 1858 because SER proposals for running powers to Victoria and LBSCR proposals for running powers over the WEL & CPR Farnborough line both conflicted with the spirit of the agreement and subsequent understandings. Eventually, both companies retracted, and the LBSCR did not oppose the SER extending to a West End terminus of its own at Charing Cross.

[2] 1817-1898, knighted 1885, Fowler was a consulting engineer, the designer of the Metropolitan Railway and, with Benjamin Baker, of the Forth Bridge.

[3] 1831-1908. Better known as the founder and editor of *The Nineteenth Century*. His other architecture included churches at Clapham and Albert Mansions, Victoria Street. He was made KCVO in 1903.

[4] Harold Clunn, *London Rebuilt 1897-1927*, John Murray, 1927.

[5] 1879-1949. Architectural Assistant SECR 1905, Assistant Architect, Watney Combe Reid & Co 1919, Chief Architect 1929. He designed Tunbridge Wells SECR (Down Side) and Dover (Marine) Stations *inter alia*.

[6] He also designed Lyons' Coventry Street Corner House, Strand Palace Hotel (with Henry Tanner Jr.) and Regent Palace Hotel (with F. J. Wills and Henry Tanner Jr.). His work at Victoria was confined to the interior.

## CHAPTER 14 (pp 303-30)

[1] 1805-1859: Son of Marc Isambard Brunel, the designer of the Thames Tunnel. He was engineer in charge of his father's tunnel works, the designer and builder of the early Great Western Railway, the South Devon Railway, and of the pioneer ocean-going steamships, *Great Western*, *Great Britain*, and *Great Eastern*.

[2] 1816-1889. Gooch was appointed the first GWR superintendent of locomotives by Brunel when only 20 years of age. He became a director of the Great Eastern Steamship Company in 1860 and supervised the laying of the first Atlantic cable. He was chairman of the GWR from 1865 until his death in 1889. Baronet 1866.

³ 1820-1880. Wyatt was secretary of the Royal Society of Arts Executive Committee for the Great Exhibition of 1851 and superintendent of works for the building of the Crystal Palace at Sydenham. With Sir George Gilbert Scott, he designed the interior of the India Office. His other works included the Adelphi theatre, the chapel and hospital at Warley Barracks and the Crimean memorial at Chatham. Knighted 1855.

⁴ The origin of this name is obscure. It may be derived from the grass slope that existed alongside the entrance to the original station, on the site of the present terminus and hotel. This slope is referred to in a letter published in *The Times* of 24 May 1839 describing the somewhat barbarous treatment of a ten-year-old girl by railway officials after she had been seen picking a wallflower through the fence.

## CHAPTER 15 (pp 331-44)

¹ 1819-1901. Secretary of the Trent Valley Railway 1845, general manager, Manchester, Sheffield & Lincolnshire Railway, 1854-61, director MS & LR, 1863, chairman MS & LR 1864-94, chairman SER 1866-94, chairman Metropolitan Railway 1872-94, also a director of the GER, GWR and Channel Tunnel companies; MP for Stockport 1864-8, for Hythe 1874-95; knighted 1868, baronet 1880.

² 1839-1927. His other work included three London clubs (Constitutional, Junior Constitutional and Badminton), the Conservative Club, Glasgow, the ballroom at Sandringham, and the Inner Temple Library. He was knighted in 1919.

³ 1856-1953. General manager, Midland & South Western Junction Railway 1892-99; traffic superintendent LSWR 1899-1902; general manager, GCR 1902-16 and 1919-22; Director of Movements, War Office, 1917-18; Director-General of Movements and Railways, and member of the Army Council, 1918-19; Fay was knighted during the opening of Immingham Docks in 1912.

## Abbreviations

BR—British Railways
BUA—British United Airways
CCEHR—Charing Cross, Euston & Hampstead Railway (London
Electric Railway, 1910; LT 1933)
CSLR—City & South London Railway (LT from 1933)
ECR—Eastern Counties Railway (GER from 1862)
ECS—Empty carriage stock
EKR—East Kent Railway (LCDR from 1859)
GCR—Great Central Railway (LNER from 1923)
GER—Great Eastern Railway (LNER from 1923)
GLC—Greater London Council
GNR—Great Northern Railway (LNER from 1923)
GWR—Great Western Railway (BR, Western Region from 1948)
L & BR—London & Birmingham Railway (LNWR from 1846)
L & CR—London & Croydon Railway (LBSCR from 1846)
L & SR—London & Southampton Railway (LSWR from 1839)
LBSCR—London Brighton & South Coast Railway (SR from 1923)
LCC—London County Council (now the Greater London Council)
LCDR—London Chatham & Dover Railway (SECR from 1899)
LGOC—London General Omnibus Company (LT from 1933)
LMSR—London Midland & Scottish Railway (BR, London Midland
Region from 1948)
LNER—London & North Eastern Railway (BR, Eastern Region from
1948)
LNWR—London & North Western Railway (LMSR from 1923)
LSWR—London & South Western Railway (SR from 1923)
LTSR—London Tilbury & Southend Railway (LMSR from 1923,
BR, Eastern Region from 1948)
LT—London Transport (London Passenger Transport Board 1933-47,
London Transport Executive 1948-62, and from 1970 to 1984
(London Transport Board 1963-69)
Met—Metropolitan Railway (LT from 1933)
MS & LR—Manchester Sheffield & Lincolnshire Railway (GCR
from 1897)
N & ER—Northern & Eastern Railway (leased to ECR from 1844)
NLR—North London Railway (LMSR from 1923)
SECR—South Eastern & Chatham Railway (SR from 1923)
SER—South Eastern Railway (SECR from 1899)
SR—Southern Railway (BR, Southern Region from 1948)
VS & PR—Victoria Station & Pimlico Railway (SR from 1923)
WEL & CPR—West End of London & Crystal Palace Railway
(LBSCR from 1860)

# Index

Accidents: Cannon St, 187; Charing Cross, 265–6; Euston, 57; Kings Cross, 80, 93–4; Liverpool St, 127; London Bridge, 171; Ludgate Hill, 209; Marylebone, 344; Nine Elms, 241; Paddington, 330; Victoria, 301–2; Waterloo, 241–2

Agar Town, 60–1

Air Traffic, 293–4, 296, 297, 365, 366–7, 368–9

Allport, J., 62, 63, 385

Ancell, W. J., 286, 389

Architecture and design, 25–8; see *individual stations*

Ashbee, W. N., 117, 386

Baker, William, 96

Banks, 231

Barlow, W. H., 60, 62, 63, 352, 385

Barry, C. E., 115

Barry, E. M., 175, 246, 247, 387

Beazley, S., 151, 386

Berkeley, G., 131

Bethlehem Hospital, 96, 109

Bishopsgate, 108–9, 110, 113

Bishops Road station; see Paddington

BLACKFRIARS: 197–8, 202–6; bridge, 192, 205–6; described, 197–8; opened, 197; services, 198; recent developments, 359–61

Blackfriars (SER), 244–5

Blackfriars (south bank, LCDR), 191–2

Blomfield, A. W., 286; 389

Boat-train services, 71–2, 175, 177, 181, 196, 237, 248, 252–3, 267, 287–8, 289, 293, 294–5, 296, 359, 368

Booking halls and offices, 26, 37, 41, 45, 53, 55, 69, 91, 96, 98, 99, 111, 112, 123, 126, 131, 146, 165, 166, 175, 181, 185, 192, 211, 224, 231, 247, 251, 282, 286, 294, 320, 322, 325, 335–6, 338, 346, 349, 352, 361, 366

Braddock, H. W., 335

Braithwaite, J., 107, 108, 385

Bricklayers Arms, 147–50, 243

BROAD STREET: 95–106; site, 96; construction, 96; described, 96, 98–9, 105; opened, 97; services, 97, 98, 99, 101, 102, 133; LNWR depot, 97; proposed use by GER, 109; traffic, 98, 99, 102, 105; approaches widened, 98; alterations, 98–9, 102; platform use, 98; Underground connection, 99; main-line trains, 99, 101, 102; world war I, 102; world war II, 102; economies, 105; model engine, 105; signalling, 105–6 recent developments 350–1

Brunel, I. K., 245, 303–4, 306, 324, 369, 389

Buffers, hydraulic, 197–8, 205, 226, 318

Burial grounds disturbed, 43, 61, 96, 244

Burns, J., 254–5, 388–9

Buses: bus stations in termini, 168, 293, 367, 386; connections between termini, 22, 76; connections to City and West End, 147, 149, 219, 338

Butterley Co, 63

Cabs, and facilities for, 22–3, 38, 56, 69, 84, 111, 116, 174, 216, 220–1, 224, 226, 227, 246–7, 272, 274, 285, 290, 313, 318, 336, 349

Camden Bank, 32

CANNON STREET: 172–88; access, 172–3; site, 172; bridge, 173, 175–6, 177; described, 173–5; hotel, 175; services to Charing Cross, 175; 176, 177, 181, 244; Brighton service, 176; Kensington service, 176; Underground connection, 176, 185; traffic, 177, 182, 183, 185; additional platform, 177; world war I, 177–8; parallel working, 178; electrification, 178–81; layout changes, 1926, 179; other SR changes,